These notes represent my private log.
Please do not read —
Not meant for publishing

Jack Whitten

EDITOR'S NOTE For six decades, Jack Whitten kept a log as a private exercise, recording and processing the experiences and experiments of his art-making as well as reflecting on the way his studio life intertwined with his daily life. From the outset, however, he was also concerned with writing itself. Early poems, stretches of imperative aphoristic writing, essays, talks, and published texts all show a stylistic sophistication, and there are occasions when even the private logs seem to address an audience. While Whitten did not share his notes with anyone as he wrote them, there were clearly moments when he had a public in mind. Whitten's decision in 2013 to allow me to read and then publish his studio notes came in part, I believe, from his feeling that the audience he had once imagined now existed and was ready to listen.

Second Edition

Jack Whitten

Notes from the Woodshed

Hauser & Wirth Publishers

Contents

Introduction

In 2013, while working together on an exhibition,[1] Jack Whitten and I were sitting in his Queens, NY, studio, a former firehouse built in the days of horse-drawn ladder trucks. He was explaining something about abstraction, about how he was expanding the word's conventional definition. It was easier to show me, and so he pulled out a sheet of paper with block lettering:

> Abstract painting that addresses subject is what I want. Before Western abstraction there was subject. I want something that goes beyond the notion of the 'formal' as subject. I want to use the formal as a means to arrive at subject. We live in a quantum world; everything is interealted. Nothing stands alone. There is no beginning + there is no end. . .

The statement easily undid the binary of abstraction=object/representation=subject, unfixed the static nature of received ideas, and put the terms of art in active and mutual relationship to each other. The writing was Whitten's, dated April 6 of that year. I was astonished by the originality of his writing—visionary, and yet totally without pretension, more intelligent than any critic writing on painting of the time. When I expressed all this, he laughed; partly because he could be so modest, deeply offhand about his accomplishments, and partly because this single sheet was truly the tip of the iceberg. We walked upstairs, where he showed me drawers of hundreds and hundreds of pages of these notes, written on everything from a 1962 notebook from his days at Cooper Union, to vellum sheets, legal pads, and large pieces of colored paper once pinned as reference points to the wall of his Lispenard Street studio in Tribeca. Whitten explained that he had been writing a studio journal for decades—since he was a student at Cooper Union. Sometimes the writing telegraphed the events of the day in true log form, as Whitten had been taught during his days in the Air Force ROTC at Tuskegee, complete with 24-hour military time notes (a habit he never dropped); sometimes it took the form of extended and fully-developed essays.

Mixed in were poems and flights of fancy, critical comments on exhibitions, books, lectures, musical performances, and recordings, and notes on the everyday—food eaten, wine drunk, birthdays and deaths celebrated and acknowledged, friends and family, pressures of money and time, etc.

In March 2009, Whitten wrote, "FROM THIS DATE FORWARD MY STUDIO LOG WILL BE KNOWN AS <u>NOTES FROM THE WOODSHED</u>."[2] For jazz musicians, to "go to the woodshed" or to "woodshed" means to practice in private, implying both the freedom to experiment in isolation and the relentless discipline of practice prior to taking ideas public. As John Coltrane (whom Whitten met and deeply admired) used the term: "The quartet has taken quite a bit of my time and recording, too, because I got to make three records a year…. I can't go up in the closet, I can't get in the woodshed and just stay in there all day and practice… Maybe I should just go back in the woodshed and just forget it."[3] The term "woodshed" appears very early in Whitten's logs as both a noun and a verb: he called his studio "the woodshed," and he said of his writing, "this note keeping is about woodsheding—New York City."[4] The addition of the phrase "New York City" indicates the site where he did it, perhaps with the ironic awareness that the city was not the woodshed's natural habitat. Certainly, he was emphasizing the idea that life as a New York painter was characterized by the need for this demanding practice.[5]

Whitten's notes of the 1970s are most redolent of what it meant to live in the pressure cooker of New York City as a competitive arena for painting; after years spent learning from Willem de Kooning, Norman Lewis,[6] and other mentors, he details a desperate search to go beyond gestural painting, sacrificing gallons of paint, hundreds of hours, many failed works, and often his own body:

<u>THE SINKING OF THE BERTHA CRUISER</u>
1 APRIL 1973 at 2200 hrs.
weapon used: one jack plane

Casulties: I received three blisters in the
process: 2 on my left hand and
one on my right hand

During the early 1970s in particular, Whitten was grappling with painting in that arena; he was hard on himself, and hard on his fellow artists. (Note: a few of his writings have been redacted here to protect the living). His struggle resolved, temporarily, with the invention of the tool that fellow painter Joe Overstreet called "the Whitmobile"— a "developer" that led to Whitten's brilliant, single-gesture canvases of the mid-1970s.[7]

Despite the enormous achievement these *Slab* paintings represented, subsequent logs do not record an artist refining a signature style; rather, they reveal an artist pushing to open his horizons out of a feeling of urgency:

I am emphasizing my being Black, with the expectation of offering another sensibility, possibly another insight into African Art other than that offered by Western Europe.

I have always considered myself to be working within the Western tradition, or in a more exalted sense a progression of that tradition. Now I sense an ending of what we call Western thought— western world-view—hence an ending of Western esthetics. The sensory-assault of technology forces upon us the beginning of another world-view. One removed from Western esthetic thinking.[8]

Here we sense the "woodshed," or private, quality of the logs: they allowed Whitten to express a scale of ambition that might have appeared unseemly, and that likely would have been met with mainstream resistance coming from a Black artist; they also allowed Whitten to work through questions of cultural identity surrounding the African diaspora, which he rarely discussed publicly during those years. His experiments with sculpture, produced during the summer (when he was not writing or painting), were similarly private, and also in part intended to work through questions posed to him by objects of African origin. Later in life he felt more comfortable fully sharing his thoughts on these subjects, as his reputation became more securely established, and also as it appeared that the world was catching up to his way of thinking. Whitten's wish to publish these logs in 2013 is emblematic of that freedom and openness.

Subsequent years and decades are each marked by distinct qualities and subjects. In the early 1980s, the writing becomes more strikingly poetic and abstract, taking the form of aphorisms or lists of categorical statements. We have chosen to reproduce many of these pages as facsimiles, to convey the power and specificity of the artist's hand. Keywords—space, light, abstraction, spirit, matter, self, grid, God, presence, geometry—appear and reappear, turned over like stones in Whitten's hand. And from the 1990s into the twenty-first century, philosophy and science—subjects important to Whitten during his college years at Tuskegee and Southern University in Baton Rouge, as well as at Cooper Union—blossom in both the logs and the more formal essays and talks included in this volume.

The writing here is abridged rather than complete, with a number of the logs and published statements omitted so as to arrive at a reasonably portable book. *Woodshed* also mirrors certain breaks in Whitten's own life and practice. Almost every spring season after 1969 ends with the note, "Gone Fishing!"—indicating Whitten's annual departure with his wife, Mary, and daughter, Mirsini, for their summer home in Crete. There is a long pause that occupies much of the 1960s, when Whitten was deeply engaged in and disturbed by the political upheaval and identity issues that characterized the era. In 2015, at my request, Whitten wrote an essay on that decade to fill the gap. Another hiatus occurred in the early 1980s, when a terrible fire destroyed Whitten's Lispenard Street home and studio just before he was to buy the building; the restoration took several years away from both his painting and his log-keeping. The last lapse took place during the early 2000s, when Whitten sold his Tribeca building and built a new studio in Woodside, Queens.[9]

Jack Whitten's voice is the heart of this book, and we have preserved it as much as possible in the facsimiles of the logs, and in retaining their original formats, spacing, punctuation, and spelling. Some of Whitten's usages are simply expedient or idiosyncratic; others are more purposeful and illuminating, allowing for a kind of wordplay that his close friend, the sculptor Mel Edwards, recognized as characteristic of their shared Southern sensibility.[10] The writing is honest, as only woodshedding can be, and offers an inspiring guide to long life as an artist. *Woodshed* crystallizes the worldview of an artist "of Universal proportions," and this vision is Whitten's ultimate gift to the future.[11] As he wrote in his final log entry, less than a month before his death on January 20, 2018, "ART IS OUR COMPASS TO THE COSMOS."[12]

Katy Siegel, 2018

Notes

1. *Light Years: Jack Whitten, 1971–1973*, Rose Art Museum, Brandeis University, September 17–December 15, 2013.
2. March 1, 2009. The earliest entry with this title is January 26–27, 1973, but the body of that entry is in blue ink, while the header, "NOTES FROM THE WOODSHED," is written in black ink, indicating it was likely added at a later date.
3. Ralph J. Gleason, "John Coltrane" [1961] in *Conversations in Jazz: The Ralph J. Gleason Interviews*, ed. Toby Gleason (New Haven and London: Yale University Press, 2016), 13.
4. As in January 8, 1975; November 20, 1974.
5. Whitten's hometown of Bessemer, Alabama, would be an example of that natural habitat, and his use of the word indicates not only the general fact of the persistent memory of the rural past in urban forms of music and art, but specifically Whitten's own serious and long-term engagement with woodcarving.
6. Lewis is the primary subject of an interview with scholar Andrianna Campbell in this volume.
7. Overstreet, cited in a November 16, 1973, entry.
8. February 15, 1976.
9. The first log entry after the fire and rebuilding is dated January 31, 1983; the move in 2001 was long planned, and was not a consequence of 9/11, although Whitten witnessed the events firsthand and was extremely disturbed by them.
10. Mel Edwards, statement in tribute delivered at Jack Whitten's memorial service, Metropolitan Museum of Art, March 3, 2018.
11. Whitten used the phrase "a man of Universal proportions" to describe Duke Ellington in a log entry made May 24, 1974, the day Ellington died.
12. Whitten's last log entry was December 27, 2017.

'60s

My first studio in New York was a storefront at 369 East 10th Street between Avenue B and Avenue C. Stanley's Bar was on the corner of Avenue B at 12th Street. The Lower East Side in 1960 was a thriving young art community and Stanley's Bar was our favorite meeting place. Every night of the week I could speak with Ishmael Reed, Calvin C. Hernton, David Henderson, and other members of the Umbra Group of Poets and Writers. Jack Kerouac and Allen Ginsberg often frequented the bar on off hours. Stanley, the Polish owner, knew Charlie Parker who was also a visitor in the early fifties. I loved to hear Stanley's stories about Charlie Parker spending hours playing the jukebox and playing Polish polkas!

Stanley, like Mike Fanelli who I would meet later in the sixties when I moved to the Lower West Side, was a friend of the artist. You could always get a hot meal on credit, cash a check without having a routine identification card; this was important because who had a bank account? The first time I ever showed a painting in public was at Stanley's . . . a small group of collage paintings from 1963. The first painting I ever sold was to the superintendent of the building where my studio was: a Spanish fellow who often came in to admire what I was doing and paid $35 for a small 1961 painting as a Christmas present for his wife.

Edios Group was a small artist co-op gallery on Avenue B in the mezzanine of the Old Charles Theatre. Stanley Moskowitz, one of the founders invited me to participate in a group show. I showed a series of collages made from rags that had been soaked in acrylic medium with oil paint applied on top. They were very earthy with siennas, raw umber, burnt umber and blacks.

The Black painters that I associated with were Joe Overstreet, William White, Bob Thompson, Emilio Cruz, Lawrence Compton and Haywood Bill Rivers. The good thing about the Lower East Side even with all the political rhetoric of race is that young artists, both Black and White, used the local bars such as Stanley's to interact. This was important because the uptown gallery scene and the 10th Street co-op galleries were mostly White.

Cooper Union offered another totally different set of experiences; this was the first time that I was in class with White students and a White professor. My education at Cooper consisted of Bauhaus aesthetics (I studied two-dimensional design with Hans Beckmann of the German Bauhaus), Ben Cunningham who was highly influenced by color theory, three-dimensional design with Professor Anthony Candido, sculpture with Leo Amino, calligraphy with the American Master Paul Standard, Bob Blackburn the Master Print Maker, Charles Cajori, a structural expressionist painter well versed in cubism, David Lund, painter, Leo Manso, painter, Jack Stewart, painter who taught me a lot about process. I also must mention Robert Gwathmey, the Southerner from Virginia who went out of his way to make me feel at home. Morris Kantor's critiques were helpful even though I was not a member of his class.

If Cooper Union offered me the Bauhaus, the Cedar Bar offered me Abstract Expressionism. Balance is an important word in my vocabulary. I have a spirit that allows me to devour everything that crosses my path. Having a high metabolic rate, I can digest everything! Meeting Bill de Kooning, Franz Kline, Philip Guston, Mark Rothko, Barnett Newman, Norman Lewis, Romare Bearden, Jacob Lawrence, and all of my professors at Cooper Union, convinced me that I had made the right decision to leave Tuskegee: New York was my home.

The tenor saxophone was my instrument of choice. I played in the Dunbar High School Marching Band in my hometown of Bessemer, Alabama. My high school band instructor, Lionel Garnier played all the classical Jazz masters for us: Miles Davis, Charlie Parker, Dizzy Gillespie, Sonny Rollins, John Coltrane, Thelonious Monk, Paul Chambers. Me and my band buddies who were interested in Jazz formed the Dunbar Jazzettes, which was a dance band. We made small change doing dances and even did local radio commercials for a used car salesman! It was a lot of fun and I sincerely thought there was a possibility of my being professional, but all of that changed when I came to New York.

Birdland, Five Spot, Minton's, Village Vanguard, Village Gate, Half Note, Jazz Gallery, and Slugg's Saloon destroyed any notion of my being a Jazz musician! What I heard in 1960 at Birdland on Monday nights changed me forever: Art Blakey and the Jazz Messengers with a young Wayne Shorter, Art Farmer, Lou Donaldson, Horace Silver . . . . and others. Art Blakey, whom I considered to be a witch doctor on drums, forced me to reconsider any interest in becoming a Jazz professional.

My first music teacher at Carver Junior High School, Mrs. Willie B. Jones, said that music was 'pleasing sound.' With this definition in mind, what was I to do with Pharaoh Sanders, Archie Shepp, Cecil Taylor, Albert Ayler, Sun Ra, Ornette Coleman, and a host of others who were changing the course of Jazz? I was at the Jazz Gallery on St. Marks place when Sonny Rollins did his first return gig from the woodshed. I saw Cecil Taylor attack the strings of the piano keyboard at the Five Spot; I witnessed Sonny Stitt and Gene Ammons in a fierce duel at McKee's Lounge in Chicago during the summer of 1961. I sat at the feet of Thelonious Monk at the Five Spot, and remember Kenny Durham scolding Ornette Coleman to get off the stand, "The nigger can't play!" No one could harness the forces of chaos more than Archie Shepp and make it into music! Most of all: John Coltrane and Eric Dolphy at the Blue Coronet in Brooklyn. The first time I had the opportunity to speak with Coltrane, "It's like a wave" he said to me. More than once I've experienced an epiphany that changed my life. Wave, and what others had said about Coltrane's music "sheets of sound" were my inspiration for my concept of planar light, i.e., light operating as a plane, came directly from Coltrane.

After a devastating critique from one of my painting professors at Cooper Union who claimed that I spent too much time on "accidents," I ran into Bill de Kooning on University Place on my way to the Cedar to chill out, and as usual his "Hi kid, how are you doing?" I told him what had happened. Bill said, "You tell that motherfucker that there is no such thing as accidents in painting!" With that said, and a couple of beers at the Cedar Bar, I felt as if I could whip the world!

More than once, Franz Kline was helpful. Franz had a way of being matter of fact. He said to me and a group of young aspiring artists one night, "the minute you step into that studio and pick up that brush, you are a part of art history and you'll never be lonely." The studio is a lonely place but I have always believed that I have a place in the history of art. I also love to tell the story of Franz Kline giving me the name of Mr. Antonelli who worked at the Astrup Canvas Co. on the Lower West Side. I told Franz that I didn't have any canvas and he said, "Go see Mr. Antonelli and tell him that Franz Kline sent you." The Astrup Co. is where Franz bought his Blue Line Cotton Duck canvas; they were large wholesalers of cotton canvas and sold end rolls to artists.

It was Robert Blackburn, who managed the printmaking workshop at Cooper Union who introduced me to Romare Bearden. I was the only Black student in my class at Cooper Union in 1960 and Bob reached out to me. He said, "You must meet Romare Bearden" and bodily took me to Romare. Romare sent me to Jacob Lawrence and it was Romy who sent me to Norman Lewis. Norman Lewis' studio was uptown on 125th Street. He lived and worked in a walk up office building. When I met Norman in 1962 he had no commercial gallery representation. His studio and living space (there was no division, he lived and worked in the same space) was very neat, and I remember his painting racks filled with paintings. I had so many questions with most of them being questions of survival.

How does one make enough money in order to do your work? How do you make a living? What was the effect of racism on his work? Problems of being a Black artist doing abstraction? Norman was helpful but not that encouraging on the prospect of making a living from one's work.

Haywood Bill Rivers in contrast to both Romare Bearden and Norman Lewis was a true Bohemian. Bill had spent a lot of time in Paris, had a pretty good grasp on the history of painting, a good painter but with no financial success to speak of . . . no gallery representation but I found the Bohemian Life attractive. When I met Romare he was just starting his first black and white collages made from Xerox copies of tribal African mixed with urban figurative imagery. They attracted me. I remember visiting his studio with all of the collage elements scattered on the floor so he could spontaneously choose from them. Even today, the image of Romy's studio floor is still with me.

I remember hitting Kate Millett on the ass and saying, "Hi baby." Kate smiled at me and said, "I don't call you nigger, do I?" Feminism was something I had never thought of. I grew up with powerful women and took for granted women as leaders. The pastor of our church, The Church of God, was Sister Griffith. Sister Watson and Sister Bettie Robinson were highly respected and considered spiritual leaders, and of course, my Mom raised us by herself. My Mother was a powerful woman. It did not take me long to understand that Kate Millett was talking about something else. What I was taking for granted was nowhere near the truth: women had no power in the country at large . . . no economic power . . . no political power . . . and certainly, as I later learned . . . no power in the art world. Kate gave me a lot to think about.

The sexual revolution affected all of us. Calvin C. Hernton was writing a book called <u>Sex and Racism in America</u>, the Lower East Side, Greenwich Village, Lower West Side were my neighborhoods and we, more than anybody, because of the multiethnic mix of people on the scene with art providing the common ground, we experienced extreme sexual cross-pollination. Sexually speaking, life was good . . . we fucked everything that moved with every color available! Calvin's research into the history of Black/White sexual identities exposed the dark and political horrors of sex: America had turned that which was free and natural . . . a gift from the Gods, into a political horror chamber!

LeRoi Jones a.k.a. Amiri Baraka was the first Black man I ever met who spoke freely and bluntly about the power of Black identity. I had met Martin Luther King in Montgomery during the bus boycott in 1957. Dr. King spoke of racial equality, the dignity of Black people, faith in the scriptures which provided the spiritual strength of overcome the legacy of slavery . . . everything that I had been taught as a child growing up in

Alabama. Roi was different. He spoke different. He acted different. He dressed different. I remember visiting him at his home with his wife Hettie Jones and their two children, Kellie and Lisa. I particularly remember a small paperweight object on his desk with the inscription "I read for information." I was very impressed with this.

So many people from so many racial backgrounds gave me so much to think about. At times I felt as if my head was exploding! Jeffrey Waite, who gave me employment, as a carpenter's helper was especially helpful. He taught me cabinetmaking . . . a skill that proved to be extremely valuable: I could always pick up my hammer, saw . . . and make a buck. Jeff also introduced me to the world of philosophy. Jeff had studied philosophy at McGill University with an advanced degree. His knowledge of books was unbelievable. More than a philosopher, he was a book collector! One day while tearing down a wall to receive a newly built cabinet, I picked up a piece of debris and excitedly said "Another one!" Jeff had been observing me collecting found objects from different sources. This day he grabbed my hand and said, "Why this one and not that one?" This was my first genuine lesson in aesthetics outside of any academic norms.

So many young men were being killed in Vietnam . . . men of my generation and I often thought . . . if I had continued at Tuskegee I would have been in the muck of war. At times I felt guilty and it was difficult for me to continue my studies at Cooper Union and to convince myself of the value of art. No one could ignore the racial implications of Vietnam . . . a lot of Black blood was spilled . . . Black men along with their White buddies were dying by the thousands. My guilt turned to shame and anger when the truth surfaced: We had no legitimate reason for being there.

After a brief marriage and the birth of my first daughter, Keita . . . survival became more urgent. The racial climate had intensified. Black people were becoming more militant and the anger of injustice exploded into outright anarchy. Political assassinations fueled the temperature of fear, and violence became American as cherry pie! America was on the brink of disaster. The 1963 bombing of the 16th Street Baptist Church in

Birmingham with the death of four little girls and partial blinding of another little girl pushed me over the edge. I didn't know what to do. Was art really that important? Those little girls were from my hometown. My worst experiences of growing up in the South had caught up with me and there was no place to hide. There was no place of comfort. For the first time in my life I experienced the absence of hope. My Grandmother Etta used to say about White people, "Their children will be better." Their children had become monsters!

My paintings became violent. It became harder to control my emotions; even hate had entered my vocabulary. Honestly, throughout horrible experiences in the South . . . I didn't feel hate . . . but now hate had penetrated my psyche. The assassination of Dr. King, the assassination of Malcolm X, of John and Robert Kennedy, Vietnam, and the resulting riots across America forced all of us to make decisions that would affect us for the rest of our lives. I was ready to acquire guns and explosives, go back to Alabama and encourage rebellion at any cost necessary. Allan Stone, my art dealer, shouted and screamed at me, "You are an artist and you better make up your mind!" He insisted that my job was in the studio. How can anyone justify staying in the studio when your people are dying? What is the artist supposed to do? Start killing White people? What justifies killing for any cause? These were and remain the most difficult questions for me considering the politics of race in America.

During the night of the Cuban Missile Crisis a bunch of us were getting high on anything available, drinking loads of alcohol, crying and making asses of ourselves in public, when George Segal the sculptor walked into Stanley's. I had met George several times through my friend Letty Lou Eisenhauer. George said, "What's going on Jack?" One young lady who was totally fucked up, crying, and screaming, "We will all be dead by morning!" George, whom I had a lot of respect for and considered to be a major artist, went on the offensive: "You are artists, I am an artist. Tonight I am going to the studio and make another sculpture and I advise you to do the same."

The conviction in his voice is something I'll never forget. Everything
was forcing me to make up my mind: Who are you Jack Whitten? What
kind of person do you want to be? What sort of world do you want?

My first one-man show at the Allan Stone Gallery in 1968 was the
highlight of the 1960s for me. Everything came together in that show.
My decision to stay in the studio had paid off. I didn't have any money;
my first marriage had fallen apart. I had a daughter to think of . . . the
responsibility of caring for someone was frightening and I dealt with it
the best I could. Romare Bearden, Jacob Lawrence, Wayne Thiebaud,
Lawrence Calcagno signed my letters of reference for the John Hay
Whitney Fellowship, which I received. This was a great help and the grant
money prevented me from going over the edge. The show got good
reviews. Allan sold a few paintings. I met Clement Greenberg for the first
time . . . I requested that he see the show, which he did, and I received
some favorable feedback.

Carl Jung, Freud, Nietzsche, Heidegger, Hegel, Husserl, Joseph
Campbell, Eastern philosophy, Zen, Black Nationalism, Vietnam, urban
riots, political assassinations, drugs, sex, family, racism, and painting all
contributed to a massive personal meltdown by late 1968. Anxiety is a
disease that has no respect for race, gender, economics, politics, or
spiritual belief. Anxiety can poison every aspect of one's being. For the
first time in my life I was forced to seek the help of a psychiatrist. A friend
of mine recommended that I see someone who had helped her. Black guy
seeing a Jewish psychiatrist? The very thought was enough to destroy
every Black cell in my body! He was nice. Patient. I liked him. Without
talking that much, he allowed me to vent everything that was bothering
me: Everything! His diagnosis? I had opened Pandora's Box. The cosmic
flood of information had blown a fuse!

I lost my taste for meat and lived primarily off of brown rice and
vegetables for almost a year. At times I could not get out of bed. I became
paranoid toward everything and everybody. Any form of drugs were out of
the question . . . even the smell of marijuana spun me out of control. I met

a Black man on Canal Street, he was a street person, smelly with red inflamed eyes, long matted greasy dirty hair, and his clothing was not fit for man or beast. His dark skin was encrusted with dirt and every quality of urban filth. He approached me and said, "What's wrong with you Brother? Men do not stand and sleep, only elephants can do that!" One of my best friends at that time, the "bread man" John Fischer said, "Do you want to kill me? Do you hate White people?" I was losing it and desperately tried to pull myself together. Another woman had entered my life: Her name was Mary Staikos, someone whom I had met at Cooper Union years before. Both of us were married at the time with no interest in romance whatsoever. Mary was born in New York City. Her father was born in Greece, but Mary had never been to Greece.

My dear friend Frank Hertz invited me to study karate with him at a local dojo. The discipline of Okinawa Karate, Shohei-ryu helped a lot. Another friend convinced me to study Hatha Yoga at the Yoga Institute, which also helped. I forgot to mention the death of my Brother Tommy, the jazz musician. Tommy died in 1967 as the result of a fire in his Grand Street apartment. Tommy lived for 28 days in intensive care at St. Vincent's Hospital. To witness the agony of such a painful death added fuel to the fire.

Mary and I were married in 1968 at our loft on Broome Street. The sculptor Melvin Edwards was my best man; Mary's cousin Harriette Andreadis was a witness. No one else in Mary's family bothered to come. In 1969, Mary wanted to visit Greece, the homeland of her parents, and I always had an interest in Greek philosophy, sculpture, and myths. We decided to take a trip to Greece in the summer of 1969. Two nights before our departure date, I had a powerful dream . . . the type of dream so vivid that I awoke violently in a sweat. I saw a tree standing in a clearing . . . heavily pruned with bare limbs. The dream was a command: Somewhere in Greece you are to find this tree and carve it into a totem. The dream did not say where in Greece, only to take your carving tools. I've always carved wood during the summer months. Before going to Greece, I spent the summers upstate New York carving wood.

We arrived in Athens, found a cheap hotel in the neighborhood of Plaka and used that as a base to travel visiting all the museums, archeological sites and going on side trips throughout the mainland. Soon our money was running out with no tree in sight, and people advised us to go to Crete because it was cheaper. They put us on an overnight ferryboat to Iraklion, Crete.

My first time in blue water with no horizon; I realized that I was in the center of a circle . . . a vast, unbelievable void of a circle. It was exhilarating! We went deck class, the cheapest ticket available . . . no cabin . . . just out in the middle of the Mediterranean. The next morning we arrived in the port city of Iraklion and I went straight to the tourist police office located in the harbor, I told them the story of my dream and they advised me to go South because it was the cheapest place on Crete. They put us on a public bus to the village of Aghia Galini. An old Cretan man befriended us on the bus and told us not to worry, that he would find us an inexpensive place to live. The bus ride across the island was amazing. We traveled through a landscape of rugged mountains, flat plains covered in grapevines, olive trees . . . it was like a fairyland. When the asphalt road turned to dirt and gravel, we were not so sure that we had made the right decision. The wind was blowing so violently, with dust and rock, our joy turned slightly to fear. Finally, after almost two hours we could glimpse the sea from a distance. It is something about the sight of the sea that automatically gives a sense of joy . . . hope and adventure.

Aghia Galini in 1969 was a small fishing village with no electricity. A little harbor at sea level nestled between rolling hills and in the distance the majestic Mt. Ida, known locally as Psiloritis. The bus pulled into the harbor and from the window I saw the tree standing in a clearing just as it appeared in my dream. The old man who befriended us was not joking: He took us to a hotel which charged one U.S. dollar a night! We found that the two of us could live comfortably getting all we wanted to eat and drink for less than five dollars a day.

The next objective was to find out who owned the tree. We were directed to the home of Strati Troullinos. My Greek was non-existent and Mary's Greek was not good enough to make Strati understand what I wanted to do with the tree. He thought I wanted to cut it down. I came up with a plan to make him understand: I went into the surrounding hills, found some wood and set up shop on the harbor beneath some trees. It worked. Strati immediately understood. He invited us into his home, led me to a back storage room, and showed me his collection of tools. He was a retired cabinetmaker! Take what you need!

The tree still stands in the harbor of Aghia Galini. Because of tourism, with cafes, restaurants, hotels, it is not as visible as in 1969 but it's still there. The face of a fisherman stares out to sea, an octopus wraps its tentacles around the trunk, fish swim in three-dimensional relief as the crest of waves from a circular motion creating a narrative of men, fish and sea. The top of the totem is a large fish with its tail pointing to the sky.

The nineteen sixties were coming to a close. I was still intact, much stronger, and braver. Greece had restored my sanity and I was ready for a new chapter in my life.

Jack Whitten
New York City
September 2015

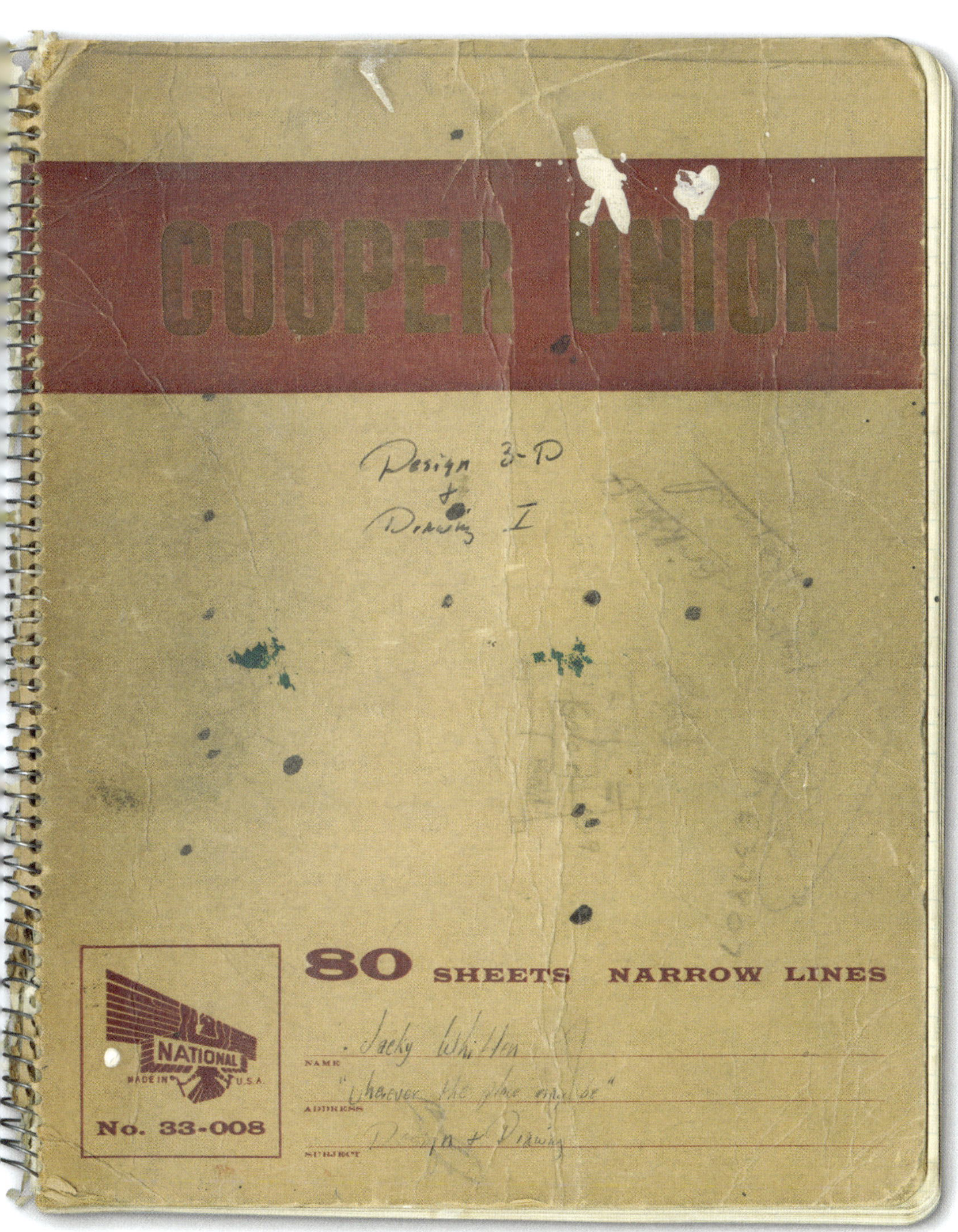

COOPER UNION
Design 3-D
&
Drawing I
80 SHEETS NARROW LINES
NATIONAL
MADE IN U.S.A.
No. 33-008
Jacky Whitten
NAME
"wherever the place could be"
ADDRESS
Design & Drawing
SUBJECT

Notes '62   in Studio

Objects do not exist without the presence of space as space is not ~~present~~ noticeable without objects. In some way space may be interchangeable with matter as energy + matter is interchangeable. Therefore everything not only belongs but also is involved with the physical + emotional construction of its sister objects e.g. no figure exist without the space that she exists in this space is as much apart of her makeup as her own physical and biological constitution. Whether the figure is in motion or at rest, this involvement is present whether in accelerated or decelerated circumstances.

To even project this idea of objects involved ~~with sister objects and in return involved~~ in the space that surrounds them further—it is important to note that when objects exist in what may be known as co-existential space, <u>at any point of this co-existantence</u> one may dominatt the other with an abrupt change of direction and physical makeup e.g. inorganic form to organic form with violent dergree of direction in form.—point to plane + vice versa diffusion of elements—destruction of picture plane—optical illusion of color etc. But it is also important to note that the dominance which one form achieves is being simultaneously destroyed by its sister form and in turn destroyed by its existence in space i.e., if dominance is achieved by one form a chain reaction occurs between its sister forms and simultaneously by the space!

Forms may be related by color only. Because one circle is ~~painted~~ yellow and another circle of the same dimension is red does not state the fact that the two circles, or of the same form. Definite forms exist only in the same family of color. Each color family behaves to its own family

<u>Space is as much apart of the object as the object is apart of space.</u> By using this spatial concept there is not real dominance of any one form by its spatial location but only by its mass and color

family is related to its sister forms. You see, spatial location could be a determining factor in the dominance of a form e.g. when playing to squares of the dimension on a white surface (one of blue and one of red) with the red square to the lower left of the picture plane + the blue square to the upper right the red square will appear to be dominant. Why?

no. 1 because of its spatial location + no. 2 because of its color family namely red.

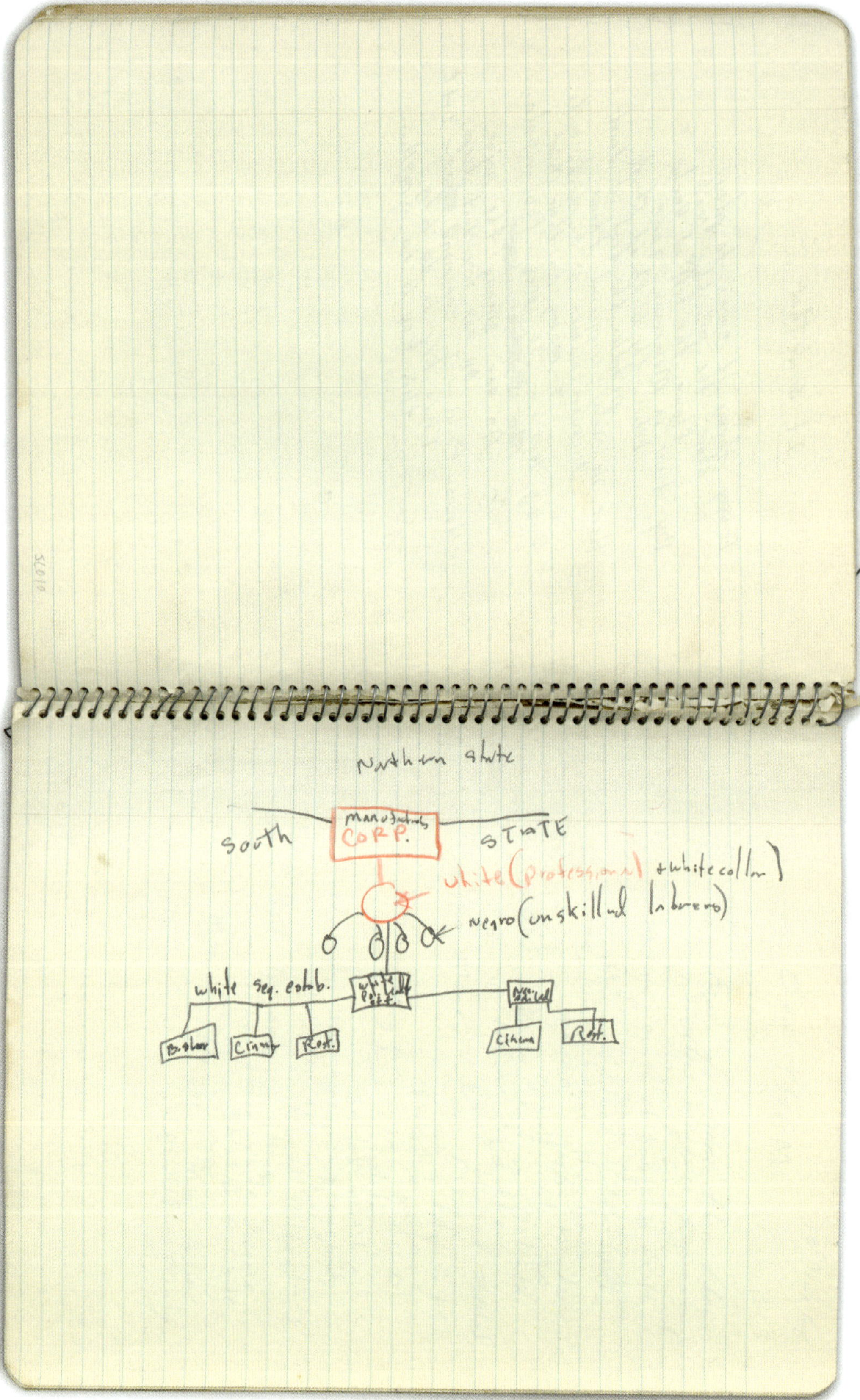

Northern white
South
manufacturing CORP.
STATE
white (professional + white collar)
Negro (unskilled laborers)
white seg. estab.
white political ...
segreg.
Barber
Cinema
Rest.
Cinema
Rest.

Extent of Spatial Tensions

The extent of reality is really amazing. While just consider all the necessary elements which evolve from this one thought. I think of space + the coherents of space. Namely, objects of inorganic + organic order (+ the tensions which exist between the coherents + the relationship which is manifested.

Considering space, space is reality. Actually space is the <u>ultimate of reality.</u> While, doesn't space defines life as well as its definition of non-living objects? To think of space as being imaginary is determental to the well-being of an open minded intellect. There is nothing imaginary about space, only to the extent that we are not aware of our spatial environment. Now, considering the fact that some people consider space as an imaginary thought or more less + imaginary being; it signifies their lack of comphensive employment of the subject. Space actually defines life + presents us with a medium in which to communicate + associate our life giving capacities. The depths of understanding life is through the super-reality aspects of space.; It provides us with the plastic thoughts of communication e.g., form, texture, color, time, existence, etc. By using those plastic thoughts we are able to determine the amount of plasticity + therefore actually associate elements by spatial tension.

Since space defines limit of scale, it imposes no limit upon the communication + association of objects. <u>At this point I must say I impose no limitations upon space.</u> The depth of its penetrative nature is no greater than the height. In other words, there is not <u>apogee</u> or <u>perigee.</u> Space defines minute particles as well as those of gigantic size beyond our comphension. Is it not true that without space life could not exist? Does matter occupy space or space occupys matter? A simple answer is that space is interchangeable + presents different spatial tensions with inter relationship as intrarelationships.

1

In a culture bounded by material thinking, completely devoid of the human being---In a culture so much mechanized that human emotions can easily blend with the oil that they pump from this earth, where the human robot has almost no soul or mind left from which to act---In such a culture, capitalistic, embedded with the richness of the world, molded and casted as a pure example of democracy (one set apart from the people), an artist lives.

Absolute dedication on the part of any man remains man's strongest character. To be capable of such dedication, -that ever searching of the whys of beauty, truth, chaos, men's actions- and then to have this dedication threatened, necessitates one to action of some kind.

Thus I stand adamently upon this principle, and say that any nation, whether democratic or communistic in its governmental supervision, cannot afford to achieve material advances without considering the non-material aspects of its society. The United States of America is doing just that! In its everlasting struggle for technical know- ledge, the nation has threatened the existence of the com- plete human being. Can such knowledge be so dear to a society as to cause the abolishment of all esthetic thinking on the part of its inhabitants?

Where are your young men, your men who thrive on creative ground; those who are able to (and indeed, can only) think esthetically? If your society be of the people,

people. Allow your few men of creative standards space and
time to record these expressions. There be no time for loss
of the arts; to jepordize its followers.

I, as an artist in these United States, feel that
we followers of art are capable of getting this country
to move toward becoming a land rich in ideas, as well as
in material goods; one where an entirely new culture belonging
solely to America can be born. And only then will this
nation be able to press sides with all the nations of the
world knowing itself fulfilled in every area. I ask the
President of the United States not to overlook the
importance of the Arts as a means of developing this
country to a degree of perfection in the eyes of the whole
world.

typed by
Florence Squires
November 4, 1962

written
4 Nov. 62

In a culture bounded by material thinking, completely devoid of the human being---In a culture so much mechanized that human emotions can easily blend with the oil that they pump from this earth, where the human robot has almost no soul or mind left from which to act---In such a culture, capitalistic, embedded with the richness of the world, molded and casted as a pure example of democracy (one set <u>apart</u> from the people), an artist lives.

Absolute dedication on the part of any man remains man's strongest character. To be capable of such dedication, -that ever searching of the whys of beauty, truth, chaos, men's actions- and then to have this dedication threatened, necessitates one to action of some kind.

Thus I stand adamently upon this principle, and say that any nation, whether democratic <u>or</u> communistic in its governmental supervision, cannot afford to achieve material advances without considering the non-material aspects of its society. The United States of America is doing just that! In its everlasting struggle for technical knowledge, the nation has threatened the existence of the complete human being. Can such knowledge be so dear to a society as to cause the abolishment of all esthetic thinking on the part of its inhabitants?

Where are your young men, your men who thrive on creative ground; those who are able to (and indeed, <u>can only</u>) think esthetically? [. . .] Allow your few men of creative standards space and time to ~~read~~ read + record these expressions. There be no time for loss of the arts; to jepordize its followers.

I, as an artist in these United States, feel that we followers of art are capable of getting this country to move toward becoming a land rich in ideas, as well as in ~~matter~~ material good; one where an entirely new culture belonging solely to America can be born. And only then will this nation be able to press sides with all the

nations of the world knowing itself fulfilled in every area. I ask the
President of the United States not to overlook the importance of
the Arts as a means of developing this country to a degree of
perfection in the eyes of the whole world.

typed by
Florence Squires
November 4, 1962
Whitten
4 Nov. 62

It Seems That

Every theme it seems to play
    above the melacoholy$_{/sp}$ scale
        floors the best of Gaucho
By time in Memorian gone
    before the birth of Christ
        paddles the fish of feast
Here in every Niggerish theme
    Nigerian women in Swedish suits
        a rosary for their chief
Swing low - - so very low – solo. . . . . . .
    ~~Mr. Einstein's key?~~
    An ear among the noise
        an ear six-foot deep.
Hocus – Pocus – I command ~~thee~~ T•H•E
    This key is to big.
        this key is to small. . . .

On Being a man

First of all I do not want to represent a nation. I do not want to represent a people nor do I want to represent myself, instead I would like to represent a man whom we <u>should</u> all know that man is man, himself.

Every black American, Every white American constantly avoids the reality of being a man insted they accept the fragmentation of man; his follies, his cruelietis his mistakes, his taboos his senseless crimes his inabilities to love his former ability to destroy, and last but not lest, his unceassingly ability to hate.

America, look at the palm of your hand. You should be able to see your face. Every man is identified by his face unfortunately many Americans do not have a face—Most of our women live beneath miles + miles of impentrable disguise and most of our men live beneath defense mechanism of an automated being. Man is not an idea. Man is a reality—without man there is no reality no existence. Our reality is psyhic$_{/sp}$. My hand shows me my face; my face shows you the man; the man represents the reality.

There is a certain profound + dynamic beauty to be found in the acceptance of one's face i.e., after one is able to see his face. Now, denial of this acceptance produces a disillusioned chaotic state of being it produces the fragmented man so commonly found in America. Conditioning processes, brainwashing or just common propaganda directed toward a group of people extensifies this denial of one's identity. The effects of these processes is quite evident in the so called Negro problem in America. It has produced a people whom the majority's only attempt at reality is a myth. It has produced a people of a whole "mythical identity" patterned from the majority of a decadent power structure.

Beneath every surface lies an identity. The amount of depth beneath this surface determines the value of its being. What is the depth of America in the year 1964? What is the depth of its people? Are the people able to see their face in the palm of their hands? Questions exist because of a deep + wanting desire for knowledge. Which one of use would dare ask ourselves "Am I A MAN?" or better yet which one of us would dare ask ourselves "DO I WANT TO BE A MAN?"

I look at my hand and see my face I will not rest until every American can do the same.

Pinkism

1969

My vision of art is that of Pinkism. Pinkism is the personality of the world expressed in pure plastic symbols. Pinkism combines all the isms of art history, especially those of contemporary times. At present I am the only true believer in Pinkism, but like all isms when introduced to the mass media it establishes instant followers. The creation of a pink world became evident to me when I started seeing pink angels on my canvas, pink horses, pink women with pink *blip*, pink cats that *blip* pink *blip*, and big pink elephants with tiny pink *blip*. I have seen pink mountains where pink stinky goats grazed upon pink grass placed within a pink holy sky. I have seen pink pigs and pink dollars. . .

Originally published in Lawrence Alloway and Sam Hunter, eds., *5+1* (New York: State University of New York at Stony Brook Art Gallery, 1969), exhibition catalogue, n.p. Reprinted courtesy of the State University of New York at Stony Brook.

'70s

Oct '72

I've done so much. I've tried everything.
I've tried the saw blade, afro comb.
I've made all sort of formal announcements
about the importance of space, volumetric surface.
About making painting real. About physical
labor used to prevent me form thinking.
Space is important; that much is true.
I still come back to surface. Please I am
trying hard not to be confused. This shit
is complicated!
    To be as clear as possible without
getting confused. I JUST WANT A SLAB
    g PAINT.

I've done so much. I've tried everything: I've tried the saw blade, afro comb. I've made all sort of formal announcements about the importance of space, volumetric surface. About making painting real. About physical labor used to prevent me form thinking. <u>Space</u> <u>is</u> <u>important</u>: that much is true. I still come back to surface. Please I am trying hard not to be confused. This shit is complicated!

To be as clear as possible without getting confused. <u>I</u> <u>JUST</u> <u>WANT</u> <u>A</u> <u>SLAB</u> of <u>PAINT</u>.

<u>NOTES FROM THE WOODSHED</u>   ~~notes on~~ methods + materials

The last experiments were concerned with paint as material with the addition of capturing subject matter. I should say not as material but paint as image. I have been using a 12' long squeege made of 6" strip of neoprene tacked to a 5" board. With this squege I am able to cover an area 12' wide by the size of my platform. First I should explain that I am working on a platform buit to the floor. The platform is 12' x 20' constructed of 2 x 4's 16" centers covered with 5/8" nova-ply which is covered with a 12' x 20' sheet of cheap linolem glued with linolem paste to the nova-ply. I tacked a piece of canvas over this and covered the whole platform with plastic to prevent the paint from reaching the linoleum. I want to keep the linoleum clean.

The platform is built perfectly flat + level. I have made a completely even surface without anything interterfering with the surface of the canvas. in other words I must be able to control everything that happens. I have not allowed for any chance elements to occur. The neoprene proved to be a perfect material because of its flexibility + toughness and easy to clean. By pouring paint at one end of the canvas I can lie down a flat even layer of color with my squeege. Therotically The painting is complete in one–two seconds, of course I must pull across several lines and do many things in between before I get what I want. For example sometimes after lieing down an area of color I would wait for the appropriate drying time + wash out a certain amount of color with hot water. By doing this I achieved the image of corroded sheets of cor-ten steel. The metallic image of the paint comes from the addition of aluminum + cooper bronzing powders to the paint.

When using bronzing poweds one must be careful to mix throughly the powders by suspending them in acrylic-meds. I do this by using a regular kitchen electric hand mixer. Not only this the powders give a metallic look but also changes the color: a bright hansa yellow lt becomes a brilliant chartreuse when adding aluminum and black becomes grey. Some colors such as ult. blue + Bocour blue or used as staining colors that is at the right time. I can apply them over an entire surface and certain areas will be affected by the staining properties and others not. Some colors are used for their transparent qualities. Colors such as hansa yel., cad. yel lt. some reds are very transparent. Most colors can be made transparent with the addition of a gel medium which acts as an extender but of course the color is not as strong.

I was asked recently about the lines and while I insist upon their bein straight instead of lyrical. I feel a kinship to both lyrical school of thought + the disciplinariness of let's say a Josef Albers—by using a guide system I managed to install a certain structural discipline which otherwise without would be totally abstract lyricalism.

My major problem at present is how to install shape into a color-field system. I used to make paintings emphasizing the total field as color removed from cubist though but at the same time having some concept of shape as image. I think that surface is very important this is the main point I take my bearings from photographs. Photographs are able to give us a special type of spatial effect depending upon the subject maintaing of a definite 2-dimensional flat surface. The surface must be maintained in painting. surface the same as a board of wood, of glass of metal that which serves as a reflection of light. A paint surface without the logical intrusion of push + pull, perspective of emphasis upon spatial locations of color—The surface alone gives us the space however deep or shallow.

Paint is used to arrive at a new surface. Paint becomes a new image not bound by geometric repretory or lyricalism. I have by devoting my energies to only surface i.e., color as surface, things such as line, form, space, movement <u>takes care of itself</u> (another word here). In the late sixties I now realize that my big mistake was trying to force a subjective image from the paint i.e., I wanted to see something that I could relate to mentally and most of the time these images took the form of faces. The face was very important to me. The psychology of relating the vision of a face, projecting the vision of a face into any pictorial disturbance meant a lot. If I could not see something within the paint it was not what I wanted. I think that Jackson Pollock also experienced this in his last black + white drip paintings: the face was so evident. When I think back now my wanting to see the face was my own face—my own identity—the fruit of earlier expeirments where I dealt exclusively with the extenstial problem of identity. My pet object during those times were to be able to see my face in the palm of my hand. When I speak of the face I do not mean drawing i.e., graphically drawing but the third vision of seeing, to see within a disturbance, a mixture of paint the psychic maniffestion of a face—surely this alone was one step removed from drawing as such—closer to Michelangelo's seeing battle scenes on the walls.

In those days I would find certain objects on the street, on the beach—in the oven—anywhere I could see this particular image— and always in the form of a face. A friend said to me one day "while did you choose that one + not this one" It really made me stop + think. You see artist never stop and ask why but I realized that this was the beginning of the development of a new esthetic one that develops out of my search for identity out of my particular unique sensibility. Now I remain free to explore the pure plactic significance of my material. I also know that one cannot make paint into a material. it is already a material but one can stop using paint for artificial means—artificial interpretation of objects. I have found it impossible to conceptualize what I want from a painting each experiment is so different. I can only work with the material aspects of each pigment; how it works under this condition, what happens when I expose it to this condition, what will hot-water do—is cold water any different—how much medium to use; how much strength is applied to the squeege. Recently I have been using a very loose arrangement of texture made by brushing on what could be called the prime coat. By having an uneven surface I am able to emphasis the shape of a certain brush stroke or sometimes such by scraping off the surface paint.

To explain further exactly how a painting is done: from the beginning a fresh piece of raw unprimed cotton-duck is tacked to the platform with its edge parallel to the outer edge of the platform (this is to maintain my parallel strafaction_{/sp}.) The tacked edge is taped in order to prevent the paint from covering the staples which allows for easier removal of the canvas after the painting is completed. The first coat of paint is rolled on with a 9" roller this is allowed to dry and then a second coat is rolled on. The third coat is brused on in order to prevent the textured effect of the roller from being noticeable in the finished painting which I find offensive. There may be a succession of three to six layers of paint brushed onto the canvas before the painting starts. After a sufficient amount of paint has being applied the squeege is used to lay down a layer of paint. Most of the time the first layer is a much lighter—brighter color than the second but sometimes I use just the opposite—there is a not set standard method of application—By working light over dark I've gotten good results + by working dark over light I've gotten good results. If I want to emphasize a certain line I use a piece of wood stripping @ ½" to 1" in width attached to the squeege at my given location so when the squeege is pulled across the canvas the strip of wood leaves a definite line cutting through the wet surface. A string stretched very tight between two points across the canvas can give a different quality of line. A piece of wood on a paper tube dropped into a wet surface leaves an impression which can later be used as shape by scraping over another color after the surface has dried. Many sutley variations of applying the paint, mixing color, breaking up of the surface goes into producing the final painting. In the final analysis I can say that the paintings or very complex to execute but I want the final image to be simple. I do not believe in very fast breaks in color contrast, to much disturbance of the surface. I don't know what I want but only what I don't want and the only way I can be sure of this is to see—to see is the nature of painting.

Working this way is very manual. The whole body comes into play. Most of time I am working on my knees, brushing on paint, using a sponge or removing water with a smaller window-cleaner type squeege. After four or five hours of working I am totally exhausted. I like the idea of working in a physical manner because it prevents me from thinking about what I am doing. I believe in the intellectual process analytical purposes— to discuss as close as possible with other painters, students what I am doing; to solve certain technical problems but when I am involved with image-making I prefer to have no mind and the physical work solves this for me.

I really don't know the meaning of what I am doing or the significance of working this way. Why the emphasis upon surface? Why the emphasis upon the total area. I can say that my most important inspiration comes from photographs, ~~more so~~ sheets of cor-ten steel—the city sidewalks, breaking a stone into—rock formations esp. like those I saw on the island of Gavdos—anything whose surface has a sense of the real. I see no paintings to excite me. I must look at my surroundings for purity for honesty for absolute materialization of matter; it is not to be found in the painting of todays art world. On the sidewalk I can see more purity of form than in any New York art gallery.

My main clue is surface. Color, form, line, movement, space, all incorporated, all executed through surface. Acrylic paint has numerous advantages over oil. First of all its fast drying is desirable for removing paintings from the platform to the racks. Its flexibility cannot be surpassed. Acrylic paintings can be rolled with no fear of cracking. I have the most undesirable factor about acrylic paints to be the quality of surface it gives. It is very difficult to arrive at a uncommercial-non-plastic look with acrylics. There is something about the painted surface aesthetically which makes us admire the matte quality over the gloss the tough New York look of tactilness more so than the manufactured plastic look. The minimalist of the early sixties got around this problem to some degree by declaring the non-individual manufactured look as an aesthetic asset in other words they publicly announced the plastic-value in manufactured art Now we understand their intentions of the manufactured look not in terms of its machiness but its importance of non-gesture. Non-gesture is the final break with Abstract-Expressionism. In giving due revelence to this important breakthrough we cannot accept the total package. that is to say "yes, non-gesture but not machined" We do with our hands but we don't do with our hands. I believe this sort of paradoxical predicament we find ourselves in to be one of the major keys of discovery in discussing the avant-garde in painting today. The avant-garde lives and for one to participates requires experience in paint handling plus the acquisition of a sound plastic vision one removed from the articifcality of the present day Photo-Realist school. The avant-garde member must be mature in ~~thought~~ history of painting plus in profound knowledge of abstract-expressionist thought, post painterly abstraction, the importance of the hard-edge movement, Morris Louis, must know the ingredients of Pop and above all ready at all times ~~to risk~~ a commitment to experimentation through risk.

There are definite ways of sidetracking the acrylic medium; by the addition of other elements such as sand or coffee, by using it as a wash instead of a solid opaque pigment, by using tension breaking to interrupt the surface (cracks is surface) by applying wet paint over semi-dry surface—Even with all these attempts it's still difficult to defeat the plasticness of acrylics.

I have experimented with using stove-blacing after completing
a painting (which of course removes all the color but certainly gives
an entire emphasis upon painting as surface) using steel-wool
afterwards with graphite or talcum powder anything to break the
surface gloss

A friend just informed me of an acrylic catalyst which the paint
to dry faster + causes some change in surface character. I have written
to Rohm + Haas and ordered this catalyst and expect to begin
experiments within the following week if my health improves. Wax
maybe another possible way of cutting the gloss—this I must try.

Painting is becoming more + more challenging. An adventure in
New York. A political fantasy with my compatriots. Painting is
becoming more harder. There is talk of the death of abstract painting
and some people even point to the rise in Realism as a triumph of
American Painting. I attribute the rise in Realism to the psychiatric
needs of middle class Americans, the bourgeoise, black art, women
searching for identity, the novo-riche collectors who wants a piece of
art instead of buying Bloomingdale reproductions and above all to
the mass output of unprepared so-called artists from our commercial
oriented art schools across the nation + Europe. Art in its advanced
stage is something more than therpy. The Mod. Day Realist gives us
art as therpy. Rothko gives us art as a dedication to Painting.

31 Jan '73

I know that the big problem today is to break through the
Color-Field Experiments. To continue the ~~drive~~ departure from
Cubism. I have some ideas on how this is possible. I mentioned
earlier that I am trying to throw shapes into a color-field system.
This is definitely the first step but I also know that those shapes
must not be represented as relational. This, At this point, is where
a change of mind is necessary. How can one present shape within a
field without designing them as relational? Here is where the

problem of total-spontaneity begins i.e., the execution of shape + field as one, the total organization of framable space into surface material. We must learn to re-structure the environment which in turn exercises our minds.

I have made a full circle. I worked so hard to build my platform and giant 12' squeege expecting to continue painting in the same manner by pulling across the surface. No Luck! One painting for Poindexter show (Midnight Stripper) and perhaps two other but the whole method is changing very rapidly. Immediately after using the squeege, I used an old technique of putting on the paint + scrubbing out only after allowing the paint to dry for a while—good results but not exactly what I want and besides the labor is too much. Two important paintings: The Pariah Way (18") + First Loading Zone @ 6'. Yesterday I did not use the squeege but threw the paint directly onto the platform + press unprimed canvas into the wet paint and afterwards tacked the wet canvas to the floor to dry taut. <u>I have made a full circle</u>: back to the photographic Image. I must work large + crop out my sizes. Cropping becomes very important. The vision is located by cropping. Next week I will experiment with a lighter weight of canvas perhaps a #12. Since I will not be using as much paint as before I can save money by using a smaller weight canvas and also the lighter weight should enable me to make better contact with the paint and will definitely cut the final weight of the painting.

Mentally I am more prepared for dealing with the Photographic Image and the experience of painting since 1965 gives me a much stronger plastic awareness. The structure is in the eye not in the hand. The emphasis in color will be placed upon strong earthy hues with very Little emphasis on brightness of hue.

The trip to California was quite nice—lovely country but couldn't live there. I don't like California Culture. [. . .]

→ Back in N.Y. back to painting—I must work—I am working very hard—that is good—doing a lot of thinking—trying very hard to tie it all together. finished a big 9½' x 13' <u>The Bertha Cruiser</u> a tough, mean, evil-painting I want more of this! I must have more of this to combat the effiminate, weak + decorative painting of N.Y. More earthy colors—darks—rusty—odd blues—rust orange—weird greys—mud—MUD—MUD

I LOVE MUD— [. . .]

David Diao told me that he is trying to enhance his image or change his image—<u>Not A BAD IDEA!!</u>

The ultimate meaning of abstraction ~~lies in~~ in painting is to be found in the true nature of the paint used. Paint is the vehicle. I am the medium. I do not believe in pre-conceived ideas in painting. The response to painting must be immediate. There must be no time to think. The idea of paint as a material is a very sound idea—but it is not enough. There is more to painting than the sheer possibilities of paint. We know the possibilities of acrylic paint—but do we know how to use those possibilities?

I have the correct sensibility for the time. I have the knowledge of paint possibilities and limitations. I have an understanding of the meaning of abstraction in painting. I know that I do not want to deal with decorations. Painting must be real for me; it must be a weapon and <u>art</u>, must be combat. IN this sense, it serves a function and has a place in society other than wall decorations. I know that my image manifests itself in the physical manipulations of paint not in the brainy world of ideas. The more I paint the more I see. There is an infinite number of possibilities. Someone must exploit one of those possibilities. Now is the TIME!

SPACE is the key word in painting today and through a concrete definition of space in today's term will be the deciding factor in abstract painting.

The paintings take another drastic change. I am going to rework the Bertha Cruiser. I have been applying a very thick impasto before destretching + tacking to the floor. I am afraid that this technique will be misunderstood as a direct influence of Bannard*—without thinking I was using a flooring chisel and chipping away the impasto the results was pure bright color shinning through a field of dark ominous undefinable color. I am convinced at this point that I am working with something that deals with denial of a present decision I will do something and immediately deny it. Now I can see this as a major element of my work through the years. I really liked the heavy impasto look—but immediately denied it by chipping it away.

The first painting of this order (Mirsini's World'), deals with fragments of color that dance across the plane spacing themselves very abartarily/sp. At first I placed the color according to a means of structuring color which I used in 67-68-69 but due to my chipping away at the color + being only able to take away a certain amount, I deny the given structure and arrive at a structure of, let us say <u>what is physically possible</u> i.e., what I can take off with my chisel. The painting is not stretched for I sort of like what happen when pull I pulled the tape (which was used for covering the staples and make them easier to remove without paint covering them), besides the flatness to the wall is nice. The triumph here is spatial. When I chipped the impasto away, it was a process of dealing with the surface. I managed to place color within a field, without getting involved with depth of positing on the plane to arrive at depth. The results is a painting very much about surface but existing within an image projecting a certain amount of air + depth. One is able to move within a flat surface.

At this point I am afraid to project my thoughts too much, for I can see a lot of possibilities opening up. First I've always wanted a means of making connections to my earlier paintings, exploring further the idea of humor, myth, politics within a painting format.

Second, I've had the feeling lately to do something new i.e., another way of handling paint. To my knowledge no one has arrived at an image by using a flooring chisel to chip paint away, but no one had used a carpenter's saw either or a shoe shine brush or an afro comb, or a plumber's plunger. . . . . . Maybe I've been doing something new all along without knowing it. Harold Diamond told me once that painters never know when they have done enough! I agree with him. How can one know? Especially if you are not getting the feedback of super-star status.

Anyway, a mister Porter from Cleveland, Ohio brought the Midnight Stripper, I hope he enjoys her as much as I did (smile!) This sale will enable me to pay Robert Perlmutter the telephone Co., Con Ed and my hospital bills plus sending Mother 100. Got Damn! that makes me feel good!! Mirsini is doing just beautiful we went for a walk today [. . .]

Good Night!

THE SINKING OF THE BERTHA CRUISER

1 APRIL 1973 at 2200 hrs.

Weapon used : one jack plane
Casulties : I received three blisters in the
process : 2 on my left hand and
one on my right hand

THE SINKING OF THE BERTHA CRUISER
    1 APRIL 1973 at 2200 hrs.

weapon used: one jack plane
Casulties: I received three blisters in the
process: 2 on my left hand and
one on my right hand

I now know that the painting which I destroyed was about the death of Picasso. <u>The Bertha Cruiser</u> was about something huge—Giant of a ship that sailed the great seas of the world and the sinking of her

If only I could read the symbolism of what I do—<u>I know but yet I don't know!</u>

So the Bertha Cruiser has sanked—I must make plans for a salvage operation immediately—a hell of a job<u>!!</u>

<u>someone must do it</u>

Bravo Picasso

I am exhausted—ill with a bad cold—too much drinking not sleeping enough—runned down and have only 3 paintings which is a triptych—<u>FRIDAY the 13th</u>

I've been thinking a lot. Saw Frank* yesterday and spent the evening with him + Lenore (Good Girl)

The best show in town is David Novros at Bykert + of course the John Walker show at Cunningham's

Had a lovely dinner with Diao + Jeannie,* Mike Todd, Walker—Novros* had some outa sight brownies at his opening—

Had a lovely evening with Novros + Dwan*—got high—good French wine—asparagus—salmon—salad—cantaloupe with ice cream + walnuts.

—Destroyed more paintings, only accepting the best results—no compromise—Spoke with Klaus* at the Bykert Gal. might be possibility of show—would like to show in Feb. '74 I hope he likes the paintings. [. . .]

The plane is still sharp—Maybe this one will be successful—will know tomorrow—

16 NOV 73

The carving went well this year — got three pieces. Picked up some good wood but it must wait until next year. I know that the carving is good for my head. Having the opportunity to work out of doors as opposed to working inside all year, frees another side of me. I expect to do plenty carving and perhaps show it.

Back to my painting — exhausting myself — sweating, crying, cursing the very ground I walk on and enjoying every minute of it. Painting is becoming harder and harder or I am becoming tougher and tougher. Haven't seen any good painting since I've been back in the city. Saw the Poons show but didn't think much of it and really believe that he stole something from me. Olitski's retrospective at the Whitney didn't impress me at all. It all seemed so cream puff and fashionable but not the real stuff. I still think he wears tinted glasses! I am convinced that painting i.e. abstract painting is experiencing a major crisis now — — plenty of abstract painting, basically good but no sign of departure just marking time. The scene has become academic and anemic — — — needs new blood — — — — <u>Where are my brothers?</u>

Joe Overstreet is back in town, just as romantic as ever. I was glad to see him. Overstreet still has the energy but sometimes I wonder about his having the necessary power to shape the next wave. He still needs crutches — politics, dumb eccentrics and vices.

I tried to maintain my cutting through with the plane to no avail. Those experiments are finished. I've tried attaching pieces of 1" rubber rods to a piece of wood and attaching this to my working tool (Overstreet calls it a "whitmobile!") no success, only a hint of something. A machine shop made two pieces of galvanized steel with a toothed edge for me but no success. I later discovered by turning the steel over to the straight edge and attaching this to my "whitmobile", I am able to use it as a huge scraper — — — some good results! Instead of cutting through the raised acrylic, I simply scrape away the wet surface to expose the color of the raised acrylic,

Plenty possibilities to work with but still a lot of
risk involved. I was hoping to eliminate some of the risk
but risk seems to be an inherent element to this type of
painting — One Never Knows Anything — Also I discovered
that attaching weights to my frame keeps the
scraper down as it passes over the picture plane. I must
admit that I am having some technical problems (Overstreet is
so funny he calls them scientific problems), for instance, I don't
like the vertical lines left by the scraper — nor the static
areas where the paint doesn't mix properly. I am learning to
pull the scraper faster across the plane and paying more
attention to the consistency of the paint, both seems to help
eliminate the vertical lines of the scraper.

I am cutting color, a loose. I think that
color is pervading me from seeing the bone of what I am dealing
with therefore I am going to black & white with maybe just a tint
of color —. sienna & blue, besides it'll be much cheaper
to work with. Sometimes I not to involved with the sensual
aspects of color and the metaphorical aspects which causes
me to forget or better yet to block out what I should be seeing,
sort of like not seeing the forest for the trees.

One real problem I am having is not knowing how much to
trust the use of a definite system for placing my visual
surfaces or relying upon total free form.
example:

system of placement
(taken from earlier paintings 66 — 68-69")

Free form (by using any means available
for paint application)
I can't show an example with a pencil
my hand is to trained.

The carving went well this year—got three pieces. Picked up some good wood but it must wait until next year. I know that the carving is good for my head. Having the opportunity to work out of doors as opposed to working inside all year, frees another side of me. I expect to do plenty carving and perhaps show it.

Back to my painting—exhausting myself—sweating crying + cursing the very ground I walk on and enjoying every minute of it! Painting is becoming harder and harder or I am becoming tougher and tougher. Haven't seen any good painting since I've been back in the city; saw the Poons* show but didn't think much of it and really believe that he stole something from me. Olitski's* retrospective at the Whitney didn't impress me at all. It all seemed so cream puff and fashionable but not the real stuff. I still think he wears tinted glasses! I am convinced that painting, i.e., abstract painting is experiencing a major crisis now - - - plenty of abstract painting, basically good but no sign of departure just marking time. The scene has become academic and anemic - - - needs new blood - - - - - <u>Where are my brothers?</u>

Joe Overstreet is back in town, just as romantic as ever. I was glad to see him. Overstreet still has the energy but sometimes I wonder about his having the necessary power to shape the next wave. He still needs crutches: politics, dumb eccentrices and vices.

I tried to maintain my cutting through with the plane to no avail. Those experiments are finished. I've tried attaching pieces of 1" rubber rods to a piece of wood and attaching this to my working tool (Overstreet calls it a Whitmobile!) no success, only a hint of something. A machine shop made two pieces of galvanized steel with a toothed edge for me but no success. I later discovered by turning the steel over to the straight edge and attaching this to my "Whitmobile", I am able to use it as a huge scraper - - - - - some good results! Instead of cutting through the raised acrylic, I simply scrape away the wet surface to expose the color of the raised acrylic.

Plenty possibilities to work with but still a lot of risk involved. I was hoping to elimate some of the risk but <u>risk</u> seems to be an inherent element to this type of painting—One Never Knows Anything—Also I discovered ~~by using wei~~ that attaching weights to my frame keeps the scraper down as it passes over the picture plane. I must admit that I am having some technical problems (Overstreet is so funny he calls them scientific problems), for instant, I don't like the vertical lines left by the scraper—nor the static areas where the paint doesn't mix properly. I am learning to pull the scraper faster across the plane faster and paying more attention to the consistency of the paint, both seems to help eliminate the vertical lines of the scraper.

I am cutting color a loose. I think that color is preventing me from seeing the bone of what I am dealing with therefore I am going to black + white with maybe just a tint of color - - sienna + blue, besides it'll be much cheaper to work with. Sometimes I get to involved with the sensual aspects of color and the metaphorical aspects which causes me to forget or better yet to block out what I should be seeing, sort of like not seeing the forest for the trees.

One real problem I am having is not knowing how much to front the ~~possib~~ use of a definite system for placing my raised surfaces or relying upon total free form.

example:

[drawing; labeled, "System of placement (taken from earlier paintings 66'–68-69")"]

[drawing; labeled: "Free form (by using any means available for paint application)
I can't show an example with a pencil my hand is to trained."]

This is a very real and important problem for it dictates the final imagery, ~~and~~ By not using the system of placement, I could eliminate a whole step i.e., it is necessary to have a stretched canvas which gives me the FOUR EDGES to work with. The placement system is BUILT UPON TENSION EXISTING WITHIN THE PLANE BOUND BY FOUR EDGES.

ANYWAY, I am back into the swing of things—paying my dues in the BIG APPLE—

STONES FROM OMALOS

I made a small 24" x 24" experiment. IT WORKED! USING STONES FROM THE BEACH AT OMALOS BENEATH A #12 COTTON DUCK FROM DAVID'S.

NO PROBLEM with placement—<u>the system is controlled chance</u>. within a given arena—2' x 2'.

I have been so flustrated—tried everything I could possibly think of. . . . The raising of the surface by using impasto was not good enough. I got some pretty good paintings but it did not please my third eye . . . . that's where real painting takes place—it's the seat of one's aesthetic.

I had a long talk with Overstreet yesterday, it helped to clear a lot of things that I've been thinking of. Joe poised the question "what are you painting for"? Money? Love? Pussy? Power? Humanity? And he insisted that I must pick one . . . . . naturally I took all of them and added one more: <u>REVENGE</u>

The last painting I did last spring was entitled <u>The Last Painting</u> some how I feel that to be correct. Correct in the sense that I am not doing relational painting anymore. I think that all painting up to this point in modern art history (EUROPEAN) has dealt with relational thinking. This experiment made tonight tends to go beyond relationships in painting (I don't think that I am explaining this to well, I am very tired tonight and will write more on this subject.

I have come along way since the Omalos experiment. Things are much clearer now. I know exactly what I must do. The Omalos experiment meant that I could remove my hands from the paint . . completely . . . . set up a situation for something to happen. I am now using pieces of coat-hanger wire beneath the canvas, ~~in order to~~ they act just as the stones but I can control it better. Also, I am incorporating the use of stain canvas, sometimes along one edge + sometimes an L shape along two edges. This gives me another space. At first I ~~considered~~ used this edge purely as a physical jesture to show the thickness of the paint but later saw much greater use. Now my slab of paint exist within another space. The first painting that showed me this was the <u>Eighth Wedge</u> (later destroyed) then immediately following <u>Storm Warning</u> then <u>A New York Lullaby</u> and tacked to the floor is <u>National High</u> or (Mellow Yellow)

I have been thinking about what I mentioned before as non-relational painting. <u>Everything happens at once</u>. All the plastic elements are conceived in one stroke across the plane. To my knowledge this is the first painting of this sort. I can see fantastic possibilities from this type of painting, it also carries me back to my earlier ideas in '66 about the photographic image in painting. . . . . . If I am correct it could be the real meaning of photo-realism or in ~~this case Abstract Photo-Realism~~ (XX I must stop trying to name what I am doing.)!

The Guggenheim notified me to send two paintings for their final judging. . . I am keeping my fingers cross I am having great difficulty in deciding which two paintings to send, maybe <u>Storm Warning</u> + <u>A New York Lullaby</u>. . . <u>I must psyche out that panel!</u>

[. . .] I find most painters just wandering—following the look of some style which they do not understand but still they follow like cattle to the slaughtering pen. <u>Nothing pleases me except my own paintings now</u> not even the upper echelon—Yes enjoyed the last Noland show and the last Frankenthaler show . . . . . but you know . . . not. moved. not moved. . . . . . . [. . .] <u>I have no more heroes!</u>

Money still remains my only problem. I cannot paint now for lack of money—I have no paint—NO canvas and I am Hot my mind is lively—My eyes can see the evidence of greatness in pigment! I have a vision—I can see it very clear.

22 Feb 74

The Santini Bros. returned the paintings from the
Guggenheim foundation. Now I must wait. I try to keep
very cool, calm + collective but my winning the Guggerheim
would make a big difference. I do not want another
year like this — so broke — no money a lich means
no materials. Mary callo me a paint addict and she is
absolutely right — I am not happy when I have no
materials to work with. I know that I must not
think about it — — — maybe Henry will see to it.

25 MARCH 74

I DID NOT GET THE GUGGENHEIM! This is
a very low blow for me. I am broke not able to
paint, a one-show at the Whitney Museum in Sept,
not really pleased with the paintings that I have — and
no Materials — but — Lennie Bocon sent me some
paint — 10 GALLONS OF VARIOUS PAINT. I now
have uncle Lennie + Uncle Sidney! Knare Radoss offad
to loan me some canvas — so with a little more
money for paint I am back in stride.
I received a letter from Emilio today, I think that
he has had it with Chicago. We must face the reality
of New York being the center of action. One cannot
escape it, what ever is going to happen — — — it
will take place in New York. It's very hard to
live here, but what can one do? all the energy is
here, the challenge of making it — the testing
ground of the art world.

22 Feb 74

The Santini Bros. returned the paintings from the Guggenheim
Foundation. Now I must wait. I try to keep very cool, calm +
collective but my winning the Guggenheim would make a big
difference. I do not want another year like this—so broke—no money
which means no materials. Mary calls me a paint addict and she
is absolutely right . . I am not happy when I have no materials
to work with. I know that I must not think about it . . . maybe
Henry* will see to it.

[drawing]

25 MARCH 74

I DID NOT GET THE GUGGENHEIM! This is a very low blow
for me. I am broke not able to Paint, a one-show at the Whitney
Museum in Sept, not really pleased with the paintings that I have—
and no materials—but—Lennie Bocour sent me from paint—
10 GALLONS OF VARIOUS PAINT. I now have Uncle Lennie +
Uncle Sidney! Kaare Rafoss offered to loan me some canvases—
So with a little more money for paint I am back in stride.

I received a letter from Emilio* today. I think that he has had it
with Chicago. We must face the reality of New York being the center
of action. One cannot escape it, what ever is going to happen . . .
it will take place in New York. It's very hard to live here but what can
one do? all the energy is here, the challenge of making it . . . the
testing ground of the art world.

Spoke with Marcia Tucker today. The aspect of a show at the
Whitney looks good . . possible date 25 August–29 Sept. it's not ideal
time but it will be the first show of the season—A chance to psyche
out everything that follows. I plan to work very hard between now
and the time to leave for Crete.

I saw Al Loving today—he was looking good. His studio entirely
activated. He had just painted the floor, it was still tacky. You could
hear yourself being glued to the floor! Al is an artist—
experimenting—continuing to grow—has not allowed himself to be
cornered—I am glad he got out of those boxes! [. . .]

I am so exciting. I can feel my juices boiling throughout my
body. Haven't paid this month's rent, but you know I am not worried
about it—I am hooked in—in harmony—in the flow of things. . .

Shifting . . . sliding to the Nth Degree
 spacing a burden on the ultra-right
  questioning the left.
   still seeking the extreme middle
Enjoying my time in SoHo
    LADY BE GOOD
        LADY BE GOOD
            LADY BE GOOD

<u>APRIL'S SHARK</u>

DARTING ZIG-ZAGGING,
   SCAVENGERING—THE BOTTOM
      OF AC-33
      RIPPING LONGITUDINAL
         A SWATH OF ~~FLESH~~ UNPRIMED COTTON DUCK

APRIL'S SHARK IS A MENACE
   TO THE ART WORLD
HE'S THE RAGE OF THE AGE
   POSSESSING AN ACRYLIC VISION
A SCAVENGER FROM THE LOWER DEPTHS

I DID NOT GET THE GUGGEHEIM! This is very low blow for me. I am broke not able to Paint, a one-show at the Whitney Museum in Sept, not really pleased with the paintings that I have—and no materials—but—Lennie Bocour sent me some paint—10 GALLONS OF VARIOUS PAINT. I now have Uncle Lennie + Uncle Sidney! Kaare Rafoss offered to loan me some canvas—So with a little more money for paint I am back in stride.

I received a letter from Emilio* today. I think that he has had it with Chicago. We must face the reality of New York being the center of action. One cannot escape it, what ever is going to happen . . . it will take place in New York. It's very hard to live here but what can one do? all the energy is here, the challenge of making it . . . the testing ground of the art world.

I have been so depressed that it has been almost a month since I've written anything or painted. An artist, without materials is like a junkie without his shit! [. . .]

The Anthony Caro show was fantastic! Simply superb. The best show in town—all year. A real master of Modern Sculpture. [. . .]

The month of April is going to be a bitch. April could make or break me. I am going to produce my entire Whitney show in April. I am abandoning the edge completely. The picture plane must speak for itself without any added device. The stretcher is the boundry, the framing eye. . . . It may be square . . rectangular, or tall + skinny, circle or triangle or oval

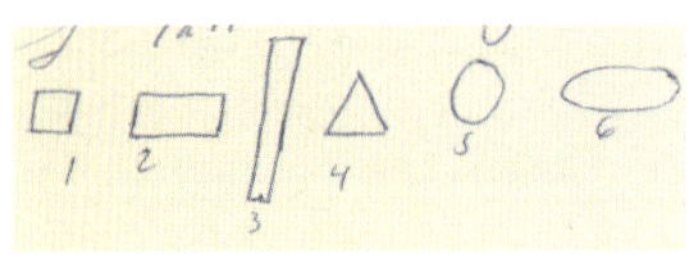 NON-RELATIONAL PAINTINGS

Ed Clark came by the studio today. He seemed impressed with the paintings—but spoke of them as action paintings—I didn't like that. [. . .]

I visited Quaytman* + Barth's* studio with Roger.* Quaytman + Barth are both good painters. Francis's works are bright—a light-hearted handling of geometry—especially the triangle. I like her triangles—they remind me of my use of the triangle as an image other than the pure geometry of the form. [. . .]

Harvey's works have always intrigued me, especially that curving device he uses. He spoke of it as that dumb curve. I've always found it interesting, but never really understood the use of it other than a device. A device for what reason? I speculate that it is a crutch used to give a more abstract presence to the total piece, without it he runs into the problem of having the actual painted surface reading as landscape. A problem I am having trouble with. <u>Abstract painting cannot be landscape</u>. At least that is what the tradition of the New York School says. Consequently, I have had to introduce certain devices to combat this tendency. My incorporation of the border edge was about this, now I am utilizing straight directional lines within the plane with no attempt to divide the total picture plane in no manner. I want a flat, continuous surface plane trapping forms in space—a natural space. Harvey's emphasis on color is purely monochromatic which leaves a lot to be desired in terms of color exploration. I find no difficulty in reacting one color to another—the difficulty is in reacting several colors without destroying the picture plane. Harvey's surface, when he allows it to crack open, adheres too close to Poons's image—Harvey should not allow this. Painters must remove their image as far as possible from another painter. There is something about horizontal structuring that automatically relates it to the landscape, this is the reason Poons turns his paintings vertical or diagonally. Ken Noland is the one abstract painter who works with a horizontal structure and prevents it from reading as landscape.

Harvey Quaytman, Frances Barth, Roger d'Amécourt

Why does Gene Davis run his stripes vertical?

[. . .] One of my problems in painting is to escape the color field—complex. I think that I have done that—by relying upon trapping more shapes, form, as I rush across the plane—modulation. [. . .]

The painting this morning on the first of April 1974 was <u>Heavy Metal,</u> * a smoky grey—with dull pinks and exciting whites pushing toward grey. I am trying to hold a middle to low value in the color. I always run into trouble in the higher registrys by having everything turning too sweet—confectionary [. . .] I want something a little more tougher—harder to deal with. I plan to work until May—then stop + make preparations for the summer.

I am very tired.

*later cut in half

Uncle Lennie called today and promised to send fifteen gals. of gel by tomorrow, that means I can work tomorrow. Bocour has been great, with his backing (even if it was a mistake) I can finish all the paintings in the Whitney show.

I visited Jake Berthot last evening. Jake is working on a series of smaller paintings done in oil, canvas tacked to plywood. Since he is using panels I suggested that he try gesso made from whiting + rabbitskin glue. I do think that Jake is a good painter [. . .]. Jake's studio is like a dungeon small and dark—no windows—a good place to brood in. I could never paint in a studio like that—so confining.

<u>Henry Aaron just hit #715</u>. My next painting must be dedicated to Him!

Harvey visited my studio. I think that we understand each other a lot—more than any other painter. After speaking with Harvey I realize that what I've been calling landscape does not explain my image. . . . It is something about naturalism—abstraction that reads of some form of naturalism Harvey understands the problem very well—A real Painter. I hope to know Quaytman better. We have something in common which could prove helpful in the future →

The ball is flying, you don't think of catching it, you catch it. . . My painting is a form of drawing. In the process of raking—raking is line—things happen. The whole painting is line. The whole painting is *one* line, let's face it. Some people take joy in the fact that nothing is happening—but Pollock, Rothko, Kline, these are my guys, these are my gods.

Do you know that Crete is the edge of the Western World? That's where we in the West draw the line. Right across those waters is Africa. Soho—the whole thing turns into a flea market. . . As for scale, I used to play tenor sax—not the soprano and not the bass clarinet or bass saxophone. Nice mellow tones. Not too big, not too small but like John Hancock's signature . . . able to be read. That's my idea of scale.

These works were painted 1973–74. The main thing is immediate raking, horizontal rakings. They're organized by chance. When I rake them in a split second, there's no way of knowing. It's a gambling situation, but you set up the situation to gamble with a lot of paint, maybe gallons of paint. . . This is my idea of history: history traveling in a straight line like my horizontals. I catch a piece of it, but it's going forever. It's part of a story that's been going on, still is going on, and always will be going on. The space I gave you is a frame that freezes a piece of action.

You take paintings built on grid systems. I don't structure like that. It gives you a play pen to play in, then you can do anything you want to. I don't have that play pen. I rake across and develop it and what happens, happens. . . You might see a face, a landscape. But it's not a crude legibility.

Whatever happens, I want to trap it in the surface. I'm really *into* surface. And I'm working with things that go very fast. It has something to do but is simpler than the "speed" of abstract expressionism. De Kooning said he wanted one skin, but he goes through several manipulations to get that skin. I want one skin too, but I want it in one physical manipulation.

Originally published in *Jack Whitten* (New York: Whitney Museum of American Art, 1974), exhibition brochure, 1–2. Reprinted courtesy of the Whitney Museum of American Art.

It's like light, like a camera trapping something in a single fix. A camera is dark, a certain amount of light enters and the amount of light is what TRAPS the image. Whatever happens on the plane of my painting has to take place instantly and has to catch and freeze something.

When I say speed I'm not talking of the emotions. I keep coming back to the word PHYSICAL. My platform is a heavy constructed platform—it's a huge architectural drawing board. It's a draughtsman's situation. The paint is applied very much like a tile setter, filling a layer of mortar. It is called "floating," and one must have the experience of knowing just how much concrete is needed to set the tiles in place. So my paint is put down, like a workman putting up a sidewalk. . . The word "develop" is important. A huge 12-ft. piece of metal attached to a wood frame, that is my DEVELOPER, which rakes across the plane. It happens very fast. De Kooning needed big house painters' brushes. I took one of those brushes and blew it up to twelve feet. I have a twelve-foot brush.
I have a vast brush: 40–50 lbs., easy.

Harsh criticism might call this landscape painting. . . But there is no most powerful region. There is no horizon line in my painting. I don't know if it's a Jungian "big dream."

On Lispenard Street I'd sit by the window and see a certain color on the street, a color someone was wearing on a shirt, I'd go back and grab that color and mix it and put it in. Take Smithson's *Spiral Jetty*. He uses tons of dirt; I use paint. Art comes from everywhere. I can be a saint and make art. I can be a stone devil and make art.

I have finished painting the Whitney show. I am pleased with what I have and plan to have a relaxing Summer with my Greek friends. This year has been very tough—tough painting I have destroyed more paintings than I have kept—this is necessary for quality—it's better to have ten very good paintings than to have thirty mediocre ones. [. . .]

I spent two days in Rochester at the Xerox headquarters—very interesting. I made a major discovery there, something that fits right into my thinking and possible financial rewards. Xerox toner can be used as a pastel or powder and made permanent by applying heat; this means no fixative necessary + no change of color. I plan to do drawings using this technique and also experiment with it on canvas—I am sure that John Walker will be interested in toner as a material to be used in executing his powdered wall pieces. Xerox is going to supply each one of us with top-plate equipment with camera—I am looking forward to playing with this machine— Great Possibilities.

Frances Barth's Paintings very just terrific at Susan Caldwell's. Frances is a good painter . . . . and a most charming woman. It is needless to say that I really like her a lot. [. . .] Motherwell at Knoedler the collages very superb—the paintings a put-on a big fat nothing! [. . .]

I have had a very hard but terrific year—some fun but mostly painting—I am ready to take on New York—the Critics + all those other Painters—TIME FOR A CHANGE IN PAINTING— ABSTRACT PAINTING IS AT AN ALL TIME LOW—MAYBE MY SENSIBILITY COULD GIVE IT A SHOT IN THE ARM.

Jacob Lawrence opened at the Whitney last night. It was a mob—a fantastic black swarm of people in color reaping the harvest of a hero. I am proud. Jake affected me more than any of the older guys—more than Romare*—more than Bill*—more than Norman*—Jake was the true Artist—the one that persevered through years of neglect. Barbara Rose wrote a History of American Art and if I remember correctly she mentioned Jake's name only once. Jake was a plastic pioneer of the Social Realist movement but he is never spoken of in those terms—Jacob Lawrence is important—Jacob Lawrence is Brave and most of ALL a Beautiful person—Yes Jacob affected me . . . . one of my first influences—He was a sign post—something permanent a part of History.

The people came last night to acclaim their harvester—First there was Horace Pippin and Second there was Jacob Lawrence. I am glad that the Whitney waited until '74 to stage a Jake Lawrence Retrospective. After all the big mouths have had their day it is quite filling that someone of Jake's stature comes in and set the record straight—ART WILL <u>TAKE CARE OF ITSELF. Whitten 74</u>

HARVEY I LOVED YOUR SHOW!!
RIGHT ON!!

I tried the toner from Xerox. executed <u>12</u> Drawings. it worked just as I expected it to—IMMEDIATE—NATURAL—SPONEITY—VERY CRISP—EVERY THING I'VE ALWAYS WANTED FROM A DRAWING—THANKS TO XEROX!

I plan to show these drawings to Rose Esman maybe she'll be interested—I must raise cash.

Very soon I will be back in Aghia Galini very excited about catching big fish—carving my wood I have a large black mulberry log waiting for me.

Mingo* is going to take Mary's studio—I hope he uses it well.

I must decide upon what to do with the studio, here at Broome st. The rent is now $300—must decide soon.

I am on my way to glory
 a child of the plane
   the square is my play box
    the triangle my source
     the circle my absolute
I am on my way to glory
I am on my way to glory
I am on my way to glory
A Child of the plane

May 24, 1974

THE DUKE WENT OUT TODAY
0310

It's not often that we have such giants of men to shape our esthetics.
All we need is one or two
     —IN MUSIC, IN painting—IN DANCE
     in writing —
All that I have heard about the Duke
proves that he was a true Artist
A man of Universal proportions

May 31, 1974

I have been drawing—putting things away, clearing the studio—
going to Crete!

Tonight is my last night to draw. I am sitting here staring at the
floor checking out all the scars—its unbelievable to think of all the
flustration, the torment the basic of hard work—LABOR—MY
PAINTINGS WORK THE HELL OF ME—THEY ARE PHYSICAL.
The drawings are just beautiful—I am trying to think of them in
terms of being dumb, yes DUMB!
I am excited about getting back to my fishing + wood carving.—
Henry* called, he is coming to the studio on Wed. Allan* is coming
on Tuesday—I HOPE! I NEED $1,000—We are leaving on Thursday
and need $1,000—BOY IS THIS CLOSE!
The Whitney will pick-up the paintings on July 1st from the
studio—I can only pray that there are no mishaps.

YES, I AM EXCITED ABOUT SHOWING AT THE WHITNEY.
NO—I DON'T EXPECT TO MAKE A MILLION DOLLARS.
It was nice to see Marcia*—I trust her to do a good job—<u>GOOD
WOMAN</u>.

ANOTHER SEASON

It has been so long since I've written anything but this note keeping is about woodsheding—New York City. The summer was lovely except for the war . . . . . very depressing. Fishing was very good this year. Plenty octopi—sword fish—shark and other smaller fish. My friend from France was there this so of course we fished our asses off. <u>Aleko</u>. I must build a house in Crete. Crete has become my second home, a good change from New York.

The excitement of returning to NY and finding my show at the Whitney installed . . . . was just fantastic? It's so good to relax for three months and come back to a show already up. We had a great party afterwards, every one was there . . dancing, eating—drinking . . Just the way I like it. Seeing the paintings installed at the Whitney gave me the opportunity to see my previous mistakes and my accomplishments. I learned something very important: <u>Only keep your best work</u>. Destroy the rest. It has a way of haunting you. The Whitney Show was well received. + John Russel gave me a short but very positive review.

The show at the Soho Center was a total success! Roger bought three paintings, Mrs. Root another and possibly another through Allan. <u>Money for Materials</u> is all I want. Poindexter expressed their desire for my joining their stable—with NO MONEY. I don't need that from such a gallery! Peter* wrote a fantastic review from the Whitney show. I was very pleased to the point of being happy and had to express my joy by writing him a letter. I hope he understands it.

I went to see David Shapiro today. [. . .] I gave him <u>OMALOS I</u> [. . .] I really like David + Lindsay.*

What's new?

[. . .] Group show at MoMA and Marden* the only thing worth viewing [. . .]. What shape should a painting take? Why not ask Stella? Shields* show was sort of fun [. . .] . . . Novros at Bykert, David built a large room with his canvases sort of like the Rothko Chapel—dark + religious [. . .] Bill Williams is coming on strong—

trying to get back into the limelight. I HOPE SO. [. . .]

At present I am busy experimenting, trying to buck the system by making my own gel + possibly some colors. I do think that the Art Supply stores are inflating the price of canvas and paints. . .too much profit!

Also. . . . . I am backtracking to 1970—Those rib paintings—reinvestingating. I have made my own blade which is equivalent to a saw blade, placed a sheet of ½" foam rubber beneath the entire canvas for exact leverage: results—I can make in one sweep (using weights to keep the blade down) an entire plane. Before I had to scan several times, with the length of my saw blade which was only @ 12" to cover the entire plane. It's remarkable what time will do for your head, for years of hard work later—I discover what I was trying to do! I am stacking the studio with materials. Plenty work this year—even if there is a depression.

Thanks to God that the Holiday season is over! Just this week I have been able to start work.

I have been experimenting with making my own acrylic gel. One failure after another. I am about ready to give up, just can't figure out the right proportions or maybe I am missing an ingredient.

I finished a painting today but doubt if the paint holds to the canvas! My home-made saw blade is working out just fine. The paintings are becoming more and more symetrical in composition—symetrical balancing—with squares + linear movements, vertical—horizontal + diagonal. The evidence of a more exacting space—3 layers. I must try to explain this later. Frontal—Middle + Back happening in a very limiting distance—as a finger pressed against the surface of a mirror. I am allowing the color to mix at will by raking wet into wet. Also I am using the same technique of mixing various hues within a stationery neutral amount of paint. Ie, a basic neutral color is mixed (scrappings from previous experiments) enough to cover the entire plane (on a 60" x 72" requires 1 ½ gallon of neutral color). This technique was used in producing all the earlier rib series. I first discovered this technique of color mixing as a solution to the problem of relational mixing i.e., the intellectual choosing ~~of color~~ and placing of color to achieve a color structure. This technique can be described as non-relational color-mixing. [. . .]

④ . 8 Jan 75

The space which appears in these painting can be
described as existing in three layers — but dye to the
process of ribbing, the three layers manifest themselves as a surface
phenomenon. The surface is a charged one — sensory charged — which
is the element which describes the emotional content: very high,
a little erratic but under control.

I cannot speak of these paintings as process. I can
but I can't. It is more of a combination of elements.
There is definite an element of drawing, a painting of forms
plus the physical process of raking and not forgetting
the all important compositional layout. ~~I most admit that
the paintings are becoming more symbolic. Maybe I am a symbolist
But FOR WHAT! IS ART TRULY THE NEW RELIGION! OK
MAYBE JUST A LITTLE BIT MORE PURER?~~
while write about that, all painters make that mistake a little
bit too much of Mondrian and his philosophical discourse on
painting. I only want to describe the experiments conducted
in the wood shed plus occasional comments on shows & other
artists.

At present the composition is a square resting in the horns
of Minos: — divided by a straight perpendicular.

All of these paintings shall be entitled Minos I – II – III
etc. Using a composition of this nature makes me think of
Renaissance composibnal studies where the figures are always
balanced against architecture or landscape and one another.
architecture / figure / landscape

↑ madonna + christ child

The space which appears in these paintings can be described as existing in three layers—but due to the process of ribbing, the three layers manifest themselves as a surface phenomenon. The surface is a charged one—sensory charged—which is the element which describes the emotional content: very high—a little erratic but under control.

I cannot speak of these paintings as process. I can but I can't. It is more of a combination of elements. There is definite an element of drawing, a painting of forms plus the physical process of raking and not forgetting the all important compositional layout. ~~I must admit that the paintings are becoming more symbolic. Maybe I am a symbolist BUT FOR WHAT! IS ART TRULY THE NEW RELIGION OK MAYBE JUST A LITTLE BIT MORE PURER?~~

While write about that, all painters make that mistake a little bit too much of Mondrian and his philosophical discourse on painting. I only want to describe the experiments conducted in the woodshed plus occasional comments on shows + other artists.

At present the composition is a square resting in between the horns of Minos: [drawing] —divided by a straight perpendicular.

All of these paintings shall be entitlted Minos I-II-III etc. Using a composition of this nature makes me think of Renaissance compositional studies where the figures are always balanced against architecture or landscape and one another.

[drawing; labeled, "architecture," "figure," "landscape," and "madonna + christ child"]

The past three weeks have been very difficult. I have been sick in bed with the flu . . . . no energy. The painting have been going very bad. Every experiment I attempted was a complete failure; times like this make you wonder why torture yourself with painting. After the very difficult month of January. . I've had a breakthrough. I have found out that by decreasing the consistency of my paint from a buttery consistency to one that allows me to pour—I am able to control the final drag much more efficiently + effectively. The paintings are a little looser with line—shape—color placed by hand: something I haven't been able to do with these paintings. I must achieve a matte surface. The rib paintings are impossible to see with a gloss surface. Tomorrow I will experiment with using gesso as a final pour which should give me a matte surface, also spoke with Ken Nelson at Bocour and he is sending me 10lbs of powdered silica.

By wetting out the silica with TAMOL or Glycol I should be able to incorporate it directly into the acrylic system with no harm. Besides the technical problem with lighting paintings possessing a gloss surface—matte paintings are much more purer in feeling than gloss.

I think that I have introduced a new type of space in painting. It can be called the conception of space through the use of a volumetric surface. A space that exists solely through surface—no attempt at overlapping—placement—or perspective. note: (as a means at arriving at a spatial solution) The space comes out of the surface. The use of gel adds more transparency to the pigment. The process of ribbing keeps the eye up front at all times. Due to the transparency of the pigment, light is allowed to pass through + refract: as a result of this refraction the color when given a definite form or shape is realized in a volume—hence volumetric space or volumetric surface (sort of like the phenomenon of viewing reflections in water. <u>I take my cue from nature</u>. Even with color I take my cue from nature i.e., presenting an all over tonal range with occasional patches of hue.

I want to put the fear of God in these paintings. I want to evoke a
spiritual—magical—cosmic existence with a material connection—
emotionally charged. . .

P.S. UNCLE LENNY sent more paint
I owe him another painting.
+ I am so broke—NEED MONEY
[. . .]

I have only one painting of value and I have been unable to ~~achieve~~ produce another. Most of my paint has turned to gray—I am two months behind in rent—phone—Lights plus—home rent + tele— I literally do not know what to do—Allan claims that he cannot help me—I need paint, stretchers and cash for more ideas to experiment with. I ordered a new design in blades from Dilorenzo should arrive this weeek. I plan to use gray paint (on unprimed canvas) with very little hue, topped with white. I am thinking of early black painters: <u>they always had a tendency to use heavy highlights.</u>

If I can override my depression and not worry about money— I am O.K. because I am ~~fairly~~ <u>secure</u> in my ideas about painting. I know what is needed. [. . .]

I received my fourth (fifth?) Guggenheim rejection today. I am not Guggenheim material. [. . .]

Painting is getting harder + harder. Maybe it is for the better—at least I like to think so. Living + working in N.Y. is getting harder + harder. Very difficult to continue without selling art. <u>I REFUSE TO ACCEPT THAT WHICH I DO NOT FEEL</u>. If it does not feel correct, I refuse to accept it! <u>REFUSE</u>!

I remain optimistic. The energy in N.Y. today is all important, not so much the product being produced. <u>The energy is still important</u>! That can of energy cannot be wrong.

The more that I think of John Walker's show the more I accept it. . . . . I still have reservations about his use of Cubist composition [. . .] . . . . Hudson's* advice to me was to do what you can. If you can not produce what your head is showing you . . . . . compromise and produce what's at hand—<u>I REFUSE. I WANT ALL OF THE APPLE</u>!

I spent last Sunday Eve. with Novros, Marden + Joanna.* A very nice evening over wine + assorted goodies! Afterwards Brice + I went to Broome St. Bar for a drink. Brice is much purer than I thought. Someone that really cares about art + civilization. He constantly spoke of Greece and asked me to visit his show at the Guggenheim especially to see his olive leaf from the olive grove of Delphi.

Yes Brice I saw your olive leaf—a real symbol. Just as real as your blocks of color. I found Brice's show to be very strong. I enjoyed it and learned something in the process: ~~that~~ the need for reduction in my own work. Brice has not done his best work. He is still too much in the shadow of Rothko. I think that the Rothko Chapel affected him very much. It is important to note that no one can reduce a Rothko, only follow suit—be influenced—copy—admire but not reduce! Abstract Expressionism as a whole can be reduced. Rothko, is not really an abstract expressionist. He is an expressionist although, but of what order?

I saw the Max Ernst show. I did not like it. Again, I learned something about my own work: I must reduce the surrealist content. It is about picking the mind for images and I have been too much influenced by that sort of thinking. [. . .]

Agnes Martin is brilliant. <u>Super</u>. <u>Strong</u>. Distinct. <u>Intellectual Suave</u>. <u>Very much together</u>. I have a lot to learn from her. [. . .]

Tonight I tried something different—spraying into a wet ribbed surface. It worked. By spraying, I am able to pull colors from beneath the ribbing to the surface and thus achieving a three layered space. I am not sure of the significant of this type of space yet but I do think that it is a step in the right direction. Toward what, who knows?

Tomorrow night I am to speak on a panel entitled Abstract Expressionism: its Continuation + Transformation. I only want to get one thing clear. That is: Abstract Expressionism as a movement is over with. ~~Secondly: the type of spirit~~

Abstract Expressionism is only an academic concern at this point in history. It is to be learned from. Talked about—discussed in terms of nostalgia—in an art history context—for the art school classroom—but it is not to be used for any serious experiment in the search for ART. and anyone using Abstract Expressionism today (except for its founders if any are alive) are only decorators.

—By adding powdered silica to the acrylic, I am able to prevent gloss. A much better solution to the problem other than varnishing.

Breakthrough

After total exhaustion — frustration — near panic . . . I experienced a major breakthrough. I have been working on 42" squares, at least ~~fifteen~~ canvases. I have destroyed all but five — and two I really like. Do you have any idea of relief the soul experiences after such an ordeal? To say I like two of my paintings is very important for me now. I plan to do two more 42" squares and then try for a larger scale.

As I have said before the paintings are beginning to be more conceptual. First I have a very simple drawing:

This limits my ~~that~~ experimenting to a fixed image — yes an imposed limitation — but any degree of exploration my occur within this limitation. ~~This~~ By using the conceptual approach I solve the problem of naturalization of image which has been a big problem for me — These paintings are totally abstract with adhering to constructive or Abstract Expressionist principles.

Also I have reduced the color structure to grey, employed only a faint acquaintance to the color wheel. The problem of locating another approach to the element of space is also solved. My past mistake about space was my thinking in terms of the thickness of paint as surface and expecting space to appear purely from the paint surface — or material surface (very much along Larry Poons ideas) Now I know that it is not only the material as surface but the manipulation of the surface plane, optically to achieve a space which is measureable: AN EXACT AMOUNT OF SPACE — MAYBE 2"!

Breakthrough

After total exhaustion—flustration—near panic . . . . I experience a major breakthrough. I have been working on 42" squares, at least <u>fifteen</u> canvases. I have destroyed all but five—and two I really like. Do you have any idea of relief the soul experiences after such an ordeal? To say I like two of my paintings is very important for me now. I plan to do two more 42" squares and then try for a larger scale.

As I have said before the paintings are beginning to be more conceptual. First I have a very simple drawing: [drawing] This limits my ~~change~~ experimenting to a fixed image—yes an imposed limitation—but any degree of exploration may occur within this limitation. By using the conceptual approach I solve the problem of naturalization of image which has been a big problem for me— These paintings are totally abstract with adhering to constructive or Abstract Expressionist principles.

Also I have reduced the color structure to grey, employed only a faint acquaintance to the color wheel.

The problem of locating another approach to the element of space is also solved. My past mistake about space was my thinking in terms of the thickness of paint as surface and expecting space to appear purely from the paint surface—or material surface (very much along Larry Poons ideas) Now I know that it is not only the material as surface but the manipulation of the surface plane, optically to achieve a space which is measurable: AN EXACT AMOUNT OF SPACE—MAYBE 2".

My talk about volumetric surface also is apparent in these new paintings. There is such a thing as a volumetric surface. I am positive that when Olitski* uses gel (or Bannard) he is trying to explain this to himself. Acrylic gel is transparent—blocks of clear acrylic plastic is transparent—glass: try visualizing a block of water with no container support. You see what I mean. When David Smith burnished the surface of his stainless steel pieces the surface became more volumetric but continued within a confined Cubist environment. I CAN SEE LARGE PAINTING WITH NO SUPPORTS JUST EXISTING OUTSIDE IN AN URBAN ENVIRONMENT.

Malraux* in <u>Metamorphosis of the Gods</u> speaks of African sculpture as being motivated by "spirits". I am aware of the fact that this is the tradition in Art which I must connect with—not the Western concept of the divine or sublime, or romantic or classical but a work of art with a function motivated by the tradition of African Sculpture—MY WAY—Not Picasso's European interruption.

Jules Olitski* André Malraux*

The paintings have changed. It is impossible for me to control them. Sometimes I wonder who or what is doing the controlling. I have three paintings of one thing + four paintings of something else and one of something else. I must learn to accept change as being inherent with my type of structure it is not a cookie-cutter-concept. One must allow for change—however rapid: as long as it is within the original boundaries.

I am painting very thin now, almost as thin as wash. The paint is first squeeged onto raw canvas and a thin coat of spray (sprayed directly onto a wet surface) and scraped with the scraper. I have spent so much time + money formulating an acrylic-gel and flatting agent and now with this new discovery none of it applies. <u>Very strange</u>. Whatever it is that I am working with, I have merely scratched the surface, if that. It is something so elusive so infinite in its ability to change—to avoid being structured—or placed in category. Sometimes it is thick, sometimes thin—always existing within obvious extremes. Sometimes transcending all extremes and sometimes existing in the extreme middle of opposite obvious extremes. I guess it is truly the extreme middle.

The paintings are hard to look at. They are a real optical experience—the change of values twist + bend the eye. The surface appears to be flat—but no it could be sculpture—It could be the beginning of a volumetric surface.

Something that is only flat out of visual appearance, but alludes to a holographic definition of forms in space—a three dimensional illusion of flatness.

May the history of Western painting die within me. [. . .]

Another major breakthrough has taken place. I am using a paint roller to apply a layer of paint and afterwards using my scraper. The paintings of mostly black + white—grey—very little color but good vibrancy—vibration of black + white value. I am also scoring ruled lines and free lines into the canvas with an ice-pick or screwdriver—or any instrument capable of cutting into the paint: this leaves an indentation into the canvas which is later filled in with a layer of paint. At times an electric drill is used to drill small indentations which later appear as dots. I am employing the use of vertical + horizontal lines plus drawing arc projections with a large homemade compass. <u>I think that the paintings are getting closer to their own space</u>. Also I learned by turning my stratations _{s/p} vertical instead of horizontal I can achieve much more vibrancy in terms of color vibrations, it also increases their abstract quality.

Roger spoke of my paintings having an European sensibility. I think that this is an awful ~~interruption~~ interpretation—it is not European but could be a new-sensibility for painting done in America. It is not the rough-hewn quality of Abstract-Expressionism (which was a regional phenomenon centered in New York, hence called New York School). And on the other hand it is not the refined slickness found in European attempts at European Abstract Expressionism: Hartung,* Soulages*—etc. These paintings are not about the New York School. I would like to prevent their having a regional look, maybe something more international in scope— something existing beyond national boundaries. Previous isms were very regional—unique to a native setting: French painting—Dutch Painting—Italian Painting—New York Painting. Perhaps it is now possible to break that tie in with history—that dependence upon history: the inbred aestetic situation which we find ourselves in— Perhaps a time to cut the umbilical cord to Western aesthetics. I can visualize an art existing beyond the aesthetic scope of a particular sub-culture within a particular regional setting—beyond the limited viewpoint of the elite, and at the same time resisting the move toward some form of Social Realism—I am talking about a new outlook to so called abstract painting.

I firmly believe that the paintings I am doing right now will put a new kink into abstract painting.

I am getting closer to understanding what I am dealing with . . . .
closer to understanding the meaning of abstract painting. I am
abstracting from landscape painting—from fields—from gardens—
from women in fields—from pussies in gardens. I have left the
landscape—viewed it from many miles above the earth's surface—
I must leave it further + further behind me. I am about to penetrate
the zone of pure abstract painting . . . . . what Mondrian spoke of
and very very few before him.

An abstract painter must start with something and go from there.
I am afraid that a lot of my peers started only from abstract paintings
(abstract paintings which someone else had arrived at) this is the
danger of an inbred aesthetic . . . . . . making to much of of a historical
reference. One must see for himself. Without seeing, and I do mean
a vision, one is only designing decorative two-dimensional planes.

I keep having the feeling that ~~I am~~ I have been preparing myself for something profoundly new and important in painting. The paintings talk to me more + more. There is something in the air.

Yes, I think I understand what De Kooning meant by painting himself out of the painting. I have the problem of working very abstractly but always seeing an image of myself in the paintin. . something which happens as a result of value-mixing in a certain way. It disturbs me very much and spoils the painting for me. I don't want to see images of myself or any one else—I want only the purity of my ideas to come through not some second-handed concept of surrealistic automation—or Jungian images.

I am being pressured toward a painters invention of geometry; a spatial concept of geometry . . . . a type of geometry which can be used to plot a painter's space . . . . . NOT A CELESTIAL SPACE TRIP . . . A TOTALLY PLASTIC SPATIAL TRIP, and I must leave this earth in order to do this . . . . one must not be earth bound!! I know as a fact that abstract painting is up against the wall I also know that I will play an important part in restoring the original importance of man as a symbol making animal.

62 X 7'2
−   8 X − 8
    54 X 64

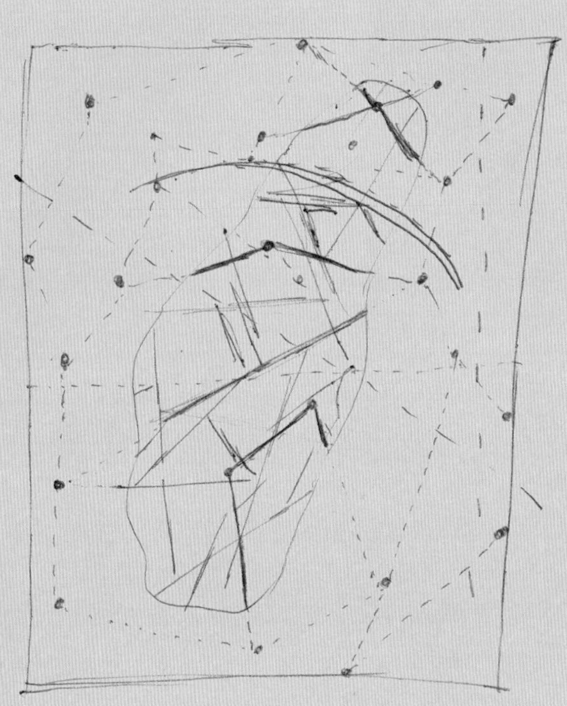

SPACE   CHART   #2

the next step will be to lose to
emphasis upon the center object — and
move toward moving from one point to
another — …. space travelling. —

I am a painter who travels through space
plotting & mapping my course — who knows
where my destination lies?? Perhaps I will
never know …….but I can always keep
travelling.   J. Whitten may '75

62 × 72
-8 × -8
54 × 64

[drawing]

<u>SPACE CHART</u> #2

the next step will be to lose to
emphasis upon the center object—and
move toward moving from one point to
another . . . . . space travelling. —
I am a painter who travels through space
plotting + mapping my course—who knows
where my destination lies?? Perhaps I will
never know . . . . . . but I can always keep
traveling!   J. Whitten May '75

The renovation is going very well. My body is exhausted from plumbing, carpentry + all the other necessary workings. I still must paint the place, do the electric, scrap the floors and build my platform plus a bunch of other smaller things like heating the place. It is a drag that painting has come to this. The amount of money involved, the work, but painters need a space in which to work, somewhere one can feel comfortable without been hassled. If I didn't know all the technical know-how of plumbing, carpentry + electricity I wouldn't have a chance today. One must be rich or the equivalent of selling plenty of paintings or definite income in order to paint. Painting is expensive today, to maintain a studio plus materials + utilities one must have a fair amount of money. No longer is it possible to live cheaply in N.Y. and produce on a professional scale. Maybe the answer is to leave N.Y.

When I am doing physical labor like this, away from my paintings, I long with such a vengeance to paint—My energy cells are overflowing—I must start painting soon. I think so much about painting and what I am going to do, however I never end up doing what I conceive of. The actual painting is always much more direct, spontaneous, as if I never thought about it. I am tired but my mind is active. Sometimes I think that not painting is also to paint. I paint whether I am in the studio or outside the studio involved with other things.

Budd Hopkins called tonight to inform me that I have just won a CAPS Award. It is only $3,500 but enough to keep the Hawk from the door long enough to formulate other plans. I cannot express how badly I need money. I am fixing up my new studio and even though I am doing all the work I still need cash!

I am excited to get back to painting. My paintings are exciting and have the promise of something new—A new sensibility plus a new plasticity makes a new aesthetic.

I am increasing the size of the platform to 14' x 24'. I expect to experiment with a large scale within the next two years. The test of a painter takes place from 12 inches to 24 feet.

I like to think of my studio as a laboratory where experiments are conducted. Having everything under my control to the absolute possible. The platform must be perfectly flat, square and able to ~~withstand the weight of~~ serve as a dance floor.

The black + white paintings have forced me to be cooler, imposed a limitation upon my work habit and structure; forced me to tighten the visual concept; provided a personal framework of references plus a stamp of originality: THEY SAY WHITTEN. I plan to continue the black + white experiments. My problems are those ~~of the~~ involving the use of geometry in the image of triangle, square, circle, point, in other words how to handle the obvious constructive imagery evident in the last two paintings. The problem of how far to push the opticality of the black + white surface modulations. The problem of what amount of emotional tension to allow in the surface. These problems are one of balance i.e., total balance: the orchestration of personal vision within the visual plastic limitations of painting . . . . two dimensional representational.

My deadline is after the New Years. I expect to be finished with the studio + working by the second week of January '76

While lecturing at Montclair State, one of the questions asked was what was the extent of my involvement with analytical cubism? I don't practice analytical cubism. The geometry in my recent works are a direct result of the wood carving. I started carving wood as an investigation into African sculpture. The first pieces were figurative of semi-abstractions of figuration. The later pieces are closer to some form of geometric rendering of abstract planes in space: hard-smooth edges without any relationship to figuration. In painting my theory was not necessarily cubism but an attempt at modern painting from a black-artist influenced or rather inspired by African sculpture very much as the early cubist were inspired by African + Oceanic Art. My question is (with the extensive knowledge of Western aesthetics, including cubism) what if one presents a new interruption of a new plasticism inspired by African Sculpture, one removed from cubist thought as we know it. I am emphasizing my being Black, with the expectation of offering another sensibility, possibly another insight into African Art other than that offered by Western Europe.

I have always considered myself to be working within the Western tradition, or in a more exalted sense a progression of that tradition. Now I sense an ending of what we call Western thought—Western world-view—hence an ending of Western esthetics. The sensory-assault of technology forces upon us the beginning of another world-view. One removed from Western esthetic thinking. One which compasses all but yet depends upon either. For the first time since the birth of Christ we ~~have the definite~~ are in the definite position of psychic-change. A new man—a new world = a new world view. New art as such is created, out of a new world view. My lifestyle will create a new esthetic.

So, instead of a progression of Western thought I find myself at the end of Western thought with nothing to fall back on except my own Being—my world view. My accumulated heritage of borrowings.

Also I cannot even afford the romanticism or I should say the escapism of indulging in my long-lost disconnected, culture: AFRICA. The toughness of my reality is just that I am <u>man</u> with exactly the same responsibilities the same enigmas that have faced all men who dared to say <u>I AM</u>. We are forced today living within the shadow of nuclear-destruction—the disintegration of society and its instititutions—the lost of spirituality— ~~we are forced to be responsible~~. . . . .

We are forced to create new values—new images—new icons—new myths another esthetic which will in turn give us a new political system.

I will start painting by the week-end. I don't know what to expect. I try not to think not to see what's around me, nor do I find myself interested in what I see: The galleries are defunct with nothing of importance to show painters of my generation are lost without nothing to go on—they are either disillusioned going insane with flustrations. We have seen in the past five years every conceivable dumb idea—amateurism + showmanship possible.

I start to paint completely alone. More alone more lonely than I have ever been. In light of all this, my creative drive to paint is at its all time height. All I know is that I will start on three squares 42" x 42" in gray—that's all I need to know!
<u>the Delta Squares</u> I, II + III —
EPSILON
destroyed four kept three

I went to Baltimore to bury my student, William Lafferty. Only now can I say without emotion that ~~that~~ I love the spirit of Bill Lafferty. Bill was the student par excellence—an ideal to be achieved by others; just recently we sorted through his works: photographs, sculptures, videos, paintings, drawings this kid had it—I never expect another student of such intelligence. A real shining star. Seldom do we have students that teach us, with bill it was always a give + take situation. We are planning an exhibition of his works at school for the 29 of March.

Everyone must know of my receiving the Guggenheim. To receive a Guggenheim in times like this is like finding a pot of gold! I expect to paint for one year without worry. I saw Henry. [. . .] He mentioned in a sly manner that my paintings which the museum owns <u>may</u> <u>be</u> exhibited in Bedford Stuyvesant. . . obvious a political gesture. I cannot afford to expend ~~the~~ energy in deciphering their logic. Whatever is done for the black artist ~~ierati~~ 99% is political motivated. One never knows the exact motive. The Modern has a Bill Williams, a Benny Andrews and a Frank Bowling, The Whitney has an Al Loving and now the Metropolitan a Whitten. My job is to paint their job is politics . . . . my salvation lies in my ability to paint . . . my freedom lies in my ability to paint . . . . painting is not only my pleasure but my arto of combat. My paintings are designed as weapons. Their objective is to penetrate and destroy the Western aesthetic. Their final objective is political in nature.

Slowly I am begginnig to recognize the true substance of my work: a structure which lies at point zero existing between two extremes. It is not just eclecticism as I previously thought but something much more original in the sense of their being obviously composed out of art history but very much within its own element of time. Always a total synthenyis/sp . . The grey paintings have the stamp of Jack Whitten . . . surely these paintings will provide the necessary excitement needed to get the ball rolling!

[. . .] Why! Why the emphasis upon sweetness, the decorative qualities? It removes all the soul from painting. [. . .] One would think that work done by black artist would be aggressive, tough and un-academic but just the opposite is true. I feel such a strong rebellious feeling against such art. I despise it! I don't even see it as art but instead decoration . . . a little bit higher than commercial work. I only hope that all the young kids who expect to paint are not influenced by these ideas. I do hope that they establish a strong reaction against such painting.

Bob Thompson's paintings were never sweet—but tough with spirit and lots of soul . . . . with tensions tied into their structuring. <u>A real involvement with art</u>. More and more I respect Bob's work. Bob was a true Artist. One to be respected. Bob used pure hue . . a complete palette but I can't call them decorative. Surely they were allegrocial, narrative and filled with litery imagery, but his emphasis upon soul searching prevented them from being decorations. [. . .]

I am using more geometry than ever before, a free-form geometry: a casual linking up of points by using straight lines. I want something more accessiable to the general public, a universal language of form without resorting to the use of naturalistic or biomorphic forms. I see something but need a language in which to express it. I think that language lies within some form of geometry. The paintings call for more drawing, more evidence of the hand but without gesture. The use of process only to reach something much more important that just process. Something which the hand is a part of. I am also toying with the idea of using drawing directly into the painting i.e., copying an exact drawing. I have never done a painting exactly from a drawing. I have always used drawing to search for material to work with. This Renaissance idea of copying directly from the drawing appeals to me.

I am depending less + less upon spontaneity, not altogether but not as a total response to structuring. My idea of always working between two extremes has advanced into a system of structuring (Plasticity) I am interested in the action which occurs when two opposing things clash. I am consciously building a plastic language which exist somewhere between a complexity of extremities. I am employing the use of surface as the unifing element: Whatever complexities exist within the painting they are ~~unified with an emphasis place upon~~ structured totally through the use of surface.

I used to speak of something being trapped within the surface. Now, my understanding is not so much to trap as in a physical sense (which still relates to a form of naturalism in painting e.g., wood, glass, rock, metal, etc.) but instead a visual use of surface in order to unify totally diverse elements. The use of variation of line, of value, of shape, of inherent space organized through the flat planar confrontation of paint surface. Yes, flat planar confrontation as in a David Smith sculpture! One must be confrontated with the painted surface. I still maintain that the space is volumetric: the extremity of surface with depth. The visualization of something physically flat, frontal but possessing the infinity of depth.

One of the main problems which I am expeirencing presently is how much information is to be given in each individual painting. What is the correct amount of information? I don't want to do minimal paintings but on the other hand I don't want to do Abstract Expressionist paintings. There exist a level of emotionality which states the exact amount of information needed within a given structure and for that painting to still maintain its maximum of performance. I am afraid that my maturity is all to important here. Not just my maturity as a painter in use of materials, techniques + theory but my maturation as a man. Our emotions are closely associated with our aging. I was much more violent as a young man, more inclined to act totally out of emotional response.

The maturity I speak of is one which is found after we have expended all the easily accessible emotions: the hot air of boyhood. Within that maturation lies the level of emotionality which expresses the exact amount of information. Surely, it is an ongoing process for we are forever in a state of psychic metabolism. We are forever defining ~~the line~~ the spatial-temporal time ~~through our personal~~ through use of our own consciousness.

More and more I am beginning to understand sensibilities as a collective phenomenon as opposed to personal phenomenon. Hence, I further believe that we arrive at esthetics through a profound use of sensibilities (or I should say a system of esthetics) i.e., the employment of our sensibilities in every day thought and action: the formation of esthetics. Esthetics is a cultivation of the senses. Of course, I believe that political systems are formulated out of esthetics.

I started to write tonight by speaking of my use of geometry. The use of geometry as a universal sign language. Finally geometry

helps to explain my being influenced by photography i.e., my being
plastically influenced. The photograph is a universal language.
A symbol of a known quantity.

My use of various tools in painting is expanding. The last two experiments employed the use of electric polishers to push around the paint. This enables me the continual removal of my hand and still being able to direct movement. I am applying white paint over a grey ground pushing it around with the machine, allowing this to dry and later raking through a field of grey which has been sprayed over the white (spraying into wet gel, the gel is applied first to prevent staining and also acts as a lubricant which allows the developer to glide more easily). Sometimes, while the white paint is still wet, I draw directly into the wet surface which gives me the same etched quality of line used in earlier experiments. I have learned to control the tone i.e., overall tone, to any degree. By using straight acrylic medium or gel directly to the ground before spraying or rolling in the neutral grey I can control the overall tone.

I am working as fast as possible dependent only upon drying time and domestic chores which are becoming more and of a drag everyday.

Mingo and Stewart* payed me a visit at the studio. I really like those guys—so serious with their work, healthy attitudes about art, not fucked up on drugs and they don't allow racial-politics to slow them down. I try to emphasize as much as possible the need for black artist to go all the way now . . . not stopping at social-realism but to press ahead and investigate what the world of the abstract has to offer. So many black artists have done mounds of preliminary work in social realism: images of protest, basic identity—nationalistic propaganda works, pseudo-surrealistic dream images—etc. Now is the time for Black Artist to research the abstract and not in the sense of duplicating past art schools and mannerisms but personal experimentations in abstract thought. No longer must we create only for the black mass. . .We are artist of the world possessing the capabilities of being universal and participating in the world art community, establish a market place on an international level. No longer must our work be stigmatized as ethnic interruptions of the various isms. If ever fame comes my way may I be prepared to use it toward influencing the direction of younger black artists.

Romare's work has achieved a huge success among black artist and white collectors. He fills a necessary vacuum in the sphere of art-politics. However, he remains a social realist dependent upon ethnic themes for subject matter and relies whole heartedly upon Cubism as a means of plasticity. I do believe that Norman Lewis at one time, maybe during the fifties saw the larger picture, was able to penetrate into abstract thought but the element of risk (the lack of) prevented the type of in depth experimentation necessary to arrive at a profound plastic language. I say the lack of risk, I must also include the circumstance of time i.e., the political climate for black artist. [. . .] Of course, some people have larger ambitions than others and are willing to pursue those ambitions at any cost, some of more inclined to accept the Romantic belief that others (presumably their dealers) will take care of their careers, as artist we can accept either course, but we must be prepared to accept the consequences, which is usually being bitter at age 65, mad with the world for not having success, poor, creatively washed up, begging for scraps from institutions and famous ~~friends~~ acquaintances, and most of all not having a substantial body of work to rely upon.

Last evening I went to the opening of "Selected Black Artist" from the Metropolitan Museum Collection of the Bedford Stuyvesant Restoration Corp in Brooklyn. I really hate Brooklyn but was curious to see the show. It was the usual presentation but with exception: there was a very tough, resistant Jack Whitten from 1975. The picture really holds up! A complicated, very complex, intriguing painting. My painting was exhibited alone—removed from the rest of the exhibition. When entering the doorway, it confronts you. . . . square in the middle. The other works were by J. Lawrence, Bearden, Woodruff,* Alston,* a Bradley etching, Van der Zee* photographs and Chase-Riboud* drawing [. . .] there was a very good Bearden and a Lawrence and the Palmer Hayden was wonderful in an ethnic manner. [. . .] There remains a need for stronger works from Black Artist. . . Stronger more exacting abstract painters.

I remain confused about being represented in a show of this nature, not me, but having the painting there under the particular circumstance. Henry purchased the painting directly from my studio for $2,000 which as far as my market today goes, it represents a fair price. The painting is part of the Metropolitan's collection. The museum purchased the painting in order to use it as a political vehicle. The painting will always be used in shows of this type so that the Metropolitan can say "Look, we have one!" Indeed, they have one but what does this do for me? Does this represent a special category for me? The most accepted black abstract artist? A pawn to keep the mass at bay? Will this painting be shown in regular museums shows at the Metropolitan as a representation of current American abstract painting?

My being black forces me into the political arena and I must gear myself to think in art-politics. To deal in order to protect my financial growth and integrity as an artist. Realizing the use that the Metropolitan has intended for my painting surely $2,000 is peanuts! If I am to be used in this manner then they must pay dearly!

Hale Woodruff, Charles Alston, James Van der Zee, Barbara Chase-Riboud

Ideally an artist should not have to participate in politics but
I cannot afford Idealism or Romanticism on any level. My policy
must be one solely based upon being an artist in society realizing the
meaning of my blackness and exercising control through diplomacy.
I will do what I have to do in order to continue my growth as an
artist and provide for the well-being of myself and family. I have
already accepted the philosophy of "THE DURATION" I have
trained myself for survival now it's left up <u>only to me</u> to maintain a
strict level of presentation of my works. note: this is not what I really
want to say but can't seem able to find the correct words. I will try
to write about this at a later date.

Earlier I wrote that I as an artist must concern myself with
painting and not waste energy on trying to decipher other people's
intentions or motives. I still believe this to be correct.

(My main purpose in life is to paint, this is my profession. I am
most happy when I am alone in the studio working. The other
problems of politics exist outside the studio.)

note: I am not sure of this. I am sure of one thing that I am
most happy when I am alone working in the studio. The distance
between art + politics is one of grey. I have thought of my
involvement in art as being one of combat—the paintings are
weapons designed to destroy oppressors i.e., the establishment.
Art is none of This! <u>Art is Art</u>.

A painting does not represent anything but itself. It shouldn't
look like anything else or make for any allusions. A painting is a
painting just as a Rose is a Rose! May God bless Gertrude Stein!

N.Y.C.

I am always interested in what exist between extremes, something that I call the extreme middle. A physical space, a magnetic field created by plastic tensions: Black to white, line to shape, center to edge, tactile surface quality to atmospheric illusion, the non-objective emphasis of imagery as opposed to that which is purely subjective, horizontal movement to vertical movement, the concrete placement of format along with the accidental, the emotional ~~cool plus~~ scale from cool to hot, the conceptual along with the spontaneity of expressionism . . . . somewhere between these extremes exist the "I", a stopping point between time zones, a resting zone, a clear crystilized space, a clearing, ~~for~~ a meeting place. . . . .

I am considering the possibilities found in the process known as layering . . . a space existing in different layers of material. This can be achieved by the use of rice papers and tracing papers, preferably rice papers because of their permanence and tough quality of fibre. In painting, gel serves the purpose of transparent papers. This kind of space has a physical presence very much like 1-2-3-4 but when injected with personal sensibilities it can acquire the character of something very mystical but not atmospheric—again my emphasis upon volumetric surface . . . a surface having volume.

My interest in art history takes me to a period of pre-photography—precisely early Italian Renaissance: Mantegna, Uccello, Fra Angelico, etc. The space inherent in these paintings, however naturalistic, the shapes occupy definite spatial zones

<u>Foreground</u>, <u>middle ground</u> + <u>background</u>

I am emphasizing pre-photography because I am convinced that after the advent of photography painting took on a totally different meaning. Once we had a machine to capture images the painters vision became one of more internal struggle: To do something the camera could not do! Also, the photograph reinforced the Artist's understandment of plasticity. The photograph assumed a love-hate relationship with the artist.

I understand that one can <u>no longer accept</u> naturalism in abstract painting: layering offers the possibility of distinct spatial zones without depending upon the type of space found in naturalism, <u>it is the surface that is all important</u>.

The field is no longer that of color-field I prefer to identify it as
<u>PSCYHIC FIELD</u>: The structuring of a plane through the use of an
emotionally charged surface. All other plastic elements taking place
within the surface of the plane . . . . a highly structured skin . . . . .
a garment for the stretcher.

An after thought of my progressions listing important decisions
made in order to arrive at this point:

1. The avoidance of the use of gesture
2. The use of Black + White instead of spectrum color
3. AVOIDING A NATURALISTIC SPACE (the space
   of surrealism)

I haven't written down my experiences in such a long time. I have been too busy. The paintings take it all. Money still remains my most depressing subject. I am in debt and can see not possible way out except selling paintings. Bob* sold one painting in August or July and since that time, nothing. My show is April 4th. Yes, I am excited. I am not quite ready but that doesn't worry me. Billy* is sending $500 for framing. I can only hope that it's enough.

The paintings are beginning to clarify themselves. It is something about <u>Systems</u>. The last painting, TAF II taught me a lesson: one step of the system deals with my applying thic aqua-tec white with a stiff bristle brush. It is too haphazard. . . too much calligraphy, a carry-over from my earlier paintings. I want something more definite as content something more thematic or recognizable. I am experimenting on TAF III with string and pieces of rag torn from one of Andrew's* old shirts. My reasoning is that I can control the amount of thickness + shape, therefore I should be able to add or subtract by using different weights of materials. I think it's important that I list the individual steps of my system.

I. Canvas is stretched to platform over foam rubber pad.
II. Gesso with AC-33 is rolled over raw canvas (four Coats)
III. Bits of string + rag are glued to canvas with gesso according to penciled in guide lines (the string is thrown in at random placement)
III. One coat of Aqua-tec white
IV. One coat of Liquitex white
V. Color is layed out according to mock-up.
V. Layer of thin white
VI. White shapes are layed in using Liquitex and squeege again according to mock-up.
VI. Arcs + pencil spacing lines are drawn
VII. Brushed layes or diluted gel-medium

VIII. SLIP rolled on

IX. RAKED

X. White relief lines added

XI. After 16 house of drying white relief lines are pulled,

XII. Canvas removed from platform

XIII. Preliminary viewing by tacking canvas to wall

IX. Decision made on stretching or destroying

X Canvas stretched + hope for the best.

The idea of system is to remove sentimental involvement which allows the material to speak more on its own, in other words a method for removing the ego. After performing all twenty steps of the system the painting works or it doesn't. Systems disallow the old-fashioned approach of being able to adjust or correct individual parts. If the painting doesn't work, the canvas is either destroyed or each step is executed in the same manner, my being able to add or remove any previous mark. Systems force the issue of total involvement with allotted space, I am forced to work the whole plane and not individual parts, in other words the final object has <u>NO mistakes</u>. It is absolute within its own system thus achieving the same status as a piece of glass, a piece of wood, a stone, steel, wool or any other material evidence of this solar system. I often give the title: Psychic system to what I am doing. A system for representing psychic-phenonomon or Psychic Realism: That which lives only in the brain, those things which one thinks they see. I also think that this solves the problem of content in abstract painting. Content is what you think you see but really there is nothing there but paint and material used. Bill de Kooning said "content is a glimpse" he was very close.

My show opens on the 4th April. I have five paintings. ~~Two of those five Only~~ I am pleased with only three of those five and I need at least six paintings. My thinking moves so fast that I can only produce two paintings that are absolutely about the same problems. When one problem is solved and I see it before on the canvas, I become bored. I cannot produce six paintings of the same idea. I am not a cookie cutter. My thinking is not stationary but moves along at a very rapid rate; therefore, each painting is a <u>representation</u> of a particular idea. The plastic concept unifies the complete works but the content of each painting could change drastically, at will. In other words I can assimilate any idea into my system. For example, the element of space can be used in different ways and still work within the system. I can use perspective in any form, simple two-point perspective, two-point plus different viewpoints whether birds eye—worm's eye etc. The frontal space of Cubism encompassing, overlapping of planes, transparency, interpenetration can be assimilated. The oriential concept of positioning on the plane can be used. The most important point to make is: all of these systems could be used at once. My system does not ~~deal~~ simply deal with one specialization but a multiplicity of things operating within one idea: that of total assimilation of art history extended to include that of contemporary thought.

The crux of this system lies within the structure of the grey slip used which is actually the <u>matter</u> ~~I take~~ or raw material. This matter can be used in any number of different ways. Matter is what unifies the whole. All plastic elements are conceived of through matter. For me, I want this raw material to be my playpen . . . . a means of doing anything I wish . . . . to exercise every fantasy, myth, every feeling of the absurd within my grasp. I intend to use color very arbitrarily: sometimes just for the sake of using color, sometimes to excite, for direction from one point to another, in order to measure a certain distance (spacing), to decorate as to decorate a geometrical figure, for atmosphere or to suggest a naturalistic space for physical positioning as to place a plane in space. Finally the intent of color should be used to establish a personal color structure.

As far as shape is concerned I want to be to use any shape at my disposal. I refuse to settle upon one dominant shape. Shape may take the form of geometry which I prefer because it bears no relationship to natural forms or it may be entirely anti-form i.e., indescriabble~/sp~ having no ~~particular~~ specific boundary. I like using both of these just as de Kooning does or Hans Hofmann does. The edge may be machine sharp or loose . . . fuzzy . . . blur it depends entirely upon mood, maybe I am a true expressionist after all. Ivan Karp once told me that I was the last of the romanticists, maybe he was correct or better yet as I have said before "I am the heir of Delacroix!"

I gave a lecture at Rockland County Comm. College yesterday and I tried to express my view of the canvas as object. I approach each canvas as ~~a new~~ virgin space, whether it is in the form of a square, rectangle, circle or triangle or shaped canvas i.e., irregular shaped. . something other than the square, rect., triangle or circle. My desire or better yet my task is to transform this virgin space. I want to transform it into an object possessing a spiritual force (this idea comes from my involvement with African sculpture, I understand African Art as having this particular esthetic and <u>it is mine given to me by birth from my African ancestry</u>!) One can say that it is an idea whose time has come. My involvement with all of these geometrical objects is the transformation of them into spiritual objects ~~their purpose being one of pure esthetic value used as a~~ to be used in the ritual of survival within a technological society. I am sure that any sane individual will agree with me of the necessity of such an object.

When I speak of a geometrical figure I am speaking of a reduction of African wood carving. My idea of a triangle is that figure which is ~~arrived~~ deducted from an African carving, the reduction of a square, or a rectangle, trapezoid, etc. These geometrical figures are the <u>matter</u> of African carving. Cubism as we know it was a borrowing of that matter. Picasso was a most beautiful thief, but in his stealing I am afraid that something was lost in Cezanne's work only to be rediscovered today by younger artist. The significance of the Cezanne show at the Modern (the Late Works) is just this: The matter that I speak of starts with Cezanne. Cezanne's emphasis upon density was about matter, in other words my grey slip.

The role which photography plays in all this is one of philosophy: it provokes a ~~new~~ revolutionary way of understanding plasticity. Western painting as we have known it be <u>ends here</u>. Man's thinking from this point on cannot be called Western thought.

The Western world is finished. Our energies as men are to be consolidated as global energies united for the survival of the species.

My wife and friends are amazed at me for being so cool. My show opens 4 April and I am not frantic. Why? Because I have done the necessary work. It is now up to Providence. My job is to get the paintings and to some degree make sure the right people see the show and other than that there is nothing I can do. The paintings must stand on their own, outside of politics, I know that my being Black will invite all inquiries of a political nature but the paintings are built to confront such inquiries. Whatever questions arise, in the end, it will be the paintings that will do the answering.

These paintings represent the best I am capable of at present. They are the sum total of my experience as an artist. I am not afraid to show them. I think the time is right. I am working on the last painting which is 6' x 7' the largest painting of the show and I am hoping for the best. The only unknown factor I can point to is: What will be the visual impact of five paintings in such a space? I do not want to ingage in overkill for that is not my sensibility. I want just enough action to present a spirited showing . . . not to overhelm. My plan is to take at least eight paintings and adjust according to my feelings toward the space.

I must admit that to some degree, I am worried about sells, I shouldn't say worried for I am too old to worry about selling paintings but frankly I would like to sell-out the show, beyond the financial significance, just the psychological significance of a sell-out would be a tremendous boost for me, <u>Bob,</u> and other black Artist. It would secure a definite position for me in terms of power + importance which I need now. Power within the gallery (my dealings with Bob Miller) and outside the gallery—school, curators, dealers— collectors and other artist. I want to be separated from the mass of nameless artists in Soho. A sell-out would accomplish just this. I am ready, the guns of April are loaded!

Very few people know the energy that passes through my body. Most people sense it but are afraid to acknowledge it. Women are either enthralled by it or run away from it. I try to live with it. I am beginning to understand that I am in touch with something. I have no other way to express this except "in touch" In touch with what, I do not know and I try not to think about it. Maybe it is what the older people back home call God. Maybe it is what ancient people meant by the spirit, in American Indian terms the "Great Spirit." I DO NOT KNOW WHAT IT IS OR WHAT TO CALL IT. I have no logic to explain what I feel or see. What's different about my work? It is in touch with what I feel and therefore expresses a certain sensibility which we are not familiar with. I am possessed with ~~visions~~ the spirit ↔ I use this word for I have nothing else. It guides me and takes over when my logic reaches its turning point. I am not dealing with a casual$_{/sp}$ situation, but a continuous stream of consequences which come in no particular intervals or particular timing. I must remain open to receive information from within. I do not know the meaning of this information for I cannot decipher it. I don't even know the value of it! My main problem is in accepting. Men are not taught to accept. I am a receiver of information and women teach me how to be more receptive. [. . .]

I am beginning to have some second thoughts about abstract painting. Abstract painting is reaching a turning point we are about to venture into another phase of painting, something that comes as a result of dealing with abstract thought, some sort of super-abstraction, somethings that goes beyond abstract painting as we know it.

I have been having these funny ideas about the transformation of things: of objects, people, places and now paintings. In painting when I start with a square space or rectangular space my work is to transform that square or rectangle into my image which up to this point deals with an abstract image i.e., abstract painting. Now, I want to transform that abstract painting which I created in my image to something which is super-abstract: an abstraction of an abstraction. I do not know which image it will take.

In terms of plasticity, I have defined the current problems of abstract painting and have gone further to solve these problems. In other words, I have summed up Western painting (I think this is what I meant earlier when speaking of the end of Western painting) My problem now is to project beyond that and my approach in solving this problem is the total transformation of Western painting. (the word Western is so limiting I must find some new work to replace it) in other others <u>SUPER ABSTRACTION</u>, I do not want another <u>ISM</u>!

A space that is achieved through a cancellation of illusion through depth and flatness of the picture plane: It is possible to arrive at a spatial solution by a cancelling-out process of <u>flatness</u> vs. <u>illusionism</u> ~~depth. In experiencing the visual~~ The illusion of depth is primarily achieved by ① placement on the plane ② overlapping of forms ③ interpenetration of forms ④ transparency ⑤ perspective ⑥ color (we could elaborate upon this as color-field theory) These represent the academic model. In modern painting, flatness of the picture plane at any cost is the raison d'etre of modern principles. By using the system of cancellation a new concept of space is made evident. We may call this space photographic primarily because it represents the same space of the photographic print. The use of a camera in the graphic reproduction of an experience produces what we call a photograph. Because we are able to read a photograph visually we are confronted with ~~the depiction~~ the illusion of space two-dimensionally i.e. something printed upon a two-dimensional plane. It is possible to arrived at the same space that exists within a photograph through the use of pigment using a canvas or other material as support and sometimes incorporating the support as surface material. note: (using pigment to produce of particular color structure)

Space could very well be the DNA of plastic elements ~~which~~ in painting. Further, our use of the two-dimensional plane in painting is totally dependent upon our perception of space. Space becomes the element which allows our involvement with line, color, texture, surface. The paradox of this says we arrive at space through our use of line, color, textures, surface.

The real plastic significance of Abstract Expressionism is that it opens the door to the possibility of the cancellation of dualities, which philosophically is what we are talking about. To say that Pollock "broke the ice" means that the cubist structure is no longer viable$_{s/p}$. This is definitely the whole significance of Jackson Pollock.

In his breaking the ice, we enter a new ball park, complete with man's total aspirations ↔ (this accounts for the reemirgances_{/sp.} of psychological symbolism through imagery in Pollocks later works black + white, black on raw canvas,); his past history, his present experiences and his future expectations. The space becomes a void very much like that of early Buddhist writings (Zen) i.e., the cancellation of dualities.

~~Due to the rashness of the void~~

Due to the infinite structuring of the void, we the only specie possessing the ability to reason must draw the boundrys. In order to produce a society based upon the principles of Humanism, man needs a finite system. ~~In other words, history repeats itself: once again man becomes the center of a universe limited only by made to his own specifications (I almost made the mistake of saying that history repeats itself, something like the Renaissance with man being the center of things, but God was the restiration or the glory of man without the absence of God~~ another mistake!

(As an insert, this point of my thinking represents the beginning of politics. Jeff* always asserted that politics grew out of aesthetics. I agree with him. My esthetics are formed now, so if I wanted to choose between politics + Art I could do so. I know that I am an artist and my enjoyment in life is centered around my practicing my art. For me to give up my art for politics is absurd at least for now. I would like to reap the harvest of my 20 year woodshedding. You may call this selfish, not willing to accept responsibility toward my race or not using my knowledge through social change i.e., revolution, which represent the only true solution to social change. The common man must bleed in order to experience change. I choose ART. I am not the common man; I have sympathy for him but I am not willing to abandon my art for his cause! The greatest success for me as an Artist is my recognition by the common man.

I <u>don't</u> expect this neither now or the near future. So, I must accept my isolation in society. But in accepting, I promise to live in a matter worthy of my value. My plan is to continue my work and enjoy myself as much as possible within my means.)

I finished KHEE II today; Although I haven't stretched it; she looks good, just like a woman! The color is coming in much stronger now even though I want to keep it under control . . . . to measure it . . . slowly. My color is about what color leaves behind, in other words, I am more interested in the tracks of the pigment. I want to show where color has been. [. . .]

My brain has been working very rapidly for the past four weeks. ~~Rest~~ Proper rest and food is very important now. At no cost must I blow my cool. The revelations have been fantastic! The cosmic puzzle is coming together. Life is an organism existing between to extreme poles. Death exist in life. There is no need for us to be afraid. Fear is simply a device for safety. Man must have something to fear in order to test his worth. Without the element of fear we are worms.

All of my plastic experiments over the past twenty years arrive at the same conclusion as the physical scientist: ENERGY, MASS, IS INTERCHANGEABLE. Piet Mondrian and Jackson Pollock both arrived at the same conclusion through the plastic construction of the two-dimensional plane. True, the visual imagery is different because they exist on opposite poles, but believe me, it's possible to move from Pollock to Mondrian. Beneath the visual imagery lies the all-powerful universal structure: THE GRID. Many contemporary artist make the mistake of using the grid as imagery or the larger mistake of accepting the grid as both content and subject matter. The grid simply represent or illustrate the atomic structure of anything shown on a flat two-dimensional plane. The Black Africans were the first to see this. They discovered it through the construction of a three-dimensional space. Picasso being influenced by African sculpture immediately saw its use as applied to two-dimensional space and called it Cubism. We must credit Cezanne as being the true discovery. Picasso simply exploited what Cezanne had discovered. Picasso was a true Capitalist.

At this point, the notion of producing so called abstract paintings is only a matter of subject matter. I have the choice of using abstraction as subject matter or realism as subject matter. Since my orientation in art as combat has stressed the abstract imagery I will continue for a while using abstraction as subject matter. Also the major battleground in painting today is located in abstraction so there exist a challenge not to be found in Realism.

Jack Whitten

N.Y.C.

The unknown will always remain mysterious, frightening something
that logic cannot comprehend: such as it should be; we must have
the unknown at all times. We cannot build our lives or our Art upon
the unknown; therefore, our responsibility is to structure the known
quantities to the fullest extent of our knowledge. By structuring
and building the known quantities we are in a better position to
accept the unknown. Man is a limited organism, limited by his own
intelligence.

I am dealing with my paintings very much in this manner. There
are certain physical characteristic about materials which I have
learned to recognize and manipulate. I know <u>a lot</u> about what one
can do with acrylic paints and canvas. I know that color can be
structured in an infinite number of ways depending upon the given
sensibilities of the artist. I am insisting upon a highly structured
organization of plasticity in order to arrive at an unknown quantity.
The only manner in which I can deal with the unknown is through
the known.

Painting is a gift. Please don't ask who does the giving or what does the giving <u>I simply do not know</u>. From now on I will cease calling what I do experiments. The word no longer applies to what I am doing. I am the receipient of visual messages. Where these messages come from, I do not know. I don't even know what to call them. I am even confused as to their use. I have been taught to say for esthetic reasons. I am not even sure of that any more. One thing I am sure of and that's how I arrived at my present presentation. In other words, I am connected to history, I learned a great deal of what I know through history and that I have projected that history.

I will no longer question what I do. My job as an artist is to keep myself physically + mentally strong in order to receive these visual messages. I can still speak of them as paintings but even this is for practical reasons. They are paintings of interior spaces and the location of objects in that particular space. Sometimes it is about the location of one object in space. By being able to locate things in space I am able to locate myself. Frankly, I think that this is what ART IS ALL ABOUT: BEING ABLE TO LOCATE YOURSELF IN SPACE. I have never believed ART to be anything weird or foreign. It must be something of the most basic nature, that which is close to home, that which lies at one's doorstep. Rothko speaks of Art as religion. . . Maybe for him it was a substitute for religion. I do not believe in art as religion. That is why the representation of the iconographic image is always centered symmetrically symbolic, an illustration of the deity either in the form of female symbolism, male symbolism or the two as a suggestion of transcendentalism: the psychic capability of going beyond the two. I find it very aggrorant for anyone to even suggest Art as being a substitute for religion. We may make art objects to be used as ritual i.e., to take part in religious services. It may even be a vehicle which aids our religious awareness, but never religion itself. There can be no substitute for belief in God. It is so obvious that historically, man has attempted to find a substitute for God. It is also obvious that historically speaking that substitute leads to moral decay and eventually destruction of state. (I need more information, I am only sure of: ART IS ALL ABOUT BEING ABLE TO LOCATE YOURSELF IN SPACE. I am not sure of or convinced of the phrase ART as Religion. I am just not sure.)

Logically speaking, if I continue my argument, I contradict myself i.e., we know that all religions teach self discovery through the finding of God and this is exactly what I understand my Art as doing. If I am able to locate objects in space I am able to locate myself. The location of objects in space is the location of the Godhead. I must do more thinking or better yet wait for more information. [. . .]

IT'S ABOUT LIGHT!

I have just completed what I call the "First Painting." I would like
to share this painting with someone . . to call in someone who would
understand without jealousy or malice but there is not one to call!
[. . .] I feel a mix of extreme joy and fear. I can always tell when I am
afraid of something: I must take a big shit! The three paintings before
this entitled the "Soho TRIO" is a message painting. It's about three
painters from the Soho area who share something in common,
myself, a woman painter and one other male. I don't know who these
people are. I must wait for more information.

I don't want to admit that I am lost or confused it's just that
I don't understand why I am doing paintings of this sort. Have I
crossed over to another sphere of painting? The light is so clear . . .
brilliant just like in Crete! The color commands the picture plane.
The whole canvas becomes an icon of color, bathed in the light of
resurrection. I am scared . . . . frighten of something that's very
beautiful! May God help me for I don't know of any other source
of comfort. My Art has become a <u>vehicle</u> which puts me in the
presence of the Godhead.
<u>I am the process.</u>

I have no explanation for my experiences in the past four weeks. It was the same as ten years ago, not as intense but definitely the same feeling. My doctor calls it anxiety, or the same symptoms as anxiety. I am much better now. I feel firm—strong and confident. My head, my body has been preparing me for something, something of significance. Whatever I went through I think it's over.

I have had some profound revelations. The most important one came when I was at my worst condition. When I rake through a field of wet paint I am taking away fifty percent, when I rake vertically over a horizontal direction I again take away fifty percent, but by combining a horizontal rake with a vertical rake I arrive at a grid which ~~adds~~ gives me a complete surface: crosshatching to arrive at 100%!

This is a very important breakthrough for me. It means I have a physical structure in which to exercise complete freedom: a structure for the spirit to manifest itself. I am still not sure of the form but I have the most important thing: content. I think that the form will take care of itself.

I am working very hard on a carpentry job for Mrs. Barnett Newman I received the job through Hester Diamond. The work is not too difficult and I need the money desperately. Working takes me from my paintings maybe that's good for now, I need time for my new brains cells to settle and adjust themselves.

"Free at last! Free at last! Thank God Almighty I'm free at Last," so said Martin Luther King. Jack Whitten is now saying the same thing. <u>I AM FREE OF ART HISTORY</u>. At last I am off the floor, it has been ten years of hard labor on the floor. I can now execute my works to the wall. There is no limitation upon scale. The whole significance of my <u>physical grids</u> is <u>visual atomic structure</u> very much the same as band-day dots in photography. This explains the connection to photography. Since 1965 I have insisted that the image was photographic but I did not have a clear understanding of what I meant. The emphasis must not be placed upon the "image" but as usual upon the plasticity of meaning in terms of painting as a medium (painting is the medium not me!) Chuck Close is illustrating what I am saying. He deals with art as the illustration of an idea. I am vastly opposed to this thinking. <u>The idea</u>, <u>the concept</u>, the <u>execution</u> ~~serves only one purpose~~ cannot be separated from painting as an activity . . . . the making of a two-dimensional plane stretched on a support in order to give rigidity to the plane. We cannot discuss which come first the painting or the idea. They are totally dependent upon each other. The attempt to separate leads to illustration + design and prevents the activity of art making. Art simply runs out of the window. I think that all great artist have always understood this. When we are reduced to illustration we lose the meaning of art.

P.S. strange that this should happen on Abe Lincoln's Birthday. . . My freedom is his birthday present!

Earlier, I spoke of gravitational fields whereas the picture plane becomes the field of gravity. Plastic tensions create the gravity. Now I am extending this to subject matter as well. Shapes, forms, are created through the use of color value (and also black + white values a mixture of both) structuring a planar gravitational field. Earlier, I also spoke of the nervous system as being the center of this energy. I would like to extend that further by saying that the nervous system, in turn, gets its energy from the cosmic system. The human form represents the cosmic system in miniature. The energy which drives the human form is the same energy which drives the universe. We exist in the same sense as planets: having our own moons, suns, etc., and depend upon the same system for survival. My paintings are an extension of my nervous system driven by the same energy which drives the universe. I guess we could say that the universe is one huge circle of energy which lives + dies upon itself. All functions are precise and operates within its own definite structure. Man is probably the most unique being within this system simply because he can individually interpret the flow of energy in an infinite number of ways: hence we have what we call ART which is an interpretation of cosmic energy.

For the present I ~~simply~~ plan to use my paintings to ~~represent the interpret the~~ show my personal interpretation of that cosmic energy.

March 25, 1979

Dear Marcel,*

The last five days have been quite hairy for me. It has taken all my self-control to maintain stability. Friday morning the anxiety took over and I had to resort to one pill. I hate taking those pills and use them only for necessity. I plan to never take another except under extreme circumstances. Anyway I thank the medical profession for making such things available. Man has always needed his various medicines and always will need it. I do not believe in placing one's total faith in the use of medicine. Man must learn to heal himself. I am beginning to understand man as being a mass of energy, generated by the same power which moves the universe. Man represents a microcosm of our universe. All the answers to creation and what which makes the universe run can be found in man.

Marcel, my work is very much involved with this sort of thinking. All of my experiments deal with what I call the DNA of plasticity: the atomic structuring of visual matter. The nature of perception is the keystone of my work. Of course in a historical sense, one must be able to grasp the whole of history, <u>chew, digest and ~~spit~~ SHIT out</u>. This requires tremendous hours of research, mental labor, physical pain all which causes a tremendous drain on one's energy supply. Intuitively, I have known this for the past ten years, this is while I've always gone to Greece for the summers. Greece has been my recharging station ~~for the past ten years~~. Man's power plant is located in his nervous system. Care must be taken at all times to keep it functioning properly. One's body chemistry is what regulates ~~the~~ all the complex functions of this system. Chemistry is controlled not only by what we eat but also by our physical surroundings: the people we meet, the air we breathe, the sounds we hear, the sights we see, weather conditions and I am sure a host of other things I haven't thought of! Man is surely a temperate beast always existing between extremes. On the cosmic scale man is zero. If extremes do not exist man will invent them. It is his nature to do so.

It was necessary for me to say this in order to say something else. I do not believe or accept your diagnosis of <u>repressed rage</u> as being the cause of my anxieties. Yes, at one time during the early sixties–late fifties I was full of rage, hatred, not so much directed at the white-man as much against my ignorance of not having an acceptable identity a knowledge of who I was. At times I would confuse it with hatred for the white-man. Of course, I cannot deny the opression of slavery inflicted upon my people because of the white man's greed of capital plus his fear of the psychological unknown of being Black. Yes, I think that deep down in every Black person's heart lies the desire of revenge. This is only human. In knowing, all the inhumane acts carried out by whites upon blacks— which continues until today in all degrees of sophistication, I cannot + categorically refuse to lose my sense of humanity! I exist in the eyes of God. My duty being the proliferation of life: That which enhances the quality of life is my reason for being.

So Marcel, I am back to the original question: What causes the symptoms of anxiety in Jack Whitten?

Jack Whitten causes his own anxieties and it's up to Jack Whitten to prevent the reoccurrence of such. Jack Whitten's ability to think creates anxieties therefore Jack Whitten's ability to think can prevent anxieties.

Marcel, your being Jewish has played an important part in helping me. We share a similar ~~memory of~~ experience with regard to oppression and still must deal with man's inhumanity to man. You have taught me the importance of constructing a system which prevents the storage of repression. Without such a system, <u>we pay</u> and the amount we pay is reflected in our mental + physical well being.

I don't think that I will be needing you again, at least not in the near future. I hope that you are always there in case I need a helping hand.

Love,
Jack

9 April 79

ART has become a monster which must be
satisfied unless it destroys you.

---

12 APRIL 1979

AFRICANO JU-JU

I have successfully made a breakthrough from
the gravitational field of flat history.
This will change the course of printing
as we know it.
Light is my guide.

Jack Whitten

ART has become a monster which must be satisfied unless it destroys you.

---

12 APRIL 1979

<u>AFRICANO JU-JU</u>

I have successfully made a breakthrough from the
gravitational field of Art history
This will change the course of painting as we know it.
Light is my guide.

Jack Whitten

I have enclosed the drawing board, it has become a drawing room: 16' x 30'. The need for privacy is so insistenant. I don't want anyone to see what I am doing or to ask questions. The only people that enter the studio area will be those people whom I invite. I think that the work will develop some sort of very private personal imagery. It has taken me ten years to get back to this. Also I am using oil paint instead of acrylic. The experimentation period is over. Now I paint straight from the heart! I don't know exactly what is going to happen but I have a general idea—I don't want anymore than this.

My biggest problem still remains money. I must work on this. It is so boring. But I am not worried,. Whatever it takes to continue my painting my am prepared to do. In December I shall be <u>40</u>, I am little concerned with this, intrigued you may say. . . not worried but curious, it's exciting for I am expecting something to click. I have done my homework and graduation exercises are over. I have definitely ended one phase of my life, now something else begins. I feel very mature as a painter and oddily enough very much alone, being alone doesn't bother me: I welcome it because later on there will be too much company. My studio is private now. A private space is so important . . . a space just for you where no one else goes unless invited and no one sees what is going on. . . . A PRIVATE RECTANGLE.

I found that I could not use the system of mark making as planned. It is to difficult and the results is not worth it. Also, that phase of the painting require something very mechanical or mathematically correct. The layout is important. I cannot do consistently enough lines . . . . this is not my thing! I am using the combs again, I had to remove one tooth to make a one inch comb. The plane is graphed in one inch squares. The comb is one inch. I systematically comb each square, one vertical, one horizontal to achieve a basket weave. The color structure is produced by viewing three layers of surface color at once, the visual mixing of color produces the structure. <u>Very impressionistic</u>!

I have been worrying a lot about the meaning of content. What should I use as image? I am not a realist. The Formalist approach is still alive for me. I am interested in the transformation of the Formalist language. The transformation of a square to be more exact interest me, but it is very hard to conceive of what I mean by the <u>transformation of a square</u>. It is like saying that the square must be born again but in my image. I am well aware that I am running into metaphysics but Ernst Cassier helps a lot with his emphasis upon symbol. Symbolism is the way out. My content or image as I conceive of it depends upon my use of the square as symbol.

Color comes alive for me—color! Lots of color: a saturation of the picture plane! I know that it is about light . . . the weaving of light. Painting has always been about light. Yes you may call me the "Light Weaver" "Ju-Ju MAN"—"SPIDER-MAN" "keeper of the flame"!

I am enjoying the use of oil-paint. It is so much more sensuous than acrylic could ever be. The oil feels more like something of the skin—more organic. Having a longer open-time helps my nerves too. I know that if I don't complete something today I can finish it tomorrow or the next day . . . it slows everything down I am not so frantic and racing against the medium.

I plan to work the smaller scale of 16"–18" 20" until I iron-out the kinks and then explode the scale slowly—42"—60"—72"—84"—96"—120". I want to do some big paintings.
MONEY, MONEY, MONEY! [. . .]

I am still working with a small scale. 16" x 16"—19" x 19". I don't have much time to paint and the paintings are changing rapidly, so the small scale is a must. I was reading Barney Newman's Book and he speaks of his major problem being what to paint. I agree with this. What to paint is my major problem at present. So far, I am sticking to geometrical figures—squares, rectangles—but I don't feel this to be my real image. Things on the street still excite me, like shapes of paper sometimes torn edges or irregular shapes: trash from packing crates—paper—rags. I still insist ~~that the art~~ upon abstract painting, the image must be of abstraction as a manner of choice. It is possible for me to use a figurative image but what's the point!

If figuration does not appeal to me, geometrics does not appeal to me nor surrealistic dream image (subconscious imagery)? What's available? Simply stated my interest is to paint the square, to paint the rectangle without putting anything into it. That is impossible. How does one paint the square without resorting to minimalist reductionism? There is something I want to say about the square or rectangle without showing anything. I keep going back to African sculpture: the element of an object possessing a presence. I don't want to put anything into the square, but the square in order for it to work for me must have a presence!

Obviously I must concentrate upon the total picture plane without using any dominant figure. The square must dominate. I could do this by using a mono-chromatic image of all the same values. This is much too academic and besides some of the early color-field painters used this idea. I can understand how the Africans managed this in sculpture: ~~the three dimensionality of sculpture~~ Function played the primary role. They were built for specific functions and this gave them a built-in plastic structure dependent upon function. In other words form followed function. I must rediscover the whole purpose of what am I painting for. What is the function of each piece? Generally speaking I can say Art for Arts sake or Arts only function being aesthetic. One thing I do know and that it is necessary. I could mention politics but I feel the political function of art to be secondary i.e. After the damn thing is created politics plays its part. The more immediate function I believe to be personal: First for me and second for the world. Art must satisfy a very specific personal longing for universality.

A desire to feel completely satisfied. A part of the total structure of things. Abstraction is the only possibility for this type of satisfaction, with figuration we are forever depicting something other than the rock-bottom meaning of universality. For this technological age abstraction is the language.

J. Whitten

Something happened today. The work changed drastically. I don't know what to do about it. My heart says yes. I felt such a mental relief. I hope my mind is not playing jokes on me. [. . .] This painting have worked me for four weeks . . grinding back to white at least four times! and each time not being satisfied. I want something solid, assertive, non-impressionistic not sweet . . . something rough, tough, male-oriented. I feel my work is becoming to soft in color, in imagery, in constraint. I want something more bold . . . more aggressive but not in a technical manner. <u>The color must assert itself!</u>

It is becoming clearer now . . . . something about what I know about as opposed to something I don't know about: The known vs. the unknown which eventually cancels out to be experience. Yes, the square is the experience! It's something about the presence of the square.

God, I hope my head is not playing jokes on me. What a horrible joke to play on any poor fool!

Jack Whitten
N.Y.C. 1310 hrs.

I must title this painting
<u>ASSERTION I</u> 1979

assertion. formal declaration:
    (1.) the act of asserting
    (2.) something asserted; positive statement; declaration

P.S. The rate of change frightens me, but I feel that I must follow.

the more you try to make it appear real the false it becomes.

That painting <u>ASSERTION I</u>, I've just been looking at it for hours, every day—every night. It's trying to tell me something. I have truly done something significant. I love this painting. I must wait and continue to look at it before starting another painting.

 I want to stay <u>hungry, lean</u> . . . . . <u>always on the edge</u>:
  only then does life speak.

 Life does not speak to those whom are comfortable. Another thing: Art is no substitution for religion, someone should have told Rothko that.

<u>God is with me</u>.

All of the movements in Art are dead. Hilton Kramer speaks of Post-Modernism. Post modernism is an accepted fact. Art must now deal with vision. The technique is not so important as long as a vision is evident. I wish that I could define what I mean by vision. The best example happened approximately twelve years ago; I was talking with Marjorie Strider about art of all things! She was explaining to me these frames that she was working with: old picture frames that she hung on walls. The act of framing made a picture. I remember telling her that if I made a picture that way, I must frame a particular space . . . . . a space which was unique to what I called vision i.e., my vision. Marjorie said "no, the art of framing <u>alone</u> ~~constituted~~ was considered enough." She did not understand what I meant by vision. When I say vision I am speaking of what I see . . . . what I see meaning something other than primary objects. Primary objects are things that are evident in nature: trees, stones, clouds, seas, sidewalks, tables, chairs, people, airplanes, etc. There are other things to be seen, but the eye must be trained to see them. Visions exist on flat two-dimensional space or three dimensional space as sculpture, and deals more with the act of seeing than any physical making, building or construction with objects. Visions can exist as a product of the hand but it is always ahead of the hand. Vision is what constitutes our psychic reality: It is more of the brain than of the hand. Myself, working as a painter, need the hand to produce the necessary object in order for vision to take place. Vision becomes evident only in a non-relational color structure. In vision color exist, it is not made to exist, in other words, it is not designed color but "<u>found color</u>." This is why I've always rebelled against any color structure of a designed nature. Color reveals vision. It may happen in any degree of the spectrum including black + white. It may take place within any surface: smooth, coarse, textured, thick, thin, matte, gloss combination of surface tension, different degrees of tactically. Vision deals with the manner in which we see: perception. I understand it to be the organic substance of seeing . . . perceiving: The DNA of visuality.

The psychology of vision deals with being able to dissolve dualities . . . . the cancelling out of opposing forces. It is what happens when opposites cancel out. The electromagnetic field comes close to giving a physical example of what happens in the process of vision. I think that my growing-up black in America gives me an advantage in dealing with the unique psychology of vision. I am a product of the cancellation of opposing races. I have been endowed with a very ~~definite~~ special sensibility because of this cancellation of opposing races. I very well know the dangers involved with psychology and I don't feel it to be my job as an artist to unravel psychological mysteries of being . . . . . as an artist I merely present <u>and dare not explain</u>! I have no desire to explain or offer explanations for what I do. Those people who are capable of seeing will see and the others must be content with the trash of our technological society. As we progress <u>into technology</u> so will our desire <u>to see</u> increase. A demand for an art-form which deals with vision is in the making. As an artist wanting to improve my lot in life, I must seize the time and present myself as an artist of vision.

<u>ASSERTION II</u> IS FINISHED. I am still working small scale. I must admit that I am confused. The paintings are back to easel painting with brush and oil paint. What's the meaning of all the experimentation in the past ten years? The emphasis upon consistency of surface? Processing? The inlaying of shape within the surface? O.K. the lack of color I understand: I imposed grey as a discipling agent i.e., black + white with later adding only small amounts of hue but I did not anticipate the return to the use of brush, unevenness of surface with tactile tensions. The image remains the same, I am still using geometrics as figure imposed in an atmosphere. What I don't understand are the reasons associated with going back to the hand. True enough, all of my experiments evolved to this point. Am I just to accept this evolution or reject it? If I do reject it, am I to continue doing scraped paintings? Something in the back of my head says to use the past ten years in order to be more sure-footed. My eye is well trained now, and also my hand. My ability to make decisions is stronger than ever. Have I been placing too much emphasis upon the <u>new</u>? ~~IMAGE~~ I have always been aware with the scraped paintings that they were <u>NEW</u>. in a New York sense of being NEW. There is so much doubt associated with painting. I am forever questing myself, doubting my performance. I make in order to tear down but the making and tearing down produces a painting. I must make a painting, destroy a painting in order to paint a painting. The color structure in Assertion I and II really have me excited. It's a joy to be using color again. I feel as if the whole spectrum is mine to play with . . . . all of it including black + white.

Hal Fondren called today. I didn't know that they had moved their gallery and dealing only by appointment. I am interested in this. [. . .]

My paintings are changing now, so it's best that I continue working without showing at least for another year. If things pick-up in March just maybe I'll commit myself to a one-man show Fall of 1980.

I am doing a small job for Annalee.* She has moved into her
Roman Palazzo as she calls it . . . a lot of marble. very nice, too bad
Barney is not around to enjoy it. The whole place is really for Barney.
It has been a pleasure doing carpentry in a room with Barney
Newman's on the walls. Some of those paintings were executed so
fast as if he knew exactly what he wanted . . . very direct, very clear—
bright color <u>not</u> trial +error. The sort of exactness that gives me a
warm rush. I love it!

I met Mr. Hulten_{s.p.}* from the Centre Beaubourg. He just
purchased a Newman for the Beaubourg's collection. I am sure that
we will meet again. I found him to be so civil a real gentleman in the
European sense. He shook hands with a carpenter who also paints.

Jack Whitten Nov. 79

It is important to know where the edge is at all times. The edge represents our space, the area in which we allot ourselves. The real fool is one who has no concept of edge. For safety measures we can hug the center but in doing this there is no possibility of discovery, exploration: we are forever attached to the womb. Man must go beyond the center to the outer edge and risk the possibility of falling over. My foot always tell me where the edge is, I can feel it . . . . . deep . . . dark . . empty establishing another space which I don't care to know about. I want to build with what I know, accept that and proceed like any other sane person in society.

The edge is different for everyone. Every man's job is to discover his own personal edge; again, and to know where it is at all times. When I choose my stretchers, the stretcher bar represents the edge but this is only a representation of something in my head. I must proceed to define that edge in terms of painting. I am always defining the edge through plasticity. I have never agreed with cropping in painting because cropping allows us to accept that which is convenient. Cropping is very good when used as a training device for the eye, but we must never use cropping to arrive at the total picture plane.

So, painting is about defining a very particular, personal space. If we are lucky enough that very particular, personal space just might represent the universal, and if it is not recognized as the universal, so what? The artist job is to define his space: establish his edge. Anything other than this is pure bullshit i.e., politics.

<u>ASSERTION III</u> 9 Nov. 79
I am having a constant battle between what I know what I think I know.

I have decided to make another tool. This time the tool is designed to leave more than taking out, it will be built to: 1/32" – 1/8". Taking out 1/32 and leaving 1/8. Essentially, I am going back to the saw paintings. I should be able to maintain a bolder image without having to stoop to impressionistic fluff. I must maintain what I have started, the process of following an experiment through is important. The past few days I have been very confused but I think that I am back on course now. Those paintings that relate to pattern paintings are only one possible direction but I don't like the connection to pattern painting, somehow the horizontal sweep is not identifiable to pattern painting although it is a pattern. Also, I feel that the horizontal sweep is more in keeping with mainstream ideas and something that I have laid claim to. The effect of obvious pattern is more informal, existing outside of formalism. Tomorrow I will purchase the necessary materials to construct the tool. I expect to make it six or eight inches wide. If this is effective I will build another larger one perhaps one foot in width.

(It did not work)

---

5 Dec. 79

After writing this, everything I have done has led to total despair nothing works—I paint just to destroy but trying to learn something. At least I know what I don't want and I feel that to be very important

Today I am forty years old. I have three dollars in my pocket and after paying the rent a remaining of twelve dollars in my bank account. Keita needs a winter coat + shoes. I have been sick and owe money for doctor bills. Mary + I are trying to raise money in order to buy the Lispenard St. building. Further, Christmas is coming in three weeks. Do you think I am worried? NO! Of course I have no money. I am an artist, what do you expect? My work is evolving and getting stronger, I have my health, my family, a great wife, great kid and I must say with no strings attached <u>we are happy</u> and enjoying our life!

I do think that the positive needs of Life overcomes all the shit. Two, three days of sunshine can mean so much. It's a matter of keeping your house clean, keep jumping the hurdles: I don't expect to ever be comfortable.

I have just finished making another tool but haven't had a chance to test it, she looks good. My greatest realization at present is: The horizontal raking is an entirely different element from the painting element. The two are not to be confused. One is one thing the other something else, but when used together produces a totally new orientation, in other words, the painting is arrived at by the interaction of these two elements . . . . . a most basic definition of Western painting in general or better yet, ART. The interacting of two elements is a basic human relationship, that which defines the universe as a whole.

I am looking for a tighter arrangement of form, something with no loose ends. I can no longer afford the ambiguity of Abstract Expressionism nor the sterility of Constructivist thought. I want something free of those movements something to exist just for what it is worth. I still insist upon its abstract nature for present but this might change unless I can speak of something that exist between realism + abstraction. I do not know of such an animal.

Anyway, I am expecting Santa Claus to come, because I still believe in Santa!

I destroyed <u>Assertion I</u>, <u>II</u> + <u>III</u>. She still continues to be elusive but I caught a big chunk of her in the <u>Lee Rider,</u> 16" square. It is definitely about space. Space is the "the new Frontier" in painting. We have pre-Renaissance space, Renaissance space, Cubist space, post Cubist space (only significant space produced after Cubism is Abstract Expressionism). The space I am dealing with is entirely different. Different in the sense of adding one: I have added one more step to that which we know about. I do not understand the entire significance of what I have done but I have truly discovered something fantastic!

$1=1$

$1+1=1$

$1+1+1=1$

Since 1964 I have been aware of seeing images. I have always accepted these images as being something to do with my personal aesthetic belief but I have never known how to use them. Those images are my source material, my universal energy supply. My problem is to convert this raw material into useable energy, the painting is supplied from this material it is my means of escaping art history. Back in the early sixties I tried to imitate these images by showing the faces on my canvas. Those faces I painted were the faces I saw in the paint. Any surface produces images. Usually I am attracted to a distressed surface as opposed to a "new" surface. Every artist must have an energy supply or "source material."

I have always been attracted to found shapes. Last year I started collecting shapes found on the streets: old discarded cardboard, wrapping papers, flatten pieces of metal, paper containers, any shape which appealed to me. My decision of choice is dictated by those shapes which exist neither as Constructivist or bio-morphic in nature. Anything that suggest something other than a known factor. Sometimes I am attracted to the pop-image of brightly colored packaging: cigarette packet covers, can labels, company trade marks

in other words artistic garbage! By using these shapes in my work
I have more freedom to deal with shapes other than Construvist
square, triangle, rectangle or surrealistic bimorphic forms. In essence
I have become a realist painter, those shapes exist as real objects but
can be read as abstraction. That which is real as opposed to that
which is abstract becomes questionable. There has been a lot of talk
about post-modernism lately, in painting I think it has something to
do with $1+1+1=1$. I have summed up the modernist tradition of
$1+1=1$. Mondrian is emerging as a real hero of modernism. Al Held
is trying very hard to understand my formula of $1+1+1=1$ but he is
still dealing with a very "spacey" neo-plasticism and all of his
followers are seeing the same: Conlon,* Robbin,* Nahas,* etc. The
next frontier of space can only be deciphered through vision and not
through design. I will remain very tight with my work meaning that
I don't want to share it with any one at present. I want to discover
who are my real peers. Frankly, abstraction is really no longer an
issue so eventually I will probably venture into more realistic subject
matter but not right now, politically it is more important for me to be
known as an abstract painter.

I turned forty and my health seems to be falling apart. I have
been so sick. I have lost all hearing in my right ear and suffering
from tinititis or ringing in the ears. It is very difficult to concentrate,
a slow torture as if someone placed an electric fan inside your
head . . . . . there is no escaping the roaring + tinklely noises. I am
trying very hard to maintain control and continue working.

Jeanne Siegel called and offered me a full days teaching at
SVA. I will be replacing Larry Zox. I really don't want to do more
teaching but I need the money. It remains a struggle to survive
and continue my work. Teaching is very hard with the lost of hearing.
Having the position at SVA means I don't have to accept any
more carpentry jobs. I will make more money and have more time
to paint.

I think that 1=1 has something to do with the type of vision found in folk art and 1+1 about Cubism are related plasticity. I need more infro on this. Mary showed me a book of Japanese woodcut by the master Harunobu* It blew my mind: the paper creates a space + their placement of form is intriguing. I am closer to early Japanese thought than imagined—maybe it's the Zen influence.

The Zen influence is strong in my work. I discovered it during my apprenticeship with Abstract Expressionism where the action was everything. The solid placement of form with no shadows but an all-over light is the order of the day.

The past two–three months have been extremely hard. I switched to oil paint all of Sept., Oct.–Nov. until recently last week I put all of the oil paint aside and pulled-out my acrylics.

Oil paint is nice. It makes you feel as if you are painting in the old-meaning of the word. It is romantic, nostalgia, very retro and I cannot afford the luxury of Romanticism. [. . .] My paintings need the fluidity, clarity and speed of acrylic. I do not accept their plastic quality but do things to change that by using additives. Acrylics are so much more practical for my lifestyle besides, I found that the smell of turpentine was sickening. [. . .] Art as icon is Mark Rothko's Art and anybody else trying to produce art as icon today is playing second fiddle to Rothko! Again there is something religious about being an artist but Art is not religion. My belief in God is stronger than ever. [. . .]

If I can maintain my health I have a chance.

'80s

I broke through their screen on the 4 Feb 80 at 1330 hours. I am hard pressed to say what lies beyond, not that I am confused but logic does not prevail here: MAN IS.

At home in Alabama when someone professed to be saved they said "I am a child of God." This is my statement today toward the history of Modern Art: "I am the heir to the modernist tradition," chosen in the same manner as my heroes before me; Rothko, KLINE, De Kooning, Newman, POLLACK, "GORKY" (God how do I love Gorky!), STILL (until 1953).

The painting which I have just finished for the P.S. I show, BARNEY'S LEGACY, is a political painting. I am laying claim to the legacy of the Abstract Expressionists. I stake my claim as the Guardian of the Flame. I, alone am entitled to this legacy and only time will give another: At present, I am alone.

I always have the feeling that I am getting closer to something to what, I don't know, as if the next painting <u>I will arrive</u>. Arrive at what? What is it that drives me + keeps my expectations up? Surely I must learn not to ask this question. Mine is not to reason why!

The paintings are becoming more joyously. The affirmation of life as Bill Williams put it. Yes, I want to celebrate the fact of my existence to shout hallahoueh before all man! Art can be used to glorify life. I want my art to serve this purpose. Death is something unavoidable so why must we celebrate it or mourn it or expect it. When death comes, I am ready. <u>Glory be to Life!</u>

The show at P.S. I has really taught me a lesson: My work cannot be shown under those circumstances. I knew that already but I continue to exhibit with Black shows for political reasons. I can never expect anything from such shows. My work does not fit into the present category of Black Art. I make in associations with African tribal or derivative motifs. Of course I know the connection between my art + Africa but it's useless to explain. For the sake of simplicity I simply say "It has the spirit" but beyond the emotional impact of the visual experience can anyone see the connection in terms of perception? I maintain that African woodcarving is a three dimensional graph the cubical structuring of such is the molecular structure of perception, in other words, the unity which exists in African wood carving is the same unity which defines the same energy which defines the universe as a whole. The two-dimensional graph serves the same purpose, which is the same structure found in photographic band-day dots. In my recognizing this simple fact and using it in my work, explains my connection to African tribal Art.

Fortunately for me at this time in history the significance of this discovery will play an important role in defining the identity of the new man. The onslaught of technology presents all of us with a new sensibility, a new esthetic, hopefully a new society with new values. I believe that the present emphasis placed upon art works of obvious "primitive" character is a direct result of this "new man vibration." In other words, we read the vibration to mean a new society with new myths, new symbols, a starting from the beginning . . . . the present day artist will create the new symbols needed for a new society. My African ancestry places me in a better position to take advantage of this "new man mentality" I more than any man represent the new race. I am the product of all men. I do not share the guilt of Christianity nor the burden of Capitalism. My spirit is one of freedom forever seeking the heights above man's folly and man's inhumanity to man. Man's greed makes war necessary. How true, back in 1964 when I painted the canvas <u>Look Mom, Look, see the Funny People!</u> that painting says it all. What am I to do? Must I also drag my spirit into the gutter? I think not. As long as the breath of life generate my physical being I will celebrate mans humanity. ~~It is the~~

Yes, my art is about self-revelation not to be confused with self-glorification. I use my art to define the self I can only hope that others can do the same. So what drives me? The search, the continuous struggle to define the self. <u>Now, I know that one never discovers the self not in a literal manner; we discover the self only to lose it.</u> The self is the sands of the river Nile, the Acropolis in Athens, a Congo fetish, a Bill de Kooning <u>Woman #1,</u> a saturn rocket to he moon, Mt. Everest. The self is all things and many more. More the better, I say, for there is no final chapter.

It is not about space as I previously thought. <u>It is about LIGHT</u>. The concept of the new will be identified by the structure of light. This frees me of pictorial space which has always hindered me from going further into space. Light can be used as an extremely abstract entity, expressing an emotional state. The object is one of the emotion i.e., the emotions as object. One could call this a representational art, the depicting of the emotions. I am not concerned with the representation aspects but rather the importance of maintaining the abstract as primary issue. I have my reasons for emphasizing the abstract as utmost necessity.

Two years ago I wrote of completing the Modernist principle or where Western Art <u>ends</u>. <u>It's all over</u>: Modernism has run its course. The grid was our gift of modernism. The grid explains the nature of visual perception, it represents the atomic structure of seeing. I am free of plasticism! The time has come to submit the mainstream to detour. Clement Greenberg mentioned that the Post-Modernists may cause more harm to Modernism than any previous assault. If only he knew how correct his hunch is. However, Clement would never accept the possibility of a Black man leading that assault!

Any painter that professes to be of any value must see the Light. This is the issue: Have you seen the light or not. No amount of gimmickry or novelty will surface. <u>the evidence of vision is to be found in the structure of Light.</u>

My desire to paint is overwhelming but my studio is not ready. I work hard every day that I am not teaching. We have no money to work with so I am doing everything myself. I am not complaining. I feel fortunate in owning this building and I am sure that one day it will pay. The privacy which this building affords will nourish my spirit. I have needed more privacy in my work, my life is enriched by it. If any luck just maybe I can get some painting done this summer. I can't afford to go for one year without working. Already I feel rusty. I try to draw, some success but it's not the same thing.

I can't afford to be sentimental about what happened. There was a very bad fire at Lispenard, we were forced into the street.* Mary, Mirsini and I lived at the studio on Crosby St. until the damage was repaired. I have not worked at my paintings since the spring of 1980. I like to think that I conducted myself as any able-thinking man would have done i.e., take care of his family, provide shelter and the necessities of life. I guess I could have been selfish, put Mirsini + Mary into an apartment + continued to paint. My decision was to purchase Lispenard and to renovate the burnt out structure. [. . .] By scraping every penny and sacrificing any thought of vacation or leisure activities we managed to put the roof back on and slowly begin the long process of renovation with small copper pennies.

Yes, I lost three years from my work. I have no regrets. The decision was mine and I am positive that I made the right decision. Lispenard is once again a livable space. The renovation is not a hundred percent complete but we are functioning. My studio is on the second floor just as it was in 1962. The space is small for me, but somehow I will manage. I give thanks to God for knowing how to do construction, having my health and the spirit to act in the face of disaster. I give thanks his guidance the belief in self-reliance and the commitment to a just cause. Considering the state of the Art world with its emphasize upon the Neo-Expressionist I couldn't have picked a better time to lie low. I haven't been painting but I've been thinking. Thinking about painting, the nature of Abstract Painting and what I must do. It is time that I penetrate the art world, establish myself as a major painter, make a decent living with my art. My objective is to quit teaching and the only way to do that is by selling my works. I need a good dealer and a respectable gallery.

*As Whitten described the events in 2017, "[In 1980] our home at 36 Lispenard Street had a major fire three weeks before we were to have the closing to purchase the building. We had to move to my studio on Broadway while renegotiating the sale. We purchased the building and spent three years of sweat equity to make it both our home and my studio."

Where must I start after three years? The only logical answer is to be found in the last black paintings. By examining the successes and failures of those paintings I should be able to find the answer to that question. Above all, I must avoid the search for a gimmick. I am a serious painter and no gimmick will surface for me. Light is still an issue but my understanding of light is a spiritual matter. That light must define a space, not a pictorial space.

A space which is actually the image: Space as Ikon. or Space as Image. I am at first constructing a series of circles, squares and possibly later rectangles, hexagons, triangles + trapezoids and pentagons. I must have something to work with or something to paint. I will paint the circle in my Image; I will paint the square in my Image. I simply want to personify those geometric figures.

I dont want to put anything into the circle as much as to make the circle as a thing within itself.

Letter to Henry Geldzahler

February 8, 1983

Dear Henry,

I've been thinking about an objective for my show and your question, 'Why 1970–80?' The content of my painting from the sixties dealt with my search for identity. They are intense emotional images arrived at through self-psychoanalytical procedures, using techniques taken from Surrealism and Abstract Expressionism. Abstract Expressionism was my academy, nothing else. They show my wrestling with the problem of selfidentity, with the everyman question of 'Who Am I?' I make no pretentious boast of having completed such an eternal quest, but I covered enough ground to allow me to continue to the next stage.

In 1970, I made a deliberate and conscious decision to start experimenting with the possibilities of paint without imposing the added burden of psychological implications. Ordinarily, in painting, decisions of this sort lead to dry formalistic paintings. This is one of the main problems with Formalism. However, I was counting on 'the perseverance of soul' to flavor my formalistic undertakings. I think I am being objective in saying that I was correct, that soul did persevere.

I want to use my exhibition at The Studio Museum as a survey, showing a precise and continuous development of experimentations dealing with the possibilities of paint, using various processes toward defining a new spatial perception in painting. By no means do I want this show presented as a retrospective exhibition. I am too young (to be dismissed so easily).

My first correspondence from The Studio Museum listed as a working title, *Jack Whitten: Ten Years—1970–1980*. This is okay with me. It's simple and direct.

All best,

Jack Whitten

Originally published in *Jack Whitten: Ten Years* (New York: The Studio Museum in Harlem, 1983), 4,
© The Studio Museum in Harlem.

BATTLE PLAN

Fall 1983

* SPACE AS MENTAL MATTER (PRESENCE)

1. Interfere with "all overness" (all overness plus hierarchy) imagery
2. Avoid planes in space
3. Structure of color depends upon Grey Content? YES!!!
* 4. It works when "physical transparency" is achieved (see through)
5. Light Structures not Heavy
   * 12. Remove all "accidental happenings"
   13. SPACE AS PRESENCE
   14. PRESERVE THE IMMEDIECY
6. Painting as "structures to Live By"
7. Remember your position is A ZERO
8. I am the Process
9. YOU MUST DO SOMETHING ABOUT THE "NATURALISTIC CONTENT", ITS CONFUSING YOUR INTENTIONS
10. ITS THE NOT KNOWING THAT GIVES ME LIFE
11. YOU MUST STOP THINKING.

5.

15. Painting as a spiritual act; a means of communicating with the spirit } 20 Dec 83
16. The technical device is a reminder of what I am not who I am
17. Geometry is only a vehicle an armature for getting "there," I need some known value, the intellect is good for this purpose. (do research a Russian Const. movement)

18. Great. ART must. be able to get beyond the self.

* 19. Necessary to modify! It works when the Spirit is present. Paintings become containers
'84 — for the spirit, a place or object to contain the spirit. (25 DEC 83)
20. The process has always been one of transformation
21. Is there such an animal as ABSTRACT REALISM?
22. Take the conceptual and crossbreed it with pure spontiety.
23. All-overness defined in terms of lightie^th nature of its source being spiritual from within.
24. There is no difineable formula ~~~~~~~~~~~
25. SPACE AIN'T NOTHING BUT TASTE!
26. The structure is trichotomy not dichotomy (my earlier interruption was } 30 Jan '84
    short-sighted of me!)
27. Inner man + Outer Space = SPIRIT
28. Am I addressing myself to a New Geometry or simply taking the old
    and locating it in another space?   } 9 FEB '84
29. In what way is my perspective differed from Renaissance perspective?
30. If I throw out masculinity, If I throw out Racicanality, If I throw out ethnicity, what am
    I left with? - What risk are involved with doing this?
31. I do not want to orchestrate Ovt History.
32. A NEW SPACE, A NEW PLACE, A NEW REINNAISANCE   10 FEB 04

33. The spirit is _not_ conceptual Knowledge. 14 FEB 84

34. EACh painting is a surprise!

35. I am not German. I have not committed any crimes against humanity. 16 FEB 84
     My soul is not tortured.

36. Each painting is found. 17 FEB 84

37. There is madness out there & somebody's got to do something about it! 27 Feb 84

38. I am an ENERGY FIELD PAINTER. 28 FEB 84

39. I am more interested in what the color leaves behind; its' tracks. 3 March

40. IF AM LOOKING FOR SOMETHING TO BASE MY LIFE UPON, A BELIEF SYSTEM,
     A REASON FOR LIVING. 6 MARCH

41. It's time that I come out of the closet. No longer can I remain anonymous. April

42. I use this energy field to produce magic objects + each one must be
     different from the other. 12 March 84

43. MAYBE EVERYTHING THAT ARTISTS SAY IS BALONEY! 18 March 84
                                                   (but such beautiful baloney!)

44. I am a carver of Light. 19 March

45. Sometimes I feel as if I am trying to steal Western civilization. 22 March 84

46. FREE THE SPIRIT!

47. The plane is a substitute for the mask. 27 March 84

48. The "presence" that I speak of is something spiritual and it exist in space. 27 March 84

49. Maybe that Joseph Campbell is correct, society is always in need of Myth. Could my
     works do fill that gap? 29 March

BATTLE PLAN
*SPACE AS MENTAL MATTER (PRESENCE)

① interfere with "all overness" (all overness plus image
  as hierarchy)

② Avoid planes in space

③ structure of color depends upon <u>Grey Content</u>? YES '84

*④ it works when "physical transparency" is achieved
  (see through)

⑤ Light Structures not Heavy

⑥ Painting as "structures<u>²</u> to Live By"

⑦ Remember your position is at zero

⑧ I am the Process

⑨ YOU <u>MUST</u> DO SOMETHING ABOUT THE
  "NATURALISTIC CONTENT", <u>ITS CONFUSING YOUR</u>
  <u>INTENTIONS</u>

⑩ IT'S THE NOT KNOWING THAT DRIVES ME NUTS!

⑪ YOU MUST STOP THINKING.

⑫ Remove all "accidental happenings"

*⑬ SPACE AS PRESENCE

⑭ PRESERVE THE IMMEDIECY

⑮ Painting as a spiritual act; a means of communicating
  with the spirit   } 20 Dec.

⑯ The technical device is a <u>reminder</u> of <u>where I am</u> not
  who I am

⑰ Geometry is only a vehicle an armature for getting "there,"
  I need some known value, the intellect is good for this
  purpose (do research on Russian const. movement)

⑱ Great ART must be able to get beyond the self

*⑲ Necessary to modify: It works when the Spirit is present.
  Paintings become containers for the spirit, a place or object
  to contain the spirit. (25 DEC 83)

'84

20. The process has always been one of transformation
21. Is there such an animal as <u>ABSTRACT REALISM</u>?
22. Take the conceptual and crossbreed it with pure spontiety.
23. All overness defined in terms of light i.e., the nature of its
    source being spiritual from within.
24. There is <u>no</u> difineable formula
25. SPACE AIN'T NOTHING BUT TASTE!
26. The structure is trichotomy not dichotomy
    (my earlier interruption was shortsighted of me!)
27. Inner man + outer space = SPIRIT

} 30 Jan. '84

28. Am I addressing myself to a New Geometry or simply
    taking the old and locating it in another space?
29. In what way is my perspective different from
    Renaissance perspective?
30. If I throw out masculinity, If I throw out Regionality,
    If I throw out ethnicity, what am I left with? What risk
    are involved with doing this?

} 9 FEB '84

31. I do not want to orchestrate Art History!
32. A NEW SPACE, A NEW PLACE, A NEW RENAISSANCE
    10 FEB 84

                              18, 31, 32, 19, 27, 3

33. The spirit is <u>not</u> conceptual knowledge. 14 FEB 84
34. Each painting is a surprise!
35. I am not German. I have not commited any crimes of against
    humanity. My soul is not tortured. 16 FEB 84
36. Each painting is found. 17 FEB 84
37. There is madness out there + somebody's got to do
    something about it! 27 Feb 84

(38) I am an <u>ENERGY FIELD</u> PAINTER. 28 Feb '84

(39) I am more interested in what the color leaves behind;
its' tracks. 3 March

(40) I AM LOOKING FOR SOMETHING TO BASE MY LIFE
UPON, A BELIEF SYSTEM, A REASON FOR LIVING.
6 MARCH

(41) It's time that I come out of the closet. No longer can I remain
anonymous. 8 March

(42) I use this energy field to produce <u>magic objects</u> + each one
must be different from the other. 12 March 84

(43) MAYBE EVERYTHING THAT ARTISTS SAY IS
BALONEY! 18 MARCH 84 (but such beautiful baloney!)

(44) I am a carver of Light. 19 March

(45) Sometimes I feel as if I am trying to steal western civilization.
22 March 84

(46) <u>FREE THE SPIRIT!</u>

(47) The plane is a substitute for the mask. 27 March '84

(48) The "presence" that I speak of is something spiritual and it
exist in space. 27 March 84

(49) Maybe that Joseph Campbell is correct, society is always in
need of Myth. Could my works fulfill that gap? 29 March

I have lost two paintings this week, not to mention the amount of wasted paint. I've been flucating between the need for imagery and impact of subject matter along with my usual formal statements. The outside has been penetrating too much. My being interviewed by Maria Nadotti from Il Tempo magazine is one example, visiting Mel Edwards another and having to deal with Joe Jacob's show at Bucknell another. I can't afford this. I've confused my concerns, my painting has suffered and it's being a continuous struggle to maintain some sense of balance. Henry's studio visit helped. His telling me that I am "no primitive" really struck home. His evaluation of me is correct. I am a very sophisticated abstract painter dealing with problematic ideas in modern painting and this I must continue to project. At no time should I allow confusing signals to emanate from the studio. I learn from my changes but they are not meant for public consumption. My best works have always fused a real sense of self with a classical <u>timelessness</u> that maintains a quiet but powerful energy flow. The energy field is definitely my thing and I should allow that to become the sole content of my works. As far as the centralized image is concerned, I don't always know what it is. Maybe it's enough to allow for a "presence." other than attempting to force a literal interruption of image.

The illusive nature of "presence" is purely a zen-inspired view of life in general. The real truth is that we never know. Sometimes we think that we know. "Presence" always exists in a time zone of knowing and not knowing. It's my knowing that gets me into trouble. Self-inflicted labor is a device used to circumvent$_{s/p}$ knowing. Labor allows us to forget what we think we know. I tire myself into submission. ~~to the in accepting~~ As a painter, I know that "presence" ~~exist is~~ exist in what I understand to be space. Space is structural. Something that occurs as a result of my thinking. I cannot use my thinking apparatus to capture "presence." If I were religious (which I do tend to believe) "presence" could be described as a God giving thing, but ultimately the Zen-master's story of trying to catch a catfish with a gourd is a much better description. One doesn't try to capture "presence", it is simply "found", or better yet, it is given.

My definition of Art as a device for filtering human emotions still remains true. In a Kantian sense it is definitely <u>a priori,</u> a must for dealing with our most elemental human responses. Somewhere between what we know of as the inner consciousness and outer self lies very fertile ground for ~~experimental~~ locating the meaning of "presence." Maybe this is what I meant by going <u>beyond the ethnic,</u> <u>the national identity of person,</u> <u>the sexual role of male + female.</u> What is left when one does this?

Cont'd   1984   <u>STUDIO LOG</u>
from spring notes

<u>1 NOV 84</u>: The most notably advance in my thinking from the 1970s was my discovery of the significance of the grid. To repeat myself: the grid is the graphic illustration of the basis of mental perception. Its roots are to be found in the plastic structure of African wood carvings. I call it the DNA of visual perception. My big problem of the eighties has been "What am I to do with this knowledge?" I know that any number of directions are available for consideration, but I do not have time or energy to pursue several directions and besides it creates problems: The public cannot follow too many directions, it misleads my intention and causes too many misinterruptions. Jack Whitten must make the decision which is a matter of choice. . . . . Who is the real Jack Whitten and what visual language most effectively represent Jack Whitten? This is a tricky problem one which runs the risk of formulating an art of Gimmick, one designed to participate in the New York art world. As usually it's a binding obligation . . . . we do but we don't do. I must be careful not to depend upon conceptual thought. I place my trust only in my personal convictions of the art making process. It's time to follow the demands of the soul. The paintings become a resting place for the soul. Space is defined through the meaning of soul. I must add that <u>soul</u> and the ownership of <u>soul</u> is not unique to black folks. Soul is available to anyone human enough to possess it. The meaning of universality is to be found in this statement. It also enforces the ability of Art to transcend all ethnic, nationalistic, sexual + religious boundaries. I am dealing with an all encompassing approach to art making. I want very much to allign myself with the primitives: in African, Oceanic, Amer. Indian—works which I feel to possess <u>soul</u>. All evidence points to the fact that Western artists learned this most important basic fact from the Primitives. My aim is to restore the

magic making in Art, to provide a resting place for the soul. I no longer call my Art Abstract Artist I don't know what best describes it. I do know that I am working out of what is generally known as abstraction but I am heading toward image. When I am carving wood I do direct carving i.e., starting with the raw material without conceptualized intent, the image is arrived at through pure plastic thinking. I want to use this approach in my painting. The beat definitely goes on and I feel myself to be a direct blood descendent of Africa.

> 12 NOV 84
>> It comes . . .
>>> ~~sometimes~~ like a thief in the night . . . .
>>> sometimes silent
>>> sometimes violent
>>>> with intent to kill . .

12 NOV.
Yes it's molecular but you must learn to deal with the condensation of molecular structure: the layers that define consciousness. Experience is the key; the common denominator of being human.

26 NOV: As long as I don't feel that the unconscious is dictating my actions I am o.k. There is difinitely a role for conceptual thought, but it's not the whole picture.

27 NOV: I have to put <u>my shit</u> on top of <u>their shit</u> just like they put <u>their shit</u> on top of <u>mine</u> . . . many moons ago!

4 Dec 84 This constant knowing + not knowing is enough to drive the average person crazy. I guess that why I am not average. It's important that I test each "feeling" to separate that which is real

from pure flirtation of excitement. Emotions become a problem. I have more than my share of emotional ecstasy, sometimes I fear too much for a sincere evaluation of feeling. These three weeks have been most severe—draining—I am weak—sick with a cold—in need of M.O.N.E.Y. surely there must be a better way!

8?? STUDIO LOG

13 OCT. I WANT TO PAINT, that WHICH I DON'T KNOW

14 OCT. MY INTEREST IS PRE-CUBIST THOUGHT- PRE EUROPEAN HISTORY

15 OCT. THE MATERIAL MAKES THE IMAGE
        THE CONTENT OF MY WORKS IS FOUND IN THE EMOTIONS
        THE ESSENCE OF FEELINS

17 OCT. I WANT TO PUT THE MAGIC BACK INTO PAINTING.

19 OCT.   IT
        YOU MUST NEVER TRY TO PAINT IT.
          IT TAKES CARE OF ITSELF.

20 OCT. IDEAS ARE THE ENEMY OF PAINTING

27 OCT. I HAVE FEELINGS OF BEING VERY MODERN AND VERY PRIMITIVE AT THE SAME TIME

3 NOV. IT LIES BEYOND THE SELF.

25 NOV. O.K. I GIVE UP. IT'S A MAGIC OBJECT.

        IT'S CORRECT TO SAY THAT IT IS MOLECULAR ARE THAT IT DEALS
    WITH MATTER BUT THAT'S ONLY THE ELEMENTAL ASPECTS, IT'S
        MINIMAL IMAGE. THE QUESTION IS: HOW DOES IT FEELT THE OBJECT? AND OUT
    OF WHAT CONTENT?
        I WANT TO SHOW THE VISUAL EQUIVALENT OF JAZZ.

17 Dec. Confusion has its own merits.

6 Jan. 86. It exists somewhere between knowing + not knowing.
    The painting is a mask, serving the same function as an African Tribal Mask

            It's about all of things which hurt, which feel good-
                Your hopes + your dreams, even fantasies
        But most of all, It's about us
                About what we are not, what we are,
            It's a Soul Space!

7 Jan 86. It's everything and yet its nothing but paint.

8 Jan. It's simply a task of taking Abstract Expressionisms and push it one more step.
            No one has been able of doing this. (Only excerpts of Abstract Expressionism has been pushed by
            certain specialists in the use of surface, color, shape, etc.)

9 Jan. The outer edge is what objectifies it; ie, the actual physical edge of the plane, in relation
            to the psychical edge.

14 Jan. I want a space, a psychic space where the mind
            May relax, an anxiety fighter a relief from the chaos of being human.
            The painting must be allowed to operate as object in order to do this.

22 JAN. FORM & COLOR ARE INTERCHANGEABLE

        ONLY THE LIGHT IS PLANAR NOT THE SHAPE-FORM
        I REJECT THE BASIC CONSTRUCTIVES IMAGE AS FORM
        THE SURREALIST IMAGE DERIVING SOLELY FROM THE UNCONSCIOUS
            IS ALSO REJECTED.
        I DO NOT DENY THE USE OF MULTIPLE LAYERS OF CONSCIOUSNESS, BUT
        THE PHYSICAL FACT OF PAINTING AS OBJECT IS MY PRIMARY CONCERN
        THE PAINTING IS FINISHED WHEN I SEE EVIDENCE OF THE SPIRIT, THE SPIRIT USES
            CERTAIN OBJECTS AS RESTING PLACES FROM THEIR CELESTIAL WANDERINGS.
        I DEPEND BOTH UPON THE SPIRITUAL AND THE MATERIAL OUT OF PSYCHIC NECESSITY.
        MY BELIEF STRUCTURE IS BASED UPON THIS EXCLAMATION.

85' <u>STUDIO LOG</u>

13 OCT. I WANT TO PAINT THAT WHICH I DON'T KNOW

14 OCT. MY INTEREST IS PRE-CUBIST THOUGHT—PRE
EUROPEAN HISTORY

15 OCT. THE MATERIAL MAKES THE IMAGE
THE CONTENT OF MY WORKS IS FOUND IN THE
EMOTIONS
THE ESSENCE OF FEELINS

17 OCT. I WANT TO PUT THE MAGIC BACK INTO PAINTING

19 OCT.   IT
                YOU MUST NEVER TRY TO PAINT IT.
                IT TAKES CARE OF ITSELF.

20 OCT. IDEAS ARE THE ENEMY OF PAINTING

27 OCT I HAVE FEELINGS OF BEING VERY MODERN AND
VERY PRIMITIVE AT THE SAME TIME

3 NOV. IT LIES BEYOND THE SELF

25 NOV. O.K. I GIVE UP. IT'S A MAGIC OBJECT
IT'S CORRECT TO SAY THAT IT IS MOLECULAR ARE THAT
IT DEALS WITH MATTER BUT THAT'S ONLY THE
ELEMENTAL ASPECTS, IT'S MINIMAL IMAGE. THE
QUESTION IS: HOW DOES IT EFFECT THE OBJECT? AND
OUT OF WHAT CONTENT?
I WANT TO SHOW THE VISUAL EQUIVALENT OF JAZZ.

17 Dec. Confusion has its own merits.

6 Jan. 86. It exists somewhere between knowing + not knowing.
The painting is a mask, serving the same function as an African
Tribal Mask
It's about all of things which hurt, which feel good.
Your hopes + your dreams, even fantasies
But most of all, It's about us
About what we are not, what we are.
It's a soulspace!

7 Jan. 86. It's everything and yet its nothing but paint.

8 Jan It's simply a task of taking Abstract Expressionisms and push it
one more step. No one has been able of doing this. (Only excerpts of
Abstract Expressionism has been pushed by certain specialists in the
use of surface, color, shape, etc.)

9 Jan. The outer edge is what objectifies it, i.e., the actual physical
edge of the plane, in relation to the physical edge.

14 Jan.   I want a space, a psychic space where the mind may relax,
an anxiety fighter a relief from the chaos of being human. The
painting must be allowed to operate as object in order to do this.

22 JAN. FORM + COLOR ARE INTERCHANGEABLE
ONLY THE LIGHT IS PLANAR NOT THE SHAPE-FORM
I REJECT THE BASIC CONSTRUCTIVEST IMAGE AS FORM
THE SURREALIST IMAGE DERIVING SOLELY FROM THE
UNCONSCIOUS IS ALSO REJECTED.
I DO NOT DENY THE USE OF MULTIPLE LAYERS OF
CONSCIOUSNESS, BUT THE PHYSICAL FACT OF PAINTING

AS OBJECT IS MY PRIMARY CONCERN
THE PAINTING IS FINISHED WHEN I SEE EVIDENCE OF
THE SPIRIT, THE SPIRIT USES CERTAIN OBJECTS AS
RESTING PLACES FROM THEIR CELESTIAL WANDERINGS.
I DEPEND BOTH UPON THE SPIRITUAL AND THE
MATERIAL OUT OF PYSCHIC NECESSITY.
MY BELIEF STRUCTURE IS BASED UPON THIS
EXCLAMATION.

I am back to zero. Tonight I cut up a large circle composed of a circle grid + threw it out! I was completely bored with the pain-taking involvement of executing all those dots! I cut it up + threw it out! The only thing I have to salvage from the past fifteen years is the fact of the hard backing; the bringing of the floor up to the wall. This is meaningful. Perhaps I have more, I've learned a lot and I've grown to hate several things in the process of learning. I want to start 1986 with a clean slate. Of course this destroys any chance of getting a gallery, no one is interested in an artist at the end of a series and beginning a completely unknown beginning.

I am black, 46 years old, angry, tired of teaching, tired of being poor. [. . .] What am I to do? I don't expect to hit the lottery nor am I in a position to show. I must stay cool, collect my thoughts, re-organize go back to the Onyx show + take the other route. I was well aware of two possibilities; I've exhausted the geometrical route which lead to the grid now I must go the other way: completely free, no geometry, loose with a minimum of color. I want to stay with grey, black + white. The white has become more meaningful especially since reading of its use in Yoruba religion.

[. . .] If I can only maintain my cool, I feel that I have a chance. I must forget about showing or trying to attract a dealer. I must work! Yes I am broke but the money will appear. May God be with me.

STUDIO LOG

3 FEB 86 I DID IT: <u>SOULSPACE I</u>, 1986 (FOR BOB KAUFMAN) 45½"x45½" A/C

A FUSION OF THE MATERIAL AND THE SPIRITUAL
THE SUBJECT MATTER IS THE TECHNOLOGICAL URBAN LANDSCAPE THE CONTENT IS TO
BE FOUND WITHIN THE EFFECTS OF TECHNOLOGY UPON THE PSYCHE
THE PAST FUSES WITH THE PRESENT. I DO NOT KNOW THE FUTURE, ALTHOUGH IT
IS PRESENT.

8 FEB. THE PLASTIC ELEMENT OF SPACE IN PAINTING IS NOT AN ILLUSIONISTIC DEVICE
IT DEALS MORE WITHIN THE DIMENSIONS IMPOSED BY PSYCHOLOGY i.e, IT'S PURELY CEREBRAL,
A PRIORI IN NATURE, JUST AS KANT SUGGESTED.

IN PAINTING, LIGHT HAS DENSITY, LIGHT IS PLANAR.
<u>FAITH IS THE ONLY THING THAT KEEPS IT TOGETHER</u>

11 FEB. THE SPACE IS PHOTOGRAPHIC, NOT THE IMAGE!

15 FEB. THROUGH ALL THE YEARS OF STRUGGLE + SACRIFIC I NEVER KNEW THE EXACT
OBJECTIVE OF MY ACTIONS, AT FIRST I SIMPLY UNDERSTOOD IT TO BE ONE OF
PERSONAL SELF REVELATION, i.e, TO SHOW THE NATURE OF SELF IDENTITY, BUT THAT
IS NOT ENOUGH. WE MUST GO BEYOND THE SELF, TO GET RID OF THE ME.
MY CAUSE IS THE SAME AS THE FIRST PRIMAL INSTINCT IN MAN:
TO UNITE WITH THE GODHEAD. ONCE THIS IS DONE ALL THINGS ARE
POSSIBLE.

23 FEB. I DON'T WANT ANYTHING THAT'S LITERAL NEITHER DO I
WANT THE OBVIOUS, AND I HATE THE DECORATIVE.
THE ACADEMIC IS AN ENEMY TO PAINTING, IT DENIS THE SPIRIT.

4 MARCH. MAYBE POLLACK WAS RIGHT, THERE IS NO EDGE, JUST MORE
OF ME!
THE ORDER COMES AFTER THE FACT

8 March: The center is not a fixed position, it is determined
by time + location of subject.

19 MARCH: IF WE EXTEND THE MEANING OF THE PAINTING AS OBJECT, THAT OBJECT (TO INCLUDE THE IMMATERIAL)
IN ITS MATERIAL FORM COULD VERY WELL BECOME SPIRIT, LIGHT FUNCTIONS AS
THE ELEMENT WHICH DE MATERIALIZES THE OBJECT AND ALLOWS IT TO BECOME SPIRIT.
ULTIMATELY I AM MORE CONCERNED WITH THE STATE OF CONSCIOUSNESS WHICH
PRESENTS SPIRIT, THE PAINTING IS THAN A BY-PRODUCT; THE WASTE.

20 MARCH: CONTENT IS HARD TOO PIN DOWN, SOMETIMES I THINK ITS ABOUT
EVERYTHING THAT I KNOW, BUT I'M NOT SURE. MY NOT KNOWING BAFFLES ME.

26 MARCH: I WANT A COLOR THAT'S FREAKY, ABSURDLY SEXY, A KINKY COLOR
STRUCTURE BUILT FROM THE EMOTIONS CONTAING A SPECIFIC POINT OF
REFERENCE
IT'S VERY DIFFICULT TO PLAY WHATS REAL OFF THAT'S WHATS
UNREAL ... MOST OF THE TIME WE DON'T KNOW, ITS HARD TO
MAKE A DISTINCTION .. I DO WANT THE ROOTE THAT OFFERS
THE MOST RESISTANCE. I GET A KICK OUT OF SLOUGHING
THROUGH MUD!

27 MARCH: HAPPY BIRTHDAY MOM. TODAY I DISSECTED THE MONSTER. I WISH YOU
UNDERSTOOD WHAT I MEAN, BUT I GUESS I CAN'T HAVE EVERYTHING. ANYWAY, ITS
YOUR BIRTHDAY PRESENT! HAPPY BIRTHDAY!

8 APRIL: YOU MAY CALL ME A STRUCTURALIST:
A ROMANTIC STRUCTURALIST | ABSTRACT STRUCTURALISM |

STUDIO LOG

3 FEB 86 I DID IT: <u>SOULSPACE I</u>, 1986 (FOR BOB KAUFMAN)
$45\frac{1}{2}$" X $45\frac{1}{2}$" A/C
A FUSION OF THE MATERIAL AND THE SPIRITUAL
THE SUBJECT MATTER IS THE TECHNOLOGICAL URBAN
LANDSCAPE THE CONTENT IS TO BE FOUND WITHIN THE
EFFECTS OF TECHNOLOGY UPON THE PSYCHE
THE PAST FUSES WITH THE PRESENT. I DO NOT KNOW
THE FUTURE, ALTHOUGH IT IS PRESENT.

8 FEB. THE PLASTIC ELEMENT OF SPACE IN PAINTING IS
NOT AN ILLUSIONISTIC DEVICE
IT DEALS MORE WITHIN THE DIMENSIONS IMPOSED BY
PSYCHOLOGY i.e, IT'S PURELY CEREBRAL, A PRIORI IN
NATURE, JUST AS KANT SUGGESTED.
IN PAINTING, LIGHT HAS DENSITY, LIGHT IS PLANAR.
<u>FAITH</u> IS THE ONLY THING THAT KEEPS IT TOGETHER

11 FEB. THE SPACE IS PHOTOGRAPHIC, NOT THE IMAGE!

15 FEB. THROUGH ALL THE YEARS OF STRUGGLE +
SACRIFIC I NEVER KNEW THE EXACT OBJECTIVE OF MY
ACTIONS, AT FIRST I SIMPLY UNDERSTOOD IT TO BE ONE
OF PERSONAL, SELF REVELATION, I.E, TO SHOW THE
NATURE OF SELF IDENTITY, BUT THAT IS NOT ENOUGH.
WE MUST GO BEYOND THE SELF, TO GET RID OF THE ME.
MY CAUSE IS THE SAME AS THE FIRST PRIMAL INSTINCT
IN MAN: TO UNITE WITH THE GODHEAD. ONCE THIS IS
DONE ALL THINGS ARE POSSIBLE.

23 FEB. I DON'T WANT ANYTHING THAT'S LITERAL
NEITHER DO I WANT THE OBVIOUS, AND I HATE THE
DECORATIVE. THE ACADEMIC IS AN ENEMY TO PAINTING,
IT DENYS THE SPIRIT.

4 MARCH. MAYBE POLLACK WAS RIGHT, THERE IS NO
EDGE. JUST MORE OF ME!
THE ORDER COMES AFTER THE FACT.

8 March: The center is not a fixed position, it is determined by
time + location of subject.

19 MARCH: IF WE EXTEND THE MEANING OF THE
PAINTING AS OBJECT (TO INCLUDE THE IMMATERIAL),
THAT OBJECT IN ITS MATERIAL FORM COULD VERY WELL
BECOME SPIRIT. <u>LIGHT</u> FUNCTIONS AS <u>THE ELEMENT</u>
WHICH DEMATERIALIZES THE OBJECT AND ALLOWS
IT TO BECOME SPIRIT. ULTIMATELY I AM MORE
CONCERNED WITH THE STATE OF CONSCIOUNESS
WHICH PRESENTS SPIRIT, THE PAINTING IS SIMPLY
A BY-PRODUCT; THE WASTE.

20 MARCH: CONTENT IS HARD TOO PIN DOWN,
SOMETIMES I THINK ITS ABOUT EVERYTHING THAT
I KNOW, BUT I'M NOT SURE. MY NOT KNOWING
BAFFLES ME.

26 MARCH: I WANT A COLOR THAT'S FREAKY, ABSURDLY
SEKY, A KINKY COLOR STRUCTURE BUILT FROM THE
EMOTIONS CONTAING A SPECIFIC POINT OF REFERENCE
IT'S VERY DIFFICULT TO PLAY WHAT'S REAL OFF THAT'S
WHATS UNREAL . . . . . MOST OF THE TIME WE DON'T

KNOW, IT'S HARD TO MAKE A DISTINCTION . . . . . I DO
WANT THE ROUTE THAT OFFERS THE MOST RESISTANCE.
I GET A KICK OUT OF SLOUGHING THROUGH MUD!

27 MARCH: HAPPY BIRTHDAY MOM. TODAY I DISSECTED
THE MONSTER. I WISH YOU UNDERSTOOD WHAT I MEAN,
BUT I GUESS I CAN'T HAVE EVERYTHING. ANYWAY, IT'S
YOUR BIRTHDAY PRESENT! HAPPY BIRTHDAY!

8 APRIL: YOU MAY CALL ME A STRUCTURALIST:
A ROMANTIC STRUCTURALIST,
ABSTRACT STRUCTURALISM

<u>STUDIO LOG</u>   '86

18 APRIL '86 : THE FLATNESS OF THE PLANE IS DETERMINED ONLY BY ITS INHERENT
   PHYSICALITY AS OBJECT NOT BY ITS PERCEPTION AS IMAGE WHICH IS PURELY ILLUSORY..

8 MAY 86 : IT IS ABSOLUTELY NECESSARY THAT EACH OF US BEAR WITNESS TO OUR IMPERFECTION

9 MAY 86 : PAINTING IS A PROCESS OF CONTINUOUS SEARCHING

12 MAY 86 : MAN HAS ALWAYS FOUND HIMSELF IN THE LANDSCAPE, HIS EXPEIRENCE
   WITH NATURE, I MUST EXTEND MY MEANING OF NATURE TO INCLUDE THE
   URBAN LANDSCAPE. HERE AND ONLY HERE WILL I FIND MYSELF.   RELIGION, POLITICS, TIME,

21 MAY 86 : MY PAINTINGS ARE ABOUT TRANSCENDENCE. I WANT THEM TO TRANSCEND RACE, SEX, OBJECT AND
   ANT KNOWN IDEA OF HISTORY. I WANT THEM TO EXIST IN A RAREIFIED MENTAL ATMOSPHERE, THE PSYCHICAL
   : A SPACE WHERE ONLY THOSE WHO HAVE PENETRATED THE DEEPEST LEVELS OF CONSCIOUSNESS CAN FANTHOM.

23 MAY 86 : IS IT POSSIBLE THAT A PAINTING COULD OPERATE AS FIGURE?

4 JUNE : THE MOST DIFFICULT PART IS THAT I NEVER KNOW WHAT I
   WANT UNTIL I SEE IT.
   I ADMIT TO HAVING A DESIRE FOR THE CONTEMPORARY SIGNIFIANCE OF THE SUBLIME

GONE FISHING ! ⟶ 12 June
                    leave 14 June 86
                    return 6 Sept 86

STUDIO LOG '86

18 APRIL '86: THE FLATNESS OF THE PLANE IS DETERMINED
ONLY BY ITS INHERENT PHYSICALITY AS OBJECT NOT BY
ITS PERCEPTION AS IMAGE WHICH IS PURELY ILLUSORY . .

8 MAY 86: IT IS ABSOLUTELY NECESSARY THAT EACH OF
US BEAR WITNESS TO OUR IMPERFECTIONS

9 MAY 86: PAINTING IS A PROCESS OF CONTINUOUS
SEARCHING

12 MAY 86: MAN HAS ALWAYS FOUND HIMSELF IN THE
LANDSCAPE, HIS EXPERIENCE WITH NATURE. I MUST
EXTEND MY MEANING OF NATURE TO INCLUDE
THE URBAN LANDSCAPE. HERE AND ONLY HERE WILL
I FIND MYSELF.

21 MAY 86: MY PAINTINGS ARE ABOUT TRANSCENDENCE.
I WANT THEM TO TRANSEND RACE, SEX, RELIGION
POLITICS, TIME, OBJECT AND ANY KNOWN IDEA OF
HISTORY. I WANT THEM TO EXIST IN A RAREFIED MENTAL
ATMOSPHERE, THE PSYCHICPHERE: A SPACE WHERE ONLY
THOSE WHO HAVE PENETRATED THE DEEPEST LEVELS
OF CONSCIOUNESS CAN FANTHOM.

23 MAY 86: IS IT POSSIBLE THAT A PAINTING COULD
OPERATE AS FIGURE?

4 JUNE: THE MOST DIFFICULT PART IS THAT I NEVER
KNOW WHAT I WANT UNTIL I SEE IT.

I ADMIT TO HAVING A DESIRE FOR THE CONTEMPORARY
SIGNIFIANCE OF THE SUBLIME

GONE FISHING!

⟶ 12 June
leave 14 June 86
return 6 Sept 86

<u>FALL '86</u>   <u>STUDIO LOG</u>

26 OCT. History has exhausted all other possible exits. Only the spirit remains free. Therefore, the subject matter must be about spirit. The paint as material is only a vehicle. What confuses me or baffles me is the question "Can I go directly to the spirit?" Do I need something other than the formal qualities of paint? If paint in its "formalness" is enough does this make me a "Formalist" I worry about this. Is it possible that I am a second generation Formalist? Can I, or is there a way to bypass the formalist approach altogether? Can paint as a medium, a vehicle put me directly in touch with spirit? How can I sidestep Idea?

If it's possible to conceive of <u>ME</u> the <u>I</u> as medium, what part is the paint playing? This is where I am confused.

Within the contradiction of pictorialness as opposed to objectness lies a presence. . . . . The Abstract Expressionists were wrong in thinking that the paint was the subject. The paint is only the medium and <u>I</u> am the director. I do not know what form the spirit takes that remains an unknown, a mystery, but I do know that it might take any form: There is no limitation placed upon the spirit. The amazing + bizarre freedom of spirit is what frightens me. It can be animate or inanimate. This I find bizaare, and I don't know the meaning of it, but I recognize its power and I wonder how can I use it to help the predicament in which mankind finds itself in today. I don't want to seem corny or preposterous but I feel that our survival as a people depend upon it.

7 NOV. The spirit is undefinable. It is faceless. By the pure necessity of its existence, it must remain a mystery. The acceptance of this is very difficult for me, but here lies the confortation of truth.

16 NOV. It's a psychic object arrived from the psychic reality.

2 DEC. There <u>must</u> be a visual eqavalient to Jazz
. . . . . . an actually object expressing the same pathos.
I want my art to show this

9 DEC. TIME <u>IS</u> A FRAGMENT OF BEING.

11 DEC. THERE IS NO IDEA. THERE IS ONLY BEING.

14 Dec. I have three possible directions:
① I can continue to mix-up the execution
② Use of screens to establish a net for trapping images
③ Direct manipulation of pigment, totally organic

16 Dec. I am beginning to experience full release, <u>something</u> still holds me. I think that politics is an obstacle to growth. My ~~native~~ cosmic desire is for full release. I still need more information to be sure. What pain is in store for me? I still worry.

25. It's like trying to see the other side of something, as if a veil of some sort separates me from it.
The molecular structure exist in the form of light not in physicality as previously thought. The problem at present is that my light source is to fragmented. I need a condenser.

17 Jan 87 The <u>It</u> is an unknown factor. I am dedicated to the preservation of mystery. Only in its political manifestation is it necessary to remove the mystery. This is the main difference between politics and art. The choice rests with the individual participant. The clarity of desire operates as an excellent condenser.

18 Jan. YOU NEVER TAKE IT; IT'S ALWAYS GIVEN TO YOU.

21 Jan. I DON'T BELIEVE IN CONCEPTUAL ART; IF YOU CAN CONCEIVE OF IT THEN IT'S NOT ART BUT AN ILLUSTRATION OF AN IDEA.

26 Jan. EXCEPT FOR THE USE OF MATERIALS THERE IS NOTHING RATIONAL ABOUT PAINTING. NOR CAN IT BE CALLED IRRATIONAL; IT EXISTS SOMEWHERE IN THE EXTREME MIDDLE.

1 FEB. THERE IS AN EDGE WITHIN THE EDGE.

2 FEB. THE CENTER CAN BE ANYTHING YOU WANT IT TO BE!

3 FEB. THE IDEA IS TO MAKE THE OPPOSITES DANCE, SING A SONG, PRAY AND HAVE A GOOD TIME!

STUDIO LOG 1987

9, FEB — THERE IS ANOTHER SIDE TO THINGS TOTALLY DIFFERENT FROM WHAT WE KNOW TO BE TRUE. THIS OTHER SIDE CONSTANTLY TEST OUR SENSE OF REALITY.

24 FEB. BILL DeKOONING WAS CORRECT IN SAYING THAT POLLOCK BROKE THE ICE: ALL OF THESE YEARS I HAVE BEEN TRYING TO SHOW WHAT'S BENEATH THE ICE.

8 MARCH: I AM WORKING WITHIN THE TRADITION OF KLINE, DE KOONING, ROTHKO, NEWMAN, POLLOCK AND SIMPLY STATED; YOU HAVE TO BE MAN [OR WOMAN] ENOUGH TO PARTICIPATE. IT IS NOT A SPACE FOR THE WEAK OF HEART; IT'S HEROIC, MYTHIC, DEALING WITH A TOTAL UNIVERSAL INVOLVEMENT WITH LIFE AND ITS ABSURDITIES.

I WANT A PICTURE OF THE OTHER SIDE.
A MENTAL PHOTOGRAPH OF THE PSYCHE

21 March: ITS POSSIBLE FOR CHANCE TO BE USED AS A CONCEPTUALIZED CONSTRUCTIVE ELEMENT. ILLUSION IS THE ANTOGNIST. THE TRUE BITCH. THE EASTERNERS CALLED IT MAYA.

22 MARCH: IT MUST BE ABLE TO EXIST OUTSIDE OF THE SELF. THE RENEWAL OF ME.

24 MARCH: I AM INTERESTED IN HOW A PAINTING IS MADE, ITS' CONSTRUCTION THAT PROCESS OF CONSTRUCTION IS DEFINITELY CELLULAR OR AS I USED TO SAY MOLECULAR. IT ALSO VIBRATES WITH AN ACCOMPANING SOUND. IT'S VIBRATION IS WHAT PRODUCES ITS' OPTICAL NATURE.

29 MARCH: I AM COMING IN THROUGH THE BACK DOOR.

2 APRIL: THE WORST POSSIBLE SCENARIO IS WHEN YOUR OWN MIND BETRAYS YOU.

5 APRIL: I CAN FEEL ITS' PRESCENCE BUT IT IS ALWAYS AT THE EDGE OF THE MIND THERE IS NO ONE ANSWER; IT'S EVERYTHING AND ONE THING AT THE SAME TIME PAINT THE POLARITY!

7 APRIL: I USE THE WALL AS METAPHOR

16 APRIL: I WANT PHYSICAL, FACTUAL INFORMATION.

19 APRIL: PAINTING IS THE PROCESS.

23 APRIL: I AM TRYING NOT TO THINK.

27 APRIL: I MUST TAKE MY BEARING FROM AFRICAN TRIBAL SCULPTURE. THE POWER IS WITHIN ME. IT MUST COME DIRECTLY FROM THE SOUL UNHINDERED BY LOGIC.

7 MAY: SPACE IS [ONLY] THE SYMBOL; REVEALED THROUGH LIGHT.

24 MAY: I AM READY. — EXPEIRENCE CAN SERVE AS METAPHOR.

10 SEPT. THE CENTER IS EVERYWHERE + NO WHERE

12 SEPT. ITS EXTREMELY COMPLICATED + EXTREMELY SIMPLE AT THE SAME TIME.

27 SEPT. I AM THE CONTENT.

29 SEPT. GOD IS A CHEMICAL... THE PROCESS OF RELEASING IT IS CALLED RELIGION.

7 OCT. YOU CAN'T DEAL WITH IT IN TERMS OF WHAT IT LOOKS LIKE, YOU MUST DEAL IN TERMS OF WHAT IT IS.

8 OCT. IT'S ABOUT NO ONE THING. THIS IS THE TRUE MEANING OF POST-MODERNISM; NO ONE CAN FIGURE IT OUT. YOU MUST SIMPLY DO IT.

11 OCT: THE SPACE IS ARRIVED AT THROUGH METABOLIC PROCESSES... A METABOLIC SPACE...

15 OCT: I AM INTERESTED IN MIND AS MATTER.

19 OCT: SPACE IS ARRIVED AT THROUGH THE MATERIAL NOT THE STORY. (a message to Cruz)

STUDIO LOG 1987

9. FEB— THERE IS ANOTHER SIDE TO THINGS TOTALLY
DIFFERENT FROM WHAT WE KNOW TO BE TRUE. THIS
OTHER SIDE CONSTANTLY TEST OUR SENSE OF REALITY.

24 FEB. BILL DeKOONING WAS CORRECT IN SAYING THAT
POLLOCK BROKE THE ICE: ALL OF THESE YEARS I HAVE
BEEN TRYING TO SHOW WHAT'S BENEATH THE ICE.

8 MARCH: I AM WORKING WITHIN THE TRADITION OF
KLINE, DE KOONING, ROTHKO, NEWMAN, POLLOCK AND
SIMPLY STATED: YOU HAVE TO BE MAN OR WOMAN
ENOUGH TO PARTICIPATE. IT IS NOT A SPACE FOR THE
WEAK OF HEART; IT'S HEROIC, MYTHIC, DEALING WITH A
TOTAL UNIVERSAL INVOLVEMENT WITH LIFE AND ITS
ABSURDITIES.
I WANT A PICTURE OF THE OTHER SIDE.
A MENTAL PHOTOGRAPH OF THE PSYCHE

21 MARCH: IT'S POSSIBLE FOR CHANCE TO BE USED AS A
CONCEPTUALIZED CONSTRUCTIVE ELEMENT. ILLUSION
IS THE ANTOGNIST. THE TRUE BITCH. THE EASTERNERS
CALLED IT MAYA.

22 MARCH: IT MUST BE ABLE TO EXIST OUTSIDE OF THE
SELF. THE REMOVAL OF ME.

24 MARCH: I AM INTERESTED IN HOW A PAINTING IS
MADE, ITS' CONSTRUCTION
THAT PROCESS OF CONSTRUCTION IS DEFINITELY
CELLULAR OR AS I USED TO SAY MOLECULAR. IT ALSO

VIBRATES WITH AN ACCOMPANING$_{s/p}$ SOUND. IT'S VIBRATION IS WHAT PRODUCES ITS' OPTICAL NATURE.

29 MARCH: I AM COMING IN THROUGH THE BACK DOOR.

2 APRIL: THE WORST POSSIBLE SCENARIO IS WHEN YOUR OWN MIND BETRAYS YOU.

5 APRIL: I CAN FEEL ITS' PRESENCE BUT IT IS ALWAYS AT THE EDGE OF THE MIND
THERE IS NO ONE ANSWER; IT'S EVERYTHING AND ONE THING AT THE SAME TIME!
<u>PAINT THE PULARITY!</u>

7 APRIL: I USE THE WALL AS METAPHOR

16 APRIL: I WANT PHYSICAL, FACTUAL INFORMATION.

19 APRIL: PAINTING IS THE PROCESS.

23 APRIL: I AM TRYING NOT TO THINK.

27 APRIL: I MUST TAKE MY BEARING FROM AFRICAN TRIBAL SCULPTURE. THE POWER IS WITHIN ME. IT MUST COME DIRECTLY FROM THE SOUL UNHINDERED BY LOGIC.

7 MAY: ~~THE~~ SPACE IS ONLY THE SYMBOL, REVEALED THROUGH LIGHT.

24 MAY: I AM READY—EXPERIENCE CAN SERVE AS METAPHOR.

10 SEPT. THE CENTER IS EVERYWHERE + NOWHERE

12 SEPT. IT'S EXTREMELY COMPLICATED + EXTREMELY SIMPLE AT THE SAME TIME.

27 SEPT: I AM THE CONTENT.

29 SEPT. GOD IS A CHEMICAL . . . 1 OCT. THE PROCESS OF REALEASING IT IS CALLED RELIGION

7 OCT: YOU CAN'T DEAL WITH IT IN TERMS OF WHAT IT LOOKS LIKE, YOU MUST DEAL IN TERMS OF WHAT IT IS.

8 OCT: IT'S ABOUT <u>NO ONE</u> THING. THIS IS THE TRUE MEANING OF POST-MODERNISM; NO ONE CAN FIGURE IT OUT. YOU MUST SIMPLY DO IT.

11 OCT: THE SPACE IS ARRIVED AT THROUGH METABOLIC PROCESSES . . . . A METABOLIC SPACE . .

15 OCT: I AM INTERESTED IN MIND AS MATTER.

19 OCT: SPACE IS ARRIVED AT THROUGH THE MATERIAL <u>NOT</u> THE STORY: (a message to E. Cruz.)

STUDIO LOG 1987

27 OCT: MY INTENTION IS TO RE-INVENT CUBISM AS PERTAINING TO A MODERN TECHNOLOGICAL SOCIETY, TAKING IT BACK TO ITS ORIGINAL SOURCE: THE AFRICAN CONTINENT. MY EMPHASIS IS PRE-HISTORY, REDEFINING THE PAST. I WANT AN ABSTRACT INTERPRETATION BUILT WITH A BLACK SENSIBILITY.

29 OCT: THE GEOMETRY REMAINS IN MY WORK BUT IT'S NO LONGER EUCLID GEOMETRY. IT IS FRACTAL GEOMETRY.

2 NOV: I ENJOY WEIRD, DIVERSE MIXTURES. THE TEXTURE OF FOOD IS IMPORTANT TO ME THATS WHY I ENJOY JAPANESE FOOD.

7 NOV: I am LOOKING FOR A SHAPE; THE PROBLEM IS, THE SHAPE THAT I SENSE HAS NO EDGE. IT IS THERE, BUT IT'S NOT THERE.

10 NOV: A PAINTING IS A PAINTING, IS A PAINTING, IS A PAINTING. AN EXTENSION OF NATURE, BUT BUILT BY ME; I AM NATURE.

17 NOV: THE HEART IS A GAUGE.

1 DEC: CHRIS... I LOVED YOU. SUMMIT IS DEDICATED TO YOU.

4 DEC: I AM PEERING THROUGH THE LOOKING GLASS.

5 DEC: D-DAY

6 DEC: IF IT IS TRUE THAT JACKSON POLLACK BROKE THE ICE, I AM SHOWING WHAT'S BENEATH THE ICE. MY INTENTION IS POLITICAL IN NATURE. MY ART IS NOT AN ART FOR ARTS' SAKE.

18 DEC: THE PAINTING MUST PRESERVE BOTH ITS PICTORIAL CONTENT AND ITS OBJECTNESS, THIS IS ACHIEVED THROUGH A METABOLIC PROCESS OF CONSTRUCT — DE CONSTRUCT.

22 DEC: BLACK MONOLITH : A TRIBUTE TO JAMES BALDWIN
        82" X 96"

29 DEC: WHAT DOES IT ALL MEAN?

1 JAN 88: WE MUST FIGHT WITH THE SPIRIT.
12 JAN 88: THERE ARE NO ANSWERS, SOMETIMES I WONDER IF THERE ARE QUESTIONS.
18 JAN 88: REALITY AS WE KNOW IT TO BE HAS ANOTHER SIDE.
24 JAN 88: LIGHT IS MY GUIDE.
25 JAN 88: I WOULD LOVE TO BE ABLE TO DISSOLVE ALL TIME ZONES AND TRAVEL PURELY BY LIGHT.
        POLY-RHYTHMIC IN MUSIC = MULTIPLE LAYERS OF LIGHT IN PAINTING THE DENSITY OF BOTH DEPENDS UPON THE DENSITY OF SOUL.

3 FEB: I WANT THE VISUAL EQUIVALENT OF JAZZ.

1 MARCH: GEOMETRY OFFERS A CHOICE OF HAVING MY CAKE AND EATING IT TO.

7 March: I MUST BE MAN ENOUGH TO ACCEPT THE MYSTERY WITHOUT BECOMING MYSTIFIED.

8 March: I PRAY THAT THE GOD OF ART BE WITH ME, PROTECT ME AND GUIDE ME WITH COMPASSION AND REVERENCE FOR ALL.

8 March: THE PURPOSE OF ART IS TO TAKE US TO A HIGHER LEVEL OF CONSCIOUSNESS.
        " IN BACK OF EVERY REALITY LIES ANOTHER

14 MARCH: I DISCOVERED AN ARC TODAY WHICH CONNECTS THE OPPOSITE CORNERS OF THE PLANE WITH ITS CENTER EXISTING OUTSIDE OF THE PLANE. I FOUND THIS ARC BY PROJECTING THE DIAGONAL BEYOND THE PERIMETER OF THE PLANE. I HAVE NAMED THIS ARC "ROMARE'S ARC" IN HONOR OF ROMARE BEARDEN. THE FIRST TWO PAINTINGS USING THIS INFORMATION ARE DEDICATED TO THE MEMORY OF ROMARE BEARDEN: ROMARE'S ARC I & ROMARE'S ARC II.

STUDIO LOG 1987

27 OCT: MY INTENTION IS TO RE-INVENT CUBISM AS PERTAINING TO A MODERN TECHNOLOGICAL SOCIETY, TAKING IT BACK TO ITS ORIGINAL SOURCE: THE AFRICAN CONTINENT. MY EMPHASIS IS PRE-HISTORY, REDEFINING THE PAST. I WANT AN ABSTRACT INTERPERTATION BUILT WITH A BLACK SENSIBILITY.

29 OCT: THE GEOMETRY REMAINS IN MY WORK BUT IT'S NO LONGER EUCLID GEOMETRY; IT IS FRACTAL GEOMETRY.

2 NOV: I ENJOY WEIRD, DIVERSE MIXTURES. THE TEXTURE OF FOOD IS IMPORTANT TO ME THAT'S WHY I ENJOY JAPANESE FOOD.

7 NOV: I am LOOKING FOR A SHAPE; THE PROBLEM IS, THE SHAPE THAT I SENSE HAS NO EDGE. IT IS THERE, BUT IT'S NOT THERE.

10 NOV: A PAINTING IS A PAINTING, IS A PAINTING, IS A PAINTING. AN EXTENSION OF NATURE, BUT BUILT BY ME; I AM NATURE.

17 NOV: THE HEART IS A GAUGE.

1 DEC: CHRIS*   I LOVED YOU. <u>SUMMIT</u> IS DEDICATED TO YOU.

4 DEC: I AM PEERING THROUGH THE LOOKING GLASS.

5 DEC: D-DAY

6 DEC: IF IT IS TRUE THAT JACKSON POLLOCK BROKE THE
ICE, I AM SHOWING WHAT'S BENEATH THE ICE.
MY INTENTION IS POLITICAL IN NATURE. MY ART IS NOT
AN ART FOR ARTS' SAKE.

18 DEC: THE PAINTING MUST PRESERVE BOTH ITS
PICTORIAL CONTENT AND ITS OBJECTNESS. THIS IS
ACHIEVED THROUGH A METABOLIC PROCESS OF
<u>CONSTRUCT-DECONSTRUCT</u>.

22 DEC: <u>BLACK MONOLITH: A TRIBUTE TO JAMES
BALDWIN</u>
82" x 96"

29 DEC: WHAT DOES IT ALL MEAN?

1 JAN 88: WE MUST FIGHT WITH THE SPIRIT.

12 JAN 88: THERE ARE NO ANSWERS, SOMETIMES I
WONDER IF THERE ARE QUESTIONS.

18 JAN 88: REALITY AS WE KNOW IT TO BE HAS ANOTHER
SIDE.

24 JAN 88: LIGHT IS MY GUIDE.

25 JAN 88: I WOULD LOVE TO BE ABLE TO DISSOLVE ALL
TIME ZONES AND TRAVEL PURELY BY LIGHT.
POLY-RHYTHMIC IN MUSIC = MULTIPLE LAYERS OF
LIGHT IN PAINTING
THE DENSITY OF BOTH DEPENDS ON THE DENSITY OF
THE SOUL.

3 FEB: I WANT THE VISUAL EQUIVALENT OF JAZZ.

1 MARCH: GEOMETRY OFFERS A CHOICE OF HAVING MY CAKE AND EATING IT TO.

7 March: I MUST BE MAN ENOUGH TO ACCEPT THE MYSTERY WITHOUT BECOMING MYSTIFIED.

~~7~~8 MARCH: I PRAY THAT THE GOD OF ART BE WITH ME, PROTECT ME AND GUIDE ME WITH COMPARSSION AND REVELENCE FOR ALL.

8 March: THE <u>PURPOSE</u> OF ART IS TO TAKE US TO A HIGHER LEVEL OF CONSCIOUSNESS.

"   " IN BACK OF EVERY REALITY LIES ANOTHER

14 MARCH: I DISCOVERED AN ARC TODAY WHICH CONNECTS THE OPPOSITE CORNERS OF THE PLANE WITH ITS CENTER EXISTING OUTSIDE OF THE PLANE. I FOUND THIS ARC BY PROJECTING THE DIAGONAL BEYOND THE PERIMETER OF THE PLANE. I HAVE NAMED THIS ARC "ROMARE'S ARC" IN HONOR OF ROMARE BEARDEN. THE FIRST TWO PAINTINGS USING THIS INFORMATION ARE DEDICATED TO THE MEMORY OF ROMARE BEARDEN: <u>ROMARE'S ARC I</u> + <u>ROMARE'S ARC II</u>.

Studio Log 1988

24 OCT: I WANT AN ART THAT REFLECT THE DIVERSITY WHICH I SEE AROUND ME.

28 OCT: I AM CONVINCED THAT ART LIES BEYOND THE SELF. I MUST BE ABLE TO GET OUTSIDE OF MYSELF. THOSE ARTIST THAT WALLOW IN THE PSYCHOLOGY OF SELF ARE PRODUCING A MINOR ART, ONLY FIT FOR THE CULT OF CONSUMPTION

—THE SURFACE (which is matter) IS ONLY A MATERIAL VEHICLE FOR THE SPIRIT [. . .]

12 NOV: I AM A CONDUIT FOR THE SPIRIT. IT FLOWS THROUGH ME AND MANIFESTS ITSELF THROUGH THE MATERIALITY OF PAINT. THIS CREATIVE ACTIVITY LIES BEYOND THE CONCEPTUAL. THE CONCEPTUAL IS ONLY A SPRING BOARD WHICH AWAKENS THE SPIRIT. THE CONCEPTUAL IS NEVER AN ENDS BUT ONLY A MEANS IN THE REALIZATION OF THE SPIRIT.

13 NOV: WHAT IS SPIRIT? A TYPE OF MENTAL i.e. cerebral MATTER CLOSELY AKIN TO THE NATURE OF THOUGHT.

17 NOV: MY ULTIMATE INTEREST IS NOT THE OBJECT BUT WHAT THE OBJECT GENERATES.

21 NOV: THERE IS A BEAUTIFUL SPACE WHICH EXIST AS A RESULT OF THE TENSION PRODUCED BETWEEN THE KNOWN AND THE UNKNOWN

22 NOV: I AM COMING THROUGH THE BACKDOOR.

26 NOV: LIGHT DETERMINES THE DEGREE OF FLATNESS
DESIRED ON THE PICTURE PLANE. MY LIGHT IS PLANAR.

4 DEC: I PAINT ABOUT WHAT I KNOW: THAT WHICH EXIST
IN MY PRESENT URBAN TECHNOLOGICAL SOCIETY. I CAN
ONLY READ ABOUT THE DISTANT PAST THROUGH
HISTORY AND I DON'T NECESSARILY TRUST HISTORY.

8 DEC: MY REFRENCE IS THE STREETS OF NEW YORK.
I WANT A HARD, CLEAR, COLD, FACTUAL REALISM.

10 DEC: THE POLITICAL SIGNIFICANCE OF WHAT I AM
DOING DEPENDS UPON MY ABILITY TO PROJECT BEYOND
ART HISTORY. THE SO CALLED MAINSTREAM MUST BE
BENT, DEFLECTED AND DETOURED IN A DIRECTION
DICTATED BY THE PROFUNDITY OF MY SENSIBILITY. THE
ALLIANCE, COMPLETED IN DEC. of '88 OFFERS SUCH A
DETOUR. THE ALLIANCE IS A PACT CONCEIVED OF AS A
MARRIAGE OF NECESSITY BETWEEN MATTER AND SPIRIT.

22 DEC: I saw Basquiat's show at A. Nosei's* today for the second
time. These paintings exist outside of art history. They are not formal
nor can I simply call them informal. They are about information:
computer banks similar to totem poles from primative cultures.
Jean-Michel is not a painter in the classical mode but an urban folk
artist, sophisticated not naive. They are spontaneous, stream of
consciouness, visual poems. I am interested in his space, because
I understand it to be non-illuisionistic, non-art historical. These
paintings fit within my meaning of totemic space, different from
what I am doing because of their use of narrative content.

My objective for 1989 is to construct a series of paintings → my content i
depicting what I mean by totemic space   in the form

<u>4 JAN 89</u>: I AM SPIRIT.

11 JAN 89: TOTEMIC SPACE IS FACTUAL +
<u>ASYMETRICALLY</u>_{sp.} → AS JAZZ IS too.

13 JAN 89: THE PAINTINGS COMES OUT OF TRUST OF
ONES' FEELINGS.
      <u>GREEN GOLD 1989</u> ©

     13 JAN: THIS UNIQUE LIGHT BENDS THE
GRAVITATIONAL FIELD AND AS A RESULT INTERFERES
WITH THE FLATNESS OF THE PICTURE PLANE. I FIND THIS
MOST DESIREABLE.

18 JAN 89: A PAINTING IS A MAGIC OBJECT.
UNFORTUNATELY WE HAVE LOST THIS SIMPLE FACT AND
I WANT TO RESTORE IT!

(CONT?)   STUDIO LOG JAN. 1989

19 JAN: IN ORDER FOR A PAINTING TO QUALIFY AS A SACRED OBJECT IT MUST EXIST
       OUTSIDE OF LOGIC. LOGIC MAY BE USED ONLY AS A SPRINGBOARD, A LAUNCHING
       PAD INTO THE UNKNOWN.
20 JAN: IN ORDER TO GROW, WE MUST LEARN TO SEE BEYOND THE LOGIC OF PUSH + PULL;
       THE FUTURE OF PAINTING DOES NOT DEAL WITH CASUAL THINKING.
         POLLOCK UNDERSTAND THIS AND WAS ABLE TO "BREAK THE ICE". UNFORTUNATELY THE
       SELF CAUGHT UP WITH HIM AND ALL THE BONES OF THE PAST WAS THURST FROM
       THE CLOSET.

25 JAN: SPACE IS A BACKDROP FOR CONSCIOUSNESS!

28 JAN: I WAS TOUCHED BY THE SPIRIT TODAY.

What joy! What an experience to behold — I AM
CONVINCED OF ITS' PRESCENCE!

Time is Totemic

30 JAN. WHATEVER OCCURS .... MY JOB i.e., RESPONSIBILITY IS TO THE OBJECT
       AS A PAINTING WHICH IS SACRED. AT ANY COST THE PAINTING MUST QUALIFY
       AS SACRED OBJECT —→ IT MUST WORK IN A PAINTERS' LANGUAGE. THE PAINTING
       IS A PAINTING, IS A PAINTING!

31 JAN: I AM AN ABSTRACT REALIST PAINTER.
          I DO ABSTRACT REALISM.

2 FEB: I AM NOT INTERESTED IN LOGIC AS AN ENDS, BUT ONLY AS A
       MEANS IN THE REALIZATION OF SPIRIT.
         "GRANDEUR HAS ITS' OWN MEANING" Ronald Josept 2 Jan 1987 on visit to my studio
3 FEB: MY MISSION IS TO RENDER EVERY PAINTING OTHER THAN
       MINE OBSOLETE.

4 FEB: THE LIGHT IS THE NET.

9 FEB: I TREAT PAINTINGS LIKE I TREAT PEOPLE... EACH ONE IS DIFFERENT.
       I MUST GO BEYOND EVERYTHING & EVERYBODY THAT HAS COME BEFORE ME.
       ONLY THERE WILL I FIND SILENCE.

14 FEB: I DON'T FIGHT FIRE WITH FIRE... I FIGHT WITH THE SPIRIT.

20 FEB: I TAKE MY CLUE FROM JAZZ.
         MEMORY CAN BE TRANSFERRED INTO PHYSICAL MATTER.
25 FEB: THESE NEW PAINTINGS ARE LITTLE BUNDLES OF PLASTIC EXPLOSIVES WRAPPED IN
       THE AESTHETICS OF NEO-MODERNISM.
2 MARCH: THE ABSOLUTE NOTION OF SPATIAL OVERLAY EXIST WITHIN THE PLANAR ACTIVITY
       OF LIGHT NOT THROUGH LINE AS PREVIOUSLY THOUGHT.

5 MARCH: MY INTEREST IN PAINTING IS INVESTIGATIONAL: AN INVESTIGATION INTO THE
       EXTENT OF INFLUENCE WHICH TECHNOLOGY HAS PLAYED IN SHAPING MY PSYCHIC — MY
       WORLD VIEW, IN PARTICULAR PHOTOGRAPHY AND ITS' USE IN MEDIA. I MAINTAIN THAT THE
       FORMAL ELEMENT OF SPACE IS THE MAJOR ISSUE IN ABSTRACT PAINTING. WHOEVER IS ABLE
       TO EXPRESS VISUALLY THE NEXT SIGNIFICENT MEANING OF SPACE IN ABSTRACT PAINTING
       CONTROLS THE AESTHETIC NECESSARY FOR SHAPING A TRULY, MODERN WORLD VIEW.
6 MARCH: LIGHT MUST HAVE A CARRIER. IN PAINTING FORM IS THE CARRIER FOR LIGHT.
7 MARCH: LIFE IS A FRAME INSIDE OF A FRAME, INSIDE OF FRAME, INSIDE OF A FRAME, INSIDE OF A FRAME,
       INSIDE OF A FRAME;

<u>STUDIO LOG JAN. 1989</u>

19 JAN: IN ORDER FOR A PAINTING TO QUALIFY AS A SACRED OBJECT IT MUST EXIST OUTSIDE OF LOGIC. LOGIC MAY BE USED ONLY AS A SPRINGBOARD, A LAUNCHING PAD INTO THE UNKNOWN.

20 JAN: IN ORDER TO GROW, WE MUST LEARN TO SEE BEYOND THE LOGIC OF PUSH + PULL: THE FUTURE OF PAINTING DOES NOT DEAL WITH CASUAL THINKING. POLLOCK UNDERSTAND THIS AND WAS ABLE TO "BREAK THE ICE." UNFORTUNATELY THE SELF CAUGHT UP WITH HIM AND ALL THE BONES OF THE PAST WAS THURST FROM CLOSET.

25 JAN: SPACE IS A BACKDROP FOR CONSCIOUSNESS.

28 JAN: <u>I WAS TOUCHED BY THE SPIRIT TODAY.</u>
<u>What joy! What an experience to behold.</u>
<u>I AM CONVINCED OF ITS' PRESENCE!</u>
Time is Totemic

30 JAN. WHATEVER OCCURS . . . . MY JOB I.E., RESPONSIBILITY IS TO THE OBJECT AS A PAINTING WHICH IS SACRED. AT ANY COST THE PAINTING MUST QUALIFY AS SACRED OBJECT → IT MUST WORK IN A PAINTERS' LANGUAGE. THE PAINTING IS A PAINTING, IS A PAINTING.

31 JAN. I AM AN ABSTRACT REALIST PAINTER.
I DO <u>ABSTRACT REALISM</u>.

2 FEB: I AM NOT INTERESTED IN LOGIC AS AN <u>ENDS</u>, BUT

ONLY AS A <u>MEANS</u> IN THE REALIZATION OF SPIRIT.
"GRANDEUR HAS ITS' OWN MEANING" Ronald Joseph 2 Jan
on visit to my studio

3 FEB: MY MISSION IS TO RENDER EVERY PAINTING
OTHER THAN MINE OBSOLETE.

4 FEB: THE LIGHT IS THE NET.

9 FEB: I TREAT PAINTINGS LIKE I TREAT PEOPLE . . . . EACH
ONE IS DIFFERENT.
I MUST GO BEYOND EVERYTHING + EVERYBODY THAT
HAS COME BEFORE ME. ONLY THERE WILL I FIND
SILENCE.

14 FEB: I DON'T FIGHT FIRE WITH FIRE . . . I FIGHT WITH
THE SPIRIT.

20 FEB: I TAKE MY CLUE FROM JAZZ.
MEMORY CAN BE TRANSFERRED INTO PHYSICAL MATTER.

25 FEB: THESE NEW PAINTINGS ARE LITTLE BUNDLES OF
PLASTIC EXPLOSIVES WRAPPED IN THE AESTHETICS OF
NEO-MODERNISM.

2 MARCH: THE ABSOLUTE NOTION OF SPATIAL OVERLAY
EXIST WITHIN THE PLANAR ACTIVITY OF LIGHT NOT
THROUGH LINE AS PREVIOUSLY THOUGHT.

5 MARCH: MY INTEREST IN PAINTING IS
INVESTIGATIONAL: AN INVESTIGATION INTO THE
EXTENT OF INFLUENCE WHICH TECHNOLOGY HAS

PLAYED IN SHAPING MY PYSCHIC—MY WORLD VIEW, IN PARTICULAR PHOTOGRAPHYAND ITS USE IN MEDIA. I MAINTAIN THAT THE FORMAL ELEMENT OF SPACE IS THE MAJOR ISSUE IN ABSTRACT PAINTING. <u>WHOEVER</u> IS ABLE TO EXPRESS VISUALLY THE NEXT SIGNIFICANT MEANING OF SPACE IN ABSTRACT PAINTING CONTROLS THE AESTHETIC NECESSARY FOR SHAPING A TRULY, MODERN WORLD VIEW.

6 MARCH: LIGHT MUST HAVE A CARRIER. IN PAINTING FOR IS THE CARRIER FOR LIGHT.

7 MARCH: LIFE IS A FRAME INSIDE OF A FRAME, INSIDE OF A FRAME, INSIDE OF A FRAME, INSIDE OF A FRAME, INSIDE OF A FRAME, INSIDE OF A FRAME

<u>STUDIO LOG '89</u>

10 MARCH: ACTUALITY IS NUMINOUS.

11 MARCH: THE NEW SPACE IS PURELY PSYCHOLOGICAL, A MATTER OF SPECIFIC CONSCIOUSNESS.
IT HAS NOTHING TO DO WITH DESIGN.

14 MARCH: "NATURE AS A SINGLE CONNECTED SYSTEM OF EVENTS UNITED BY LAWS IS THE FINAL
AND MOST DIFFICULT OUTCOME OF ABSTRACTION"
COULD THIS STATEMENT REPRESENT MY THINKING?

15 MARCH: THE NUMINOUS IS IDENTIFIABLE BY THE QUALITY OF WONDER. THIS MORNING ON MY WAY
TO CLASS I RECOGNIZED THE NUMINOUS IN A CHILDS' FACE; THERE WAS A DISTINCT QUALITY
OF WONDER AS HE CHASED A BIRD!
IN REFERENCE TO JAZZ, IT OCCURED TO ME THAT MY STRUCTURES ARE POLY-RHYTHMIC.

16 MARCH: EACH PAINTING IS A FOUND OBJECT

19 MARCH: I HAVE SUMMED UP THE MEANING OF MATERIALITY AND THE ONLY THING THAT I AM LEFT
WITH IS THE OBJECT.

31 MARCH: COGNITION WHICH TAKES PLACE AT THE EDGE OF CONSCIOUSNESS, INTEREST ME A LOT!
TODAYS' PAINTING IS TO SYNTHETIC, FAR TO RATIONAL, NO EVIDENCE OF SPIRIT
EXCEPT ON A SUPERFICIAL LEVEL.

12 APRIL: "SEEK AND YE SHALL FIND"

13 APRIL: S.P. DOESN'T SEE.

15 APRIL: LOVE IS NOT AN INTELLECTUAL IMPOSITION OF WILL.

19 APRIL: WHAT IS THE PRICE OF GLORY?

20 APRIL: IT IS NOT AS DIFFICULT AS I HAVE MADE IT SEEM.

21 APRIL: MORALITY DOES NOT DICTATE ART.
I READ IN THE <u>NEW YORK TIMES</u> TODAY THAT THE BATTLESHIP I<u>OWA</u> SUFFERED
A CATASTROPHIC EXPLOSION WHICH RESULTED IN THE DEATH OF 47 SAILORS.
THE TURRET WAS REINFORCED WITH 17¼" OF ARMORED STEEL.
I WANT MY THINKING TO PENETRATE THIS DEGREE OF ARMOR.
A LASER CONCENTRATION OF LIGHT DESIGNED TO PENETRATE SEVERAL LAYERS
OF CONSCIOUSNESS, STEREOTYPES, FALSEHOODS AND SYMBOLS OF POWER.

8 MAY: IT'S TIME TO TURN IT LOOSE.

18 MAY: ABSTRACTION IS A MASK.
I MUST QUALIFY THIS BY SAYING THAT ABSTRACTION IS THE WESTERN EQUIVALENT
OF THE MASK AS USED IN NON-WESTERN SOCIETIES.

19 MAY— GONE FISHING

STUDIO LOG '89

10 MARCH: ACTUALITY IS NUMINOUS.

11 MARCH: THE NEW SPACE IS PURELY PSYCHOLOGICAL,
A MATTER OF SPECIFIC CONSCIOUNESS. IT HAS NOTHING
TO DO WITH DESIGN.

14 MARCH: "NATURE AS A SINGLE CONNECTED SYSTEM
OF EVENTS UNITED BY LAWS IS THE FINAL AND MOST
DIFFICULT OUTCOME OF ABSTRACTION"
COULD THIS STATEMENT REPRESENT MY THINKING?

15 MARCH: THE NUMINOUS IS IDENTIFIABLE BY THE
QUALITY OF WONDER. THIS MORNING ON MY WAY TO
CLASS I RECOGNIZED THE NUMINOUS IN A CHILDS' FACE.
THERE WAS A DISTINCT QUALITY OF WONDER AS HE
CHASED A BIRD!
IN REFERENCE TO JAZZ, IT OCCURRED TO ME THAT MY
STRUCTURES ARE POLY-RHYTHMIC.

16 MARCH: EACH PAINTING IS A FOUND OBJECT

19 MARCH: I HAVE SUMMED UP THE MEANING OF
MATERIALITY AND THE ONLY THING THAT I AM LEFT
WITH IS THE OBJECT.

31 MARCH: COGNITION WHICH TAKES PLACE AT THE
EDGE OF CONSCIOUNESS, INTEREST ME A LOT!
TODAY'S PAINTING IS TO SYNTHETIC, FAR TO RATIONAL,
NO EVIDENCE OF SPIRIT EXCEPT ON A SUPERFICIAL
LEVEL.

12 APRIL: "SEEK AND YE SHALL FIND"

13 APRIL: S.P. DOESN'T SEE.

15 APRIL: LOVE IS NOT AN INTELLECTUAL IMPOSITION OF WILL.

19 APRIL: WHAT IS THE PRICE OF GLORY?

20 APRIL: IT IS NOT AS DIFFICULT AS I HAVE MADE IT SEEM.

21 APRIL: MORALITY DOES NOT DICTATE ART.
I READ IN THE <u>NEW YORK TIMES</u> TODAY THAT THE BATTLESHIP <u>IOWA</u> SUFFERED A CATASTROPHIC EXPLOSION WHICH RESULTED IN THE DEATH OF 47 SAILORS. THE TURRET WAS REINFORCED WITH $17\frac{1}{4}$ OF ARMORED STEEL. I WANT MY THINKING TO PENETRATE THIS DEGREE OF ARMOR. A LASER CONCENTRATION OF LIGHT DESIGNED TO PENETRATE SEVERAL LAYERS OF CONSCIOUNESS, STEREOTYPES, FALSEHOODS AND SYMBOLS OF POWER.

8 MAY: IT'S TIME TO TURN IT LOOSE.

18 MAY: ABSTRACTION IS A MASK.
I MUST QUALIFY THIS BY SAYING THAT ABSTRACTION IS THE WESTERN EQUIVALENT OF THE MASK AS USED IN NON-WESTERN SOCIETIES.

19 MAY— GONE FISHING

STUDIO LOG   FALL '89

7 Sept. 89: THE PAINTING AS FOUND OBJECT.

20 Sept 89: ANY WORKABLE DEFINITION OF WORLDVIEW TODAY, MUST INCLUDE
        THE OPINION OF THE MINORITY.

12 Oct: LOOK FOR A SPECIFIC QUALITY OF LIGHT

13 OCT: TENSION EXIST BETWEEN KNOWING + NOT KNOWING

    I CAN NO LONGER AVOID THE SIGNIFICANCE OF WILL.
        REALITY HAS NO EDGE.

17 Oct: ALL OF MY KNOWLEDGE ABOUT PAINTING MUST BE FOCUSED ON THE
        CANVAS AS SHAPE. THE CANVAS IS THE FORM. A FUNCTIONAL FORM. (9Nov)
9 NOV: I MUST INTERCEPT THE INTERGITY OF THE SQUARE.   FOR WHAT PURPOSE?
        THIS IS ANTI-FORMALISM

        NOT ONLY IS THE SPACE IDENTIFIABLE BY A SPECIFIC QUALITY OF LIGHT
        BUT A CANCELLATION OF ILLUSION AND NON-ILLUSION (THESE TWO MUST BE SPLIT)

11 NOV: MY POSITION HAS ALWAYS BEEN ONE OF WORKING THROUGH THE MAINSTREAM OF WESTERN ART.
    MY OBJECTIVE IS ONE OF PROJECTION i.e., to DEFLECT, TO BEND, TO HAMMER OUT A FORM
    DEPENDENT UPON THE DICTATES OF MY SENSIBILITY. I HOPE THAT THIS IS CLEAR TO
    ANYONE INTERESTED.

18 NOV: I AM NOW LOOKING THROUGH THE LOOKING GLASS.

25 NOV: MY ART IS ABOUT REACHING LAYERS OF CONSCIOUNESS. EACH LAYER REACHED
        IS HISTORICALLY DEEPER THAN THE ONE PRECEEDING.

26 NOV: ABSTRACT SURREALISM

27 NOV: I AM AN ABSTRACT PAINTER OUT OF CHOICE .... THE CHOICE WAS MINE.

4 DEC: MY SHIT GOES ON TOP.
        IN ORDER FOR ART TO QUALIFY AS BEING GREAT, IT MUST MAKE
        LOVE WITH NATURE.

9 DEC: $X = Y - Z^{10}$

14 DEF: I AM THE CONDUIT.

4 JAN 90: SPACE AS SUSPENSION IN TIME.

20 JAN 90: I DO NOT ACCEPT THE SEPARATION OF SPIRIT FROM MATTER.

24 JAN: PAINTING IS MY ONLY SALVATION.
        VIRGIN SPACE

27 JAN: MY OBJECTIVE IN PAINTING IS TO SUM UP MODERNIST THEORIES
        AND TO LAUNCH INTO VIRGIN SPACE. I WANT TO PROJECT INTO ANOTHER SPHERE.

28 JAN: LIGHT AS A CARRIER OF INFORMATION.
        THE PRIMARY ISSUE IS SPACE.

17 FEB: GOD IS THE GLUE THAT HOLDS IT ALL TOGETHER.

23 FEB: I WANT TO TAKE IT ALL OUT!

18 MARCH: I DON'T WANT IT TO BE ABOUT SEX, ART, RELIGION OR POLITICS

30 MARCH: THE ENVIRONMENT ENCOMPASSES THE TOTAL DEFINITION OF SYMBOL: SEX, RELIGION,
        POLITICS, PHILOSOPHY, CULTURE, SENSIBILITY ... TIME/SPACE, SELF ... etc.
        THE CENTER DICTATES THE EDGE.

16 APRIL: I AM TRULY A WEAVER OF LIGHT:
        AN ABSTRACT RECONSTRUCTIVIST

STUIDO LOG FALL '89

7 Sept. 89: THE PAINTING AS FOUND OBJECT.

20 Sept 89: ANY WORKABLE DEFINITION OF WORLDVIEW TODAY, MUST INCLUDE THE OPINION OF THE MINORITY.

12 Oct: LOOK FOR A SPECIFIC QUALITY OF LIGHT

13 OCT: TENSION EXIST BETWEEN KNOWING + NOT KNOWING
I CAN NO LONGER AVOID THE SIGNIFICANCE OF WILL.
REALITY HAS NO EDGE.

17 Oct: ALL OF MY KNOWLEDGE ABOUT PAINTING MUST BE FOCUSED ON THE CANVAS AS SHAPE. THE CANVAS IS THE FORM. A FUNCTIONAL FORM. (9 NOV.) FOR WHAT PURPOSE?

9 NOV: I MUST INTERCEPT THE INTERGITY OF THE SQUARE
THIS IS ANTI-FORMALISM
NOT ONLY IS THE SPACE IDENTIFIABLE BY A SPECIFIC QUALITY OF LIGHT BUT BY A CANCELLATION OF ILLUSION AND NON-ILLUSION (THESE TWO MUST BE SPLIT)

11 NOV: MY POSITION HAS ALWAYS BEEN ONE OF WORKING THROUGH THE MAINSTREAM OF WESTERN ART. MY OBJECTIVE IS ONE OF PROJECTION i.e., to DEFLECT, TO BEND, TO HAMMER OUT A FORM DEPENDENT UPON THE

DICTATES OF MY SENSIBILITY. I HOPE THAT THIS IS
CLEAR TO ANYONE INTERESTED.

18 NOV: I AM NOW LOOKING THROUGH THE LOOKING
GLASS.

25 NOV: MY ART IS ABOUT REACHING LAYERS OF
CONSCIOUNESS. EACH LAYER REACHED IS HISTORICALLY
DEEPER THAT THE ONE PRECEEDING.

26 NOV: <u>ABSTRACT SURREALISM</u>

27 NOV: I AM AN ABSTRACT PAINTER OUT OF
CHOICE . . . . . THE CHOICE WAS MINE.

4 DEC: MY SHIT GOES ON TOP.
IN ORDER FOR ART TO QUALIFY AS BEING GREAT, IT
MUST MAKE LOVE WITH NATURE.

9 DEC: X=Y-Z[10]

14 DEC: I AM THE CONDUIT.

4 JAN 90: SPACE AS SUSPENSION IN TIME.

20 JAN 90: I DO NOT ACCEPT THE SEPARATION OF SPIRIT
FROM MATTER.

24 JAN: PAINTING IS MY ONLY SALVATION.
<u>VIRIGN SPACE</u>

27 JAN: MY OBJECTIVE IN PAINTING IS TO <u>SUM UP</u>
MODERNIST THEORIES AND TO LAUNCH INTO VIRGIN
SPACE. I WANT TO PROJECT INTO ANOTHER SPHERE.

28 JAN: LIGHT AS A CARRIER OF INFORMATION.
THE PRIMARY ISSUE IS SPACE.

17 FEB: GOD IS THE GLUE THAT HOLDS IT ALL TOGETHER.

23 FEB: I WANT TO TAKE IT ALL OUT!

18 MARCH: I DON'T WANT IT TO BE ABOUT SEX, ART,
RELIGION OR POLITICS

30 MARCH: THE ENVIORNMENT ENCOMPASSES THE
TOTAL DEFINITION OF SYMBOL: SEX, RELIGION,
POLITICS, PHILOSOPHY, CULTURE, SENSIBILITY . . . TIME /
SPACE, SELF . . . etc. THE CENTER DICTATES THE EDGE.

16 APRIL: I AM TRULY A WEAVER OF LIGHT:
AN ABSTRACT RECONSTRUCTIVIST

'90s

STUDIO LOG   SPRING '90

21 APRIL: THE PAINTING BECAME OBJECT, THE OBJECT BECAME SPIRIT.
   MY PREVIOUS THOUGHT WAS THAT THE SPIRIT LIVES IN THE OBJECT, I.E.,
   THE OBJECT AS CONTAINER FOR THE SPIRIT.... THE OBJECT MUST BECOME SPIRIT
   THE OBJECT IS THE SPIRIT. FOR A PAINTER, WE MUST HAVE THE OBJECT.
   PAINT CONTINUES TO BE MEDIUM. MY PAINTING IS THE FORM OF RECONSTRUCTION
   I AM RECONSTRUCTING THE SPIRIT WHICH HAS BEEN MISSING FROM AMERICAN ART
   SINCE THE ABSTRACT EXPRESSIONISTS.

30 APRIL: THE IMAGE IS LOCATED IN THE MARRIAGE OF FRACTAL + EUCLID GEOMETRY.
   INTELLUCTUAL AGRESSION IS A DESIREABLE TRAIT.
   INTELLIGENCE TO BE WORTH ANYTHING MUST BE CONFORTATIONAL (i.e. if it is to qualify as non-academic)
   CHARLIE PARKER WAS CONFORTATIONAL.
   ABSTRACT SYMBOLISM   RECONSTRUCTIONISM

4 MAY: A MEMORIAL PAINTING SERVES AS A REPOSITORY FOR THE SPIRIT OF THE DECEASED.

5 MAY: THE SPIRIT IS NON-REPRESENTIONAL.

10 MAY: ULTIMATELY, IT'S NOT SO MUCH ABOUT HOW MUCH YOU KNOW BUT
   HOW MUCH YOU CAN FORGET.
   CONSCIOUNESS IS ALWAYS A MATTER OF BEING FORMED I.E.,
   THE PROCESS OF FORMING TRULY THE MEANING OF PLASTICITY IN
   THE PAINTER'S LANGUAGE.

11 MAY: I WANT THE VISUAL EQUAVALENT OF JAZZ.
   THERE IS NO SUCH THING AS ONE WAY.
   IT IS MY DUTY AS AN ARTIST TO COMMERATE THAT WHICH IS IMPORTANT AND NOBLE
   ESPECIALLY IF IT SIGNIFIES PARTICULAR ASPECTS OF MY INDIVIDUAL CULTURE.

13 MAY: SEEING IS A MATTER OF CONSCIOUNESS. ONES DEPTH OF SEEING DEPENDS UPON
   THE DEPTH OF CONSCIOUNESS. CONSCIOUNESS IS A PROCESS OF LAYERING. THE LAYERS MUST
   BE PENETRATED IN ORDER TO REVEAL CONSCIOUNESS. HISTORY IS AN ACCUMULATION
   OF LAYERS. ANYONE INTERESTED IN IDENTITY MUST LEARN TO PENETRATE HISTORY.
   → A TREE IS NOBLE. LAST NIGHT VANDALS DESTROYED THREE TREES ON CHURCH ST. IN FRONT
   OF THE POST OFFICE. I WILL MAKE A TRYPTYCH AS A MEMORIAL TO THESE THREE TREES.

17 MAY: THE PSYCHIC INTERSECTION IS AN ABSOLUTE BALANCE OF HORIZONALITY + VERTICALITY
   WHICH IS THE CROSS + WHICH IS THE ELEMENTAL BASIS OF THE GRID ∴ THE
   GRID IS AN ALL ENCOMPASSING SYMBOL OF ART, NATURE, RELIGION
   THIS IS THE MEANING OF P.M.'S PLUS + MINUS
   ALL OF THIS CONFIRMS MY CONCEPT OF FUSION POLLOCK + MONDRIAN   FRACTAL + EUCLID

19 MAY: THE SPIRIT IS A PRIORK
   LIFE IS THERE IS NO OTHER EXPLANATION!

21 MAY: AS FAR AS COLOR IS CONCERNED, MY OBJECTIVE IS TO ESTABLISH A STANDARD
   BY WHICH ALL COLOR IS COMPARED. THIS OBJECTIVE IS MY COLOR AS ISSUE.
   (FOUND COLOR) like found object.

26 MAY: PLEASURE HEALS.

27 MAY: I DON'T HAVE ANY SKELETONS IN MY CLOSET. THIS SIMPLE FACT OF
   HISTORY ALLOWS ME TO GLORIFY THE AFFIRMATION OF LIFE, THE PURSUIT OF HAPPINESS.
   GOD BLESS ART!.

6 June: FINALLY, I AM ABLE TO USE THE REWARDS OF MEMORY
   WITHOUT EVERY GESTURE DICTATED BY ITS CRITERIA.

2 JULY 90: GONE FISHING

STUDIO LOG SPRING '90

21 APRIL: THE PAINTING BECAME OBJECT, THE OBJECT BECAME SPIRIT.
MY PREVIOUS THOUGHT WAS THAT THE SPIRIT LIVES IN THE OBJECT, I.E., THE OBJECT AS CONTAINER FOR THE SPIRIT . . . . THE OBJECT MUST BECOME SPIRIT <u>THE OBJECT IS THE SPIRIT</u>. FOR A PAINTER, WE MUST HAVE THE OBJECT. PAINT CONTINUES TO BE MEDIUM. MY PAINTING IS THE FORM OF RECONSTRUCTION I AM RECONSTRUCTING THE SPIRIT WHICH HAS BEEN MISSING FROM AMERICAN ART SINCE THE ABSTRACT EXPRESSIONISTS.

30 APRIL: THE IMAGE IS LOCATED IN THE MARRIAGE OF FRACTAL + EUCLID GEOMETRY. INTELLUCTUAL AGRESSION IS A DESIREABLE TRAIT.
INTELLIGENCE TO BE WORTH ANYTHING MUST BE CONFORTATIONAL. (i.e. if it is to qualify as non-academic) CHARLIE PARKER WAS CONFORTATIONAL.
　　　<u>ABSTRACT SYMBOLISM</u>　　<u>RECONSTRUCTIONISM</u>

4 MAY: A MEMORIAL PAINTING SERVES AS A REPOSITORY FOR THE SPIRIT OF THE DECEASED.

5 MAY: THE SPIRIT IS NON-REPRESENTATIONAL

10 MAY: ULTIMATELY, IT'S NOT SO MUCH ABOUT HOW MUCH YOU KNOW BUT HOW MUCH YOU CAN FORGET. CONSCIOUNESS IS ALWAYS A MATTER OF BEING FORMED I.E., THE PROCESS OF FORMING TRULY THE MEANING OF PLASTICITY IN THE PAINTER'S LANGUAGE.

11 MAY: I WANT THE VISUAL EQUIVALENT OF JAZZ.
THERE IS <u>NO</u> SUCH THING AS <u>ONE</u> WAY.
IT IS MY DUTY AS AN ARTIST TO COMMENRATE
THAT WHICH IS IMPORTANT AND NOBLE ←
ESPECIALLY IF IT SIGNIFIES PARTICULAR ASPECTS
OF MY INDIVIDUAL CULTURE.

13 MAY: SEEING IS A MATTER OF CONSCIOUNESS.
ONES DEPTH OF SEEING DEPENDS UPON THE DEPTH
OF CONSCIOUNESS. CONSCIOUNESS IS A PROCESS OF
LAYERING. THE LAYERS MUST BE PENETRATED IN
ORDER TO REVEAL CONSCIONESS. HISTORY IS AN
ACCUMULATION OF LAYERS. ANYONE INTERESTED
IN IDENTITY MUST LEARN TO PENETRATE HISTORY.
→ A TREE IS NOBLE. LAST NIGHT VANDALS DESTROYED
THREE TREES ON CHURCH ST. IN FRONT OF THE POST
OFFICE. I WILL MAKE A TRYPTCH AS A MEMORIAL TO
THESE THREE TREES.

17 MAY: THE PSYCHIC INTERSECTION IS AN ABSOLUTE
BALANCE OF HORIZONTALITY + VERTICALITY WHICH IS
THE CROSS + WHICH IS THE ELEMENTAL BASIS OF THE
GRID ∴ THE GRID IS AN ALL ENCOMPASSING SYMBOL OF
<u>ART</u>, <u>NATURE,</u> RELIGION
[drawing; triangle labeled, "A," "N," "R," with arrow to pyramid
labeled, "A," "N," "R," "T."]
THIS IS THE MEANING OF P.M.'S PLUS + MINUS
ALL OF THIS CONFIRMS MY CONCEPT OF FUSION
<u>POLLOCK +</u> <u>MONDRIAN</u> <u>FRACTAL</u> + <u>EUCLID</u>

19 MAY: THE SPIRIT IS A PRIOR
<u>LIFE IS</u> THERE IS NO OTHER EXPLANATION!

21 MAY: AS FAR AS COLOR IS CONCERNED, MY OBJECTIVE
IS TO ESTABLISH A <u>STANDARD</u> BY WHICH ALL COLOR IS
COMPARED THIS OBJECTIVE IS MY COLOR AS ISSUE.
(FOUND COLOR) like found object.

26 MAY: PLEASURE HEALS.

27 MAY: I DON'T HAVE ANY SKELETONS IN MY CLOSET,
THIS SIMPLE FACT OF HISTORY ALLOWS ME TO GLORIFY
THE AFFIRMATION OF LIFE, THE PURSUIT OF HAPPINESS.
<u>GOD BLESS ART!</u>

6 JUNE: FINALLY, I AM ABLE TO USE THE REWARDS OF
MEMORY WITHOUT EVERY GESTURE DICTATED BY
ITS CRITERIA.

2 JULY 90: GONE FISHING

STUDIO LOG   FALL 1990

25 SEPT: LINE IS ONE WAY TO INTERRUPT THE APPEARANCE OF OVER-ALL COMPOSITION.

3 OCT: THERE IS A GREAT PLEASURE IN BEING THE FIRST ONE TO SEE A GREAT PAINTING.

6 OCT: IDEA IS THE ENEMY OF ART.

7 OCT: BEING IS AN ONGOING PROCESS

13 OCT: SPACE IS THE ISSUE.

16 OCT: OTHER THAN THE ACTUALITY OF OBJECT, EACH PAINTING IS AN EVENT, A HAPPENING.

28 OCT: I AM NOW PICKING-UP WHERE POLLOCK STOPPED

29 OCT: THERE IS NO ME.

2 NOV: LIFE IS A MULTI-DIMENSIONAL PLANE.

4 NOV: I AM INTERESTED IN THE SUBLIME BUT ONLY AS IT APPLIES TO THE
MODERN TECHNOLOGICAL SOCIETY. THE POSSIBILITY OF A NEW WORLDVIEW
IS LOCATED WITHIN THIS NEW INTERPRETION OF THE SUBLIME.

I AM THE MEDIUM. THE PAINT IS ONLY A VEHICLE.

I NOW HAVE THE CAPABILITY TO CHANGE THE COURSE OF ART HISTORY.
USE YOUR MIND BUT TRUST YOUR HEART.

"IT'S A SIGN OF MATURITY WHEN YOU CAN EAT YOUR DINNER
FROM THE STUDIO FLOOR"   FRANK BOWLINGS 4 NOV 90

5 NOV: 46" SQUARE ARCS FROM A CENTER POINT 166" TO EDGE OF CIRCUMFERNCE
~~KELL'S~~ ARC $\wedge R = 166"$ 2,116 SQ. IN.
JACK'S ARC

15 NOV: THE FORCE IS WITH ME.

17 NOV: I AM THE UNIVERSE

2 DEC: SPACE IS ALWAYS "THE LAST FRONTEIR"

15 DEC: IF I DARE TO REWRITE HISTORY, I MUST START FROM THE BEGINING.

16 DEC: I WANT A PICTURE OF THE INSIDE

22 DEC: MY ULTIMATE DESIRE IS TO CHANGE THE COURSE OF ART HISTORY.

8 JAN 91: JACKSON POLLOCK DISCOVERED THE SOURCE OF THE RAW MATERIAL ....
IT IS MY JOB TO MANUFACTURE AND USE THIS RAW MATERIAL THROUGH RECONSTRUCTION.

18 JAN 91: GOD IS THE ONLY REALITY. EVERYTHING ELSE IS MYTH.

GOD IS THE CENTER

19 JAN 91: I HAVE DISCOVERED THE DNA OF SEEING.
THE MARRIAGE OF FRACTAL + EUCLID GEOMETRY.
PAINTING IS A FORM OF PRAYER — IT ALLOWS ME TO COMMUNICATE
WITH THE GODHEAD.

20 JAN: GOD IS THE LIGHT; THEREFORE, MY PAINTINGS ARE
ABOUT GOD .... THE RECONSTRUCTION OF GOD AS A BELIEF SYSTEM.
GOD HAS ALWAYS BEEN DISCOVERED THROUGH THE IMMEDIACY OF CULTURE.
I AM NOT A CHRISTIAN. I AM AN ARTIST.
ART IS MY RELIGION.

9 FEB: THE PAINTING IS A SHADOW OF AN ABSTRACT THOUGHT.

11 FEB: A MODERN CONTEMPORARY INTERPRETATION OF ANIMIST
BELIEF INTEREST ME. WHAT IS THE EQUIVALENT OF
ANIMISM IN A MODERN TECHNOLOGICAL SOCIETY?

<u>STUDIO LOG</u>   <u>FALL 1990</u>

25 SEPT: LINE IS ONE WAY TO INTERRUPT THE APPEARANCE OF OVER-ALL COMPOSITION.

3 OCT: THERE IS A GREAT PLEASURE IN BEING THE FIRST ONE TO SEE A GREAT PAINTING.

6 OCT: IDEA IS THE ENEMY OF ART.

7 OCT: BEING IS AN ONGOING PROCESS

13 OCT: SPACE IS THE ISSUE.

16 OCT: OTHER THAN THE ACTUALITY OF OBJECT, EACH PAINTING IS AN EVENT, A HAPPENING.

28 OCT: I AM NOW PICKING UP WHERE POLLOCK STOPPED

29 OCT: <u>THERE IS NO ME</u>.

2 NOV: LIFE IS A MULTI-DIMENSIONAL PLANE.

4 NOV: I AM INTERESTED IN THE SUBLIME BUT ONLY AS IT APPLIES TO THE MODERN TECHNOLOGICAL SOCIETY. THE POSSIBILITY OF A NEW WORLDVIEW IS LOCATED WITHIN THIS NEW INTERUPRETION OF THE SUBLIME.
   <u>I AM THE MEDIUM</u>. <u>THE PAINT IS ONLY A VEHICLE</u>. I NOW HAVE THE CAPABILITY TO CHANGE THE COURSE OF ART HISTORY.
   USE YOUR MIND BUT TRUST YOUR HEART.

"IT'S A SIGN OF MATURITY WHEN YOU CAN EAT YOUR DINNER FROM THE STUDIO FLOOR" FRANK BOWLING.
4 NOV 90

5 NOV: 46" SQUARE ARCS FROM A CENTER POINT R=166" TO EDGE OF CIRCUMFERNCE 2,116 sq. in.
~~KELLY'S~~ ARC
JACK'S ARC

15 NOV: <u>THE FORCE IS WITH ME.</u>

17 NOV: I AM THE UNIVERSE

2 DEC: SPACE IS ALWAYS "THE LAST FRONTIER"

15 DEC: IF I DARE TO REWRITE HISTORY, I MUST START FROM THE BEGINNING.

16 DEC: I WANT A PICTURE OF THE INSIDE.

22 DEC: MY ULTIMATE DESIRE IS TO CHANGE THE COURSE OF ART HISTORY.

8 JAN 91: JACKSON POLLOCK DISCOVERED THE SOURCE OF THE RAW MATERIAL . . . . . .
IT IS MY JOB TO MANUFACTURE AND USE THIS RAW MATERIAL THROUGH RECONSTRUCTION.

18 JAN 91: <u>GOD IS THE ONLY REALITY.</u> <u>EVERYTHING ELSE IS MYTH.</u>
<u>GOD IS THE CENTER</u>

19 JAN 91: I HAVE DISCOVERED THE <u>DNA</u> OF SEEING.
THE MARRIAGE OF FRACTAL + EUCLID GEOMETRY.
PAINTING IS A FORM OF PRAYER—IT ALLOWS ME TO
COMMUNICATE WITH THE GODHEAD.

20 JAN: GOD IS THE LIGHT, THEREFORE, MY PAINTINGS
ARE ABOUT GOD . . . . THE RECONSTRUCTION OF GOD AS
A BELIEF SYSTEM. GOD HAS ALWAYS BEEN DISCOVERED
THROUGH THE IMMEDIACY OF CULTURE. I AM NOT A
CHRISTIAN. I AM AN ARTIST. ART IS MY RELIGION.

9 FEB: THE PAINTING IS A SHADOW OF AN ABSTRACT
THOUGHT.

11 FEB: A MODERN CONTEMPORARY INTERPRETATION OF
ANIMIST BELIEF INTEREST ME. WHAT IS THE EQUVALENT
OF ANIMISM IN A MODERN TECHNOLOGICAL SOCIETY?

An artist is one who
reconstructs nature
Nature is a metaphor for God.
What we think of nature
in the form of trees, mountains, water, sky, etc.,
is God's metaphor for being.
Art is ~~the~~ my metaphor being.

STUDIO LOG '91

23 FEB: I AM AN ANTI-CUBIST PAINTER.
AFRICAN ART HAD NOTHING TO DO WITH CUBISM BUT
CUBISM HAD A LOT TO DO WITH AFRICAN ART.

24: FEB: IF I DESIRE TO REMOVE <u>ME</u> FROM THE PAINTING I
MUST CONCEPTUALLY ALLOW A SYSTEM TO OPERATE ON
PURE <u>RANDOMNESS</u>.
AT RANDOM IS ONE WAY TO ACHIEVE A TOTAL NON-
RELATIONAL IMAGE
i.e. <u>A PRIORI</u>—BUT AS USUAL, THE <u>A POSTERIOR</u> DUE TO
MIND → (interruption) WILL APPEAR AS RELATIONAL. . .
THERE IS NO WAY TO AVOID THIS
     RECONSTRUCTED NATURALISM
       A RECONSTRUCTION OF NATURE

2 MARCH: AS I WORKED, I WATCHED MY BLACK SCALES
FALL TO THE FLOOR.
IT'S THE REVERSE OF PICKING COTTON

10 MARCH: NOW IS THE TIME TO REMOVE ALL THE
SENTIMENT ABOUT PAINTING FROM MY PAINTINGS.

16 MARCH: I HAVE JUST COMPLETED <u>DATA II</u>. IT DEFIES
INTERPUTATION VERY AGGRESSIVELY.

25 MARCH: GOD IS NON-RELATIONAL
"VISIBLE SUBSTANCE TO THINGS FELT"
"OUT OF EMOTION COMES FORM"   MARTHA GRAHAM, 96
"CHART THE GRAPH OF THE HEART"   1 OF APRIL 1991
"THE THING ITSELF"

9 APRIL: <u>LIGHT</u>, <u>OBJECT</u>, <u>SHADOW</u>—TRANSLATED AS ABSTRACT SYMBOL.

20 APRIL: SHAPE . . . . . OR FORM AS MELODY

25 APRIL: I DON'T WANT ANY IMAGE WHICH IS POSSIBLY MADE BY THE CAMERA.
THE IMAGE MUST COME OUT OF THE PROCESS
AVOID AT <u>ALL COST</u> AN ILLUSTRATION OF ANY KNOWN IMAGE.

13 MAY: I STARTED DE-CLOAKING <u>EINSTEIN'S VIOLIN</u> AT 01105 AND COMPLETED IT AT 1600.

[. . .]

26 MAY: CARACAS WAS A GAS!
<u>DIGITAL EXPRESSIONISM EINSTEIN'S VIOLIN</u>: DEDICATED TO THE MEMORY OF MARTHA GRAHAM. MAY 1991 BEARDEN WAS RIGHT "YOU ARE ONLY AS GOOD AS WHAT YOU FIND"! THE PAITNING IS A PHYSICAL POEM

17 JUNE: It is time to go fishing. I need a rest. It has been a good year very productive, not too much money, but we survived. IN Sept. I start with definition of shape within a specific pattern.

STUDIO LOG '91

8 OCT. I AM IN THE STUDIO. THE WEATHER HAS CHANGED.
ITS COOL. BILLIE HOLIDAY IS SINGING "AUTUMN IN NEW YORK"
WHAT COULD BE BETTER? I AM STARTING MY FIRST PAINTING.
BACK FROM GREECE & READY TO GO!

28 OCT: ART IS A MANNER OF IDENTITY. I IDENTIFY WITH THE IMAGE.
THE IMAGE IS A REPRESENTATION OF MY BEING. MY WORLDVIEW IS INCORPORATED
WITHIN THE IMAGE.

I AM PROBABLY THE MOST FREEEST MAN ON THE PLANET.
I HAVE NO BONES IN THE CLOSET. I HAVE NO GHOST TO CONTEND WITH.

MY COLOR STRUCTURE IS BASED UPON THE CONCEPT OF "FOUND COLOR"
THAT WHICH INTRIGUES ME THE MOST IS THAT WHICH EXIST ON THE EDGE OF CONSCIOUSNESS
GOD IS A GENERATOR

30 OCT. THE ONLY CONCEPT OF TIME THAT WE TRULY KNOW OF IS ENTIRELY
WITHIN THE NOW.

8 NOV. IN ORDER FOR A STRUCTURE TO QUALIFY AS SIGNIFICANT FORM IT MUST BE OF THE NOW.
NORMAN ROCKWELL ←——→ JACKSON POLLOCK
CHUCK CLOSE ←——→ JACK WHITTEN

10 NOV: EACH "ACRYLIC CHIP" REPRESENT A PARTICLE OF LIGHT

11 NOV: MY PAINTINGS ARE NO LONGER PAINTINGS IN THE TRADITIONAL SENSE.
.... THEY ARE THE PHYSICAL OBJECT AS ORGANIC EQUIVALENT
OF THE PHOTOGRAPH. FOR IMAGERY, I SHOULD BE ABLE TO
SHOOT WHERE THE CAMERA CANNOT SHOOT.

14 NOV: THEY ARE ACRYLIC MOSAICS

I DON'T DEAL IN RHETORIC.

26 Nov: I PLAN TO STAY WITH THE GRID STRUCTURE FOR NOW...
THERE IS SOME UNFINISHED BUSINESS THAT MUST BE
CLARIFIED

14 DEC: I AM BEGINNING TO SEE THE LIGHT!

16 DEC: I AM THE SUBJECT

17 DEC: THE CONCEPT OF THE FLAT TWO-DIMENSIONAL GRID SERVED
UP WELL TO A CERTAIN POINT — BUT — NOW THAT FLAT 2-D
GRID MUST BE CONCEIVED AS A THREE DIMENSIONAL GRID
(THIS EXPLAINS A. HELD'S INVOLVEMENT WITH GEOMETRICAL ILLUSIONISM)
I.E., 3-D IN ALL DIRECTIONS. THIS ALLOWS THE POSSIBILITY OF OTHER
DIMENSIONS TO EXIST AS PURE MENTAL CONSTRUCTS. (ISOMETRIC GRID)
PICTORIAL CARVING

4 JAN 92 — — I AM INVESTIGATING A CONCEPT OF DIGITAL AUTOMATISM

18 JAN: — TIME IS THE TIMEKEEPER

19 JAN: THE ACT OF FORMING IS MORE IMPORTANT THAN THAT OF FORM.

25 JAN: IT'S ABOUT DECODING PERCEPTION INSTITUTED BY VISUAL STIMULI.

<u>STUDIO LOG</u> '91

8 OCT. I AM IN THE STUDIO. THE WEATHER HAS CHANGED. IT'S COOL. BILLIE HOLIDAY IS SINGING "AUTUMN IN NEW YORK" WHAT COULD BE BETTER? I AM STARTING MY FIRST PAINTING. BACK FROM GREECE + READY TO GO!

28 OCT: ART IS A MANNER OF IDENTITY. I IDENTIFY WITH THE IMAGE. THE <u>IMAGE</u> IS A <u>REPRESENTATION</u> OF MY <u>BEING</u>. MY WORLDVIEW IS INCORPORATED WITHIN THE IMAGE.
    I AM PROBABLY THE MOST FREEEST MAN ON THE PLANET. I HAVE NO BONES IN THE CLOSET. I HAVE NO GHOST TO CONTEND WITH.
MY COLOR STRUCTURE IS BASED UPON THE CONCEPT OF "FOUND COLOR." THAT WHICH INTRIGUES ME THE MOST IS THAT WHICH EXIST ON THE EDGE OF CONSCIOUNESS
    <u>GOD</u> <u>IS</u> <u>A</u> <u>GENERATOR</u>

30 OCT. THE ONLY CONCEPT OF TIME THAT WE TRULY KNOW IF IS ENTIRELY WITHIN THE <u>NOW</u>.

8 NOV. IN ORDER FOR A STRUCTURE TO QUALIFY AS SIGNIFICANT FORM IT MUST BE OF THE <u>NOW</u>.
    NORMAN ROCKWELL ↔ JACKSON POLLOCK
    CHUCK CLOSE ↔ JACK WHITTEN

10 NOV: EACH "ACRYLIC CHIP" REPRESENT A PARTICLE OF LIGHT

11 NOV: MY PAINTINGS ARE NO LO LONGER PAINTINGS IN THE TRADITIONAL SENSE . . . . . THEY ARE THE PHYSICAL OBJECT AS ORGANIC EQUIVALENT OF THE PHOTOGRAPH.

FOR IMAGERY, I SHOULD BE ABLE TO <u>SHOOT</u> WHERE THE CAMERA CANNOT <u>SHOOT</u>.

14 NOV: THEY ARE <u>ACRYLIC</u> <u>MOSAICS</u>
I DON'T DEAL IN RHETORIC

26 NOV: I PLAN TO STAY WITH THE GRID STRUCTURE FOR NOW . . . THERE IS SOME UNFINISHED BUSINESS THAT MUST BE CLARIFIED

14 DEC: I AM BEGINNING TO SEE THE LIGHT!

16 DEC: I AM THE SUBJECT

17 DEC: THE CONCEPT OF THE FLAT TWO-DIMENSIONAL GRID SERVED UP WELL TO A CERTAIN POINT—<u>BUT</u>— NOW THAT FLAT 2-D GRID MUST BE CONCEIVED AS A <u>THREE DIMENSIONAL GRID</u> (THIS EXPLAINS A. HELD'S INVOLVEMENT WITH GEOMETRIC ILLUSIONISMS) I.E., 3-D IN ALL DIRECTIONS. THIS ALLOWS THE POSSIBILITY OF OTHER DIMENSIONS TO EXIST AS PURE MENTAL CONSTRUCTS. (ISOMETRIC GRID) PICTORIAL CARVING

4 JAN 92 — — I AM INVESTIGATING A CONCEPT OF DIGITAL AUTOMATISM

18 JAN: — TIME IS THE TIMEKEEPER

19 JAN: THE ACT OF <u>FORMING</u> IS MORE IMPORTANT THAT THAT OF <u>FORM</u>.

25 JAN: IT'S ABOUT DECODING PERCEPTION INSTITUTED BY VISUAL STIMULI.

STUDIO LOG 1992

27 JAN: SPACE IS A THING WITHIN A THING, A PLACE WITHIN A PLACE
SURROUNDED BY TIME... TIME HAS NO BOUNDARY.
THE BOUNDARY OF SPACE IS DEFINED ONLY VIA THAT WHICH CONFINES IT, E.G.
OBJECT OR PLACE. THEREFORE, LINE COULD BE USED AS A DEFINITION OF SPACE
OR SHAPE-FORM ... EVEN THAT WHICH IS IN THE PROCESS OF FORMING.
SPACE IS ACTIVE
THE SUBJECT IS BEING (THE SAME AS ITS' ALWAYS BEEN) THE SUBJECT
NEVER CHANGES ONLY THE VEHICLE CHANGES. SYMBOL IS VEHICLE.
— MEMORY CAN BE A LIABILITY, KNOWLEDGE OF THE PRESENT IS THE
GREATEST ASSET.

8 FEB. ILLUSION IS JUST A SKIN AN OUTER MEMBRANE. WE MUST LEARN
TO PRICK IT OR SIMPLY PASS THROUGH IT.

9 FEB: I AM A COMPRESSIONIST

27 FEB: ART IS THE OPPORTUNITY TO PLAY GOD.

29 FEB: ALL I WANT IS TO RESTORE ART TO ITS' ORIGINAL PURPOSE -
"TO GIVE BACK INFINITY" E. CRUZ 10 MARCH

14 MARCH: TODAY, I BITE OFF THE HEAD OF CHRIST,

17 MARCH: SPOKE WITH HENRY TODAY, HE AGREED TO WRITE THE ESSAY FOR
MY CATALOGUE FOR GALLERY SHOW IN MAY.
AN INTERESTING COMMENT ABOUT THE NATURE OF IMAGE IN MY WORK
"LIKE IN PHYSICS ..... TRYING TO HAMMER WATER"
"CREDIT MARVELS AND GET AWAY FROM THE HEAVINESS OF BEING"
SEAMUS HEANEY

25 MARCH: GESTURE AS LIGHT — GESTURE CAPTURING LIGHT S.H.

10 APRIL: I AM AN ANIMIST.

18 APRIL EASTER: SPACE IS MY SUBJECT.

12 MAY: MY GOD BE WITH ME.

12 JUNE: GONE FISHING,

STUDIO LOG 1992

27 JAN: SPACE IS A THING WITHIN A THING, A PLACE WITHIN A PLACE
SURROUNDED BY TIME . . . TIME HAS NO BOUNDARY.
THE BOUNDARY OF SPACE IS DEFINED ONLY ~~BUT~~ VIA
THAT WHICH CONTINES IT, E.G., OBJECT OR PLACE.
THEREFORE, LINE COULD BE USED AS A DEFINITION OF
SPACE OR SHAPE-FORM . . . EVEN THAT WHICH IS IN THE
PROCESS OF FORMING.
    SPACE IS ACTIVE
THE SUBJECT IS BEING (THE SAME AS ITS' ALWAYS BEEN)
THE SUBJECT NEVER CHANGES ONLY THE VEHICLE
CHANGES. SYMBOL IS VEHICLE.
— MEMORY CAN BE A LIABILITY, KNOWEDGE OF THE
PRESENT IS THE GREATEST ASSET.

8 FEB. ILLUSION IS JUST A SKIN AN OUTER MEMBRANE. WE
MUST LEARN TO PRICE IT OR SIMPLY PASS THROUGH IT.

9 FEB: <u>I AM A COMPRESSIONIST.</u>

27 FEB: ART IS THE OPPORTUNITY TO PLAY GOD.

29 FEB: ALL I WANT IS TO RESTORE ART TO ITS' ORIGINAL
PURPOSE –
    <u>"TO GIVE BACK TO INFINITY" E. CRUZ 10 MARCH</u>

14 MARCH: <u>TODAY, I BITE OFF THE HEAD OF CHRIST.</u>

17 MARCH: SPOKE WITH HENRY TODAY, HE AGREED TO
WRITE THE ESSAY FOR MY CATALOGUE FOR GALLERY
SHOW IN MAY.
AN INTERESTING COMMENT ABOUT THE NATURE OF
IMAGE IN MY WORK
 "LIKE IN PHYSICS . . . . . TRYING TO HAMMER WATER".
 "CREDIT MARVELS AND GET AWAY FROM THE
HEAVINESS OF BEING"
 SEAMUS HEANEY

25 MARCH: GESTURE AS LIGHT—GESTURE CAPTURING
LIGHT S.H.

10 APRIL: <u>I AM AN ANIMIST.</u>

18 APRIL EASTER: <u>SPACE</u> IS MY SUBJECT

12 MAY: MY GOD BE WITH ME.

12 JUNE: GONE FISHING,
⟶

<u>STUDIO LOG</u>   <u>FALL '92</u>

27 OCT: MY USE OF IMAGE IS A MATTER OF FAITH.
        → DIGITIAL IMAGING

1 NOV: A PAINTING IS A PAINTING, IS A PAINTING, IS A PAINTING, IS A PAINTING.
    MY PAINTINGS ARE OBJECTS DESIGNED FOR THE SPIRIT TO HAVE A PLACE OF REST. (CHARTERS)
                                                              (CHARACTERS)

5 NOV: I AM NOT IN IT FOR PROFIT.

8 NOV: THERE MUST BE SOME WAY TO BYPASS THE TIME ZONES: PAST · PRESENT · FUTURE = BEING

25 NOV: I SIT AND WATCH BENEATH MY FEET
        THE PASSAGE OF TIME

29 NOV: AT 13:30 HRS I STARTED OPERATION DELTA.
    IT IS NOT SO MUCH ABOUT SPACE AS PREVIOUSLY THOUGHT... IT IS MORE
    ABOUT A THING. SPACE IS A BY-PRODUCT.
        THIS CLOSES THE GAP BETWEEN MY SCULPTURE & MY PAINTING.

10 DEC: EACH PAINTING IS A PART OF SOME GIGANTIC WHOLE.

17 DEC: DELTA OPERATION TERMINATED AT 17:30. (8²76² Gestalt) FOR NEW MUS. SHOW
                                                          SKIN DEEP

23 DEC: TO AVOID AT ALL COST:
1. FORMALISM
2. SLICKNESS
3. CORPORATE IMAGE
4. LITERAL
5. NARRATIVE
6. MALE-FEMALE CATEGORY
7. ABSTRACT EXPRESSIONISM
8. EXCESSIVE USE OF COLOR
9. CHRISTIAN ICONOGRAPHY
10. BLACK BOURGEOIS AESTHETIC
11. OTHER ARTISTS
12. ABSTRACTION AS DESIGN
13. NATURALISM
14. POST-MODERNISM
15. APPROPRIATION
16. DECORATIVE
17. ILLUSTRATION
18. ART HISTORY
19. SELF PITY
20. EXCESS EMOTIONAL BAGGAGE

THE "DIZ"
6 JAN 1993
75

I MUST DO ONE FOR THE "DIZ"
A MASK FOR JOY

4 JAN: LIFE IS AN ABSTRACTION—

1 JAN 93: MY AMBITION IS TO RE-INVENT NATURE IN MY IMAGE.

2 JAN 93: THE PAINTING IS A <u>MASK</u>, VERY SPECIFIC IN ITS USE AS <u>OBJECT</u>.
    THE REINVENTION OF NATURE IS NECESSARY IN ORDER TO DISCOVER A RAW MATERIAL
    I.E. gather IN ORDER TO BUILD THE PAINTING. (SUBSTANCE IS LOCATED WITHIN MATERIALITY)

3 JAN 93: 1910 HRS. I FINISHED FANCY TRIANGLE; FOR EDVINS—
    I WANT MY ART TO SERVE AS A BRIDGE: TO BRIDGE THE GAP
    THAT EXIST BETWEEN PEOPLE. SO <u>NUMBER ONE</u> "MAKE IT SO"!

<u>STUDIO LOG</u> <u>FALL '92</u>

27 OCT: MY USE OF IMAGE IS A MATTER OF FAITH.
   └→ DIGITAL IMAGING

1 NOV: A PAINTING IS A PAINTING, IS A PAINTING,
IS A PAINTING, IS A PAINTING
MY PAINTINGS ARE OBJECTS DESIGNED FOR THE SPIRIT
TO HAVE A PLACE OF REST ~~(CHARGERS)~~ (CHARACTERS)

5 NOV: I AM NOT IN IT FOR PROFIT.

8 NOV: THERE MUST BE SOME WAY TO BYPASS THE TIME
ZONES: PAST-PRESENT-FUTURE=BEING

25 NOV: I SIT AND WATCH BENEATH MY FEET
  THE PASSAGE OF TIME

29 NOV: AT 13:30 HRS I STARTED OPERATION DELTA.
IT IS NOT SO MUCH ABOUT SPACE AS PREVIOUSLY
THOUGHT . . . IT IS MORE ABOUT A THING . . SPACE IS
A BY-PRODUCT.
THIS CLOSES THE GAP BETWEEN MY SCULPTURE +
MY PAINTING

16 DEC: EACH PAINTING IS A PART OF SOME GIGANTIC
WHOLE.

17 DEC: DELTA OPERATION TERMINATED AT 17:30.
(5th and 6th Gestalt) FOR NEW MUS. SHOW <u>SKIN DEEP</u>

23 DEC: TO AVOID AT ALL COST:
1. FORMALISM
2. SLICKNESS
3. CORPORATE IMAGE
4. LITERAL
5. NARRATIVE
6. MALE-FEMALE CATEGORY
7. ABSTRACT EXPRESSIONISM
8. EXCESSIVE USE OF COLOR
9. CHRISTIAN ICONOGRAPHY
10. BLACK BOURGEOIS AESTHETIC
11. OTHER ARTISTS
12. ABSTRACTION AS DESIGN
13. NATURALISM
14. POST-MODERNISM
15. APPROPRIATION
16. DECORATIVE
17. ILLUSTRATION
18. ART HISTORY
19. SELF PITY
20. EXCESS EMOTIONAL BAGGAGE

1 JAN '93: MY AMBITION IS TO REINVENT NATURE IN MY IMAGE.

2 JAN 93: THE PAINTING IS A <u>MASK</u>, VERY <u>SPECIFIC</u> IN ITS USE AS <u>OBJECT</u> THE REINVENTION OF NATURE IS NECESSARY IN ORDER TO DISCOVERY A RAW MATERIAL I.E., MATTER IN ORDER TO BUILD THE PAINTING. (SUBSTANCE IS LOCATED WITHIN MATERIALITY)

3 JAN 93: 1910 HRS. I FINISHED <u>FANCY TRAINGLE: FOR EDVINS.</u>
I WANT MY ART TO SERVE AS A BRIDGE: TO BRIDGE THE GAP THAT EXIST BETWEEN PEOPLE. SO <u>NUMBER ONE "MAKE IT SO"!</u>

4 JAN: LIFE IS AN ABSTRACTION-

THE "DIZ"*
6 JAN 1993
<u>75</u>

I MUST DO ONE FOR THE DIZ
<u>A MASK FOR JOY</u>

STUDIO LOG '93

5 MARCH: ULTIMATELY, IT'S THE UNKNOWN QUANTIES THAT INTEREST ME THE MOST ACCORDING TO THE ART MAGAZINE + THE WHITNEY ANNUAL, WE SUPPOSE TO KNOW EVERYTHING AS LITERAL MESSAGE ART. I FIND THIS RATHER NAIVE, BOY SCOUTISH + BORING. WHILE NOT LEAVE IT TO MADISON AVE + THE TABLOIDS?

6 MARCH: THE MESSAGE IS CODED WITHIN THE PROCESS.
ABSENCE OF SELF IS THE ONLY WAY TO DECODE.

7 MARCH: I COMMUNICATE TO THE SPIRIT THROUGH THE RITUAL OF WORK.

8 MARCH: <u>NATURE DOES NOT THINK</u>.

12 MARCH: LIGHT IS THE <u>KEY</u> TO UNDERSTANDING PAINTING. IT DEFINES THE MEANING OF SPACE + TIME + MY RELATIONSHIP TO IT.
THERE IS NO <u>IN</u> AND THERE IS NO <u>OUT</u>.
THESE ARE ONLY CATEGORIES OF LEARNING (elaborate further)

14 MARCH: SPACE, TIME + LIGHT ARE INTERDEPENDENT, INTERRELATED INTER I WANT TO EXPRESS THIS INTERDEPENDNESS IN MY PAINTINGS.
COSMIC BOPPER: FOR THE DIZ DOES THIS!

16 MARCH: FRACTAL SENSATIONS (RIGHT ON!)

17 MARCH: THE SPACE IS <u>FACTUAL</u>.

22 MARCH: THE PRESENT IS COMPOSED OF THE PAST AND THE FUTURE: THIS IS MY UNDERSTANDING OF TIME.

29 MARCH: MET THORNTON DIAL IN BESSEMER, ALA. …DEFINATELY A CONNECTION FELT GOOD!
I AM NOT LOOKING FOR AN <u>ISM</u>.

3 APRIL: LOVE TRAVELS AT THE SPEED OF LIGHT.

4 APRIL: RIGHT ON MEL EDWARDS! GREAT SHOW
FINALLY IT ALL COMES DOWN TO WHAT YOU KNOW HOW TO DO.

22 APRIL: COLOR TRAVELS AT THE SPEED OF LIGHT UNDER CERTAIN CIRCUMSTANCES.

30 APRIL: I WORK WITH ALCHEMY OF THE MIND.
THE SHIT IS COMING IN THROUGH COLOR CODES! ARNETTE STOPPED BY, UNDERSTOOD THE COSMIC BOPPER
COMPLETED THE RUSSIAN BIRD: FOR NUREYEV

4 MAY: THIS IS THE DIGITAL AGE. I ACKNOWLEDGE THAT,
THE DIGITAL IS <u>NOT NECESSARILY</u> ONE OF SCIENCE + TECHNOLOGY <u>BUT</u>
ALSO FOUND IN NATURE. I PREFER THAT FOUND IN NATURE.

6 MAY: MY SUBJECT MATTER IS PEOPLE.

28 MAY: STOP TRYING TO MAKE IT SOMETHING. IT IS WHAT IT IS.

31 MAY: I HAVE NO FEAR.

5 JUNE: RIGHT ON, MEL EDWARDS! GREAT OPENING!
SAM WAS THERE.

10 JUNE: GONE FISHING!

STUDIO LOG '93

5 MARCH: ULTIMATELY, IT'S THE UNKNOWN QUANTIES THAT INTEREST ME THE MOST. ACCORDING TO THE ART MAGAZINE + THE WHITNEY ANNUAL, WE SUPPOSE TO KNOW EVERYTHING AS LITERAL MESSAGE ART. I FIND THIS RATHER NAÏVE, BOY SCOUTISH + BORING. WHILE NOT LEAVE IT TO MADISON AVE + THE TABLOIDS?

6 MARCH: THE MESSAGE IS CODED WITHIN THE PROCESS. ABSENCE OF SELF IS THE ONLY WAYS TO DECODE.

7 MARCH: I COMMUNICATE TO THE SPIRIT THROUGH THE RITUAL OF WORK.

8 MARCH: NATURE DOES NOT THINK.

12 MARCH: LIGHT IS THE KEY TO UNDERSTANING PAINTING. IT DEFINES THE MEANING OF SPACE + TIME + MY RELATIONSHIP TO IT.
THERE IS NO IN AND THERE IS NO OUT.
THESE ARE ONLY CATEGORIES OF LEARNING (elaborate further)

INTERELATED
14 MARCH: SPACE, TIME + LIGHT ARE INTEREDEPENDENT, I WANT TO EXPRESS THIS INTERDERENDNESS IN MY PAINTINGS.
COSMIC BOPPER: FOR THE DIZ DOES THIS!

16 MARCH: FRACTAL SENSATIONS (Right on!)

17 MARCH: THE SPACE IS FACTUAL.

22 MARCH: THE PRESENT IS COMPOSED OF THE PAST AND
THE FUTURE: THIS IS MY UNDERSTANDING OF TIME.

29 MARCH: MET THORNTON DIAL IN BESSEMER ALA. . . .
DEFINITELY A CONNECTION
    FELT GOOD!
I AM NOT LOOKING FOR AN <u>ISM</u>.

3 APRIL: LOVE TRAVELS AT THE SPEED OF LIGHT.

4 APRIL: RIGHT ON MEL EDWARDS! <u>GREAT SHOW</u>
FINALLY IT ALL COMES DOWN TO WHAT YOU KNOW
HOW TO DO.

22 APRIL: COLOR TRAVELS AT THE SPEED OF LIGHT
UNDER CERTAIN CIRCUMSTANCES.

30 APRIL: I WORK WITH ALCHEMY OF THE MIND.

<u>THE SHIT</u> <u>IS COMING</u> IN <u>THROUGH</u> <u>COLOR CODES</u>!
COMPLETED THE RUSSIAN BIRD: FOR NUREYEV
ARNETTE STOPPED BY
UNDERSTOOD THE <u>COSMIC BOPPER</u>

4 MAY: THIS IS THE DIGITAL AGE. I ACKNOWLEDGE THAT.
THE DIGITAL IS <u>NOT NECESSARILY</u> ONE OF SCIENCE +
TECHNOLOGY <u>BUT</u> ALSO FOUND IN NATURE. I PREFER
THAT FOUND IN NATURE.

6 MAY: MY SUBJECT MATTER IS PEOPLE.

28 MAY: STOP TRYING TO MAKE IT SOMETHING. IT IS
WHAT IT IS.

31 MAY: I HAVE NO FEAR.

5 June: RIGHT ON, MEL EDWARDS! GREAT OPENING!
    SAM WAS THERE.

10 June: GONE FINISHG!

ial to be rendered.

STUDIO LOG   FALL '93

26 SEPT.: ONE MUST LEARN TO RECOGNIZE THE PRESENCE OF SPIRIT AND TO ACKNOWLEDGE ITS' PRESENCE. I ACKNOWLEDGE ITS' PRESENCE BY CONSTRUCTING AN OBJECT WHICH ALLOWS OR INVITES THE SPIRIT TO REST. THIS IS MY JOB AS AN ARTIST.
YOU CAN IDENTIFY THE PRESENCE OF SPIRIT WITHIN A SPECIFIC QUALITY OF LIGHT
THIS AND ONLY THIS IS THE ART OF PAINTING.

16 OCT.: IMAGE IS A MATTER OF FAITH (W.L.P. SAYS THAT FAITH IS THE LAST FRONTIER)

17 OCT.: THE GRID HAS BEEN BROKEN!
FREEDOM IS AT HAND!

19 OCT.: CONCENTRATE MORE ON RHYTHMN-FLOW, LESS ON IMAGERY
IMAGERY IS A RESIDUE OF PROCESS.

24 OCT.: THE ARTIST ROLE IN SOCIETY IS TO EXPAND CONSCIOUSNESS.
NINETY NINE PERCENT OF THE PAINTINGS I SEE TODAY, DO NOT EXPAND MY CONSCIOUSNESS.
THIS IS UNFORTUNATE BECAUSE I NEED HELP IN WHAT I AM DOING.

25 OCT.: I AM AN EXPLORER, I SHOW WHAT I HAVE FOUND.
I AM NOT AN ILLUSTRATOR.

26 OCT.: MY SUBJECT IS THE PSYCHOLOGY OF SPACE.

31 OCT.: THE BESSEMER BOOGIE COMPLETED 1730 hrs.
I DEDICATE THIS PAINTING TO THE MEMORY OF VIVIANE BROWNE...REST IN PEACE.
BILL DeKOONING SAID THAT POLLOCK "BROKE THE ICE"
I AM SHOWING WHAT'S UNDERNEATH THE ICE.
THE FORCE IS WITH ME.

1 NOV.: THE PAINTING MUST BE BUILT, LIKE BUILDING A STONE WALL & IT MUST EXIST IN THE MIND AS A STONE WALL EXIST.

13 NOV.: I DEAL WITH CONSCIOUS HISTORICAL PROGRESSIONS AND I AM VERY MUCH AWARE OF THE BURDEN THIS ENTAILS. I HAVE ACCEPTED THIS RIGHT FROM THE BEGINNING. SO BE IT!

14 NOV.: MATERIAL AS METAPHOR.

20 NOV.: I HAVE AND DEMAND THE RIGHT TO INVESTIGATE ANY SUBJECT WHICH IS PART OF THE EXPERIENCE OF BEING HUMAN
P.S. MARY + I had dinner with Jake Lawrence & Gwen the other night very pleasurable evening!

28 NOV.: I AM VERY INTERESTED IN HOW THE SUBLIME IS APPLIED THE MODERN TECH. SOCIETY. HOW IS THIS POSSIBLE? CAN THE SUBLIME ACT AS SUBJECT?

3 DEC.: IT IS THE ESTHETICS OF JAZZ

12 DEC.: I AM A FOLLOWER... A FOLLOWER OF THE SPIRIT!
ULTIMATELY ART MUST HAVE A PURPOSE, MY PURPOSE IS TO MAKE OBJECTS THAT REDUCE THE TENSION ASSOCIATED WITH CONTEMPORARY LIFE...A HEALING PROCESS.

16 DEC.: I WANT TO DEAL ONLY WITH PHYSICAL FACT.

18 DEC.: IN TRULY GREAT PAINTING FORM + CONTENT IS INSEPERATIBLE s/p.

3 JAN 94 - EXPERIENCE IS THE SUBJECT.

5 JAN: THE METAPHOR HAS SHIFTED TO HEALING ......
IT IS A SACRED ART DEDICATED TO THE GLORIFICATION OF GOD!

9 JAN: IT'S THE REVERSE OF PICKING COTTON!

10 JAN: I DO NOT SEPARATE SPIRIT FROM MATTER.

11 JAN: I DON'T WANT ONLY THE MEMORY OF LIFE. I ALSO WANT THE NOW OF LIFE. PRESERVATION OF MEMORY IS IMPORTANT BUT THE PSYCHIC LIABILITY OF BAGGAGE CAN PREVENT ME FROM EXPERIENCING THE FLUID NATURE OF BEING NOW... PRESENT.
14 JAN. THEREFORE, THE PAINTINGS HAVE MULTIPLE MEANINGS. 28 BLACK HOLES COMPLETED 14 JAN 94

13 JAN: THE POST-MODERNIST ASPECT OF WHAT I AM DOING IS ITS' MULTI-DIMENSIONALITY.... A REFLECTION OF ITS' MULTI-RACIAL ORIGIN. THIS SHIT IS ANCIENT BUT EXTREMELY NEW AT THE SAME TIME....THAT IS WEIRD!!

<u>STUDIO LOG FALL '93</u>

26 SEPT.: ONE MUST LEARN TO RECOGNIZE THE PRESENCE OF SPIRIT AND TO ACKNOWEDGE ITS' PRESENCE. I ACKNOWLEDGE ITS' PRESENCE BY CONSTRUCTING AN OBJECT WHICH ALLOWS OR <u>INVITES</u> THE SPIRIT TO REST. THIS IS MY JOB AS AN ARTIST. YOU CAN IDENTIFY THE PRESENCE OF SPIRIT WITHIN A SPECIFIC QUALITY OF LIGHT. THIS AND ONLY THIS IS THE ART OF PAINTING.

16 OCT: IMAGE IS A MATTER OF FAITH (W.L.P. SAYS THAT FAITH IS THE LAST FRONTIER)

17 OCT: <u>THE GRID HAS BEEN BROKEN!</u>
    <u>FREEDOM IS AT HAND!</u>

19 OCT: CONCENTRATE MORE ON RHYTHMN-FLOW, LESS ON IMAGERY
IMAGERY IS A RESIDUE OF THE PROCESS.

24 OCT: THE ARTIST ROLE IN SOCIETY IS TO EXPAND CONSCIOUNESS.
NINETY NINE PERCENT OF THE PAINTINGS I SEE TODAY, DO NOT EXPAND MY CONSCIOUNESS. THIS IS UNFORTUNATE BECAUSE I NEED HELP IN WHAT I AM DOING.

25 OCT. I AM AN EXPLORER, I SHOW WHAT I HAVE FOUND. I AM NOT AN ILLUSTRATOR.

26 OCT: MY SUBJECT IS THE PSYCHOLOGY OF SPACE.

31 OCT: <u>THE BESSEMER BOOGIE</u> COMPLETED 1730 hrs.
I DEDICATE THIS PAINTING TO THE MEMORY OF VIVIANE
BROWNE . . . . REST IN PEACE.
BILL DeKOONING SAID THAT POLLOCK "BROKE THE ICE"
I AM SHOWING WHAT'S UNDERNEARTH THE ICE.
   <u>THE FORCE IS WITH ME.</u>

1 NOV: THE PAINTING MUST BE BUILT, LIKE BUILDING A
STONE WALL + IT MUST EXIST IN THE MIND AS A
STONEWALL EXIST.

13 NOV: I DEAL WITH CONSCIOUS HISTORICAL
PROGRESSIONS AND I AM VERY MUCH AWARE OF THE
BURDEN THIS ENTAILS. I HAVE ACCEPTED THIS RIGHT
FROM THE BEGINNING. <u>SO BE IT!</u>

14 NOV: MATERIAL AS METAPHOR.

20 NOV: I HAVE AND DEMAND THE RIGHT TO
INVESTIGATE ANY SUBJECT WHICH IS PART OF THE
EXPEIRENCE OF BEING HUMAN.
   P.S. MARY + I had dinner with Jake Lawrence + Gwen the
   other night
   very pleasureable evening!

28 NOV: I AM VERY INTERESTED IN HOW THE SUBLIME IS
APPLIED THE <u>MODERN TECH. SOCIETY.</u> HOW IS THIS
POSSIBLE? CAN THE SUBLIME ACT AS SUBJECT?

3 DEC: <u>IT IS THE ESTHETICS OF JAZZ</u>

12 DEC: I AM A FOLLOWER . . . A FOLLOWER OF THE SPIRIT!
ULTIMATELY ART MUST HAVE A PURPOSE. MY PURPOSE IS
TO MAKE OBJECTS THAT <u>REDUCE</u> THE TENSION
ASSOCIATED WITH CONTEMPORARY LIFE . . . A HEALING
PROCESS.

16 DEC. I WANT TO DEAL <u>ONLY</u> WITH PHYSICAL FACT.

18 DEC: IN TRULY GREAT PAINTING FORM + CONTENT IS
INSEPERATIBLE$_{s/p}$

3 JAN 94. – <u>EXPERIENCE IS THE SUBJECT.</u>

5 JAN THE METAPHOR HAS SHIFTED TO <u>HEALING</u> . . . . .
    IT IS A SACRED ART DEDICATED TO THE
GLORIFICATION OF GOD!

9 JAN: IT'S THE REVERSE OF PICKING COTTON!

10 JAN: I DO NOT SEPARATE SPIRIT FROM MATTER.

11 JAN: I DON'T WANT ONLY THE MEMORY OF LIFE. I ALSO
WANT THE NOW OF LIFE. PRESERVATION OF MEMORY IS
IMPORTANT BUT THE PSYCHIC LIABILITY OF BAGGAGE
CAN PREVENT ME FROM EXPERIENCING THE FLUID
NATURE OF $\underline{\underset{NOW}{BEING}}$ ∴ PRESENT

13 JAN: THE POST-MODERNIST ASPECT OF WHAT I AM
DOING IS ITS' MULTI-DIMENSIONALITY . . . . A
REFLECTION OF ITS' MULTI-RACIAL ORIGIN. THIS SHIT IS
ANCIENT BUT EXTEREMLY NEW AT THE SAME
TIME . . . . THAT IS WEIRD!!

14 JAN. THEREFORE; THE PAINTINGS HAVE MULTIPLE
MEANINGS.
<u>28 BLACK HOLES</u> COMPLETED 14 JAN 94

11 Jan 94:

I DON'T WANT THE <u>MEMORY</u> OF LIFE
I WANT THE <u>NOW</u> OF LIFE.
PRESERVATION OF MEMORY IS IMPORTANT BUT
THE PSYCHIC LIABILITY OF BAGGAGE CAN
PREVENT ME FROM EXPEIRENCING THE
FLUID NATURE OF <u>BEING</u> · PRESENT.
NOW.

I DON'T WANT THE <u>MEMORY</u> OF LIFE
I WANT THE <u>NOW</u> OF LIFE.
PRESERVATION OF MEMORY IS IMPORTANT BUT THE
PSYCHIC LIABILITY OF BAGGAGE CAN PREVENT ME FROM
EXPERIENCE THE FLUID NATURE OF $\frac{BEING}{NOW}$: PRESENT.

STUDIO LOG '94

31 JAN: SPACE IS A SUSPENSION. . . IN WHAT ? ? (I DON'T KNOW YET)
IT'S FLUID, & FLOWS LIKE WATER . IT IS A SUBSTANCE

9 FEB: TIME IS WHAT MOVES IT, WE ONLY GO ALONG FOR THE RIDE TO NOWHERE.

13 FEB. THE PURPOSE OF ART IS TO GIVE FORM TO CONSCIOUNESS.

16 FEB: I DON'T DEAL IN ABSOLUTES; I LEAVE THAT TO GOD.

17 FEB. GOD IS FLUID . . . IN MOTION . EVER CHANGING . IT'S THE DOGMA THAT'S STATIC.

MEMORY IS ONLY PART OF IT.

SPACE IS SUSPENDED IN TIME !!

20 FEB: PROCESS ALONE CAN DICTATE IMAGERY i.e, PROCESS AS SYMBOL-SUBJECT-VECHICLE.

3 APRIL: SPACE IS ONLY A FEELING. MY JOB AS AN ARTIST IS TO MAKE THAT FEELING INTO A PHYSICAL OBJECT.

9 APRIL: THE SUBJECT IS ME.

14 APRIL: TIME IS A MOTHERFUCKER !

15 APRIL: THERE IS AN INTERSECTION IN TIME WHERE THE PAST CANCELS THE PRESENT . . .
. . . . . THE SELF IS LOCATED AT THAT INTERSECTION, IT IS A POINT ON A PLANE KNOWN AS SPACE. ALL OF MY LIFE I HAVE BEEN TRYING TO LOCATE THAT POINT. MAY GOD BE WITH ME.

17 APRIL: COMPLETED BLACK MONOLITH, II : FOR R.W. ELLISON   1605 HRS.

SPIRIT + MATTER = LIFE   (FORGET ABOUT DEATH IT'S A PART OF LIFE)
CONTENT IS ELUSIVE . . . . VERY FLUID . — ALWAYS IN MOTION, IT IS IMPOSSIBLE TO DETERMINE CONTENT THROUGH CONCEPTUALITY. ONE MUST FIND IT THROUGH FORMAL ANALYSIS.

19 APRIL: THE VIEWER IS A WITNESS TO THE PAINTING AS FACTUAL OBJECT.
THEY EXPEIRENCE ITS SUCHNESS.

21 APRIL: THE OBJECT THAT I SPEAK OF IS A SCULPTURE OF A PAINTING i.e, a three DIMENSIONAL REPRESENTATIONAL OF A TWO-DIMENSIONAL PLANE.

7 MAY: MORE THAN ANYTHING . . . I WANT TO BE FILLED WITH THE SPIRIT.

3 MAY: BESSEMER BOOGIE WAS ORIGINALLY DEDICATED TO VIVIAN BROWNE BUT TODAY'S
N.Y. TIMES CHANGED THAT !
ALEXANDRA, SOUTH AFRICA
"AN ERUPTION OF JOY SWEPT THE VAST BLACK GHETTOS OF SOUTH AFRICA TONIGHT AS NELSON MANDELA CLAIMED HIS PRESIDENTIAL VICTORY WITH A BIT OF BOOGIE DANCING ON TELEVISION THAT WAS INSTANTLY IMITATED BY STREET THRONGS ACROSS THE LAND "
I AM SINCERELY VIVIAN BUT BESSEMER BOOGIE IS A HOMAGE TO NELSON MANDELA.
OFTEN I RECEIVE MY INFORMATION BEFORE THE CONCRETE ACTION. I CAN ONLY ACCEPT, I HAVE NO CONTROL ON THE TYPE OF INFO OR TIME OF RECEPTION.

11 MAY: MY INTEREST IS THE METAPHYSICS OF SPACE.

CLEM PASSED

"ABSTRACTION IS THE ONLY STREAM THAT LEADS TO AN OCEAN "
I AM THE OCEAN.

20 MAY: THE PAINTING AS IMAGE.
I USE DRAWING AS A MEANS OF ELIMINATING THAT WHICH IS NON-ESSENTIAL.

21 MAY: THE PURPOSE OF ART IS TO EXPAND CONSCIOUNESS
WHEN ART PERFORMS THIS FUNCTION, IT IS ALSO POLITICAL.
IT'S A VIRTUAL SPACE

24 MAY: I AM A TIME TRAVELER.
THE SPACE IS CLEMENT: COMPLETED 25 MAY 1994   KRITI
HOMAGE TO CLEM GREENBERG   TIME TO GO FISHING ! ——

STUDIO LOG '94

31 JAN: SPACE IS A SUSPENSION.   IN WHAT?? (I DON'T KNOW YET)
IT'S FLUID, + FLOWS LIKE WATER . . . IT IS A SUBSTANCE

9 FEB: TIME IS WHAT MOVES IT + WE ONLY GO ALONG FOR THE RIDE TO NOWHERE.

13 FEB: THE PURPOSE OF ART IS TO GIVE FORM TO CONSCIOUNESS.

16 FEB: I DON'T DEAL IN ABSOLUTES; I LEAVE THAT TO GOD.

17 FEB: GOD IS FLUID . . . . . IN MOTION . . . EVER CHANGING. IT'S THE DOGMA THAT'S STATIC.
MEMORY IS ONLY PART OF IT.
SPACE IS SUSPENDED IN TIME!!

20 FEB: PROCESS ALONE CAN DICATATE IMAGERY i.e., PROCESS AS SYMBOL-SUBJECT-VEHICLE.

3 APRIL: SPACE IS ONLY A FEELING. MY JOB AS AN ARTIST IS TO MAKE THAT FEELING INTO A PHYSICAL OBJECT.

9 APRIL: THE SUBJECT IS ME.

14 APRIL: TIME IS A MOTHERFUCKER!

15 APRIL: THERE IS AN INTERSECTION <u>IN TIME</u> WHERE THE PAST CANCELS THE PRESENT . . . . THE SELF IS LOCATED AT THAT INTERSECTION; IT IS A POINT ON A PLANE KNOWN AS SPACE. ALL OF MY LIFE I HAVE BEEN TRYING TO LOCATE THAT POINT. MAY GOD BE WITH ME.

17 APRIL: COMPLETED <u>BLACK MONOLITH, II: FOR R.W. ELLISON</u> 1605 HRS.
    SPIRIT + MATTER = LIFE (FORGET ABOUT DEATH IT'S A PART OF LIFE)
CONTENT IS ELUSIVE . . . . VERY FLUID . . . ALWAYS IN MOTION. IT IS IMPOSSIBLE TO DETERMINE CONTENT THROUGH CONCEPTUALITY. ONE MUST FIND IT THROUGH FORMAL ANALYSIS.

19 APRIL: THE VIEWER IS A WITNESS TO THE PAINTING AS FACTUAL OBJECT. THEY EXPERIENCE ITS SUCHNESS.

21 APRIL: THE OBJECT THAT I SPEAK OF IS A SCULPTURE OF A PAINTING i.e., a three DIMENSIONAL REPRESENTATIONAL OF A TWO-DIMENSIONAL PLANE.

7 MAY: MORE THAN ANYTHING . . . . I WANT TO BE FILLED WITH THE SPIRIT.

3 MAY: <u>BESSEMER BOOGIE</u> WAS ORIGINALLY DEDICATED TO VIVIAN BROWNE BUT TODAY'S <u>N.Y. TIMES</u> CHANGED THAT!
    ALEXANDRIA, SOUTH AFRICA
        "AN ERUPTION OF JOY SWEPT THE VAST BLACK
        GHETTOS OF SOUTH AFRICA TONIGHT AS NELSON
        MANDELA CLAIMED HIS PRESIDENTIAL VICTORY

WITH A BIT OF BOOGIE DANCING ON TELIVISION
THAT WAS INSTANTLY IMITATED BY STREET
THRONGS ACROSS THE LAND"
I AM SINCERELY VIVIAN BUT <u>BESSEMER BOOGIE</u> IS A
HOMAGE TO NELSON MANDELA.
OFTEN I RECEIVE MY INFORMATION BEFORE THE
CONCRETE ACTION. I CAN ONLY ACCEPT, I HAVE NO
CONTROL ON THE TYPE OF INFO OR TIME OF
RECEPTION.

11 MAY: MY INTEREST IS THE METAPHYSICS OF SPACE.
   <u>CLEM* PASSED</u>
"ABSTRACTION IS THE ONLY STREAM THAT LEADS TO AN
OCEAN"
<u>I AM THE OCEAN.</u>

20 MAY: THE PAINTING AS IMAGE.
I USE DRAWING AS A MEANS OF ELIMINATING THAT
WHICH IS NON-ESSENTIAL.

21 MAY: THE PURPOSE OF ART IS TO EXPAND
CONSCIOUNESS
WHEN ART PERFORMS THIS FUNCTION IT IS ALSO
POLITICAL.
   <u>IT'S A VIRTUAL SPACE</u>

24 MAY: I AM A TIME TRAVELER.
<u>THE SPACE IS CLEMENT</u>: COMPLETED 25 MAY 1994
HOMAGE TO CLEM GREENBERG   TIME TO GO FISHING! →
KRITI

<u>STUDIO LOG 1994 N.Y.C.</u>

18 Sept: No Religion, No Politics, No sex, No Autobiographical pretense, or Historical References, No Identities whatsoever, No commerce or Market ideologies. I WANT ART.

<u>SPACE IS A SUSPENSION</u>

20 Sept: My interest is a self-constructed gestalt.

24 Sept: It's my culture that I am putting back together. Due to Slavery, it was factured and its' my job as an artist to put it back together.

25 Sept: FOLLOW THE LIGHT + YOU WON'T GET LOST!

31 Sept: I want to put the magic back into art; American Art especially has become anemic.

2 OCT: LIFE IS A COSMIC PUZZLE.

4 OCT. THE ILLUSION MUST BE FLATTEN
    <u>NATURAL SELECTION, I</u> COMPLETED
    DEDICATED TO THE MEMORY OF H. GELDZAHLER
(only a dedication not meant as symbolism H.G.)

14 OCT: THE PAINTING AS FOUND OBJECT

3 DEC: SPIRITS ARE SUSPENDED IN SPACE. . . . .
    THEREFORE, THE PAINTING AS FOUND OBJECT
COULD QUALIFY AS A SPIRIT. <u>I</u> <u>LIKE</u> <u>THIS</u> <u>VERY</u> <u>MUCH</u> !!
IT TAKES ME BACK TO AFRICA.

IF AN ARTIST IS TRULY GREAT . . . . THEY MUST BE ABLE
TO ADD ANOTHER CIRCLE TO THE CONCENTRIC CIRCLE
OF LIFE. . . . THIS IS THE COSMIC CONSCIOUNESS.

10 DEC: ART IS MY CROSS TO BARE
    OBJECT = IMAGE (this is my contribution to art history)

17 DEC: "It ain't what you do it's the way which you do it" "that's
what jazz is all about" <u>old blues</u>

18 DEC: ULTIMATELY, ONE MUST ADDRESS THE
QUESTION: <u>What is the purpose of my art</u>?

21 DEC: "KEEP YOUR EYE ON THE PRIZE"
THE PURPOSE OF MY ART IS SELF IMPROVEMENT. I
STRIVE TO BE A BETTER PERSON. MENTALLY, MOST
IMPORTANT SPIRITUAL + MORAL. I WANT TO REDEFINE
THE MEANING OF BEING CIVILIZED BECAUSE I HAVE NOT
ENCOUNTERED ANY GOOD EXAMPLES, EXCEPT FOR A
FEW PEOPLE.
    <u>I AM THE IMAGE ∴ I AM THE OBJECT.</u>

28 DEC: 1610 HRS. COMPLETED <u>THE HAIRDRESSER: FOR
SISTER</u>

<u>1995</u>

8 JAN: PURPOSE HAS BEEN BOTHERING ME FOR SOME
TIME. I'VE ALWAYS KNOWN THAT I AM THE FIRST AND
MOST IMPORTANT RECIPIENT FOR ANY BENEFITS FROM
MY ART, BUT SOMETHING EVEN MORE IMPORTANT FOR
ME AND OTHERS IS TO RECLAIM OUR CULTURE . . . . THAT

which WHAT WAS LOST AS A DIRECT RESULT OF THE SLAVE TRADE. THIS PAINTING IS ABOUT RECLAIMING THE IMAGE OF THE MASK. THE MASK GIVES FOCUS AN ANCHOR FOR IDENTITY. IDENTITY AS A PEOPLE WAS LOST. WE HAVE SUFFERED FOR THIS. MY ART IS A TOOL USED FOR THE PURPOSE OF RECLAIMING MY LOST CULTURE AND DIRECTING IT INTO THE PRESENT.
THE MASK COMPLETED JAN. 95

19 JAN: ART MUST TRANSCEND DOGMA. THE PAINTING AS FOUND OBJECT ALLOWS ME TO PAINT WITHOUT CONSIDERING MEANING + AVOID AUTOMATISM. THERE IS NO STORY. THE STORY LIES ONLY IN THE FACT OF FINDING.

9 Feb: SYNTHETIC MATTER

11 FEB: ABSTRACTION AS IMAGE.

13 FEB: COMPLETED: WINDOWS OF THE MIND: A MONUMENT CELEBRATING THE ART OF PAINTING [ILLEGIBLE: 2440 HRS]

14 FEB: IT IS VERY IMPORTANT FOR ME NOT TO SEPARATE IDEA FROM CONTENT FROM PROCESS. THE PAINTING MUST ALWAYS BE SEEN WITHIN THE CONTEXT OF FORMING. THE PAINTING IS NOT AN ILLUSTRATION OF THE IDEA.

<u>STUDIO LOG – '95</u>

10 APRIL: YOU <u>MUST NOT</u> THINK IN TERMS OF CREATING THE SPACE; YOU MUST THINK OF MAKING THE OBJECT THAT MAKES THE SPACE.

11 APRIL: IT IS THE SPACE THAT'S CONCRETE

13 APRIL: LIFE IS A TIME MACHINE

20 APRIL: WHAT IS TODAY'S DEFINITION OF REALISM?

26 APRIL: ABSTRACTION AS A MODERNIST CONVENTION ENDED WITH THE GRID.

30 APRIL: JANEY WASHBURN DIED TODAY. I JUST SPOKE TO BILL. (DID THE SOCCER TARGET FOR JANEY)

6 MAY: I MUST WORK AGAINST SOL LEWITT. SAW THE ACE GALLERY SHOW, 100% CONCEPTUAL. <u>WORK</u> <u>AGAINST</u> <u>THE</u> <u>CONCEPTUAL.</u>
<u>MY ART IS PERCEPTUAL ART</u>
I WALK WITH TWO SHADOWS: ONE FROM ME + ONE FROM GOD.

7 MAY: IN PERCEPTUALISM, THE PAINTING AS OBJECT <u>ONLY</u> ACTS AS A CATALYST; THE REAL PAINTING EXIST <u>ONLY</u> IN THE MIND. THE MIND SEES THE PAINTING. THIS IS WHAT THE ANCIENTS MEANT BY INNER EYE. IMAGE IS ONLY A FEELING. AND NOT NECESSARILY A FEELING ABOUT SOMETHING. FEELING CAN EXIST AS PURE PHENOMEON. I am SURE THAT THIS IS WHAT DROVE

HUSSEREL CRAZY i.e., with EXCITMENT TO PROVOKE THOUGHT. I HAVE ARRIVED AT THIS CONCLUSION THROUGH A SYSTEMATIC DIGESTION OF MODERNISM. THIRTY ONE YEARS OF ANALYSIS, A TOTAL + THOROUGHLY DISECTION OF THE WESTERN MIND. <u>NOW STARTS THE REAL POST-MODERNIST EPOCH</u>. MAY THE $\frac{POWER}{GOD}$ BE WITH ME. I AM GOING TO NEED IT!

8 MAY: THE STRUCTURE IS DIGITAL. THE DIGITAL STRUCTURE SIGNIFIES THE TIME; THE SPACE IS INDIGENOUS TO THE STRUCTURE. I AM AT THE INTERSECTION WHERE SPACE-TIME CANCELS OUT. THE MEANING OF DIMENSIONAL TIME CEASES TO BE OF IMPORTANCE. I AM WHERE I'VE ALWAYS WANTED TO BE . . . . . WITHIN THE <u>NOW</u>.

11 MAY: FINISHED <u>SELF PORTRAIT</u> TODAY. THE WORLD'S FIRST PERCEPTUAL PAINTING. (OF CONCEPTUAL AWARENESS)
BILL RUBIN. . EAT YOUR HEART OUT!

15 MAY: MY JOB AS A PAINTER IS TO CREATE THE RIGHT VISUAL CONDITION WITHIN THE OBJECT WHICH ALLOWS THE IMAGE TO EXIST. IMAGE AND OBJECT IS NOT THE SAME. THE OBJECT ONLY ACTS AS A PHYSICAL REPRESENTATION OF THE IMAGE. THE IMAGE ONLY EXIST IN THE BRAIN. IN AFRICAN SCULPTURE, WHEN WE SPEAK OF PRESENCE, <u>PRESENCE IS IMAGE</u>. THE OBJECT MUST HAVE A SPECIFIC PHYSICAL QUALITY FOR IMAGE TO EXIST; THEREFORE, IMAGE IS A METAPHYSICAL MANIFESTATION. IT IS DEPENDENT UPON MATTER. IMAGE IS EIDETIC, PHOTOGRAPHIC IN STRUCTURE, NOT

PHOTOGRAPHIC AS IN MECHANICAL REPRODUCTION
BUT PHOTOGRAPHIC ORGANICALLY PERCEIVED. EIDETIC
IMAGERY HAS THE SAME STRUCTURE OF LIGHT
RECOGNIZABLE IN MECHANICAL PHOTOGRAPHY.

7 June: I have plenty to think about. Tomorrow I leave for Aghia
Galini. . . The wood carving is calling me strongly. Hopefully my
back will hold out + allow me to work. . .
GONE FISHING

STUDIO LOG

11 SEPT 95. THE PAINTING IS A MAGIC OBJECT.
16 SEPT: SELLING IS A BY-PRODUCT OF ART.
21 SEPT: MY INTENTION IS TO BRING BACK THE HEROIC
IN AMERICAN ART.

26 Sept.
First, The object as image manifest itself abstractly through sensation
and afterwards slowly defines the specifics of pictorial image with all
the richness of illusion, meaning + metaphor. ~~expressed~~ The painting
~~becomes a~~ is a "physical poem."
~~A prodcedure of formal thinking~~
Conceptualized formal programming is the means used in
constructing the painting. . . . . The formal is a tool which serves a
greater end.

29 Sept. Saw the Tim Hawkinson show at ACE Gallery today.
Very interesting . . . definitely connecting to me—use of
materials is astounding—very talented guy! I don't feel the Spirit
to be present but he is trying.
Left Ace + walked home met a Black hobo (long braids—total
hair in wades— dirty) sitting on road—at entrance to tunnel. I
attempted to give him some money which he refused saying that he
doesn't take dollars—nor talk to people—but he tell me that a
Brother had moved to the Midwest and brought land—that he was
living well. (This man was unusual + remainded me of a Black man
who said to me in 1968 that "What's wrong with you men don't sleep
while standing—Only horses + elephants."
This man said to me "YOU HAVE THE LIGHT."
30: KNOWN + UNKNOWN

6 OCT. VIRTUAL IMAGERY
    DON CHERRY 20 OCT 95

Content is transmitted through light, not through form 18 OCT

29 OCT. COMPLETED <u>MEMORY SITES</u>, 1995 (Dedicated to
YITZHAK RABIN 1922–1995, made dedication after his ass. on
4 NOV 95)
    This painting addresses man's inhumanity to man.

1 NOV: MY USE OF $\frac{\text{SYMBOL}}{\text{METAPHOR}}$ MUST ALWAYS BE
GROUNDED IN NECESSITY AS PROJECTED THROUGH
EXPERIENCE!

3 NOV: EXPERIENCE IS THE SUBJECT.

12 NOV: <u>CODE</u> AS A CARRIER OF INFORMATION (THIS IS A
GREAT POSSIBILITY, AN ALTERNATIVE OPTION IN the USE
OF IMAGE AS SUBJECT) CODE IS AN ALTERNATIVE TO
IMAGE.

13 NOV: I AM VERY INTERESTED IN STRUCTURES THAT
OCCUR BEFORE THE ADVENT OF HUMAN CONSCIOUNESS.
(PRE-LOGIC)

28 NOV: SPECIFIC EMOTIONS HAVE SPECIFIC VISUAL
PATTERNS.

2 DEC: → <u>JAZZ IS A PATTERN</u>

8 DEC: IT IS TIME: GIVE ALL OF IT TO GOD.

11 DEC: COMPLETED <u>MESSAGE FROM NORMAN</u> (This
painting is an example of code as image, a carrier of information.
I especially built it to be musical, a celebratory expressive musical
structure. 59" x 123" (Goodbye to all of that modernist shit!)
including <u>Mondrian</u>!

12 DEC: These are <u>Organic Grids</u> I work with.

13 DEC: THE OBJECT CAN ONLY → ATTRACT THE SPIRIT
THROUGH THE MAKER, THE MAKER MUST BE OF
SPIRIT. . . ALL MAKERS ARE NOT OF SPIRIT. THIS IS MOST
EVIDENT IN OBJECTS THAT CLAIM TO ADDRESS THE
SUBLIME: THE SUBLIME IS SPIRIT.

STUDIO LOG 1996

3 JAN: MY NEXT PAINTING IS A SELF PORTRAIT. I WANT IT TO BE CLEAR,
   VERY DIRECT + GRAPHIC... A DOCUMENT ART IN BLACK WALNUT + RECYCLED
   GLASS. MAY THE SPIRIT BE WITH ME.

6 JAN: I PRAY FOR CLARITY OF BEING.

7 JAN: IF THE GRID IS ORGANIC, THEREFORE THE COMPUTER AS METAPHOR IS ORGANIC:
   AN ORGANIC COMPUTER. THESE STRUCTURES COULD BE REFERRED AS
   PHYSICAL PHOTOGRAPHS, AN EDETIC IMAGE, PRODUCED BY MATERIALITY.
   ITS SUBSTANCE A PRODUCT OF THE EMOTIONS.
   ABSTRACTION WAS A MODERNIST INVENTION. IT IS NO LONGER AN ISSUE.
   ABSTRACTION AS MODERNIST INVENTION ENDED WITH THE GRID. FROM NOW ON
   ABSTRACTION PART II IS DERIVED FROM PRE-MODERNIST SENSIBILITIES. IN MY
   PARTICULAR CASE, OF AFRICAN ORIGIN... PRE-SCIENTIFIC... PRE-LOGIC, AN EXPRESSION
   OF THE MIND IN ITS NATURAL STATE. A FUNCTIONAL TOOL USED TO RECONSTRUCT A
   RUPTURED CULTURE. MY TASK IS ONE OF RECONSTRUCTION.

   THE BODY IS A CONTAINER FOR THE SPIRIT.

17 JAN: IT'S IN THE GEOMETRY. WE MUST RECONSTRUCT OUR CULTURE THROUGH THE GEO.

25 JAN: THERE IS NO BEGINNING AND NO END.

27 JAN: TOM DIED TODAY.

30 JAN: ART IS JUST A FEELING.

3 FEB: THE PAINTING AS HYBRID OBJECT, ENCOMPASSING DIVERSE ELEMENT OF KNOWN QUALIFIERS e.,
   FORMAL, INFORMAL, REPRESENTATIONAL, MODERNIST + POST-MODERNIST ISMS. MY OBJECTIVE IS
   TO MAKE USE OF PLURALISM: PLURALISM IS A CONCEPTUAL ARMATURE. THIS GIVES ME AN
   ENORMOUS AMOUNT OF FREEDOM. THE UNIVERSE BECOMES MY SANDBOX!
   — MAKE IT SO —   THE PAINT IS REAL. IT'S CONCRETE.

14 FEB: REALITY IS THAT OF THE PAINT.... THE PAINT IS REAL. IT'S CONCRETE.

18 FEB: FINALLY MADE CONTACT WITH THE ORIGINAL MIND AT 01140.

22 FEB: COMPLETED T.C.'S CORNER FOR MY UNCLE THOMAS CUNNINGHAM.
   I TRULY LOVED HIM.
   HIS CORNER WAS TILLARY AT FLATBUSH IN BKLYN.

24 FEB: I FIRST WROTE IN 1964(?) THAT THE IMAGE IS PHOTOGRAPHIC; THEREFORE
   I MUST PHOTOGRAPH MY THOUGHTS. I HAVE BEEN TRYING TO UNDERSTAND THIS
   EVER SINCE. MORE IMPORTANT; THE SPACE IS PHOTOGRAPHIC.
   AND, IF, OR — OR BUT (SAUL TOLD ME THIS TODAY, TAKEN FROM WILSON)
   HENRY USED TO SAY: EITHER OR, MAYBE, BUT- NEITHER NOR -OR BOTH
   + THEN SOME! THE NEW PAINTING IS ABOUT FREEDOM!
   ART HAS ALWAYS BEEN ABOUT FREEDOM. THE ARTIST JOB IS TO
   CONTINUE THE EXPANSION OF FREEDOM ... TO UNVEIL ANOTHER LAYER
   OF CONSCIOUSNESS. ANYWAY, THE NEW PAINTING IS RECOGNIZABLE
   BY ITS SPACE WHICH IS PHOTOGRAPHIC, IMAGE COULD BE INCLUDING
   IF ONE DESIRES. IT'S A MATTER OF CHOICE.

3 MARCH: SPACE IS NOT A RELATIONAL FORMAL ELEMENT IN PAINTING; IT MUST BE
   STRICTLY A PRIORI.

8 MARCH: VISUAL ALCHEMY OF PERCEPTION.

19 MARCH: "CONCENTRATION ON THE BASICS, ELIMINATION OF ALL SUPERFLOUS THINGS AND OF ALL FALSEHOODS"
   ODYSSEUS ELYTIS 1911-1996

29 MARCH: THE PAINTING IS A MASK.   (COMPLETED MASK, II TODAY)
                            PHOTOGRAPHED
   "EXPEIRENCES HAVE ALREADY BEEN PHOTOGRAPHED IN THE SUBJCONSCIOUS."
                            HERBERT GENTRY (S.M.H. INTERVIEW WITH ED CLARK+K. CONNELL)
2 APRIL: IF THIS IS TRUE, MY INTEREST IS IN DIGITALIZING THE SUBCONSCIOUS.

3 APRIL: RON BROWN WAS KILLED IN AIR CRASH IN FORMER YUGOSLAVIA TODAY.
   I DEDICATED MASK II TO RON (IT'S A BIRD'S BEAK, SEE FACE OF R.B.)
                   RAGE
8 APRIL: PUSH THE ANGER INTO THE MATERIAL, COMPRESS IT.
              ANGST
12 APRIL: RECONSTRUCTIONISM—RECONSTRUCTIONIST—RECONSTRUCTION—RECONSTRUCT
   CONSTRUCT ⎫
   DECONSTRUCT ⎬= CONCEPTUAL ABSTRACTION
   RECONSTRUCT ⎭

14 APRIL: I MUST RELIE MORE ON WHAT I SEE (VISION)

STUDIO LOG 1996

3 JAN: MY NEXT PAINTING IS A SELF PORTRAIT. I WANT IT TO BE CLEAR, VERY DIRECT + GRAPHIC . . . . A DOCUMENTARY IN BLACK WALNUT + RECYCLED GLASS. MAY THE SPIRIT BE WITH ME.

6 Jan: I PRAY FOR CLARITY OF BEING.

7 JAN: IF THE GRID IS ORGANIC, THEREFORE THE COMPUTER AS METAPHOR IS ORGANIC: AN ORGANIC COMPUTER. THESE STRUCTURES COULD BE REFERRED AS PHYSICAL PHOTOGRAPHS, AN EDETIC IMAGE, PRODUCED BY MATERIALITY.
ITS' SUBSTANCE A PRODUCT OF THE EMOTIONS. ABSTRACTION WAS A MODERNIST INVENTION. IT IS NO LONGER AN ISSUE.
ABSTRACTION AS MODERNIST INVENTION ENDED WITH THE GRID. FROM NOW ON ABSTRACTION PART II IS DERIVED FROM PRE-MODERNIST SENSIBILITIES. IN MY PARTICULAR CASE, OF AFRICAN ORIGIN . . . . PRE-SCIENTIFIC . . . . . . PRE-LOGIC, AN EXPRESSION OF THE MIND IN ITS NATURAL STATE. A FUNCTIONAL TOOL USED TO RECONSTRUCT A RUPTURED CULTURE. MY TASK IS ONE OF RECONSTRUCTION.
THE BODY IS A CONTAINER FOR THE SPIRIT.

17 JAN: IT'S IN THE GEOMETRY. WE MUST RECONSTRUCT OUR CULTURE THROUGH THE GEO.

25 JAN: THERE IS NO BEGINNING AND NO END.

27 JAN: TOM DIED TODAY.

30 JAN: ART IS JUST A FEELING.

3 FEB: THE PAINTING AS HYBIRD OBJECT, ENCOMPASSING DIVERSE ELEMENT OF KNOWN QUALIFIERS e.g., FORMAL, INFORMAL REPRESENTATIONAL, MODERNIST + POST-MODERNIST ISMS. MY OBJECTIVE IS TO MAKE USE OF PLURALISM: PLURALISM IS A CONCEPTUAL ARMATURE. THIS GIVES ME AN ENORMOUS AMOUNT OF FREEDOM. THE UNIVERSE BECOMES MY SANDBOX!
—MAKE IT SO—

14 FEB: REALITY IS THAT OF THE PAINT . . . . THE PAINT IS REAL. IT'S CONCRETE.

18 FEB: FINALLY MADE CONTACT WITH THE ORIGINAL MIND AT 01140.

22 FEB: COMPLETED <u>T.C.'S CORNER</u> FOR MY UNCLE THOMAS CUNNINGHAM. I TRULY LOVED HIM.
HIS CORNER WAS TILLARY AT FLATBUSH IN BKLYN.

24: FEB: I FIRST WROTE IN 1964 (?) THAT THE IMAGE IS PHOTOGRAPHIC; THEREFORE I MUST PHOTOGRAPH MY THOUGHTS. I HAVE BEEN TRYING TO UNDERSTAND THIS EVER SINCE. MORE IMPORTANT: <u>THE SPACE IS PHOTOGRAPHIC</u>. AND, IF, OR—OR BUT (SAUL TOLD ME THIS TODAY, TAKEN FROM WILSON) HENRY USED TO SAY: EITHER OR, MAYBE, BUT—NEITHER NOR—OR BOTH + THEN SOME! THE NEW PAINTING IS ABOUT FREEDOM!

ART HAS ALWAYS BEEN ABOUT FREEDOM. THE ARTIST JOB IS TO CONTINUE THE EXPANSION OF FREEDOM . . . TO UNVEIL ANOTHER LAYER OF CONSCIOUNESS. ANYWAY, THE NEW PAINTING IS RECOGNIZABLE BY ITS SPACE WHICH IS PHOTOGRAPHIC, IMAGE COULD BE INCLUDING IF ONE DESIRES. IT'S A MATTER OF CHOICE.

3 MARCH: SPACE IS NOT A RELATIONAL FORMAL ELEMENT IN PAINTING; IT MUST BE STRICTLY A PRIORI.

8 MARCH: <u>VISUAL ALCHEMY</u> OF PERCEPTION.

19 MARCH: "CONCENTRATION ON THE BASICS, ELIMINATION OF ALL SUPERFLOUS THINGS AND OF ALL FALSEHOODS"
    ODYSSEUS ELYTIS 1911–1996

29 MARCH: THE PAINTING IS A MASK (COMPLETED MASK II TODAY)
"EXPERIENCES HAVE ALREADY BEEN PHOTOGRAPHED IN THE SUBCONSCIOUS."
    HERBERT GENTRY (S.M.H. INTERVIEW WITH ED CLARK + K. CONWILL)

2 APRIL: IF THIS IS TRUE, MY INTEREST IS IN DIGITALIZING THE SUBCONSCIOUS.

3 APRIL: RON BROWN WAS KILLED IN AIR CRASH IN FORMER YUGOSLAVIA TODAY. I DEDICATED MASK II TO RON (IT'S A BIRD'S BEAK, SEE FACE OF R.B.)

8 APRIL: PUSH THE $\overset{\text{RAGE}}{\underset{\text{ANGST}}{\underline{\text{ANGER}}}}$ INTO THE MATERIAL, COMPRESS IT.

12 APRIL: RECONSTRUCTIONISM—RECONSTRUCTIONIST—RECONSTRUCTION—RECONSTRUCT

$$\left.\begin{array}{l} \text{CONSTRUCT} \\ \text{DECONSTRUCT} \\ \text{RECONSTRUCT} \end{array}\right\} = \text{CONCEPTUAL ABSTRACTION}$$

14 APRIL: I MUST RELIE MORE ON WHAT I SEE (VISION)

8 APRIL: SOUL IS THE SPIRIT WITHIN YOU

9 APRIL: I AM THE FREE-EST PERSON ON THE PLANET!
I HAVE NO BAGGAGE—NO BONES IN THE CLOSET!

7 APRIL: <u>NOW</u> MORE THAN EVER <u>BEFORE</u> IT'S <u>CRUCIAL</u> TO
PUT THE MAGIC BACK INTO PAINTING
<u>PIC'ASS'O</u> IS <u>NO</u> <u>LONGER</u> <u>RELEVANT</u>
THIS IS THE 21 CENTURY
ONLY <u>I</u> AM RELEVANT!

28 APRIL: COMPLETED <u>MASK, III: FOR</u> <u>THE</u> <u>CHILDREN</u> OF
<u>DUNBLANE, SCOTLAND</u>

7 MAY: THE FORMAL ISSUE IN ABSTRACT PAINTING
TODAY IS NOT <u>SHAPE,</u> <u>SURFACE,</u> <u>FORM</u> OR <u>CONTENT</u>. . . .
<u>THE ISSUE IS SPACE</u>.

6 JUNE: <u>GONE FISHING</u>

TRIBLES   TRIBBLE

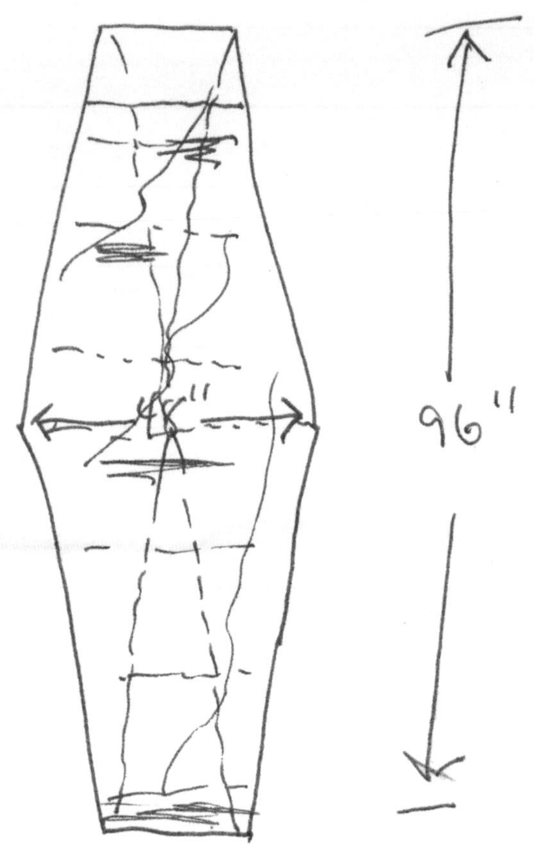

I saw it on Star Trek
9 NOV 96

November 9, 1996

TRIBLES TRIBBLE

[drawing; labeled, 48" wide and 96" high]

I saw it on Star Trek
9 NOV 96

<u>STUDIO LOG</u>   1996

23 SEPT: BACK FROM FISHING, IMMEDIATELY STARTING
<u>ELLA</u> SERIES, I PLAN THREE SMALL INTENSE
STRUCTURES.
THE NECESSITY OF ABSTRACTION IS MORE PRESSING
THAN EVER. I SPENT LOTS OF TIME THINKING THIS
SUMMER. . . . THE DIGITAL MUST BE CONCEIVED AS
DERIVED FROM NATURE . . . <u>NOT MAN</u> . . IT'S ORGANIC.
IT CAN BE CONSTRUCTED ON A GRID PATTERN BUT
THE PATTERN MUST BE ORGANIC NOT MACHINED.

24 SEPT: THE PAINTING MUST BE BUILT . . . LIKE YOU ARE
BUILDING A STONE WALL.
        ART, LIKE RELIGION DEPENDS UPON FAITH.
        DIGITAL ABSTRACTION IS ORIGINAL MIND.

26 SEPT: THE PAINTING IS ~~JUST~~ AN OBJECT EXPRESSING
A FEELING ABOUT SOMETHING.

25 SEPT: CORRECTION: DIGITAL ABSTRACTION IS
<u>PRESENT</u> MIND.
WE ARE NOT IN SPACE, WE ARE ON SPACE. . . SPACE IS
A PLANE.
        LEGBA—GOD OF THE CROSS ROADS
WHAT HAPPENS WHEN ILLUSION + NON-ILLUSION
CANCEL EACH OTHER?

8 OCT: CAN INTUITION BE CONCEPTUALLY
STRUCTURED?
        I AM A THIEF, I HAVE STOLEN THE LIGHT!
        | HIPISM | THE QUALITY OF BEING HIP ABOUT LIFE.

10 OCT: I WANT TO PROVE THAT PAINTING HAS THE BUILT
IN ABILITY TO REINVENT ITSELF. IF IT IS LIKE YOGURT
THEN LETS PASS ON THE CULTURE.
NATURE IS DIGITAL

19 OCT:

$$\left.\begin{array}{l} \underline{\text{CONTENT}} \\ \text{MATERIAL} \\ \text{as MATTER} \end{array}\right\} \quad \frac{\text{COLOR}}{\text{FORM}} \quad = \text{SYMBOL}$$

24 OCT: SPIRIT IS A METAPHOR FOR THAT WHICH IS NOT
SEEN.

6 NOV: EXPERIENCE IS ONLY THE CATALYST.

9 NOV: ALL PAINTING IS ABOUT PERCEPTION, IT JUST
DEPENDS UPON WHICH LEVEL ONE IS TALKING ABOUT.
I AM TALKING ABOUT THE MOLECULAR LEVEL.
TRANSPARENCY IN COLOR STRUCTURE IS NOT A
FORMAL ISSUE.
IT IS AN AUTOBIOGRAPHICAL ISSUE. THE QUESTION IS:
DO WE HAVE ANYTHING TO HIDE?
THE PAINTING IS AN ORGANIC OBJECT.

12 NOV: FOR A PAINTING TO QUALIFY AS ABSTRACT,
ULTIMATELY, IT MUST DEFY ORAL INTERPERTATION. s/p

15 NOV: FIVE SKANDHAS: CONSTITUENTS OF
PHENOMENA
    ① FORM   ② FEELING   ③ PERCEPTION
    ④ MENTAL FORMAL/TIME   ⑤ CONSCIOUSNESS

17 NOV: WHAT HAPPENS IF I PHYSICALLY REMOVE THE CENTER? CONTEMPLATION UPON THE NATURE OF BEING IS THE CONTENT;
THE PAINTING AS OBJECT IS A VEHICLE USED TO INVESTIGATE BEING
IT'S A PHILOSOPHICAL INQUIRY, THEREFORE METAPHYSICAL

21 NOV: <u>DUMP THE CENTER</u>! (the equivalent of dumping the mass in sculpture) Psychologically going for broke, dangerous but necessary, takes a lot of faith

"You have to believe it before you can see it" → <u>ART MUST HAVE MYSTERY</u>!
→ EACH PAINTING IS CONCEIVED OF AS A MASK

23 NOV 96 Loch Ness → MY GRID IS ORGANIC, IT GROWS AS THE PAINTING PROGRESSES

+ FRIEND

14 DEC: COMPLETED THE MINGO ALTERPIECE : FOR MY STUDENT GEORGE MINGO

18 DEC: I AM A PART OF NATURE.

2 DEC : I revisited the grid today. Painting is like riding a comet, she swings way out
on an orbit & returns. My job is to stay on top! The 'broken grid series' was fun
with a lot of freedom & very romantic but let's face it everything is grided.
I plan to start a series of bold black & white, 'Revisited GRID SERIES', Digital
Abstraction Part II. Since Franz Kline is more & more important to me,
even more so than DeKooning, I will dedicate this series to Franz.
Also, I have been thinking about the Formal..... the Formal could be conceived
of as 'Personal Myth'. This notion of the Formal attracts me very much.
I shall try to penetrate this notion with the 'Revisited Grid Series'
✻ FIRST ONE IS TO BILL

SPIRIT

MATTER — ENERGY

This is what my subject is.
7 Jan 97

1997

7 JAN: THE UNIVERSE IS NOT CASUAL.

8 JAN: SPIRIT
         MATTER — ENERGY
         } THIS ALLOWS ME TO RECONSTRUCT REALITY.

14 JAN: BLACK AESTHETICS IS ALL INCLUSIVE. (NOT TO BE CONFUSED WITH SO CALLED BLACK ART)

16 JAN: AT SOME POINT IN LIFE, ONE MUST STOP CHASING & LET IT COME TO YOU.

25 JAN: IT'S THE THIRD ENTITY THAT I WANT.

31 JAN: I AM A HISTORICAL FACT.

20 MARCH: ABSTRACTION IS THE ESSENCE OF BEING.

22 MARCH: IS THERE AN ABSTRACT REALISM?

27 MARCH: THE DRAWING IS A CATALYST.

1 APRIL: THE PHILOSOPHY OF JAZZ IS THE EXPANSION OF FREEDOM, FROM INSIDE → OUT
OUT IS ALWAYS EXPANDING THE PARAMETERS OF FREEDOM. JAZZ IS ALL INCLUSIVE.

10 APRIL: YES GOD! BRIGHT MOMENTS 1995 FOR RASAAN ROLAND KIRK
THE PAINTING IS AN EXTENSION OF NATURE, THEREFORE I AM A MEGACEPTUALIST.

14 APRIL: I WANT THAT WHICH IS A MATTER OF FACT.

15 APRIL: COMPLETED THE GREAT WHITE: FOR BILL DE KOONING   1430 HRS.

6 MAY: MY PAINTING PROCESS IS NOT LABOR INTENSIVE IT'S LOVE INTENSIVE.

7 MAY: COMPLETED THE GINSBURG MANDALA: FOR ALLEN GINSBURG

17 MAY: I AM A DIGITAL EXPRESSIONIST.

22 MAY: GONE FISHING

see you in sept

STUDIO LOG '96

14 DEC: COMPLETED <u>THE</u> <u>MINGO</u> <u>ALTERPIECE</u>: FOR MY STUDENT + FRIEND GEORGE MINGO

18 DEC: I AM A PART OF NATURE.

26 Dec: I revisited the grid today. Painting is like riding a comet, she swings way out on an orbit + returns. My job is to stay on top! The 'broken grid series' was fun with a lot of freedom + very romantic but let's face it everything is grided. I plan to start a series of bold black + white, '<u>Revisited</u> <u>GRID</u> <u>SERIES</u>', <u>Digital</u> <u>Abstraction</u> <u>Part II</u>. Since Franz Kline is more + more important to me, even more so than DeKooning, I will dedicate this series to Franz. Also, I have been thinking about the Formal . . . . . the Formal could be conceived of as 'Personal Myth.' This notion of the Formal attracts me very much. I shall try to penetrate this notion with the 'Revisited Grid Series' *FIRST ONE IS TO BILL

1997

7 JAN: THE UNIVERSE IS <u>NOT</u> CASUAL.

[drawing; triangle labeled, "SPIRIT," "MATTER," "ENERGY"; arrow pointing at center of triangle] This is what my subject is. 7 Jan 97

8 JAN: [drawing; triangle labeled, "SPIRIT," "MATTER," "ENERGY"]} THIS ALLOWS ME TO RECONSTRUCT REALITY

14 JAN: BLACK AESTHETICS IS ALL INCLUSIVE. (NOT TO BE CONFUSED WITH SO CALLED BLACK ART)

16 JAN: AT SOME POINT IN LIFE, ONE MUST STOP CHASING + LET IT COME TO YOU.

25 JAN: IT'S THE THIRD ENTITY THAT I WANT.

31 JAN: I AM A HISTORICAL FACT.

20 MARCH: ABSTRACTION IS THE ESSENCE OF BEING.

22 MARCH: IS THERE AN ABSTRACT REALISM?

27 MARCH: THE DRAWING IS A CATALYST.

1 APRIL: THE PHILOSOPHY OF JAZZ IS THE EXPANSION OF FREEDOM, FROM INSIDE → OUT
OUT IS ALWAYS EXPANDING THE PARAMETERS OF FREEDOM. JAZZ IS ALL INCLUSIVE.

10 APRIL: YES GOD! BRIGHT MOMENTS, 1995 FOR ROSSAN ROLAND KIRK
THE PAINTING IS AN EXTENSION OF NATURE; THEREFORE I AM A MEGACEPTUALIST.

14 APRIL: I WANT THAT WHICH IS A MATTER OF FACT.

15 APRIL: COMPLETED THE GREAT WHITE: FOR BILL DE KOONING 1430 HRS.

6 MAY: MY PAINTING PROCESS IS NOT LABOR INTENSIVE
IT'S <u>LOVE</u> <u>INTENSIVE</u>.

7 MAY: COMPLETED <u>THE</u> <u>GINSBURG</u> <u>MANDALA</u>: <u>FOR</u>
<u>ALLEN GINSBURG</u>

17 MAY: I AM A DIGITAL EXPRESSIONIST.

22 MAY: <u>GONE FISHING</u>
see you in Sept

STUDIO LOG 1997

19 Sept: MY OBJECTIVE IS TO DIVERT MODERNIST THEORY.

20 Sept: IT LIES BEYOND THE HAND ONLY THE EYE CAN PENETRATE IT.

21 Sept: I AM SMOKING A COHIBA + DRINKING RAKI FROM ANO MEROS!
RIGHT ON!!

"A MARRIGAGE BETWEEN THE SUBCOUSCIOUS, THE FUNCTIONAL + THE SURREAL" DENNIS YI

22 SEPT: COLOR IS A SURFACE,

26 SEPT: YOU CAN DO THIS BY RECONSTRUCTING PAINTING.

27 SEPT: ART DEALS WITH THE EXPANSION OF FREEDOM.

30 SEPT: WE LOST ROY YESTERDAY.
DIGITIAL EXPRESSIONISM DISSECTS PERCEPTION AT THE MOLECULAR LEVEL

3 OCT: THE GRID OPERATES IN THE SAME MANNER AS 'MUSIC NOTATION PAPER'; EACH OF MY CHIPS OF PAINT IS A NOTE CARRYING BOTH SOUND + LIGHT.

6 OCT: "BALANCE IS THE GREATEST POWER"

7 OCT: THE MUSICALITY OF COLOR IS 'CALL + RESPONSE' [CINDY]

9 OCT: THE BODY IS A BATTERY + NEEDS CONSTANT RECHARGING.
I DON'T KNOW QUITE HOW TO PUT THIS BUT: JAZZ CAN BE MADE PHYSICALLY,
THEREFORE THE PAINTING AS OBJECT COULD BE EXPRESSED AS PHYSICAL JAZZ.
IN MY TALK AT MOMA, I SPOKE OF SEEKING AN EQUIVALENT TO JAZZ, i.e, A PHYSICAL
EQUIVALENT.... JAZZ CONSTRUCTED AS OBJECT - WHICH IS THE PAINTING.

13 OCT: EACH VALUE HAS A SOUND.

30 OCT: WE LIVE IN A MULTIDIMENSIONAL WORLD THEREFORE THE ART OF PAINTING MUST REFLECT
THIS, PRIMARILY THE [FORMAL] ELEMENT OF SPACE IN PAINTING. I AM A SPACE PAINTER.
I CHOOSE THE USE ABSTRAKTION BECAUSE IT ALLOWS A BROADER NOTION OF FREEDOM.

1 NOV: COMPLETED THE TOWER OF DI : [FOR] DIANA PRINCESS OF WALES 1930 HRS.
MAY SHE REST IN PEACE

20 NOV: THE PAINTING AS SACRED OBJECT?
THIS COMES CLOSER TO WHAT I AM FEELING; AN OBJECT OF DEVOTION.
MUSIC PLAYS A ROLE IN THIS; THUS THE CONNECTION TO JAZZ. IT LIES BEYOND THE FORMAL
I INSIST THAT THE FORMAL IS ONLY A TOOL USED TO CONSTRUCT A SACRED OBJECT.
MY NEXT PAINTING IS DEDICATED TO ROY LICHTENSTEIN SACRED OBJECT NUMBER ONE
I WILL ATTEMPT TO DUMP THE CENTER.

27 NOV: THE MOST DIFFICULT IN PAINTING IS TO ELIMINATE THE NOTION OF IDEA.
MY ONLY RECOURSE IS TO TRICK MYSELF IN ORDER TO DETOUR THE IDEA.
IF THERE IS ANYTHING TO DERAIL, IT IS IDEA. I HATE THE NOTION OF IDEA!
THE ONLY WAY IS TO FORGET ABOUT MEANING AND INSIST UPON THE PAINTING
AS BEING.... i.e, INSIST UPON THE PAINTING ONLY AS A FEELING.
IT EXIST ONLY AS A FEELING. (ABOUT NOTHING IN PARTICULAR)

ABSTRACT NATURALISM: THE MATERIAL DEPICTION OF SOUL.

30 NOV: EARLIER, I SPOKE OF DIGITAZING THE UNCONSCIOUS, ABSTRACT NATURALISM IS THE RESULTS.
I AM TRYING TO EVADE THE IDEA BY SIMPLY FORGETING ABOUT IT + LET
IT TAKES ITS' OWN COURSE; THE IDEA HAS ITS' OWN CONSCIOUNESS.

9 DEC: PAINT IS MATTER, AND CAN SERVE AS A METAPHOR FOR SPIRIT.

VISION HAS NO MIND.

13 DEC: GOD IS A METAPHOR FOR LOVE, EMPATHY... HUMAN COMPASSION; IT IS A
NECESSARY INGREDIANT FOR VISIONARY ART

17 DEC: I MUST RECONSTRUCT NATURE IN MY IMAGE.

STUDIO LOG 1997

19 Sept: MY OBJECTIVE IS TO DIVERT MODERNIST THEORY.

20 Sept: IT LIES BEYOND THE HAND ONLY THE EYE CAN PENETRATE IT.

21 Sept: I AM SMOKING A COHIBA + DRINKING RAKI FROM ANO MEROS! RIGHT ON!!
"A MARRIAGE BETWEEN THE SUBCONSCIOUS, THE FUNCTIONAL + THE SURREAL" DENNIS YI

22 SEPT: COLOR IS A SURFACE.

26 SEPT: YOU CAN DO THIS BY RECONSTRUCTING PAINTING.

27 SEPT: ART DEALS WITH THE EXPANSION OF FREEDOM.

30 SEPT: WE LOST ROY* YESTERDAY.
DIGITAL EXPRESSIONISM DISSECTS PERCEPTION AT THE MOLECULAR LEVEL

3 OCT: THE GRID OPERATES IN THE SAME MANNER AS 'MUSIC NOTATION PAPER'; EACH OF MY CHIPS OF PAINT IS A NOTE CARRYING BOTH SOUND + LIGHT.

6 OCT: "BALANCE IS THE GREATEST POWER" CINDY

7 OCT: THE MUSICALITY OF COLOR IS 'CALL + RESPONSE'

Roy Lichtenstein

9 OCT: THE BODY IS A BATTERY + NEEDS CONSTANT
RECHARGING.
I DON'T KNOW QUITE HOW TO PUT THIS BUT: <u>JAZZ</u> <u>CAN</u>
<u>BE</u> <u>MADE</u> <u>PHYSICALLY</u>, THEREFORE THE PAINTING AS
OBJECT COULD BE EXPRESSED AS PHYSICAL JAZZ. IN MY
TALK AT MOMA, I SPOKE OF SEEKING AN EQUIVALENT
TO JAZZ, i.e., A PHYSICAL EQUIVALENT . . . . JAZZ
CONSTRUCTED AS OBJECT . . . WHICH IS THE PAINTING.

13 OCT: EACH VALUE HAS A SOUND.

30 OCT: WE LIVE IN A MULTIDIMENSIONAL WORLD
THEREFORE THE ART OF PAINTING MUST REFLECT THIS,
PRIMARILY THE FORMAL ELEMENT OF SPACE IN
PAINTING. I AM A SPACE PAINTER. I CHOOSE THE USE
ABSTRACTION BECAUSE IT ALLOWS A BROADER NOTION
OF FREEDOM.

1 NOV: COMPLETED <u>THE</u> <u>TOWER</u> <u>OF</u> <u>DI</u>: FOR <u>DIANA</u>
<u>PRINCESS</u> <u>OF</u> <u>WALES</u> 1930 HRS.
    MAY SHE REST IN PEACE

20 NOV: THE PAINTING AS SACRED OBJECT?
THIS COMES CLOSER TO WHAT I AM FEELING; AN OBJECT
OF DEVOTION.
MUSIC PLAYS A ROLE IN THIS, THUS THE CONNECTION
TO JAZZ. IT LIES BEYOND THE FORMAL
I INSIST THAT THE FORMAL IS ONLY A TOOL USED TO
CONSTRUCT A SACRED OBJECT. MY NEXT PAINTING IS
DEDICATED TO ROY LICHTENSTEIN <u>SACRED</u> <u>OBJECT</u>
<u>NUMBER</u> <u>ONE</u>
I WILL ATTEMPT TO DUMP THE CENTER.

27 NOV: THE MOST DIFFICULT IN PAINTING IS TO
ELIMINATE THE NOTION OF IDEA. MY ONLY RECOURSE IS
TO TRICK MYSELF IN ORDER TO DETOUR THE IDEA. IF
THERE IS ANYTHING TO DERAIL, IT IS IDEA. I HATE THE
NOTION OF IDEA! THE ONLY WAY IS TO FORGET ABOUT
MEANING AND INSIST UPON THE PAINTING AS A
BEING . . . . i.e., INSIST UPON THE PAINTING ONLY AS A
FEELING.
IT EXIST ONLY AS A FEELING. (ABOUT NOTHING IN
PARTICULAR)
     ABSTRACT NATURALISM: THE MATERIAL DEPICTION
OF SOUL.

30 NOV: EARLIER, I SPOKE OF DIGITAZING THE
UNCONSCIOUS, ABSTRACT NATURALISM IS THE RESULTS.
I AM TRYING TO EVADE THE IDEA BY SIMPLY FORGETING
ABOUT IT + LET IT TAKE ITS' OWN COURSE; THE IDEA HAS
ITS' OWN CONSCIOUNESS.

9 DEC: PAINT IS MATTER AND CAN SERVE AS A METAPHOR
FOR SPIRIT.
     VISION HAS NO MIND.

13 DEC: GOD IS A METAPHOR FOR LOVE,
EMPATHY . . . . HUMAN COMPASSION; IT IS A NECESSARY
INGREDIANT FOR VISIONARY ART

17 DEC: I MUST RECONSTRUCT NATURE IN MY IMAGE.

STUDIO LOG 1998

3 JAN: THE SIGNAL IS NOT ELECTROMAGNETIC IT'S BIO MAGNETIC.

7 JAN: MY PAINTINGS EXIST ON THE EDGE OF REALITY.... THERE IS A GAP OF ALLOTTED
SPACE ---- ANOTHER FRONTIERE OF BEING. I FIND IT VERY FREE, AN OPEN SPACE
WITHOUT RESTRAINT + NO BOUNDRIES! I LIKE IT HERE.

8 JAN: 1215 hrs. COMPLETED THE DARK MIRROR: FOR ROY
SPACE IN MY PAINTING IS METAPHYSICAL.

11 JAN: WHAT DO I WANT? I WANT THAT WHICH EXIST BEYOND THE SEXUAL, BEYOND THE
NARRATIVE, BEYOND THE ETHNIC, BEYOND THE AUTOBIOGRAPHICAL, BEYOND THE POLITICAL,
.... I WANT THAT WHICH IS .... THAT WHICH IS NATURAL + HOLISTIC ..
I DON'T WANT POUSETTE DART'S COSMIC RELIGIOUS- TRANSCENDTAL WANDERINGS,
NO NEW AGE PHILOSOPHICAL IDEAS; IT'S BETTER TO HAVE NO IDEAS!
I WANT THAT WHICH IS FOUND .... PURE WITHOUT IDEOLOGY. FORGET ABOUT
BLACKNESS, FORGET ABOUT WHITENESS - ANY COLOR WILL DO!

15 JAN: FOLLOW THE LIGHT! NO PLAN, NO SKETCH, NO IDEA.
JUST FOLLOW THE LIGHT!

17 JAN: THE PAINTING IS IN THE HAND OF GOD.
JAZZ IS A BELIEF SYSTEM; THEREFORE IT COULB BE CONSIDERED
AS A RELIGION. IT IS MOST DEFINITELY A PHILOSOPHY.
MONK, BIRD, BUD, JOHN COLTRANE, DIZ, MILES - ...,
ALL THOSE CATS WERE PROPHETS!

24 JAN: PICKANNINY ABSTRACTION

25 JAN: IT'S SUPER BOWL SUNDAY + I AM WORKING ON BLACK, GOLD AND JAZZ
THE SPIRIT IS WITH ME, SO STRONG ... ITS' AS IF I AM
BEING RECLAIMED AS A CHILD OF GOD. ... NOT IN ITS'
CHRISTIAN CONTEXT BUT SOMETHING + MYSTERIOUS AND
WONDERFUL. I FEEL IT TO BE TOTALLY AFRICAN IN ORIGIN.

I 'AM A BACKDOOR MAN!

27 JAN: IT'S TRUE, I CAME IN THROUGH THE BACKDOOR OUT OF
BESSEMER, ALA. MY TOOL WAS VISUAL ALCHEMISTRY, I AM A VISUAL
ALCHEMIST, TAUGHT BY GEORGE WASHINGTON CARVER AT TUSKEGEE. I WAS THERE
FOR TWO YEARS VISITING HIS STUDIO.
1515 HRS. FINISHED BLACK-GOLD + JAZZ
DEDICATED TO THE MEMORY OF CHARLIE PARKER
I PAINT WHAT ONLY THE MIND CAN SEE.

29 JAN: MY INTEREST IN SUBJECT MATTER IS ONLY AS A CATHERYST.

7 FEB: COMPRESSIOISM : THE ACT OF COMPRESSING ALL EMOTIONS
INTO A COHERENT WHOLE, NOTHING IS
LEFT OUT. IT'S ALL IN THERE ... THE WHITE + THE BLACK.

19 FEB: COMPLETED BLACK MONOLITH III FOR BARBARA JORDAN 1430 HRS.

8 MARCH: 1320 HRS. STARTED EL NIÑO. DEDICATED TO THE MEMORY OF CHARLIE PARKER.
THE SUBLIME CAN ONLY BE EXPERIENCED THROUGH THE PERCEPTUAL.

10 MARCH: ICY COMETS EXCITE ME.

12 MARCH: 1955 BIRD DIED.

19 MARCH: ORNETTE'S BIRTHDAY 68 HE IS THE GREATEST! (WBGO made a mistake. Mel said it's the 9th)
IT'S ABOUT WHAT I SEE IN REAL TIME - THE EVERY DAY OCCURENCES ...
LIKE TODAY HAVING LUNCH AT FU KEE'S, IT WAS THE CHINESE NAPKIN HOLDER THAT
CAUGHT MY EYE. A PERFECT IMAGE OF NOWNESS. THE CRATING MATERIAL RETRIEVED
FROM CANAL STREET WHICH I WILL USE AS SUPPORT.
THE GRID FOR ME IS MUSIC NOTATION PAPER; I USE IT TO LAY DOWN
PIECES OF PULSATING LIGHT OF A SPECIFIC DENSITY LOCATED IN EACH TESSERAE.
PAINT IS THE MATERIAL WHICH MATERIALIZES THE LIGHT STRAIGHT
FROM MY EMOTIONS. I CAN RECORD ANY SUBJECT WHICH I CHOOSE.
RIGHT NOW I AM CHOOSING ABSTRACTION AS SUBJECT.

<u>STUDIO</u> <u>LOG</u> <u>1998</u>

3 JAN: THE SIGNAL IS NOT ELECTROMAGNETIC IT'S
BIOMAGNETIC.

7 JAN: MY PAINTINGS EXIST ON THE EDGE OF
REALITY . . . . THERE IS A GAP OF ALLOTTED SPACE . . . . .
ANOTHER FRONTIERE OF BEING. I FIND IT VERY FREE,
AN OPEN SPACE WITHOUT RESTRAINT + NO BOUNDARIES!
I LIKE IT HERE.

8 JAN: 1215 hrs. COMPLETED <u>THE DARK MIRROR</u>: <u>FOR ROY</u>
SPACE IN MY PAINTING IS METAPHYSICAL.

11 JAN: WHAT DO I WANT? I WANT THAT WHICH EXIST
BEYOND THE SEXUAL, BEYOND THE NARRATIVE, BEYOND
THE ETHNIC, BEYOND THE AUTOBIOGRAPHICAL,
BEYIND THE POLITICAL, ... I WANT THAT WHICH IS . . .
THAT WHICH IS NATURAL + HOLISTIC . . I DON'T WANT
POUSETTE DART'S COSMIC RELIGIOUS-TRANSCENDTAL
WANDERINGS, NO NEW AGE PHILOSOPHICAL IDEAS;
IT'S BETTER TO HAVE NO IDEAS! I WANT THAT WHICH IS
FOUND . . . . . PURE WITHOUT IDEOLOGY. FORGET ABOUT
BLACKNESS, FORGET ABOUT WHITENESS—ANY COLOR
WILL DO!

15 JAN: <u>FOLLOW</u> <u>THE</u> <u>LIGHT</u>! <u>NO PLAN</u>, <u>NO SKETCH</u>,
<u>NO IDEA</u>.
<u>JUST</u> <u>FOLLOW</u> <u>THE</u> <u>LIGHT</u>!

17 JAN: THE PAINTING IS IN THE HAND OF GOD.
JAZZ IS A BELIEF SYSTEM; THEREFORE IT COULB BE
CONSIDERED AS A RELIGION. IT IS MOST DEFINITELY A
PHILOSOPHY. MONK*, BIRD*, BUD*, JOHN COLTRANE, DIZ,
MILES* . . . . ALL THOSE CATS WERE PROPHETS!

24 JAN: <u>PICKANINNY</u> <u>ABSTRACTION</u>

25 JAN: IT'S SUPER BOWL SUNDAY + I AM WORKING ON
<u>BLACK,</u> <u>GOLD</u> <u>AND</u> <u>JAZZ</u> THE SPIRIT IS WITH ME, SO
STRONG . . . ITS' AS IF I AM BEING RECLAIMED AS A CHILD
OF GOD . . . . NOT IN ITS' CHRISTIAN CONTEXT BUT
SOMETHING + MYSTERIOUS AND WONDERFUL. I FEEL
IT TO BE TOTALLY AFRICAN IN ORIGIN.
<u>I AM A BACKDOOR MAN!</u>

27 JAN: IT'S TRUE, I CAME IN THROUGH THE BACKDOOR
OUT OF BESSEMER, ALA. MY TOOL WAS VISUAL
ALCHEMISTRY, I AM A VISUAL ALCHEMIST, TAUGHT BY
GEORGE WASHINGTON CARVER AT TUSKEGEE. I WAS
THERE FOR TWO YEARS VISITING HIS STUDIO.
    1515 HRS. FINISHED <u>BLACK-GOLD</u> + <u>JAZZ</u>
    DEDICATED TO THE MEMORY OF CHARLIE PARKER
I PAINT WHAT ONLY THE MIND CAN SEE.

29 JAN: MY INTEREST IN SUBJECT MATTER IS ONLY AS
A CATALAYST.

7 FEB: <u>COMPRESSIOISM:</u> THE ACT OF COMPRESSING ALL
EMOTIONS INTO A COHERENT WHOLE. NOTHING IS LEFT
OUT. IT'S ALL IN THERE . . . . THE WHITE + THE BLACK.

19 FEB: COMPLETED <u>BLACK</u> <u>MONOLITH</u> <u>III</u> FOR BARBARA
JORDAN 1430 HRS.

8 MARCH: 1320 HRS. STARTED <u>EL NIŇO</u> DEDICATED
TO THE MEMORY OF CHARLIE PARKER.
THE SUBLIME CAN ONLY BE EXPERIENCED THROUGH
THE PERCEPTUAL.

10 MARCH: ICY COMETS EXCITE ME.

12 MARCH: 1955 BIRD DIED.

19 MARCH: ORNETTE'S BIRTHDAY ⑥⑧ HE IS THE GREATEST!
(WBGO made a mistake: Mel* said it's the 9th)
IT'S ABOUT WHAT I SEE IN REAL TIME—THE EVERY DAY
OCCURENCES . . . LIKE TODAY HAVING LUNCH AT FU
KEE'S, IT WAS THE CHINESE NAPKIN HOLDER THAT
CAUGHT MY EYE . . . . A PERFECT IMAGE OF NOWNESS . .
THE CRATING MATERIAL RETRIEVED FROM CANAL
STREET WHICH I WILL USE AS SUPPORT.
THE GRID FOR ME IS MUSIC NOTATION PAPER; I USE IT
TO LAY DOWN PIECES OF PULSATING LIGHT OF A
SPECIFIC DENSITY LOCATED IN EACH TESSERAE. PAINT
IS THE MATERIAL WHICH MATERIALIZES THE LIGHT
STRAIGHT FROM MY EMOTIONS. I CAN RECORD ANY
SUBJECT WHICH I CHOOSE. RIGHT NOW I AM CHOOSING
ABSTRACTION AS SUBJECT.

STUDIO LOG 1998

J. Whitten

21 MARCH: MY PAINTINGS ARE ANIMIST STRUCTURES, THEY INCORPORATE SPIRIT IN MATTER. THE MATTER, WHICH IS THE PAINT IS A CARRIER FOR SPIRIT. SPIRIT EMBODIES INFORMATION. INFORMATION IS OF ANY SPECIFIC QUALITY DICTATED BY SUBJECT-MATTER CHOSEN BY ME. IT'S STRICTLY A MANNER OF CHOICE e.g. ABSTRACTION AS SUBJECT-MATTER, PORTRAITURE AS SUBJECT MATTER, LANDSCAPE AS SUBJECT MATTER, WOMAN AS SUBJECT MATTER, THE SUBLIME AS SUBJECT MATTER, ETC. IT'S LITERALLY ANYTHING I WANT IT TO BE.

IT'S VISUAL ALCHEMY

22 MARCH: FIGURE/GROUND SHARE A TOPOLOGICAL RELATIONSHIP, THEY ARE INTERCONNECTED.

23 MARCH: I LIKE THE NOTION OF 'OUTSIDER FORMALISM'.

26 MARCH: THE SPIRIT WAS PRESENT TODAY + ENTERED THE PAINTING. I LEFT IT THERE.

28 MARCH: IT'S POSSIBLE WORKING PURELY WITH THE ORGANIC TO CONSTRUCT A NEW IMPRESSIONISM DERIVED FROM THE TECHNOLOGICAL SENSIBILITY YOU COULD REFER TO THIS STRUCTURE AS TECHNO-IMPRESSIONISM.

I LIKE THE TYPE OF COLOR THAT SNEAKS UP ON YOU FROM BEHIND THE MIND IT'S AMBUSH COLOR!

JAZZ IS PURE JOY — AN AFFIRMATION OF LIFE EXPRESSING THE EXPANSION OF FREEDOM THIS IS WHAT I WANT FROM THE PAINTINGS. ... PURE JOY! + EXPANSION OF FREEDOM.

THE ABSTRACT AND THE REPRESENTATIONAL ARE RECIPROCALS. WHEN THEY CANCEL EACH OTHER OUT ..... ANOTHER DISTINCT AND SPECIFIC STRUCTURE EXIST. THIS IS MY STRUCTURE; I LAY CLAIM TO THIS SITE. IT'S MINE BECAUSE I WAS THE FIRST HERE ..... IT'S MINE!

31 MARCH: I TREAT THE PAINTING LIKE A WOMAN: GIVE IT WHATEVER SHE WANTS.

4 APRIL: <u>I</u> <u>AM</u> <u>A</u> <u>FREE</u> <u>MAN</u>!
I AM THE LONG RANGER LOOKING FOR A HORSE! WHERE ART THOU SILVER?

6 APRIL: ART HISTORY MUST BE COMPRESSED INTO A MODERN SIGNIFICANT RECOGNIZABLE FORM; FOR ME AT MY VISIT IN HISTORY THIS IS MODERNISM PART THREE.

7 APRIL: LADY DAY'S BIRTHDAY

12 APRIL: EASTER SUNDAY 1630 HRS. COMPLETED EL NINO: FOR CHARLIE PARKER.

25 APRIL: MY LIFE IS NOT A METAPHOR IT'S AN ACTUALITY.—

29 APRIL: BALANCE IS THE KEY TO LIFE.

6 MAY: THERE IS NOTHING SACRED ABOUT ART, ONLY LIFE IS SACRED.

21 MAY: GONE FISHING!

See You in Sept.

<u>STUDIO</u> <u>LOG</u> <u>1998</u>   J. Whitten

21 MARCH: MY PAINTINGS ARE ANIMIST STRUCTURES, THEY INCORPORATE SPIRIT IN MATTER. THE MATTER, WHICH IS THE PAINT IS A CARRIER FOR SPIRIT. SPIRIT EMBODIES INFORMATION. INFORMATION IS OF ANY SPECIFIC QUALITY DICTATED BY SUBJECT-MATTER CHOSEN BY ME. IT'S STRICTLY A MANNER OF CHOICE E.G. ABSTRACTION AS SUBJECT-MATTER PORTRAITURE AS SUBJECT MATTER, LANDSCAPE AS SUBJECT MATTER, WOMAN AS SUBJECT MATTER, THE SUBLIME AS SUBJECT MATTER, ETC. IT'S LITERALLY ANYTHING I WANT IT TO BE.
     <u>IT'S</u> <u>VISUAL</u> <u>ALCHEMY</u>

22 MARCH: FIGURE / GROUND SHARE A TOPOLOGICAL RELATIONSHIP, THEY ARE INTERCONNECTED.

23 MARCH: I LIKE THE NOTION OF 'OUTSIDER FORMALISM'.

26 MARCH: THE SPIRIT WAS PRESENT TODAY + ENTERED THE PAINTING. I LEFT IT THERE.

28 MARCH: IT'S POSSIBLE WORKING PURELY WITH THE ORGANIC TO CONSTRUCT A NEW IMPRESSIONISM DERIVED FROM THE TECHNOLOGICAL SENSIBILITY YOU COULD REFER TO THIS STRUCTURE AS <u>TECHNO-IMPRESSIONISM</u>.
I LIKE THE TYPE OF COLOR THAT SNEAKS UP ON YOU FROM BEHIND THE MIND
IT'S <u>AMBUSH COLOR!</u>

JAZZ IS PURE JOY—AN AFFIRMATION OF LIFE EXPRESSING THE EXPANSION OF FREEDOM
THIS IS WHAT I WANT FROM THE PAINTINGS . . . . <u>PURE JOY!</u>—<u>EXPANSION</u> OF <u>FREEDOM!</u>
THE ABSTRACT AND THE REPRESENTATIONAL ARE RECIPIROCAL _{s/p}
WHEN THEY <u>CANCEL</u> EACH OTHER <u>OUT</u> . . . . . . ANOTHER <u>DISTINCT</u> AND <u>SPECIFIC</u> STRUCTURE EXIST.
    <u>THIS IS MY STRUCTURE</u>; I LAY CLAIM TO THIS SITE.
    IT'S MINE BECAUSE IT WAS THE FIRST HERE . . . . . .
    <u>IT'S MINE!</u>

31 MARCH: I TREAT THE PAINTING LIKE A WOMAN: GIVE IT WHATEVER SHE WANTS.

4 APRIL: <u>I</u> <u>AM</u> <u>A</u> <u>FREE</u> <u>MAN</u>!
          I AM THE LONG RANGER LOOKING FOR A HORSE!
          WHERE ART THOU SILVER?

6 APRIL: ART HISTORY MUST BE COMPRESSED INTO A MODERN SIGNIFICANT RECOGNIZABLE FORM; FOR ME AT MY VISIT IN HISTORY THIS IS MODERNISM PART THREE.

7 APRIL: LADY DAY'S BIRTHDAY

12 APRIL: EASTER SUNDAY 1630 HRS. COMPLETED <u>EL NIÑO</u>: FOR CHARLIE PARKER.

25 APRIL: MY LIFE IS NOT A METAPHOR IT'S AN ACTUALITY.—

29 APRIL: BALANCE IS THE KEY TO LIFE.

6 MAY: THERE IS NOTHING SACRED ABOUT ART, ONLY LIFE IS SACRED.

21 MAY: <u>GONE FISHING</u>!
See you in Sept.

<u>STUDIO LOG '98</u>

4 OCT: I WANT TO REMOVE <u>ME</u> FROM THE PAINTING.

6 OCT: THE KEY TO REAL POWER LIE IN AESTHETICS. IF ONE CAN ESTABLISH AN ESTHETIC WHICH DEFINE TIME AS PRESENT IN THE MODERN TECHNOLOGICAL SOCIETY, THE POWER IS THEIRS.

8 OCT:

<u>OBJECTIVES</u>

1. REMOVE THE EUROPEAN SIGNIFANCE OF TOUCH IN PAINTING.
2. INSIST UPON THE PAINTING'S AFRICAN HERITAGE.
3. REMOVE THE NOTION OF ME.
4. STOP RELYING UPON GHOST TO DO THE PAINTING.
5. DON'T WALLOW IN THE PAST AND. WITH GOD'S HELP AVOID ROMANTIC NATIONALISM.
6. THE PAINTING IS NOT AN ILLUSTRATION OF ANYTHING.
7. ELIMINATE THAT WHICH QUALIFIES AS NARRATIVE.
8. ALLOW THE PAINT AS MATERIAL TO TAKE CARE OF THE BLACK THING.
9. DON'T SUCCUMB TO POPULIST ESTHETICS.
10. LEARN TO UNDERSTAND EXISTENCE AS BEING POLITICAL.
11. EXCEPT THE FACT THAT THERE ARE MULTIPLE DIMENSIONS IN TIME.
12. DON'T EVER BEG FOR ANYTHING.
13. EXCEPT GOD'S GUIDANCE. AND FOREVER BE FREE.
14. LEARN TO LIVE BY THE PHILOSOPHY OF JAZZ.
15. ONLY FOOLS WANT TO BE FAMOUS (AVOID AT ALL COST)
16. THE PAINTING SHOULD NEVER EXIST AS A SQUARE, RECTANGLE, TRIANGLE OR ANY OTHER EUCLIDEAN FIGURE.
17. ABSTRACT EXPRESSIONIST GESTURE IS A NO-NO.
18. THE FIGURE IN PRESENT DAY PAINTING IS OBSOLETE UNTIL I REINTRODUCE IT AS A MODERN CONCEPT.
19. THE EUCLIDEAN GRID IN PAINTING IS OBSOLETE. IT MUST BE REPLACED BY THE FRACTAL GRID.
20. STAY AWAY FROM FALSE PRIMITIVE PATTERNS.
21. AVOID ART-WORLD STRAGETIES.
22. INSIST UPON PAINT ON CANVAS.
23. ERASE ALL KNOWN ISMS.
24. REVERSE THE ABSTRACT EXPRESSIONIST'S NOTION OF SPEED, SLOW IT DOWN.
25. BALANCE THE APPOLOIAN AND THE DIONYSION AT 50/50.
26. I MUST CHANGE THE COURSE OF ART HISTORY.
27. DON'T EVER USE THE PARASE AVANT GARDE.
28. LEARN TO HATE THE HISTORY OF ART. AND ABOVE ALL DON'T TRUST IT.
29. THE PAINTING AS OBJECT MUST EXIST ON ITS OWN TERMS.
30. USE SCIENCE AS METAPHOR.
31. BE THANKFUL AND PAY HOMAGE TO HORACE PIPPIN.
32. REMAIN TRUE TO MY SELF.

STUDIO LOG '98

4 OCT: I WANT TO REMOVE <u>ME</u> FROM THE PAINTING.

6 OCT: THE KEY TO REAL POWER LIE IN AESTHETICS. If ONE CAN ESTABLISH AN ESTHETIC WHICH DEFINE TIME AS PRESENT IN THE MODERN TECHNOLOGICAL SOCIETY, THE POWER IS THEIRS.

8 OCT: <u>OBJECTIVES</u>

1. REMOVE THE EUROPEAN SIGNIFANCE OF TOUCH IN PAINTING.
2. INSIST UPON THE PAINTING'S AFRICAN HERITAGE.
3. REMOVE THE NOTION OF ME.
4. STOP RELYING UPON GHOST TO DO THE PAINTING.
5. DON'T WALLOW IN THE PAST AND WITH GOD'S HELP AVOID ROMANTIC NATIONALISM.
6. THE PAINTING IS NOT AN ILLUSTRATION OF ANYTHING.
7. ELIMINATE THAT WHICH QUALIFIES AS NARRATIVE.
8. ALLOW THE PAINT AS MATERIAL TO TAKE CARE OF THE BLACK THING.
9. DON'T SUCCUMB TO POPULIST ESTHETICS.
10. LEARN TO UNDERSTAND EXISTENCE AS BEING POLITICAL.
11. EXCEPT THE FACT THAT THERE ARE MULTIPLE DIMENSIONS IN TIME.
12. DON'T EVER BEG FOR ANYTHING.
13. EXCEPT GOD'S GUIDANCE. AND FOREVER BE FREE.
14. LEARN TO LIVE BY THE PHILOSOPHY OF JAZZ.
15. ONLY FOOLS WANT TO BE FAMOUS (AVOID AT ALL COST)

16. THE PAINTING SHOULD NEVER EXIST AS A SQUARE, RECTANGLE, TRIANGLE OR ANY OTHER EUCLIDEAN FIGURE.
17. ABSTRACT EXPRESSIONIST GESTURE IS A NO-NO.
18. THE FIGURE IN PRESENT DAY PAINTING IS OBSOLETE UNTIL I REINTRODUCE IT AS A MODERN CONCEPT.
19. THE EUCLIDEAN GRID IN PAINTING IS OBSOLETE, IT MUST BE REPLACED BY THE FRACTAL GRID.
20. STAY AWAY FROM FALSE PRIMITIVE PATTERNS.
21. AVOID ART-WORLD STRAGETIES.
22. INSIST UPON PAINT ON CANVAS.
23. ERASE ALL KNOWN ISMS.
24. REVERSE THE ABSTRACT EXPRESSIONIST'S NOTION OF SPEED, SLOW IT DOWN.
25. BALANCE THE APPOLOIAN AND THE DIONYSION AT 50/50.
26. I MUST CHANGE THE COURSE OF ART HISTORY.
27. DON'T EVER USE THE PHRASE AVANT GARDE.
28. LEARN TO HATE THE HISTORY OF ART AND ABOVE ALL DON'T TRUST IT.
29. THE PAINTING AS OBJECT MUST EXIST ON ITS OWN TERMS.
30. USE SCIENCE AS METAPHOR.
31. BE THANKFUL AND PAY HOMAGE TO HORACE PIPPIN.
32. REMAIN TRUE TO MY SELF.

STUDIO LOG '98

10 NOV: 1310 HRS. COMPLETED "FLYING HIGH": A TRIBUTE TO BETTY CARTER
17 NOV: STUART, YOUR QUESTION: "WHERE DO THOSE SHAPES COME FROM"?
       THEY ARE DIRECTLY DERIVED FROM THE EMOTIONAL SPACE, INTERNAL
       WITHOUT ANY INTELLECTUAL CHECK & BALANCES... THEY ARE DIRECT + SPONTANEOUS!

   THE PAINTING IS A MAGIC OBJECT.

19 NOV: THE PAINTING IS LIKE A WOMAN; YOU MUST GIVE HER WHAT SHE WANTS.
28 NOV: MEL STOPPED BY + WE HAD A GLASS TOGETHER... SUPER!!
29 NOV: COMPLETED BRILLANT CORNERS: HOMAGE TO MONK   1300 HRS.
                                                    T.S.
       MADE FIRST SPIRIT BOTTLE FOR MY JUNGLE JUICE.

       MONK'S TUNE

                     1999

7 JAN: I NEED MY FREEDOM.
14 JAN: IN THE BEGINNING, ART WAS SACRED, MAGIC AND PROFOUND. MY OBJECTIVE
       TODAY AS AN ARTIST IS TO RESTORE ITS' SACREDNESS, ITS' MAGIC
       AND ITS' PROFUNDITY. MY BLACKNESS WHICH IS DERIVED FROM AFRICA,
       EVOLVED THROUGH THE MIDDLE PASSAGE AND MATURED IN AMERICA.
       I AM NOT PROUD OF BEING AN AMERICAN, BUT I PROTECT IT.
       BECAUSE ITS ALL I HAVE. IN ALL TRUTH, THIS BLACKNESS IS MY
       MAJOR ASSET. MY SURVIVAL IN THE MODERN TECHNOLOGICAL SOCIETY
       DEPENDS UPON IT.
16 JAN: IT IS POSSIBLE FOR THE PAINTING TO BE FORMAL AND STILL CARRY
       SPECIFIC INFORMATION, EVEN NARRATIVE.... TO BE BOTH ABSTRACT AND
       REAL IN A MOST CONCRETE MANNER: THIS IS WHAT I WANT...
         FORMAL AND INFORMAL SIMULTANEOUSLY. SO BE IT... MAKE IT SO.
     I MAKE MAPS BECAUSE THEY EMPOWER ME TO EXPLORE NEW TERRITORY.
     I AM AN EXPLORER.
18 JAN: I FEEL THEREFORE I AM. OF COURSE I AM AWARE AND USE THE
CONCEPTUAL TOOL OF THOUGHT BUT ULTIMATELY IT IS FEELING THAT GROUNDS ME.
              LISTEN TO THE PAINTING.

       HOUSTON CONWILL VISITED THE STUDIO TODAY. WE HAD A MARVELOUS TALK!
19 JAN: THE PAINTING MUST BE LIKE A GOOD FUCK. IT MUST BE INTOXICATING!
       I AM NOT A DESIGNER; I AM NOT AN ILLUSTRATOR...
              I AM A VISIONARY ARTIST... I PAINT VISIONS.
24 JAN: MY STRUCTURES ARE ANALOGOUS TO NATURE.   HOMAGE TO
       COMPLETED THE PREDOMINACE OF TAN, BLACK AND BLUE; FOR THE DUKE
          OF ELLINGTON FOR HIS CENTENNIAL.   1610 HRS.

9 FEB: I WILL ATTEMPT TO DUMP THE CENTER.
27 FEB: COMPLETED THREE OPENINGS: DEDICATED TO JAKI BYRD 1643 HRS.
     THE FUCKING IS DUMPED + I DID IT!

STUDIO LOG '98

10 NOV: 1310 HRS. COMPLETED FLYING HIGH: A TRIBUTE TO BETTY CARTER

17 NOV: STUART, YOUR QUESTION: "WHERE DOES THOSE SHAPES COME FROM"?
THEY ARE DIRECTLY DERIVED FROM THE EMOTIONAL SPACE, INTERNAL WITHOUT ANY INTELLECTUAL CHECK + BALANCES . . . THEY ARE DIRECT + SPONTANEOUS!

THE PAINTING IS A MAGIC OBJECT.

19 NOV: THE PAINTING IS LIKE A WOMAN, YOU MUST GIVE HER WHAT SHE WANTS.

28 NOV. MEL STOPPED BY + WE HAD A GLASS TOGETHER . . . . . SUPER!!

29 NOV: COMPLETED BRILLIANT CORNERS: HOMAGE TO T.S. MONK 1300 HRS.
MADE FIRST SPIRIT BOTTLE FOR MY JUNGLE JUICE.
→ MONK'S TUNE

1999

7 JAN: I NEED MY FREEDOM

14 JAN: IN THE BEGINNING, ART WAS SACRED, MAGIC AND PROFOUND. MY OBJECTIVE TODAY AS AN ARTIST IS TO RESTORE ITS' SACREDNESS, ITS' MAGIC AND ITS' PROFUNDITY. MY BLACKNESS WHICH IS DERIVED FROM AFRICA, EVOLVED THROUGH THE MIDDLE PASSAGE AND MATURED IN AMERICA. I AM NOT PROUD OF BEING AN AMERICAN, BUT I PROTECT IT BECAUSE IT'S ALL I HAVE. IT ALL TRUTH, THIS BLACKNESS IS MY MAJOR ASSET. MY SURVIVAL IN THE MODERN TECHNOLOGICAL SOCIETY DEPENDS UPON IT.

16 JAN: IT IS POSSIBLE FOR THE PAINTING TO BE FORMAL AND STILL CARRY SPECFIC INFORMATION, EVEN NARRATIVE . . . . TO BE BOTH ABSTRACT AN REAL IN A MOST CONCRETE MANNER: THIS IS WHAT I WANT . . . . FORMAL AND INFORMAL SIMOULTANOUSLY. SO BE IT . . . MAKE IT SO.
I MAKE MAPS BECAUSE THEY EMPOWER ME TO EXPLORE NEW TERRITORY. I AM AN EXPLORER.

18 JAN: I FEEL THEREFORE I AM. OF COURSE I AM AWARE AND USE THE CONCEPTUAL TOOL OF THOUGHT BUT ULTIMATELY IT IS FEELING THAT GROUNDS ME. LISTEN TO THE PAINTING.
HOUSTON CONWILL VISITED THE STUDIO TODAY. WE HAD A MARVELOUS TALK!

19 JAN: THE PAINTING MUST BE LIKE A GOOD FUCK. IT MUST BE INTOXICATING! I AM NOT A DESIGNER; I AM NOT AN ILLUSTRATOR . . . I AM A VISIONARY ARTIST . . . . .
I PAINT VISIONS.

24 JAN: MY STRUCTURES ARE ANALOGOUS TO NATURE.
COMPLETED <u>THE PREDOMINACE</u> OF <u>TAN, BLACK AND
BLUE</u>: HOMAGE TO <u>THE DUKE</u> OF <u>ELLINGTON FOR HIS
CENTENNIAL.</u> 1610 HRS.

9 FEB: I WILL ATTEMPT TO DUMP THE CENTER.

27 FEB: COMPLETED <u>THREE OPENINGS</u>: <u>DEDICATED TO
JAKI BYRD</u> 1643 HRS.
THE FUCKING center IS DUMPED + I DID IT!

STUDIO LOG 1999

2 MARCH: NOW THAT I HAVE SUCCESSFULY DUMPED THE CENTER, MORE
FREEDOM IS IN THE OFFER. FOLLOWING THE PHILOSOPHY OF JAZZ WHICH
DEALS WITH THE EXTENSION OF FREEDOM ... FREEDOM IS AN EVOLVING
CONCEPT ... ALWAYS IN THE PROCESS OF EMERGING, EXPANDING THE PARAMETERS
OF FEELING. I CAN BE MORE PLAYFUL NOW ... NOT SO SERIOUS
WHICH YOUNGER ARE AFRAID OF AND RIGHTFULLY SO. WE SHOULDN'T TAKE
OURSELVES SO SERIOUS. ART MUST OFFER FUN + JOY OF LIFE.

5 MARCH: MOM, THE SPIRIT IS WITH ME. I CAN FEEL SISTER BETTY ROBINSON'S PRESENCE
VERY STRONGLY; SHE IS MY GOLDEN STANDARD.

7 MARCH: O.K., NOW IT'S TIME TO STOP BEING SO SERIOUS.
LET'S HAVE FUN!

17 APRIL: IF ANYBODY ASK WHAT I
AM DOING, TELL THEM THAT
I AM
DIRECTING
MATTER.

Stanley Kubrick: 26 July, 1928 — 7 March 1999
Speaking of "2001"   (70)

"tried to create a visual expeirence, one that
bypasses verbalized pigeonholing and directly penetrates
the subconscious with an emotional and philosophic
content." ... just as music does.. You're free to speculate
as you wish about the philosophical and allegorical meaning"

9 MARCH: MY WORK IS ABOUT EMBRACING THAT WHICH I AM.
I HAVE EXPEIRENCED THE REVERSAL OF CASUALTY.... MANY TIMES.

TUZ MARCH: COMPLETED CLOCKING: FOR STANLEY KUBRICK 1655 HRS.
WILL START THE YANKEE CLIPPER; FOR JOE DiMAGGIO
IMMEDIATELY!

13 MARCH: THE ISSUE OF ABSTRACTION VS. FIGURATION MUST BE SOLVED; I WILL
ATTEMPT TO SOLVE THIS PROBLEM WITH SEVEN CHARACTERS.

20 MARCH: I HAD TO RE-WORK IT. ... WASN'T WORKING I.E, NOT PENETRATING THE
SYMBOL OF STANLEY KUBRICK DEEP ENOUGH. NOW IT'S WORKING! 1530 HRS.
I AM BEGINNING TO LIKE THE NOTION OF A PAINTING AS AN. TO
ONTOLOGICAL OBJECT. I LIKE THAT.. THE MAGIC OBJECT IS CORNEY.
THE GRAPH DOES NOT SIT ON THE PLANE.. IT'S OUTSIDE OF THE PLANE
IN YOUR HEAD. THIS IS THE REAL MEANING OF GRAPHISM.

4 APRIL: EASTER SUNDAY AND I HAVE HAD A GOOD DAY IN THE STUDIO. I AM WORKING
ON THE YANKEE CLIPPER' FOR JOE DiMAGGIO. I MUST DO SOMETHING TO
CELEBRATE JOE WILLIAMS I LOVED HIM; HE WAS TRULY A MESSENGER!
I AM WILLING + READY TO DO WHATEVER GOD COMMANDS OF ME.
MY INITATION IS COMPLETE. I AM MATURE ENOUGH FOR THE NEXT PHASE.

6 APRIL: THE SUBJECT IS ONLY A VECHICLE FOR ANOTHER HIGHER ORDER OF CONSCIOUSNESS.
THE CENTER IS NOT PHYSICAL; IT IS TOTALLY CEREBRAL !! MY GOD !!

I WANT THE PAINTING TO OPERATE ON PRESENCE' NOT THE PICTORIAL.

11 APRIL: COMPLETED THE YANKEE CLIPPER'. FOR JOE D. MAGGIO   1310 HRS.

WILL START SEVEN SHADES OF BLUE: FOR JOE WILLIAMS IMMEDIATELY
AND THEN IT'S TIME TO GO FISHING! FREE AT LAST!

STUDIO <u>LOG</u> <u>1999</u>

2 MARCH: NOW THAT I HAVE SUCCESSFULLY DUMPED
THE CENTER, MORE FREEDOM IS IN THE OFFER.
FOLLOWING THE PHILOSOPHY OF JAZZ WHICH DEALS
WITH THE EXTENSION OF FREEDOM . . . . . FREEDOM IS
AN EVOLVING CONCEPT . . . ALWAYS IN THE PROCESS OF
EMERGING, EXPANDING THE PARAMETERS OF FEELING. I
CAN BE MORE PLAYFUL NOW . . . . NOT SO SERIOUS
WHICH YOUNGER ARE AFRAID OF AND RIGHTFULLY SO.
WE SHOULDN'T TAKE OURSELVES SO SERIOUS. ART MUST
OFFER FUN + JOY OF LIFE.

5 MARCH: MOM, THE SPIRIT WITH ME. I CAN FEEL SISTER
BETTY ROBINSON'S PRESENCE VERY STRONGLY; SHE IS
MY GOLDEN STANDARD.

7 MARCH: O.K., NOW IT'S TIME TO STOP BEING SO SERIES.
<u>LET'S</u> <u>HAVE</u> <u>FUN!</u>

Stanley Kubrick: 27 JULY 1928–7 MARCH 1999
    Speaking of "2001"   ⑦⓪
"tried to create a visual experience, one that bypasses verbalized
pigeonholing and directly penetrates the subconscious with an
emotional and philosophic content . . . just as music does . . . You're
free to speculate as you wish about the philosophical and allegorical
meaning"

9 MARCH: MY WORK IS ABOUT EMBRACING THAT WHICH I
AM.
I HAVE EXPEIRENCED THE REVERSAL OF
CASUALTY . . . . MANY TIMES.

12 MARCH: COMPLETED <u>CLOCKING</u>: FOR STANLEY
KUBRICK 1655 HRS.
WILL START THE <u>YANKEE CLIPPER</u>: FOR JOE DIMAGGIO
IMMEDIATELY!

13 MARCH: THE ISSUE OF ABSTRACTION VS. FIGURATION
MUST BE SOLVED; I WILL ATTEMPT TO SOLVE THIS
PROBLEM WITH <u>SEVEN</u> <u>CHARACTERS</u>.

20 MARCH: I HAD TO RE-WORK IT . . . . WASN'T WORKING
i.e, not PENETRATING THE SYMBOL OF STANLEY KUBRICK
DEEP ENOUGH. <u>NOW</u> <u>IT'S</u> <u>WORKING</u>! 1530 HRS.
I AM BEGINNING TO LIKE THE NOTION OF A PAINTING AS
AN ONTOLOGICAL OBJECT. I LIKE THAT . . THE MAGIC
OBJECT IS TO CORNEY.
THE GRAPH DOES NOT SIT ON THE PLANE . . IT'S
OUTSIDE OF THE PLANE IN YOUR HEAD. THIS IS THE REAL
MEANING OF GRAPHISM.

4 APRIL: EASTER SUNDAY AND I HAVE HAD A GOOD DAY IN
THE STUDIO. I AM WORKING ON THE <u>YANKEE CLIPPER</u>:
FOR JOE DIMAGGIO. I MUST DO SOMETHING TO
CELEBRATE JOE WILLIAMS I LOVED HIM; HE WAS TRULY A
MESSNEGER!
I AM WILLING + READY TO DO WHATEVER GOD
COMMANDS OF ME.
MY INITATION _{s/p} IS COMPLETE. I AM MATURE ENOUGH
FOR THE NEXT PHASE.

6 APRIL: THE SUBJECT IS ONLY A <u>VECHICLE</u> FOR ANOTHER
HIGHER ORDER OF CONSCIOUNESS. <u>THE</u> <u>CENTER</u> <u>IS</u> <u>NOT</u>
<u>PHYSICAL</u>, <u>IT IS</u> <u>TOTALLY</u> <u>CEREBRAL</u>!! <u>MY GOD</u>!! I WANT

THE PAINTING TO OPERATE ON <u>PRESENCE</u> NOT THE <u>PICTORIAL</u>.

11 APRIL: COMPLETED <u>THE YANKEE CLIPPER: FOR JOE DiMAGGIO</u> 1310 HRS.
WILL START <u>SEVEN SHADES OF BLUE</u>: FOR JOE WILLIAMS IMMEDIATELY AND THEN IT'S TIME TO GO FISHING! FREE AT LAST!

<u>17 APRIL</u>: IF ANYBOBY ASK WHAT I AM DOING, TELL THEM THAT I AM DIRECTING MATTER.

<u>STUDIO LOG 99</u>

22 APRIL: 1612 HRS. COMPLETED <u>PORTRAITS IN BLUE</u>: FOR JOE WILLIAMS.

22 APRIL: "TO BE CREATIVE ONE HAS TO BE OPEN" ROY DeCARAVA
            "GOD GEOMETERIZES"   "LIFE IS A GIFT"
         "THE INTELECT IS A SERVANT FOR THE SPIRIT"

4 MAY: COMPLETED THE FIRST PART OF <u>20 APRIL 1999</u> 1315 HRS,
     WHAT'S DIFFERENT ABOUT ME IN RELATION TO OTHER PAINTERS
   WHO WORK WITH PAINT AS MATTER, I USE AFRICA AS SOURCE,
     MY ART HISTORICAL REFERENCES ARE DIFFERENT.

14 MAY: RECEIVED THE NEWS FROM MANOLIS THAT NAPOLEON "THE BLUE EYED DEVIL"
      DIED, MARY & I ARE VERY SAD WE ADMIRED HIM... HE BUILT OUR
   OCTOPUS GATE & OUR ALUMINUM WIND SCREENS. WE WILL TRULY MISS HIM.
   OUR LOVE AND CONDOLENCES TO HIS FAMILY. WE PLAN TO VISIT HIS
   VILLAGE & GIVE OUR SYMPATHIES. MAY GOD BLESS HIS FAMILY.

19 MAY: LEAVE FOR AGHIA GALINI TOMORROW

         GONE FISHING!

STUDIO LOG 99

22 APRIL: 1612 HRS. COMPLETED PORTRAITS IN BLUE:
FOR JOE WILLIAMS.

22 APRIL: "TO BE CREATIVE ONE HAS TO BE OPEN" ROY
DeCARAVA
"GOD GEOMETERIZES" "LIFE IS A GIFT"
"THE INTELECT IS A SERVANT FOR THE SPIRIT"

4 MAY: COMPLETED THE FIRST PART OF 20 APRIL 1999
1315 HRS.
WHAT'S DIFFERENT ABOUT ME IN RELATION TO OTHER
PAINTERS WHO WORK WITH PAINT AS MATTER, I USE
AFRICA AS SOURRCE; MY ART HISTORICAL REFERENCES
ARE DIFFERENT.

14 MAY: RECEIVED THE NEWS FROM MANOLIS THAT
NAPOLEON "THE BLUE EYED DEVIL" DIED, MARY + I ARE
VERY SAD WE ADMIRED HIM . . . HE BUILT OUR OCTOPUS
GATE + OUR ALUMINUM WIND SCREENS. WE WILL TRULY
MISS HIM. OUR LOVE AND CONDOLENCES TO HIS FAMILY.
WE PLAN TO VISIT HIS VILLAGE + GIVE OUR SYMPATHEIES.
MAY GOD BLESS HIS FAMILY.

19 MAY: LEAVE FOR AGHIA GALINI TOMORROW
    GONE FISHING!

<u>STUDIO LOG '99</u>

1 OCT: I AM PUTTING THE BLACK EXPERIENCE INTO PAINT.
THAT'S MY GOAL . . . . . THAT'S MY OBJECTIVE

3 OCT: MEMORY IS IMPORTANT BUT I DON'T INTEND ON WALLOWING IN IT.

13 OCT: I WENT TO THE CAMPBELL FUNERAL PARLOR TODAY TO PAY MY RESPECT TO 'BAGS'* SPOKE WITH SANDRA + OFFERED MY SYMPATHY.
    BAGS WAS QUIET, SERENE, LIKE ASLEEP AGAINST AN IVORY BACKDROP WEARING HIS GOLD VIBRAPHONE ON HIS LAPELS AS ALWAYS. HE WAS HOLDING A PAIR OF BRIGHT GREEN MALLETS IN HIS HANDS WITH A LITTLE CIRCLE IN THE MIDDLE. I KNEW IMMEDIATELY THAT THE PAINTING WHICH I AM PRESENTLY WORKING ON WAS FOR 'BAGS.' MY MIND ALWAYS DOES THIS TO ME: ACTUAL PHYSICAL NATURE SERVES AS A CATALYST THROUGH EXPERIENCE OF THE PRESENT TO PROJECT THAT WHICH IS TRUE; THEREFORE, BAG'S GROOVE: FOR MILT JACKSON.

14 OCT: COMPLEXITY CAN BE CONTROLLED THROUGH SIMPLICITY.
ONE MUST LEARN TO COMPRESS.

16 OCT: HETTIE* INFORMED ME OF PETAH'S DEATH TODAY.

19 OCT: <u>THERE</u> <u>IS</u> <u>NO</u> <u>CENTER</u>; IT IS ONLY ANOTHER ILLUSION.

22 OCT: THE TRANSITIONAL AESTHETICS OF POST-
MODERNISM HAS PASSED; WE ARE NOW ENTERING THE
THIRD PHASE OF MODERNISM. IT IS BEYOND MEISM.
ONE MUST BE ABLE TO PROJECT BEYOND THE SELF . . . .
BEYOND ETHNIC, GENDER, POLITICAL + RELIGIOUS
BARRIERS.
THIRD PHASE MODERNISM DEALS WITH COMPRESSION:
TO COMPRESS ALL OF OUR MISTAKES, OUR FAILURES
AND OUR SUCCESSES. IT MUST ALL BE IN THERE.
OPPOSITES HAVE BEEN DISSOLVED

28 OCT. MY OBJECTIVE AS AN ARTIST HAS NEVER BEEN
TO BECOME FAMOUS OR TO BECOME A MILLIONAIRE.
MY OBJECTIVE IS TO BECOME A BETTER PERSON . . .
TO ACHIEVE A HIGHER LEVEL OF CONSCIOUNESS . . . TO
EXPAND THE NOTION OF FREEDOM . . . TO BECOME
LOVE . . . TO PRESERVE IDEALISM AS A NECESSARY
INGREDIENT OF BEING. I WANT A WORLDVIEW FOR THE
NEXT MILLENNIUM.
I AM A COMPRESSIONIST.

2 NOV. THE SACRED CAN BE ENCODED INTO GEOMETRY.

14 NOV: BYZANTINE ART HAS INFLUENCED MY THINKING;
I AM INTERESTED IN THE PAINTING AS SACRED OBJECT
. . . . TO SANTIFY THE OBJECT.

23 NOV: THE PAINTING AS A SACRED SURFACE SIGNIFYING
A SACRED SPACE.

28 NOV: IDEA IS ARMATURE.

18 DEC: PLAY OFF TWO EXTREMES; SHOW THE EXTREME CENTER.

28 DEC: "YOU CAN'T RUSH ART" from Toy Story II

29 DEC: ART MUST THE QUESTION, HOW DO WE SEE THE WORLD? THIS IS THE ISSUE PARTICULARLY IN ABSTRACT PAINTING.

'00s

<u>STUDIO LOG 2000</u>

3 JAN: TRY LINE AS FIGURE.

8 JAN: THE PAINTING IS AN OBJECT: THIS IS A CORRECT CERTAINTY, EVERYONE AGREES UPON THAT. THE CRITICAL QUESTION REMAINS AS USUAL; "WHAT KIND OF OBJECT?" EACH ARTIST MUST ANSWER THAT. FOR ME THE ANSWER IS; THE PAINTING AS OBJECT OF IDENTITY, NOT A NARRATIVE EXPRESSING IDENTITY BUT A CONCRETE REALITY OF MATTER. ABSTRACT AUTOBIOGRAPHICAL OBJECTS. IDENTITY ICONS

23 JAN: I AM MAKING THREE OF THESE IDENTITY ICONS FOR THE NEW MILLENIUM; THEY ARE ABSTRACT AUTOBIOGRAPHICAL OBJECTS EXISTING WITHOUT THE USE OF NARRATIVE. THE NARRATIVE BORES ME. I HATE STORYTELLING! NARRATIVE MUST BE COMPRESSED INTO MATTER, THERE IS NO NEED TO SAY IT. WE MUST SHOW IT.

4 FEB: I WANT TO CHANGE THE COURSE OF ART HISTORY.
ART HISTORY IS A RIVER AND I CAN CHANGE ITS COURSE THROUGH PSYCHIC ENGINEERING. MAKE IT SO!

7 FEB: THE PAINTING IS A MUSICAL INSTRUMENT ENGINEERED TO PRODUCE SOUND.
THIS IS MY CONNECTION TO JAZZ. THANK GOD FOR MONK!
IF THE PAINTING CAN PRODUCE SOUND THEREFORE IT CAN LEARN TO TALK I.E., LANGUAGE.... REMEMBER THE AFRICAN TALKING DRUM?

15 FEB: OH LORD, WHAT MUST I GIVE UP?

26 FEB: THERE IS A SPACE WHICH LIES BETWEEN PAINTING + SCULPTURE I CALL THIS SPACE INTERPLANAR SPACE. THE OBJECT IS NOT PAINTING OR SCULPTURE ITS A LAMINATE

29 FEB: PHILIP GUSTON IS CORRECT, THE PLANE IS IMAGINARY. HE IS ALSO CORRECT ABOUT FRANK STELLA: IT'S NOT WHAT YOU SEE IS WHAT YOU GET <u>IT</u> IS MUCH MORE MAGICAL THAN THAT! OF COURSE STELLA HAS PROVEN THAT HE CANNOT PENETRATE THIS. PHILIP COULD. MY DISAGREEMENT WITH PHILIP: THE PLANE IS MULTIPLE OCCUPING MULTIPLE DIMENSION. THERE IS AN UNEXPLORED GAP OF SPACE BETWEEN PAINTING + SCULPTURE. <u>I</u> AND <u>ONLY</u> <u>I</u> AM EXPLORING THIS. THERE IS <u>NO ONE ELSE</u>! THE PAINTING IS FINISHED WHEN THE SPIRIT ENTERS.

13 MARCH: I MET A GREEK LAST SATURDAY + I ASKED HIS NAME.
O <u>LAZARUS EMAI</u>! HE SAID. SUCH AN ANCIENT NAME
I SAID. SO POWERFUL! LAZARUS ROSE FROM THE DEAD,
TODAY I START TOTEM 2000 #<u>VI</u>. THE SPIRIT IS WITH ME.

14 MARCH: EVERYTHING IS IN GOD'S HAND. I FIRMLY BELIEVE THAT MAN HAS NOTHING WITH IT; WE SIMPLY + NAIVELY THINK THAT WE DO. PRAISE BE TO GOD! MOTHER ARE YOU LISTENING?

23 MARCH: I HAVE JUST CROSSED THROUGH TO ANOTHER LEVEL;
TOTEM 2000 #VI FOR ANNUNCIATION ; FOR JOHN COLTRANE

6 APRIL: THAT OTHER IS IDENTIFABLE BECAUSE OF ITS' MOTION.
THE SHIT VIBRATES!

HAPPY BIRTHDAY LADY DAY! 29 APRIL 1899
HAPPY BIRTHDAY DUKE!
LOVE, Jack 4 MAY RON CARTER

18 APRIL: HAPPY BIRTHDAY CHARLIE MINGUS!
I REMEMBER WHEN YOU GAVE ME THOSE CARROTS
+ TOLD ME TO "EAT MY CARROTS!" 20 APRIL: HAPPY BIRTHDAY HAMP!
23 MAY: GONE FISHING! SEE YOU IN SEPT.

<u>STUDIO LOG 2000</u>

3 JAN: TRY LINE AS FIGURE.

8 JAN: THE PAINTING IS AN OBJECT: THIS IS A CORRECT CERTAINTY, EVERYONE AGREES UPON THAT. THE CRITICAL QUESTION REMAINS AS USUAL, "WHAT KIND OF OBJECT?" EACH ARTIST MUST ANSWER THAT. FOR ME, THE ANSWER IS: <u>THE PAINTING AS OBJECT OF IDENTITY</u>. NOT A NARRATIVE EXPRESSING IDENTITY BUT A CONCRETE REALITY OF MATTER. ABSTRACT AUTOBIOGRAPHICAL OBJECTS. <u>IDENTITY ICONS</u>

23 JAN: I AM MAKING THREE OF THESE IDENITY ICONS FOR THE NEW MILLENIUM; THEY ARE ABSTRACT AUTOBIOGRAPHICAL OBJECTS EXISTING WITHOUT THE USE OF NARRATIVE. THE NARRATIVE BORES ME. I HATE STORYTELLING! NARRATIVE MUST BE COMPRESSED INTO MATTER, THERE IS NO NEED TO SAY IT. WE MUST SHOW IT.

4 FEB: I WANT TO CHANGE THE COURSE of ART HISTORY. ART HISTORY IS A RIVER AND I CAN CHANGE ITS COURSE THROUGH PSYCHIC ENGINEERING. MAKE IT SO!

7 FEB: THE PAINTING IS A MUSICAL INSTRUMENT ENGINEERED TO PRODUCE SOUND. THIS IS MY CONNECTION TO JAZZ. THANK GOD FOR MONK! IF THE PAINTING CAN PRODUCE SOUND THEREFORE IT CAN LEARN TO TALK I.E., LANGUAGE . . . . REMEMBER THE AFRICAN TALKING DRUM?

15 FEB: OH LORD, WHAT MUST I GIVE UP?

26 FEB: THERE IS A SPACE WHICH LIES BETWEEN
PAINTING + SCULPTURE
I CALL THIS SPACE <u>INTERPLANAR SPACE</u>. The OBJECT is
NOT PAINTING OR SCULPTURE IT'S A LAMINATE

29 FEB: PHILIP GUSTON IS CORRECT, THE PLANE IS
IMAGINARY. HE IS ALSO CORRECT ABOUT FRANK STELLA:
IT'S NOT WHAT YOU SEE IS WHAT YOU GET. <u>IT</u> IS MUCH
MORE MAGICAL THAN THAT! OF COURSE STELLA HAS
PROVEN THAT HE CANNOT PENETRATE THIS. PHILIP
COULD. MY DISAGREEMENT WITH PHILIP: THE PLANE IS
MULTIPLE OCCUPING MULTIPLE DIMENSION. THERE IS
AN UNEXPLORED GAP OF SPACE BETWEEN PAINTING +
SCULPTURE. <u>I</u> AND <u>ONLY</u> I AM EXPLORING THIS. THERE IS
<u>NO</u> ONE ELSE! THE PAINTING IS FINISHED WHEN THE
SPIRIT ENTERS.

13 MARCH: I MET A GREEK LAST SATURDAY + I ASKED HIS
NAME?
O <u>LAZARUS</u> <u>EMAI</u>! HE SAID. SUCH AN ANCIENT NAME I
SAID . . . SO POWERFUL! LAZARUS ROSE FROM THE DEAD.
TODAY I START TOTEM 2000 #VI. THE SPIRIT IS WITH ME.

14 MARCH: EVERYTHING IS IN GOD'S HAND. I FIRMLY
BELIEVE THAT MAN HAS NOTHING WITH IT. WE SIMPLY +
NAIVELY THINK THAT WE DO. PRAISE BE TO GOD!
MOTHER ARE YOU LISTENING?

23 MARCH: I HAVE JUST CROSSED THROUGH TO ANOTHER
LEVEL.
<u>TOTEM</u> <u>2000</u> #VI ~~FOR~~ ANNUNICATION: FOR JOHN
COLTRANE

6 APRIL: THAT OTHER IS IDENTIFIABLE BECAUSE OF ITS'
MOTION. THE SHIT VIBRATES!
HAPPY BIRTHDAY LADY DAY!
        LOVE, JACK

18 APRIL: HAPPY BIRTHDAY CHARLIE MINGUS!
I REMEMBER WHEN YOU GAVE ME THOSE CARROTS +
TOLD ME TO 'EAT MY CARROTS!'

20 APRIL: HAPPY BIRTHDAY HAMP!*

29 APRIL 1899 HAPPY BIRTHDAY DUKE!

23 MAY: GONE FISHING! SEE YOU IN SEPT.

BACK FROM EGYPT STUDIO LOG 2001

8 FEB. I WANT TO ERASE THE LINE BETWEEN PAINTING + DRAWING
   PAINTING i.e., MAKING MUST BE DIRECT WITH NOTHING IN BETWEEN.
   SAW THE SOL LEWITT RETRO SHOW TODAY AT THE WHITNEY MUSEUM.
   THEY WERE BOLD, BIG, BEAUTIFUL, INTELLECTUALLY SOUND, VERY CONCEPTUAL
   BUT ULTIMATELY ONLY DESIGNS.. ELEGANT WALL PAPER.

9 FEB: WENT TO SEE THE SHOW AFRICAN FORMS AT MUSEUM OF AFRICAN ART
   FANTASTIC, MUCH MORE USEFUL INFORMATION THAN SOL LEWITT. I AM
   MUCH CLEARER ABOUT WHAT I AM DOING. THE PAINTING AS DEVOTIONAL OBJECT
   BEYOND MERELY DECORATIVE, ELEGANT DESIGNS. GEOMETRY SERVES A HIGHER PURPOSE,
   A BRIDGE TO THE UNKNOWN.

8 MARCH: AFRICA WAS A MOTHERFUCKER! I AM READY FOR WORK + WILL WORK
   STRICTLY FROM VISION.

10 MARCH: THE PAINTING IS ORGANIC. IT TAKES ITS OWN DAMN TIME!
   MY GRIDS ARE ORGANIC, STRAIGHT OUT OF NATURE, THEREFORE, STRAIGHT
   OUT OF AFRICA. I UNDERSTAND THIS SINCE MY TRIP TO SENEGAL + GAMBIA.
   SHAPE, i.e., FORM CAN BE BUILT BY SEGMENTING THE ALL-OVER.
   THIS IS A VERY SOPHISCATED CONCEPT THAT HAS ALWAYS EVADEING
   MY THINKING. IT'S MUCH CLEARER NOW.

16 MARCH: I AM NOW WORKING WITH RECONSTRUCTED GESTURE i.e.,
   FOR EXAMPLE, TAKE A BASIC ABSTRACT EXPRESSIONIST GESTURE
   AND RECONSTRUCT IT. THIS ALLOWS ME TO BY PASS GESTURAL
   ABSTRACTION AND REACH DEEP INTO THE PSYCHE + LOCATE
   PURE SHAPE or FORM.

23 MARCH: ERASING THE BOUNDRY BETWEEN DRAWING + PAINTING GIVES
   ME MORE FREEDOM.. IT IS AN EXPANSION OF FREEDOM.
   THAT'S WHAT I WANT.. AN EXPANSION OF FREEDOM: THIS IS
   MY REAL PLASTIC CONNECTION TO JAZZ. JAZZ IS A PHILOSOPHY
   OF LIFE, IT DEALS WITH THE EXPANSION OF FREEDOM.
   I CAN IMPROVISE + STRUCTURE AT THE SAME TIME
   MY NEXT TEN YEARS OF WORK WILL DEAL WITH THIS.

31. MARCH I FINISHED JAKE'S PAINTING TODAY; IT WENT
   MUCH FASTER THAN I EXPECTED. TRULY, JAKE
   WAS WITH ME!

1 APRIL; IN ORDER TO DO WHAT I AM DOING IN PAINTING, THE
   PAINTER MUST BE ABLE TO GO BEYOND THE NOTION OF SELF.
   THEY MUST TAKE CARE OF IDENTITY ISSUES FIRST, JUST AS I DID
   IN THE 1960'S. ONLY THEN CAN ONE PENETRATE A
   HIGHER PLANE OF THOUGHT.

BACK FROM EGYPT <u>STUDIO</u> <u>LOG</u> <u>2001</u>

8 FEB. I WANT TO ERASE THE LINE BETWEEN PAINTING +
DRAWING
PAINTING i.e., MAKING MUST BE DIRECT WITH NOTHING
IN BETWEEN.
SAW THE SOL LEWITT RETRO SHOW TODAY AT THE
WHITNEY MUSEUM.
THEY WERE BOLD, BIG, BEAUTIFUL, INTELLECTUALLY
SOUND, VERY CONCEPTUAL BULT ULTIMATELY ONLY
DESIGNS . . ELEGANT WALLPAPER.

9 FEB: WENT TO SEE THE SHOW <u>AFRICAN</u> <u>FORMS</u> AT
MUSEUM of AFRICAN ART. FANTASTIC, MUCH MORE
USEFUL INFORMATION THAN SOL LEWITT. I AM MUCH
CLEARER ABOUT WHAT I AM DOING. THE PAINTING AS
DEVOTIONAL OBJECT BEYOND MERELY DECORATIVE,
ELEGANT DESIGNS. GEOMETRY SERVES A HIGHER
PURPOSE: A BRIDGE TO THE UNKNOWN.

8 MARCH: AFRICA WAS A MOTHERFUCKER! I AM READY
FOR WORK + WILL WORK STRICTLY FROM VISION.

10 MARCH: THE PAINTING IS ORGANIC. IT TAKES ITS' OWN
DAMN TIME! MY GRIDS ARE ORGANIC, STRAIGHT OUT
OF NATURE, THEREFORE, STRAIGHT OUT OF AFRICA. I
UNDERSTAND THIS SINCE MY TRIP TO SENEGAL + GAMBIA.
SHAPE, i.e., FORM CAN BE BUILT BY SEGMENTING THE
ALL-OVER. THIS IS A VERY SOPHISCATED CONCEPT THAT
HAS ALWAYS EVADEING MY THINKING. IT'S MUCH
CLEARER NOW.

16 MARCH: I AM NOW WORKING WITH RECONSTRUCTED
GESTURE i.e., FOR EXAMPLE, TAKE A BASIC ABSTRACT
EXPRESSIONIST GESTURE AND RECONSTRUCT IT. THIS
ALLOWS ME TO BYPASS GESTURAL ABSTRACTION AND
REACH DEEP INTO THE PSYCHE + LOCATE PURE SHAPE or
FORM.

23 MARCH: ERASING THE BOUNDARY BETWEEN DRAWING
+ PAINTING GIVES ME MORE FREEDOM . . IT IS AN
EXPANSION OF FREEDOM. THAT'S WHAT I WANT. . AN
EXPANSION OF FREEDOM; THIS IS MY REAL PLASTIC
CONNECTION TO JAZZ. JAZZ IS A PHILOSOPHY OF LIFE, IT
DEALS WITH THE EXPANSION OF FREEDOM. I CAN
IMPROVISE + STRUCTURE AT THE SAME TIME
MY NEXT TEN YEARS OF WORK WILL DEAL WITH THIS.

31: MARCH I FINISHED JAKE'S PAINTING TODAY; IT WENT
SO MUCH FASTER THAN I EXPECTED. TRULY, JAKE WAS
WITH ME!

1 APRIL: IN ORDER TO DO WHAT I AM DOING IN PAINTING,
THE PAINTER MUST BE ABLE TO GO BEYOND THE NOTION
OF SELF. THEY MUST TAKE CARE OF IDENTITY ISSUES
FIRST, JUST AS I DID IN THE 1960'S ONLY THEN CAN ONE
PENETRATE A HIGHER PLANE OF THOUGHT.

STUDIO LOG

APRIL 7: REALITY IS A CAMOUFLAGE

APRIL 8: MY PAINTINGS HAVE A LIFE OF THEIR OWN.
RIGHT ON TIGER!!

14 APRIL: JUST FINISHED BODY AND SOUL: FOR GEORGE
SEGAL 1924–2000

16 APRIL: IF I HAVE TIME . . SOMETHING MUST BE DONE
FOR JOHN LEWIS of the MJQ . . . SOMETHING IN BLACK +
WHITE . . . VERY FORMAL
BE EXTREMELY AMERICAN + BLACK AT THE SAME TIME

22 APRIL: I MUST LEARN TO REMOVE MYSELF FROM THE
PAINTING . . . MORE DISTANCE IS NECESSARY.

26 APRIL: A MISTAKE WITH MY USE OF VISION: VISION yes,
but constructed VISION . . THAT WHICH COMES AND IS USED
TO BUILD UPON.

30 APRIL: THE AVOIDANCE OF FETISH IS NECESSARY IN
ORDER TO PENETRATE THE SUBLIME.

1 MAY: THERE IS NO HORIZON!
THE SPIRIT IS WITH ME.

23 MAY: GONE FISHING!!

On September 11, 2001

I was on Lispenard Street, where I had lived since 1962, with some firement that morning because of a gas leak on our block. Do you remember the voice of somebody saying, "Holy shit!" from the first video clip that was available on TV? That's my voice. Anyway, all of a sudden, there was this horrible sound coming our way, and we all looked up to see this enormous plane flying right over our heads, and it went directly into the North tower. And when it hit, the first thing you saw was this big crystal burst—before you saw any smoke, before you saw any flame, the sky was just filled with crystal glass, which was hard to see on the video. It was like this huge chandelier, that's what you saw. One of the firemen said, "Oh, it's a horrible accident," and so did my tenant and a few others among my neighbors. But my gut feeling was, "Hey man, that was no goddamn accident." I had two years of Air Force ROTC at Tuskegee, so I know that you can muscle a plane's steering and take it off course. Believe me, that plane was like an arrow shooting at a target. The firemen stopped what they were doing, got into their trucks, and took off immediately toward the Trade building; while some of us were still arguing about whether or not it was an accident, the second plane hit the South tower. Watching those poor people jumping out of the building was the most terrifying and horrible experience. To think that close to 3,000 people were murdered in my neighborhood—nobody gets over that, you really don't. So I made a vow to do something about it.

I moved to Tribeca in 1962. What that means is I saw the first bulldozers that went down there and dug the first hole, the dedication, all of that. I saw all of that. And I saw it step by step, all those years it took to build those structures. I was right up the street. Went down there with my bike practically every day, 'cause I was very interested in the whole construction of that, the architecture, everything that was going into it. So, I'm a person who can say that I saw the thing from the beginning

Originally published as "9/11," in Stuart Horodner, ed., *Jack Whitten: Memorial Paintings* (Atlanta: Atlanta Contemporary Art Center, 2008), 52. Reprinted courtesy of Atlanta Contemporary Art Center.

to the end. I watched it go up step-by-step, and I watched it go down step-by-step. That's the absolute truth. That gives me a kind of conviction. One of the most powerful accounts we have when something horrible goes down in history is the fact that somebody witnessed it. Even if there's no documentation; even if the perpetrators went out of their way to hide all documentation. The fact that somebody can stand up and say, "Hey man, I saw this, I witnessed it."

2008

—STUDIO LOG—

27 FEB 06: Back in the studio: I've started 9•11•01 with mixed
emotions. [. . .]

It's been so long between paintings: . . . . it's like starting new.
I'm frighten, not knowing where or how to start. The painting for
9•11•01 is something I must do. The new studio is great! A dream
come true. I sincerely feel blessed to have such a space. May God
be with me.

19 MARCH: There is no need to rush: history is on my side. Art is
dependent upon time/space. My time is now. Space is an overlay; it
wraps around time, very much like a cocoon. I could call my space
"cocoon space" as a description. My interest is the 'global mind' I
have no need nor interest in the local. Local shit bores me! I have no
interest in the autobiographical identity issue bullshit, especially
from Black artist. The shit is boring! Get over it. Move on + stop
wallowing in memory. The now is much more exciting. Please do not
show me anything that doesn't go beyond the self!

24 MARCH: MY AMBITION IS TO RECONSTRUCT NATURE.

30 MARCH: 01000–1830

31 MARCH: Implied Geometry i.e., geometry used to suggest a
EUCLIDEN STRUCTURE without totally defining it; not forming a
parameter, As in Tiepolo's painting used by Appiah* on the cover of
his new book COSMOPOLITANISM: The implied equilateral
triangle that commandeers the plane; I want this frontal boldness
for 9•11•01
Reconstruction allows me to bypass gravity; Gravity is no longer
an issue.
0900–1830

PAINT AS OBJECT

1 APRIL: 1300–1900

2 APRIL: 1500–1930 MY AGENDA IS PAINTING

3 APRIL: The real significance of acrylic collage is PAINT AS OBJECT. My first example of acrylic collage is thin skins of acrylic paint which were removed with a carpenter's block plane from the thick surfaces of early 1973 process paintings. These skins were glued to paper + also to canvas. These represent the first acrylic collage paintings. At first, these collages were thought of as shapes. I used these skins exclusively throughout the 1980s to construct the <u>SITE</u> paintings. In 1990, the skins became thin sheets of acrylic squares placed upon a grid. It was not until 2005 that I conceptually thought of them as actual object i.e., the paint as object. My understanding of AB/EX painters is paint was subject and later both Johns + Stella insistence upon the painting as object. Now the paint is object used in the service of building the painting as object which is a strange ironic twist upon the history of painting. Paint as object gives me the freedom to do anything I want. I can use anything as subject or a combination of things. If there is anything of value to be used from Post Modern aesthetics, this is the most valuable asset worthy of preserving. It is all coming together.

—STUDIO LOG—

cont. from 3 APRIL: My only request is more time from God: Give me my health + more time + I promise to do the rest. History is mine.

[. . .] The painting <u>9•11•01</u> is a promise to all those people murdered. To think that I saw @ 3,000 people killed in my neighborhood is a horrible thought. My objective in this painting is to put their suffering in paint. This is my job + I owe it to all those poor people. <u>9•11•01</u> is not meant to be a nice painting: There will be no decoration or feel good fantasies. What I saw will haunt me forever. Boiled flesh, bone, blood, piss, feces, personal belongings, construction debris, toxic chemicals, concrete emotions, hair + body parts . . . . . these are the elements to work with. It is a painful painting for me to make + ask for God's help.

4 APRIL: 1200–1900

6 APRIL: 01100—   Great opening last night; Good to see everybody. . . Good show!
This show will hold-up anywhere in the world! Nice mix.
RECONSTRUCTION OF NATURE GIVES ME THE OPPORTUNITY TO PLAY GOD. I ENJOY THIS! WHAT A FANTASTIC OPPORTUNITY! I HAVE ALWAYS ENVIED THE NOTION OF GOD. I ENVY BIRDS; I AM VERY JEALOUS OF THEM. THE AIRPLANE IS O.K., BUT IN FLIGHT WITHOUT ANY MECHANICAL DEVICE OTHER THAN FLESH + BONE IS MIRACLEOUS. MY NEXT BET IS TO PLAY GOD. ANYBODY WILLING TO PLAY WITH ME? ANY LADIES IN PARTICULAR?
[. . .]

7 APRIL: 1200–1800

8 APRIL 1200–1900 COOPER SATURDAY PROGRAM CAME TO
STUDIO M.G.* IS DOING A GREAT JOB. THIS YOUNG LADY
IS SPECIAL. NICE BUNCH OF KIDS.

11 APRIL: 1300–1930 OFF TO L.A. . . . . MAY GOD BE WITH ME.

15 APRIL: 1200–   WE BURIED BILLY: Brother,* Toots,* Jesse*
+ I. It was extremely sad. One of the most sad things ever to do.
Now, he is at rest; no suffering.
I LOVED MY BROTHER.

16 APRIL EASTER American: 1300–1900 [. . .]
→ When I am working, I simply follow the density of Light.
Particular i.e., specific densities create their own image, therefore
I don't have to worry about image; it takes care of itself.

18 APRIL: 01100–1900 YOU GOTTA BE ABLE TO THINK LIKE
JOHN COLTRANE TO DO WHAT I AM DOING IN PAINTING:
THE LIGHT EXIST IN SHEETS, JUST LIKE COLTRANE TOLD
ME. THE SHIT FALLS ACROSS THE PLANE; THEREFORE,
IT'S PLANAR LIGHT. (COLTRANE USED THE WORD 'WAVE')
MY AMBITION IS TO CHANGE THE COURSE OF ART HISTORY.

20 APRIL: 01030–1930 GERALD JACKSON TOLD ME TO
"IT'S TIME TO TAKE IT OUT!" I HEAR YOU GERALD + I
UNDERSTAND YOU.

21 APRIL 0900–1900

25 APRIL 1200–1830

Martha Gutierrez, James "Brother" Monroe Cross (Whitten's brother), Martha "Toots" Tunson (Whitten's sister), Jesse Whitten (Whitten's brother)

27 APRIL 01000–1900   MY COLOR STRUCTURE IS A
<u>FRAGMENTED COLOR</u>, i.e., IT IS BUILT UPON
FRAGMENTATION WHICH IS A DIRECT RESPONSE TO
COLLAGE WHICH IS A FRAGMENTED FORM. <u>I</u> <u>FOUND</u> <u>MY</u>
<u>IMAGE</u> <u>IN</u> <u>PAINT</u> <u>TODAY</u>.
JAZZ MUST BE TRANSLATED PHILOSOPHICALLY; IT IS NOT
GOOD ENOUGH TO TRANSLATE ONLY A NARRATIVE
'JAZZY LOOK' IT MUST BE METAPHISALLY SO WITHIN THE
MATERIAL WHICH IN MY CASE IS PAINT. (TO MANIFEST
ITSELF IN THE MATERIAL. THIS IS MOST DIFFICULT!)

March 2, 2006

— NIGGERISM —

Take every known philosophical premise shake in bag of flour and
fry in hot cast iron skillet of pure lard. Simmer in World Art History
for Five Hundred years and serve immediately. Niggerism should be
served hot preferably in a warm climate near the sea. If seaside is not
available, urban environment may be substituted with no loss of
flavor but enjoyment factor could be hindered. I prefer a round table
of granite or other natural stone. Guest should be dressed with
minimal amount of clothing or whatever weather conditions dictate.
Less attire contributes to sensual fulfillment; this is of paramount
importance for fullness of experience.

Do not overcook. Process of simmering requires ultimate control
of intuitive knowledge. Avoid any mechanical timing device. When
removing from hot skillet, do not place on paper towel ~~for~~ to absorb
fat. Place in ceramic covered bowl, set aside for Five Hundred years
until remaining ingredients are ready. Cook must be willing to travel,
for most ingredients are hard to come by and are not readily availabe
in local markets. If ingredients are not found in global marketplace,
cook must be able to create substitutes. Be warned . . . the creation
of substitute ingredients must adhere to precise cultural norms. Taste
must not be ~~sacrificed~~ comprised for lack of practical availability.
Extreme measures may be necessary to maintain quality control.
Experimentation is of utmost necessity. Do not depend upon store
bought produce. Seek alternatives. If a particular ingredient is not
located within the immediate culture, cook must investigate other
cultures. It is a proven an acceptable fact that two or more cultures is
better than one. Keep in mind that all ingredients are inclusive
without adhering to fundamental premises. It is enjoyable to mix +
contaminate ingredients that doesn't provide adequate flavor. The
success of this dish totally depends upon flavor. Flavor is the
psychological underpinning of cooking.

Be careful of invited guest: Establish priorities in connection to objective. Objective should be one of enjoyment. One is invited to have fun and if person is not capable of having fun, do not invite! Age is not a criteria. Sex of guest is not a criteria. Sexual persuasion is not a criteria. Religious views are not a criteria + is not encouraged. Belief in God is not a criteria. Politicians not invited. Pope may be present if he abides by rules. Not necessary to believe in Heaven or Hell. Must accept philosophical notion of death in life. Everything happens in Life. Color of skin not a criteria.

Not necessary to have money but donations accepted. toward payment of expenses. Memory as tool of self-identity is accepted as long as its weight does not impede objective of enjoyment. Cook prefers that racial identities be checked at the door. Professional Racists not invited. Consumption of alcoholic beverages, wine + raki in particular is encouraged in moderation. Guest must be able to dance. Dancing is ritual + Cook recognizes dance as important ingredient of cooking + physical exercise. Rest and relaxation is a must. Knowledge of World Art History is a primary criteria. Application of critical thinking to all matters concerned is constructed as work in progress

—STUDIO LOG—

28 APRIL 06: 01100–1900 / 29 APRIL 01100–1830 / 30 APRIL 01030–1600

2 MAY 06: 01130–1900 WE ARE <u>ON</u> THE PLANET NOT <u>IN</u> IT! THE HISTORY OF PAINTING HAS BEEN CONFUSING ON THIS POINT. MY SPACE IS LIKE LOOKING THROUGH A LENS. IT ALLOWS ME TO SEE THE OTHER SIDE. THE OTHER SIDE OF WHAT? I DON'T KNOW.

3 MAY: 01100–1900

4 MAY: 0900–1900   5 MAY: 00900–1900 / 6 MAY 01100–<u>RECONSTRUCTED GESTURE</u> WILL EXPLAIN LATER.

7 MAY: 1500–1900 I AM PUTTING EVERYTHING I KNOW ABOUT PAINTING INTO <u>9/11/01</u>.

8 MAY: 0800–1900 JAZZ MUSICIANS IMPROVISE: I WANT MY COLOR TO BE IMPROVISATIONAL i.e., CREATE A CONCEPTUAL STRUCTURE AND GO AGAINST IT. . . . . . TO DESTROY IT! TO MAGNIFY IT! TO FRACTURE IT! TO PRESS IT INTO A MOLECULAR SPACE! 100% FRACTALITY!

9 MAY: 01000–1900

10 MAY: 01000–1900 I AM TRYING TO DEFEAT HISTORY.

11 MAY: 01000–1900 I AM MANIPULATING MATTER . . . . . . HAMMERING IT . . . . MOLDING IT INTO ANY FORM of STRUCTURE I WANT.

12 MAY: 0930–1900   13 MAY: 01130–1600 14 MAY: 1300–1730

15 MAY: 0930–1900 (OBSOLETE) KELLIE,* MY INTENTION IS TO RENDER THE WORD 'ABSTRACTION' PASSE; SOMETHING OF THE PAST. I WILL SUBSTITUTE <u>PRESENCE</u> IN PLACE OF <u>ABSTRACTION</u>. I AM TAKING IT BACK TO ITS ORIGINAL SOURCE WHICH IS AFRICA. I HAVE THE VISUAL DNA + I AM GOING TO USE IT!

16 MAY: 01000–1930 17 MAY: 0830–1900 IN JAZZ, TO IMPROVISE, ONE MUST KNOW THE <u>KEY</u>, THE <u>MELODY</u>, THE <u>TIME</u>. KNOWING THIS ALLOWS YOU TO IMPROVISE WITH OTHERS. I USE THIS SAME SYSTEM IN PAINTING: I KNOW THE <u>SUBJECT</u>, THE DENSITY OF A PARTICULAR <u>LIGHT</u> + I KNOW THE <u>BEAT</u>. THE DIFFENENCE IS I AM NOT IMPROVISING WITH A GROUP. I IMPROVISE WITH <u>MYSELF</u>, THE <u>CULTURE</u> + THE <u>TIME OF DAY</u> i.e., <u>NOW</u>

18 MAY: 0900–1600   19 MAY: 0900–1930   20 MAY: 0900–
THE PAINTING AS OBJECT IS EQUIVALENT TO NATURE I.E., IT RUNS PARALLEL TO NATURE . . . . . . NOT THE SAME AS NATURE OF COURSE, BUT PARALLEL . . IT'S ANALOGOUS PAROUSIA—PRESENCE, ARRIVAL, BEING, SUBSTANCE (A NEAT GREEK WORD, SOUNDS GOOD TO ME!)
I PUT ON THE LAST TESSARAE AT 1540 HRS (9•11•01)
        WHAT A RELIEF!! <u>TIME TO GO FISHING!!</u>

Disaster in the studio: I worked all year on the memorial painting 9•11•01 10' x 20' Returned from Greensboro, North Carolina, for the Hard Time–High Time show at Weatherspoon Museum, went to studio on Monday morning. The painting had pulled loose from the wall! Extremely upset + depressed. Realized that I must regain my composure + deal with its' rescue methodically. Managed to remove most of the objects like shop-vac, paint cans, flower pots, from underneath. A REAL MESS!

No sign of canvas rupture. I am truly thankful nor I or anyone was hurt. Painting is @ 500 lbs. Enlisted Mel Edwards, Guy Goodwin, Tom Tryforos + four students for work in rescue. Constructed two heavy-duty pulley systems to cieling with heavy rope as safety harness. Was able to remove all wood strips with contact cement (from sliding doors) no visible damage. Returned painting to floor face down + sponged <u>back</u> with water in order to pull canvas taut. It's working! Next Friday, crew will return to hoist painting back to wall.

The symbolism of 9•11 is very much in this painting, that's obvious. Scary but true. No one has said that painting can be dangerous.

Saw the Richard Serra show at Gagosian. Fantastic! a marvelous example of materiality as applied to sculpture. I feel a connection to him. Even his surfaces were very painterly in connection to process. There is no message other than the material. I LIKE THIS. It's a good lesson for me: concentrate more on material + process; allow the painting to speak for its self; get rid of all symbolic gestures; develop planar edge only as perimeter if object; no framing devices; no centering devices; avoid pure notion of spectrum color structures; concentrate upon minerals as in elements of iron, cobalt, sulfur, copper, lead, silica, etc.

Very important for me to hold the line. Remove all sentiment. Allow the 'surface as symbol.' Remove all narrative references. I want an extreme but truthful notion of abstraction—The fact of my making the painting is political; There is no need to preach!

Guy Goodwin said: 'Jack Whitten dissects painting' I like this. Painting is organic. It continues to evolve, very much like a specic of animal, plant. It grows without ever developing a final characteristic except for the fact of its being. To put painting under a microscope + dissects as if I am cutting a frog apart! To study its cellular structure, skin, bone, vessels circulatory system, nervous system. The studio becomes a lab for experimentation. I must make sure to have everything I need in the studio. My ambition now is to establish the next course for painting, that which will define painting for the next hundred years!

I am capable of this. I read about what the scientist are doing in technology of all disciplines both physical scienes and biological scienes. These people explore by specializing: I want to do the same in painting.

My mentor is George W. Carver. Carver specialized in peanuts. Where is my peanut? In my case, I must invent the peanut.

—STUDIO LOG—

28 OCT 06—I grow space in my garden; during the summer time in Aghia Galini, I grow Chinese, Japanese + a variety of vegetables including amarath which I like very much. In New York during the fall, winter + spring . . . . I grow space. Space comes in many varieties but I am especially interested in a particular variety which I have cultivated. I call it multidimensional space; it is a space which I breeded for the modern technological society. It encompasses a world view. With this space I can navigate the modern society. My compass is mind i.e., world mind. It's been around for a long time but I recently rediscovered it. My plan is to patent this space because I invented it. The paintings are my patent. There is no protection from the government or any established patent office; therefore I must paint in order to secure my discovery.

SPACE GARDEN '06

31 OCT: Space is organic; you can grow it; you can manipulate it; therefore you can use it for any purpose. Light and space are totally reciprocal: one depends upon the other for cognition. Soul is defined through light + space. J.C.* knew this. Charlie Parker knew, Miles knew, Monk knew + K.D.* knew. They all taught me. I continue to learn from the jazz musicians. Saying that space is organic does not prevent or deter its' physicality, that's why its' application to painting is one of construction. The painting is constructed! It's like building a house, a cabinet or any other structure. It can exist as concept + remain perceptual but painting as object exist only through matter.

10 NOV: I have just discovered a work on paper from 1964; written on the surface is a statement, "I AM SOUL". Is it possible that I found what I am looking for in 1964 but perhaps did not take it seriously or simply did not understand its' significance? What is soul?

We as blacks say that we possess soul, which is a certain feeling about life + myself. Soul encompasses a worldview. Is soul the same as God? I do not know. Can soul be used as a substitute for God? I am bored with the concept of God. Monk had soul. Miles had soul. Yardbird had soul. John Coltrane had soul. All of the major jazz musicians had soul. I have soul; I am soul. How does this understanding of soul apply to what I am doing in painting? The formal element of space is mine! I own space! Space is my subject. Could soul be my content? This requires more thought. <u>IT MIGHT BE THAT I'VE ALWAYS HAD WHAT I AM LOOKING FOR.</u>

29 NOV: David Budd once told me that 'something was swept under the rug after Pollock' Whenever I pressed him for clarification he could never give me a straight answer. I've just finished Francis Frascina's <u>Pollock + After</u>. In Rosalind E. KRAUSS essay: <u>Greenber on Pollock</u>, she quotes Greenberg: 'The picture plane as a total object represents space as a total object.' She proceeds to critique Greenberg 'The stolid neutrality of 'space as object,' materialist and literal, would cede its place to the idea of the pictorial field as 'mirage'. . . . Could this be what David was trying to express?

Greenberg's original assessment of Pollock was correct but if Rosalind's critique is correct then Greenberg's later assessment was a total failure! <u>Space as object interest me</u>. My recent works on paper were conceived as 'Space Gardens," i.e., a place to cultivate space . . . . . if it can be cultivated, as in growing, therefore its' an object. David Budd gave me valuable information; information that I could not understand at that time and obvious he did not understand, but he felt it! Budd is right + I think that 'space as Object is the key!

All of my years of experimentation of space as object continues to be a tough nut to crack! I am approaching ⑥⑦ I do not know how much time I have left. If I can prove through paint 'space as object' then it has all been worth the effort. Stella felt this but he could not produce it. I know of <u>no</u> <u>one</u> but myself who is capable of doing it. Whatever time I have left, it will be spent on pursuing this one objective: Space as Object.

Space as Object

It can look like a lot of things but never can it look like anything in particular. It should always exist between things; even its' presence should remain unknown, and unidentifiable. It can relate to figure, landscape, symbol, geometry of any type, text, history → of any degree, i.e., sexual, religious, autobiography = IT CAN BE ANYTHING!
OBJECTIVE: TO TRANSCEND ALL KNOWN SYMBOLS; THEREFORE, ITS' STRUCTURE IS LOCATEN WITHIN THE SUBLIME AS NONE SPIRITUAL ENTITY. (BUT LEAVES THE DOOR OPEN) The light is purely physical i.e., concrete not mystical. We know that light is physical not only through personal + subjective observation but also from sciene. Light can be compressed, it can be slowed down, stretched out + hammered into various viscosities as in fluid dynamics. Light has temperature: extremely cold as in liquid hydrogen or hot is plasmic fluidness measured in Kelvins. It can be non-visibable to the naked eye only with the help of instruments designed for that purpose. Light can be structured for specific purposes, e.g., to carry information as in optical fibre.

My list of light's physical properties is not complete because I do not know its' total dimensions but the amount I know convinces me of being on the right track. This is a unique period of history: we have advance knowledge of the micro + the macro simultaneously; this is the first time in history that this has occurred. I think that a particular worldview is encoded ~~within~~ because of this . . . . a worldview that did not exist previously. A worldview that requires flexibility, of thought, mobility in movement, non-static, always in motion with no center. Dimensions are multiple interdependent entities capable of digestion space/time. Light feeds these dimensions and <u>mind</u> is the residue. I would like to think that mind is the

controlling factor . . . an ends within itself, but I think not. . . . .
There is something else out there! Please do no ask me to explain
this; it's only a hunch.

In no way am I pleased or comfortable with my thinking. I can
not accept Mattisse's notion of the 'easy armchair' My blackness
does not allow me. The ultimate pressure + stress of survival is too
severe. I do not have Mattisse's luxury!

Van Eyck's <u>LUCA MADONNA</u>, Cranach's <u>Venus</u>, Anonymous
artist's <u>Dance of the Rats</u>, Botticelli's <u>Venus</u>? Medieval wood carvings
of Christian Symbolisms, Worm's Cathedral (St. Peter's Cathedral)
I saw + learned so much in Frankfurt, Heildenberg, Sperey: Art has
the ability to transcend history! My joy is I am a part of this! I extend
the tradition which crosses all borders race, gender + belief systems.
Art is total freedom like Jazz it expands the notion of freedom. Jazz
is art.

N.Y.C. J.W.
6 Dec 06

STUDIO LOG

My past is catching up with me; All of that funky 1960's psychedelic expressionism raises its' ugly head! I don't know what to do . . . should I embrace it or exterminate every impulse. Everything I've been trying to get rid of is insisting upon prominence. My recent editing of early works on paper from 1963 to the present is what ignited this. The photographic aspect I embrace for I think that it's correct. It's all the psychic imagery which I used to call Psychic Realism is what's bothering me. How much of this stuff should I accept? Is imagery necessary? Abstraction has become meaningless. Does what I am doing define Modernism's Third Phase? Is there such a thing as Third Phase Modernism?

All systems must be tested. I am not dealing with religion: I am constructing concrete mind. Does concrete mind contain images? Automatism was an invention of early surrealists; I am not a surrealist! + I cannot accept automatism. Space as Object explains only the formal aspect of my structures but all that other shit, I still do not know. What am I supposed to do? Is there anyone whom I can talk to? If I saw evidence in another painter's work, I would feel better but there is no one. I am lonely. There is no one to talk to.

The image is photographic; therefore, I must photograph my thoughts. This statement was the beginning of my journey dating to 1964. The photograph is the only graphic representation that illustrate my thinking but I am not talking about mechanics. This stuff is totally mental! Mind as matter is my mantra + paint is my matter. I think that I am own the right track but some feedback would certainly help. The need for clarity of thought, clarity of process, clarity of purpose (in connection to identity issues) keeps me focused.

<u>Looking for Billy</u> is a series of current works on paper.

Billy's death still grieves me. I am hurting + logically acceptable of time. It takes time to overcome death, But my Southern background stews in sentiment. [. . .]

Back to painting. I want to do, I am already planning to do a painting for Billy whether he likes it or not! Everything i.e., my foundation constructed for the past forty-two years . . . . I am convinced . . . . it's a sound foundation, built on the bedrock of Southern Sensibility. I've drilled deep, my foundation will hold! As I move further from the present I am also moving closer to the present. It's the MICRO/MACRO of my Being. Every time zone is embraceable. I have no problem with past and I face the future with optimism.

—STUDIO LOG—

9 JAN 07: Painting is the art of seeing: This statement is a known fact, there is nothing new in this; what's new is my saying it at this particular point in history. We have always known this but we were sidetracked by all sorts of conceptualized strageties about painting done by people who were not capable of seeing. I CAN SEE! The present crisis in painting is not my problem. Market driven strageties are destroying painting. My job is to paint what I see. It is not a quest for truth, for spirituality or any other symbolism. It is not a critique of society or its political systems or any other problematic concerns of civilizations. It is simply about seeing. Therefore I am a keeper of the flame. All significant artists before me, throughout history, have simply painted what they see.

Seeing is the mind's eye. Literally simplistic understanding of retinal responses to light is not painting. . . . That is illustration. Light is physical, painting is mental i.e., mental light. Let us not confuse the light of nature with the light of mind. They are two different realities. Physical realities are grounded in material matter. Mental realities are grounded in Mind as matter. Physical components of light is used through raw matter (paint) in order to manifest mind into object (the painting as object) = SPACE AS OBJECT.

11/Jan: Went with Tom* to see the Brice Marden show. Tom's eye is growing with good instinct. Brice's show is impressive . . . a real accomplishment. It shows consistency, perservence, control, restraint, order, conceptual, pretty good sensual content. There are a lot of good things in this show <u>but</u> ultimately I find it to cautious + totally without risk. He is not an innovator! Brice is a classical painter very much within the modernist tradition of Classicism. This is a good thing but it is not the mark of genius. It is very good painting.

Art is <u>organic</u> + painting is a particular <u>specic</u> of art. Art evolves the same as any organic being + like organisms in nature. . . It's all in the genes.

13 JAN

Went to Benny Andrews memorial today at the Great Hall. It was good to see Jack White, Adger,* DANNY JOHNSON, Ed C.,* D. Driskell,* John Moore, Tyrone,* Stanley Whitney, Michael Brenson, David Hammons, Lowery,* Richard Mayhew: There is a community with lots of Integrity. . . Everybody is doing their thing, Benny did his. . . his way. He is different from me but that's the way it should be. The good thing is everybody is doing their thing. We are intact as a people!

Alice Coltrane just died. She was good, enjoyed her music.

Now, we have lost a lot of people: It sends me a signal. . . . . I must go forward without any stops—no cleaver conceptualizations—<u>I</u> <u>must</u> <u>let</u> <u>it</u> <u>all</u> <u>hang</u> <u>out</u>. At 67 I don't know how much time I have left. Death doesn't frighten me. I am always prepared. LIFE IN DEATH IS MY MOTTO. SO BE IT. I want thirty more years more years if GOD is willing.

14 JAN: I MUST DISSOLVE THE NOTION SELF IN ORDER TO DO THIS THE notion of SELF IS AN INTELLECTUAL INVENTION. IT'S GOT NOTHING TO DO WITH PURE MIND: I WANT PURE MIND: NO ETHNITICITY, NO NATIONALISM, NO GENDER, NO POLITICS, NO GOD
PURE MIND IS A SPIRITUAL EQUALVENT TO MINIMALISM i.e., NO ATTACHMENTS TO ANY THING OTHER THAN MIND
—I AM TIRED OF BEING TESTED—

—STUDIO LOG 07—

29 MARCH: I am now working totally by call and response without concern for imagery. The tessera is placed (laminated) on the canvas; the next tessera response to an exact density of light recorded in the brain from the first tessera. This exact density of light carries a sound which I can hear mentally, hence call + response. Blues and therefore Jazz started from this humble beginning of slaves working in the fields.

31 MARCH: The essence of flatness is COMPRESSION. Physical properties along with its psychological implications is compressed into the skin of paint. The painting as object is skin and only skin. The stretcher bar or any other support is a separate entity; including its depth i.e., thickness of bar or configuration of shape <u>is NO issue</u> in paintings' three-dimensionality. Everything is located within the skin. Clem's emphasis upon flatness as spatial element is part of the dialogue. When compression is complete i.e., absolute, the spatial element takes care of itself. It is a mistake for painters to attempt to control space; it only leads to further examples of pictorial illusionism. Space is already built into matter.

Multi-dimensional space is the soul of matter and therefore beyond our control. At this juncture one is nature. Pollock was right.

Knowing all of this is important + very invigorating intellectually, ... but what + how must I use this Knowledge? I AM A PAINTER. MY AGENDA IS TO PAINT. Obviously there is a lot of shit involved with saying this. What do you want Whitten?

'Stone is a forehead where dreams grieve
Without curving waters and frozen cypresses
Stone is a shoulder on which to bear Time
With trees formed of tears and ribbons and planets'

F.G.L.*

12 APRIL: How about debunking the whole notion of abstraction? More Later. Very sorry to hear of Sol Lewitt's death. I learned so much from him. He made me question what is painting; His work was a challenge to my thinking about painting.

My paintings are antidote to the speed of today's society.

A place to rest + enjoy quiet.

ABSTRACTION IS A THING OF THE PAST. IT IS OVER! OBSOLETE! ITS' ROLE WAS TO SHOW THE UNIT I.E., THE MOST BASIC COMPONENT OF PAINTING IS THE 'POINT' (•) THIS IS THE BASIS OF ALL FORM. THE NEXT PHASE OF MODERNISM I.E., THE THIRD PHASE WHICH INCLUDES ME, IS TO SHOW WHAT'S POSSIBLE. FINALLY I HAVE REMOVED MYSELF FROM THE PAINTING. RIGHT ON!!

STUDIO LOG

27 MAY 07: IT'S TIME TO GO FISHING! We leave for Aghia Galini tomorrow. Manolis called; it has been raining. Thank God!

So nice to leave for the summer with a show at PS1. I have done my part. It's up to the Art Public. Hope Alex* can get some results. It's been a good year in the studio; The E-Stamp paintings will be shown at Alex's 12 Sept—PS1,—Berlin in the summer + Dusseldorf in the Fall . . . not bad for a kid from Bessemer.

Transcendence is outside of me. It's not 'I' that must transcend 'ME' The material i.e., the paint as matter must transcend must transcend its physical properties . . . to transform its' self into 'psychic reality' It's not me! Therefore, I am free to roam! Spirituality takes care of its' self. I have no control of that, Art history has confused the hell out of me! Fuck art history! Especially Modernist Western Art History. It's time for payback. It has made me suffer, now its' time that I make it suffer! I always knew that history was organic. So, lets make it suffer!

My plan for the summer: ① Catch octopus ② Catch Fish ③ Carve wood ④ take care of my olive trees + garden ⑤ Drink lots of wine + Raki [. . .] Have a good summer.

Jack

Studio Log

5 Oct 07: ~~The doxa of~~ Making a painting is a pure organic a prior act arrived at as a fact ~~of evolunationary processes.~~ history. ALL dimensions of Space/time is compressed into a single act. It is a spontaneous product of nature; ~~a surrogate of the self.~~ nature being a surrogate of the self. ~~All aprior mental conditions including the present with unknown advances of sensations vibrating from The past, present + future must~~ the future is compressed into a single act. Subject is a necessary instigator acting as a detonator for the possibility of expeirence. Expeirence confirms my existence as a human being. Without the conscious ~~act of~~ awarness of expeirence my existence is only a residue of nature.

My studio is stocked with various materials from different ~~manufactures~~ sources. The bulk of my supplies are unprocessed raw materials. Some are taken directly from nature e.g., ink from cuttlefish + octopus which I catch egg shell from the Libyan Sea where I spend the summer months, various herbs which grow in the countryside near my house such as, thyme, pokeberry, onions, rosemary, sage, chamomile, bones, blood, walnut shells, coffee + tea pomegrante, tree barks various insects which I catch! I also use inorganic products such as, rust graphite, mica, silica, recycled glass, pulverized mylar, a numerous variety of powdered pigments, gold + silver leaf, bronzing COPPER powders, mineral, earth, ash, stone, IORN RUST wood dust, floor sweepings!

My mediums ~~include~~ are primarily acrylic polymers, acrylic gel mediums, urethane both gloss + matte. Because of extreme experimental processes I tend not to use oil I prefer acrylic because of their flexible tough surface films and their ability to be used ~~as suspensions.~~ Sometimes I use acrylic paint manufactured from different manufactures. I also use suspensions along with coating processes. The three processes are: 1. paint 2. suspension 3. coating.

(Acrylics may be used as:) The rapid availability of a wide range of materials allows me to react to a specific subject: The subject dictate the materials + processes used. Depending upon the nature of subject processes may be dry, wet, transparent, opaque, with various combinations. I insist that the process be a spontaneous ~~active activity~~ done in the silence of the private environment of the studio. My ~~pre-~~methdology of making a painting consist of three separate processed:

CONSTRUCTION—DECONSTRUCTION—RECONSTRUCTION

The first process of construction is the most difficult + the most mysterious: the subject must be <u>translated</u> ~~into matter via~~ <u>metaphysically</u> ~~transportation~~ into matter. ~~is the most difficult~~ Deconstruction is a manual process which involve any number of procedures which may include <u>heat</u> (both dry + wet), cold (freeze), grinding, sanding cutting ~~breaking into tesserae~~. Reconstruction is the ~~lamination~~ process of ~~choosing~~ selecting + laminating the acrylic tesserae onto canvas as acrylic paint collage. This is to most sensitive process because the act of seeing + require the most experience + feeling ~~is~~ simultaneously guided by <u>call</u> + <u>response</u> to extremely sensitive singals of light emanating directly from the brain. This is where color structure is born. It is can be cerebral or visceral depending upon the emotional response to subject. Content is also constructed at this juncture existing outside of any conceptualized ~~conscious awareness~~ consciousness; At this point ~~the brain~~ MIND is must already be previously programmed to act. The Reconstruction process will make or break the painting; If this process is effective then we know the painting works. ALL information that defines the painting is carried by light. This includes all emotions encoded ~~as~~ within expression.

The history of a people, in my personal case, that of the slave: uprooted, torn + dismembered, piece by piece, fragmented, +

scattered to various geographical locations far removed from orgins of birth, language, religion, political constructs, family, adrift in the <u>MIDDLE</u> <u>PASSAGE</u>, abandoned by all known civilized norms of behavior: This to must be addressed.

All people must insist upon + indeed deserve the right to livilhood. Charity is only a necessity provided by others to those less unfortunate to the access of livihood for any legitamate or non-legitamate reason. Charity must never be allowed to become habitual for it saps the spirit + prevents any development of both spiritual + physical manifestion of a people.

Tuskegee Institute, now known as Tuskegee University, in Tuskegee, Alabama ~~was~~, originally funded by Rich American Capitalists + founded upon the premise that Black People must be educated in the manual arts of agriculture, brick laying, tailoring, carpentry, mechanics i.e. ~~skilled~~ trade skills that provided skilled labor to the Capitalists industries ~~of the Capitalistic regimes~~. In term, these learned skills would provide a livilhood to a disenfranschied people. This concept was wholeheartedly accepted + promoted by leading Negro educators of the late ~~nineteen~~ eighteen + early nineteen century such as Booker T. Washington. ~~My~~ Du Bois a leading social philosopher of American Pragmatism rebelled + sought to establish as emphasis upon the humanities to be included as a necessary universal ingredient of education. I am here today because of Du Bois. My first advance schooling was at Tuskegee Institute as a pre-med student and AFROTC. As a young man possessing talent in both music + Art I was not encouraged to study arts out of fear of economic realities. In other words the theory was: I would not be able to make a living.

A disinfrancished people living on the margins of society always bear the blunt of economic repression. Economic repression provide the breeding ground for social unrest. It discourages stable family units. Inhibits spiritual growth. Prevents + indeed aid in the destruction of the physical body by denying excess to quality food + quality medical services. Education which is the <u>guarantee</u> for any progressive advances in the general health of society must be open to all and adhere to established universal standards of learning. Without excess to quality education a chronic lower class is established. This chronic lower class will continue to fester + openly bleed the life force from any society.

I am what I am because of the culture that forms me. No one can escape the influence of culture. We are the culture. My interest in art is that of a tool: Art as tool can be used to shape culture. A friend recently accused me of being naive. I thought about that accusation seriously. I did not take it lightly. I like folk-art and the main reason that I like it is because of its naviety! How marvelous it must be to experience naviety and idealism in our Modern Technological Society! The jaded, hypocritical, nilists, old fashion greed, narcissciatic gore of instant self. gratification, apathetic scorn for the homeless + powerless ~~aggreavated~~ promoted by the globalization of capital without any regard of country, race, gender religion, the continuous rape of the planet perperuated by a chosen few solely for profit: IS THIS WHAT WE WANT OF OUR CULTURE?

My paintings instruct me how to live. They instruct me how to construct the structural components ~~of living~~ of my life. In the silence of the studio, I have learned to listen to my paintings. They don't yell at me nor do they command. They are not vindictive. They do not threaten. There is no carrot + stick scenario of any kind. There are no promises or rewards. Guilt is no issue. They have taught me to erase the notion of revenge however ~~horofic~~ the profundity of its' premise. ~~Inclusiveness is a necessary ingredient of art. To exclude is a form of hate~~ Freedom is only possible when there is no need for the OTHER. By eliminating the need of the OTHER, we expeirence the expansion of freedom. This is what ~~I want. This is what I got.~~ my paintings have taught me.

I am still learning from them

J. Whitten
Oct 07 N.Y.C.

*SEE FINAL EDITING SENT TO MUMOK FOR 7 NOV TALK
IN VENNA

—STUDIO LOG—'07

3 DEC 07: "The image is photographic; therefore, I must photograph my thoughts" I wrote this on my studio wall in 1964. Today in the Dentist office while staring at the baseboard which was a bland institutional beige like color, worn from use, I was observing my usual edietic imagery expressed as landscape. . .
I HAD A REVELATION: <u>THE</u> <u>SPACE</u> <u>IS</u> <u>EDIOGRAPHIC.</u>
Automatically I said the space is photographic which is misleading (there is no mechanical instrument involved, only the brain!) The ancient Greek word 'edios' which means <u>image</u>, later applied to <u>ICON</u> is more apporiate. Our word photographic is also Greek / PHOTO (as in light) GRAPHIC (as in draw) = TO DRAW WITH LIGHT or TO COPY WITH LIGHT i.e., of course using a mechanical process which is the camera. This revelation clarifys (I'VE ALWAYS INSISTED UPON CLARITY) It is a mistake to say the space is photographic. Maybe mistake is not the right word; There was no other graphic example except the photo of what I was feeling. Art is structured feelings. Now, I can structure my feelings using space as a tool. <u>LIGHT</u>—<u>SPACE</u>—<u>TIME</u> is interconnected. The image can be anything of my choosing. This is a tremendous expansion of freedom! I am a Jazzman. I adhere to Jazz as a Philosophy. The expansion of freedom is the philosophy of Jazz.

    <u>Ediographic space</u> gives me a spatial concept to work with. ALL spatial concepts throughout our history of art embodies a worldview. I must define this worldview: It's first of all ① multidimensional ② all inclusive ③ transparent ④ man + only man as responsible creature without dependence upon concept of God: ⑤ Ethics as necessary survival tool ⑥ dissolution of national boundaries which includes ethnicity + nationalistic identities. ⑦ No fixed center of the universe (to be continued)

4 DEC: Now that I have more freedom, I can let go. The only important thing is <u>to follow the light.</u> Everything else takes second place including the importance of subject. If there is subject, I will find it in the material. Once in California I accomied my Brother Bill on a fabric buying expeidation; it was lots of fun! I did not understand fully what was going on. Finally I asked Bill 'Where do your ideas for design of clothing comes from?' He thrust the fabrics in my face + rubbed them with his fingers: From the material! He said.

Now I understand. The paint as matter is the material + light is carried within the material. <u>Light is matter</u>. All information is carried within the light. If I let go + follow the light . . . the world is my oyster!

I am aware of the spiritual signifance of this and I accept this. Spirituality is a necessity. It's ancient and it can be modern. I want a modern concept of spirituality. This spirituality must <u>not</u> depend upon any known belief system: It's not Christian—not Buddhist—Not Islam—Not Hindu Not Jewish—Not Orthodox—If I follow the light . . . . THE Belief SYSTEM AS SUBJECT WILL REVEAL ISTELF IN OTHER WORDS: I WILL FIND <u>IT</u> or MAYBE <u>IT</u> WILL FIND ME.

Tomorrow is my birthday, I am thankful for my health + thankful for my family. I have a lot to be thankful for. The universe has been good to me.

6 DEC. B.B. KING SAID "I HAVE A SWEET LITTLE ANGEL' RENAISSANCE PAINTERS ACTUALLY PAINTED ANGELS! THEY BELIEVED IN ANGELS! WHAT IF I BELIEVE IN ANGELS? COULD THE <u>PAINTING</u> BE AN ANGE? MARY IS AN ANGEL, THEREFORE IF I MADE A PAINTING OF MARY IT WOULD BE AN ANGEL.

MAKE IT SO! <u>BAR CODE #I: RUTILANTION FOR MARY,</u> 2007 80" x 36"

—STUDIO LOG '08—

4 JAN: We Lost MIKE GOLDBERG. ED CLARK IS LEFT. That generation is over . . . . all second generation ab/ex. Mike didn't like the term but that's history. He was a good painter. I always enjoyed talking to him. We met in the early sixties probably at the Cedar Bar. I knew his paintings from Allan Stones + Martha Jackson plus several shown at 10 St. Gallery. His death hurts + I hate so badly that I didn't visit him. [. . .] I'm sorry Mike. . . . I wanted very much to see you.

7 JAN: NOT TO BELIEVE IN GOD IS AN INTELLECTUAL LUXURY THAT I CANNOT AFFORD. I AM IN DEBT TO GOD. MY PLAN IS TO USE MY LIFE AS COLLATERAL. I HAVE NO INTEREST IN INTEREST.

8: JAN: I SAW THE NINTH CIRCLE TODAY: PROCEED WITH CAUTION.

12 JAN: IT WAS A VERY RISKY SITUATION + I WAS RIGHT TO BE CAUTIOUS: IT WAS LIKE BREAKING THROUGH THE 'LIGHT BARRIER'. I'M O.K. FOUND SOME GOOD STUFF: LIGHT IS COMPOSED OF MULTIPLE LAYERS. . . . I DIDN'T THINK THAT IT WAS SO FLAT. . . THEY ARE THIN FLAT LAYERS LIKE PHILO DOUGH . . . . SOFT + FLAPPY. . . IT IS DEFINITELY NOT HARD NOR IS IT ATMOSPHERIC. MY MISTAKE FOR YEARS I THOUGHT IT WAS ATMOSPHERIC! BUT NOTHING FLOATS IN IT. . . IT IS INLAID LIKE MOSAIC BUT MULTIPLE LAYERS OF MOSAIC. IT REMINDS ME OF VIEWING AN ARCHELOGICAL SITE WHERE THE LAYERS OF TIME ARE EXPOSED. FREEDOM HAS EXPANDED; IT IS JAZZ. EVERYTHIG WE EXPERIENCE IS COMPRESSED INTO

LIGHT . . . INCLUDING SPACE. ALL THAT I AM—MY WHOLE IDENTITY IS COMPRESSED INTO LIGHT. <u>I AM FREE MAN.</u>

19 JAN: I HAVE INVENTED NATURE. OR ANOTHER WAY OF PUTTING IT, I HAVE DISCOVERED ANOTHER TYPE OF NATURE; ONE THAT EXIST ONLY IN THE MIND. I REMEMBER E. KANT'S NOTION OF NATURE BEING WHATEVER THE MIND IS CAPABLE OF PERCEIVING. BILL RUBIN TOLD ME THAT THERE IS NO SUCH THING AS A PERCEPTUAL PAINTING. HE WAS ONLY HALF RIGHT. THE <u>IDEA</u> i.e., THE PERCEPTION CAN EXIST MATERIALLY. I AM TELLING YOU WHAT I HAVE FOUND! MIND IS MATTER + IT CAN MANIFEST ITSELF THROUGH LIGHT. EVERYTHING IS COMPRESSED IN LIGHT INCLUDING SPACE—MEMORY—TIME. IT'S JUST AS THE BIBLE SAID "LET THERE BE LIGHT." <u>RIGHT ON!</u> I HAVE MY RAW MATERIAL + I CAN MAKE ANYTHING I WANT. THERE ARE NO BOUNDARIES IN SPACE. <u>JAZZ EXTENDS FREEDOM.</u>

29 JAN: When they ask what am I doing? Tell them that I am following Paul Cezanne's footsteps. Tell them that I am reconstructing nature.... I am reconstructing nature in my image. . . Tell them that I am a child of God. Tell them that I am free. Tell them that I have been to the mountaintop. Tell them that God is with me. Also tell them that I listen to B.B. King, Satchmo, Dizzy, Miles. Tell them that I listen to Saint Coltrane & the Duke of Ellington. Tell them that I listen to James Brown. Tell them that I take evening walks with Kenny Dorham, Monk and the Count of Basie. Tell them that I saw the 'Bird' last evening riding a pink pony. Tell them that Bags said hello. Dexter, the Jolly Green Giant was present so was the 'Hawk', and the 'Judge' presided over a jam session. Tell them that the scene is clean. Tell them that we bathe ourselves in Light. Tell them that there is another side... No! tell them that there are many sides. Then tell them that there are many levels & Most of all tell them that the center is dependant totally upon where we are at any given location in space/time. Tell them that memory is necessarry. Tell them that Memory is the indivisable remainder! Tell them that Memory is who we are & tell them not to fear death. Please do not wallow in Memory. Please do not seek revenge.

Tell them that we have the power of
the blues. BLUE POWER. Listen & pay
attention to the Blues. The Blues shall set
you free! Do not deny the presence of any
people. Always acknowledge that we are one.
Color was an accident of nature & race was
predicated by men. Tell them not to lose
their energy over questions of race. Be one
with Nature. Learn to flow like a river,
to fly like a bird, to crawl like a snake,
to swim like a fish. To be alert & fast,
like a hawk. Know your colors & camouflage
yourself when needed. Do not be afraid to
retreat but at the same time do not be afraid
to attack. Learn to trust & depend upon
the power of BLUE. Respect others, especially
women. Do not be afraid of Gay People. They
are different & they have something you do not
have. Pay attention to gay people & learn.
Do not be afraid of work. Work defines
life. Without work we are nothing.

2 FEB: I PROMISE THE NEXT PAINTING IS FOR JAMES BROWN

⁎ BAR CODE II R²⁰08 PAYBACK.
     THE FIRST RHYTHM ONE HEARS WAS THE MOTHERS' HEARTBEAT;
THEREFORE, I HEARD MONK BEFORE I WAS BORN. JAZZ HAS ALWAYS
BEEN WITH ME BUT ANNIE BELL DIDN'T KNOW IT! THATS O.K.
SHE HEARD THE RHYTHM OF GOD AND IT WAS NOT MADE AS
A RESULT OF TWO THINGS STRIKING. THIS WAS & IS THE
ORIGINAL SOUND: THAT WITHOUT STRIKING.

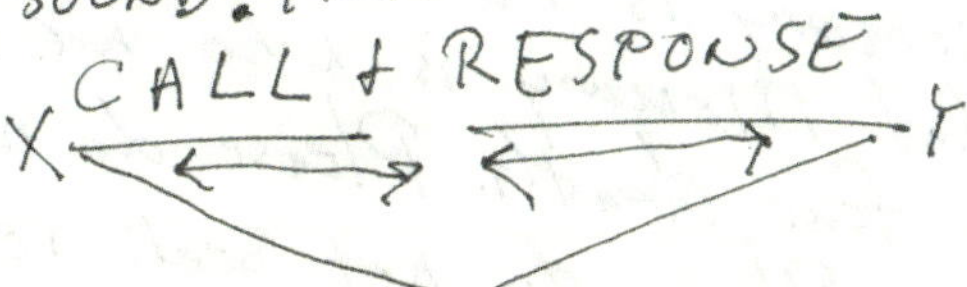

—STUDIO LOG '08—

29 JAN: When they ask 'what am I doing'?

Tell them that I am following Paul Cezanne's footsteps: tell them that I am reconstructing nature . . . . . . I am reconstructing nature in my <u>image</u>.

Tell them that I am a child of God. Tell them that I am free. Tell them that I have been to the mountaintop. Tell them that God is with me. Also tell them that I listen to B.B. King, Satchmo, Dizzy, Miles. Tell them that I listen to Saint Coltrane + the Duke of Ellington. Tell them that I listen to James Brown. Tell them that I take evening walks with Kenny Dorham, Monk and the Count of Basie. Tell them that I saw the 'Bird' last evening riding a pink pony. Tell them that Bags said hello. Dexter, the Jolly Green Giant was present so was the 'Hawk' and the 'Judge' presided over a jam session. Tell them that the 'scene is clean' Tell them that we bathe ourselves in Light. Tell <u>them</u> <u>that</u> <u>there</u> is another side . . . No! <u>tell</u> <u>them</u> <u>that</u> <u>there</u> <u>are</u> <u>many</u> <u>sides</u>. Then <u>tell them that there are</u> many levels + most of all tell them that the center is dependent totally upon where we are at any given location in space / time.

Tell them that memory is necessary. Tell them that memory is the 'indivisable remainder' Tell them that memory is who we are + tell them not to fear death. Please do not wallow in memory. Please do not seek revenge.

Tell them that we have the power of the blues. <u>BLUE</u> <u>POWER</u>. Listen + pay attention to the Blues. The Blues shall set you free! Do not deny the prsence of any people. Always acknowledge that we are one. Color was an accident of nature + race was predicated by men. Tell them not to lose their energy over questions of race. Be one with Nature. Learn to flow like a river, to fly like a bird, to crawl like a snake, to swim like a fish. To be alert + fast like a hawk. Know your colors + camouflage yourself when needed. Do not be afraid to retreat but at the same time do not be afraid to attack. Learn to trust + depend upon the power of BLUE. Respect others, especially women. Do not be afraid of Gay People. They are different + they have something you do not have. Pay attention to gay people + learn.

Do not be afraid of work. Work defines life. Without work we are nothing.

2 FEB: I PROMISE THE NEXT PAINTING IS FOR JAMES BROWN
*BAR CODE, II 2008 PAYBACK.
THE FIRST RHYTHM ONE HEARS WAS THE MOTHERS' HEARTBEAT; THEREFORE, I HEARD MONK BEFORE I WAS BORN. JAZZ HAS ALWAYS BEEN WITH ME BUT ANNIE BELL DIDN'T KNOW IT! THAT'S O.K. SHE HEARD THE RHYTHM OF GOD AND IT WAS NOT MADE AS A RESULT OF TWO THINGS STRIKING. THIS WAS + IS THE ORIGINAL SOUND: THAT WITHOUT STRIKING

CALL + RESPONSE
[drawing; triangle labeled "X" and "Y" at either end, with arrows underneath "CALL" and "RESPONSE"]
THE GAP WHERE THIS SOUND IS FORMED

STUDIO LOG 08

6 FEB: <u>THE</u> <u>ME</u> <u>PERIOD</u> <u>IS</u> <u>OVER</u>. We are free as a people. I am the whole. I am the beginning. I am the ancient one. I am the modern one. I have been selected to see the world. I am filled with joy. The Lord is with me. From now on I must go without fear. I must present myself without prejudice. History is with me we walk in the presence of the Lord. What is the Lord? The Lord is the energy that governs the universe. One cannot question the Lord nor can anyone fully understand the Lord. The Lord exist beyond intelligence. Reason is important for it serves as a catalyst to our making sense of space/time. The universe has its' own structure. We are only a part of this structure. It <u>allows</u> us to be here.

I have always said that wolrdvew is compressed in space (I am speaking of the formal element of space in painting) My space is recognizable as <u>inlay</u>. I have created an inlaid space in painting. This space was first recognizable in ancient mosaics. Modern art i.e., moderism has been trying to rediscovery this space. This is what modern painting is about. Of course we have plenty examples of 'off shoots' as in plants some of them are interesting but none of them have the power to convert energy into worldview.

No one is talking about this; therefore, I must write. This is what attracts + this is what I am interested in painting.

ZIZEK!* I HAVE DISCOVERED A 'PARRALLEX VIEW' IN FIGURE GROUND! <u>FANTASTIC</u>!

8 FEB: COMPLETED BAR CODE #II, <u>LATERAL SHIFT</u> AT 1530 HRS.

It's amazing! <u>A</u> <u>truly</u> <u>magnificent</u> <u>painting</u>! Everything I know about black, white, gray went into this painting. Lateral shift is a metaphysical term. . . Zizek explains it as a parallax existing in the gap between nounmenon + phenomenal. I think that he is correct.

I've been consciously working with this notion since the early 70's
It's interesting to note for the record, my dentist, Dr. Lehrer was
fitting a crown for my front teeth. Ajusting a little bit back + forth.
Sort of trial + error until it fit perfectly. Each time the adjunct tooth
would affect its position, refering to the tooth, I said 'Its's lateral
shift' Dr. Lehrer said yes they work lateral to each other. I said
"That's a beautiful title for a painting" It is so marvelous to find art
in experience. The back pocket rule continues to be true.

Connie Butler just left. What a smart, thoughtful lady. We had a
good talk about what I am doing + how to proceed with discussion
at MoMA in March. I hope we have a responsive audience, my
advice was seek clarity. Be blunt. Be provocative don't be afraid to
discuss the political in my work. Compression is the key word for me.
The information is compressed into matter. I am a metaphysician. I
study matter + its application as paint. Paint as matter is the raw
material. I can construct anything I want.

You might like to know that the bar code for <u>LATERAL SHIFT</u>
was taken from <u>THE N.Y. TIMES</u> check it out!

People must understand that I am a painter. I have studied +
taught painting all of my adult life. I study painting as painting. I
<u>start</u> with painting to <u>arrive</u> at → social issues, i.e., identity elements
1. gender 2. race 3. politics etc. It is not the other way around. Young
black artists + indeed artists of all colors are putting the cart before
the horse! First build the horse the other uses come afterwards. [. . .]

—STUDIO LOG 08—

5 MARCH: Meaning ~~is~~ has become the enemy of art. There are things in life that should have no meaning. They are simply there. . Like Mt. Everest. Art is such a thing. As long as I know that I am in the presence of it: that's good enough. Art will take care of itself.

I have often said that Fundamentalism is the greatest threat to world peace. It never occurred to me that Fundamentalism also applys to art. [. . .] Fundamentalism in politics, in religion is a known fact. But art?

The insistence upon meaning is a simplistic either-or philosophical situation that left unchecked will suffocate art. Only the bourgeois mind need + insist upon meaning. The artist does not need meaning. Presence is good enough.

Today, because of Puralism we must be very specific about our intentions in art. The artist, from a personal-subjective point of view must <u>state</u> their intentions. There are risks in doing this for the artist don't necessarily understand their intentions. We must be willing to take the risk. For me, my intentions are based upon a specific art historicalness:

<u>SLAVERY</u> <u>SEVERED</u> <u>MY</u> <u>AFRICAN</u> <u>ROOTS</u>. Since then I have been actively reconstructing my roots. This has not been easy. Because of art, this reconstruction process has been collective. I have always known that I am doing something that is much larger than I. Luckily, first phase European Moderism provided me with the tools of understanding what happened. Because of contamination, enough evidence remained; it was just a manner of decoding the evidence. Second phase American Moderism required further decoding because of a vast quanity of additional evidence. Fortunately, my being born in 1939 + reared in the south, educated + having the opportunity to travel + meet historical figures I have been given the time to sift through the evidence. I am thankful for that.

I have digested a lot of information + now find myself in a position to construct the third phase of global modernism. So my intentions are historical: it starts in Africa passes through Europe through the New World of America and continues to travel outwards i.e., globally. I am shaping global aesthetics. My objective in painting is <u>constructing worldview</u>.

DECLINATION: a bending or sloping downward; deviation from the horizontal or vertical. ② an oblique variation from some definite direction ③ the angle formed by a magnetic needle with the line pointing to true north. ④ a polite declining or refusal ⑤ (archaic) decline, deterioration; decay ⑥ (astronomy) the angular distance of a heavenly body north or south from the celestial equator.

* NOTE: SEE <u>HOMECOMING</u>: <u>FOR MILES</u>, 1992

Even abstraction must become specific in its intentions. I do not accept abstraction as an ends within itself. Abstraction for me is a means, not an end. Same with formalism, for me it serves only as a means not an end. I must clarify this further.

Opening tonight at American Academy must run!

<u>HOMECOMING</u>: <u>FOR MILES</u>, aka <u>DECLINATION</u>
Homecoming, aka, <u>DECLINATION</u>: FOR MILES
1992

noumenon—of mind—an object reached by intellectual intuition, without the aid of the senses.

phenomenal—apparent to or perceptible <u>by the senses.</u>

13 MARCH 08: The talk with Ms. Butler at MoMA went well; i was pleased. [. . .]

Last night went to hear ZIZEK AT N.Y.P.L. He is on to something. [. . .] I understand his use of the <u>GAP</u> and its difinitely applicable to painting. Toward the end of AB/EX people, including myself spoke of the problem of abstraction vs. figuration. <u>THIS IS INCORRECT</u>. THERE IS NO PROBLEM IN ABSTRACTION VS. FIGURATION. THERE IS NO PROBLEM IN PAINTING VS. SCULPTURE. <u>THE REAL</u> <u>ISSUE</u> <u>IS</u> <u>THE GAP</u>! The GAP is a third entity existing in another space/time. Sort of like an alternative universe. I do not understand all of this but I can smell it! The GAP IN PAINTING is identifiable in painting through the structure of compressed space. My earlier use of multidimensional space is correct but it must be compressed further i.e., compressed into the skin of paint. I am so excited about this; Thanks to ZIZEK for clarifying this. Of course its' my original theory of 'extreme middle' from the early sixties but clarity improves everything!

I do not agree with ZIZEK's concept of God as the big other. If this is the case it would impose a limit upon freedom. I am a jazzman + I'll stick to my philosophy as jazz being an expansion of freedom. Remember what MLK said: Let freedom ring! Let freedom ring! Let freedom ring in all aspects of our lives. I let it ring loud + clear in the studio. I let it ring loud + clear in the bedroom. I let it ring on every street corner in America + I let it ring throughout the planet. Let freedom ring, let freedom ring. When freedom rings it <u>EXPANDS</u>!

What I am doing is the reverse of picking cotton. I had a Jeep Eagle from 1986 that wouldn't go in reverse! I had it fixed. I've fixed my mind to go in reverse or forward when necessary. Most of the time I am in forward gear but sometime I go in reverse just to change course Back in 1954–55?? I went with old man Wesley to pick cotton. I was determined to pick 100 lbs. We went into the fields at 6:00 A.M. Wesley finished hiss 100 at 4:00! It took me until 7:00 PM! But I did it. For $8.

It makes me feel good to reverse the process. [. . .]

15 MARCH: The spirit is in the abstract. It lies beyond logic— beyond reason. It lies in the great void where God resides. It makes itself known only through presece. You can't paint it you can only provide the ground for it to exist. The ground is the painting. The painting is a receiver. Under the right conditions it receives the spirit through light.

15 MARCH CONTD. All information is within the light. All knowledge resides in the light. The light is the univeral unit. The unit is the same as the molecular: <u>THE BIT</u>. <u>MOLECULAR— UNIT—BIT</u> is the same thing. The bit is the holy grail of painting. Painters have been chasing the bit for hundreds of year. It took the third phase of modernism to discover. <u>I AM THE THIRD PHASE</u>. I have the bit at my disposable + I can use it for anything I want!

I am a jazzman. The bit is encoded in jazz. One must understand jazz in order to decode the bit. My advice is for everyone to listen to Monk—Max*—Satchmo*—Duke— Count*—Bird—Diz—Bags—Ronc.*—Lady Day*—Ella*— Sarah*—Bud—Miles—Coltrane—K.D.— Mingus*—Sonny— Prez*—Hawk*—Judge*—Dexter*—Ornette—Clifford B.*— The Shadow*—Art B.*—Paul C.*—+Paul Q.*—all the greats! Above all . . . . one must know African art for this is the genesis. Without African art there would be no modernism. We as black Americans must take African art and construct it as modern. This is what I am doing. I have the modern/contemporary equalivant of African art. Therefore, the painting is a mask. Therfore, the painting is functional; it serves a specif purpose through the nature of its content.

16 MARCH: Went to the <u>whack</u>! Show at P.S. 1 today. It was good to see in retrospective a lot of stuff from the past. I do not understand why Mira Schor is not represented. She should be in that show. Most of it is <u>boring</u>, <u>no poetry</u>, mostly <u>propoganda</u>, <u>exhibitionism</u>, <u>self pity</u>, <u>not sensual</u>. I am convinced that the feminist movement was a necessary act of history but when that history becomes institutazized as an end within itself. . . . It's a mistake. So much of this show is purely sensibility with no plastic thought. Most is just poor art a good example of art as therapy. I must maintain my critique in dealing with young women . . . . . be firm in insisting upon using the feminine as sensibility along with the plastic. Do not rely upon sensibility alone. Use it to structure the plastic.

—STUDIO LOG 08—

27 MAY: There is a gap between knowing + not knowing. I am attracted to the gap. At present, this is what excites me the most. I have always been aware of this, but now it is absolute cognitive! In the 60's I called it the extreme middle. [. . .] In African art it's called presence. All great art has this presence. It's purely mental i.e., it exist only in the mind. When matter is used in a particular way it excudes prescence. I want to be able to go directly to presence without any hindrace. I am even willing to through out <u>subject</u> rub out <u>object</u> + depend solely upon the <u>verb</u>, <u>to act.</u> (Zen?)

The bar codes have taught me a lot but I don't know what they have taught me! They are intruiging they defy analysis. Modernist strip paintings? I don't think so. They are bar codes! I like them because they tease the mind. They are smart + devilish. They can be more than one thing simultaneously. I like this brutal fact! BAR CODE #IV LOTTO: (the pink, red, yellow + white with black) is a gift for Robert Rauschenberg. It's a take off on a lotto ticket!

6 JUNE: Mel,* Bill,* Pat,* Jayne,* Mary + I met for dinner last night; a very nice eveing: I can depend upon Mel + Bill . . . they are mega buddies! I am very excited about Obama's victory. It could have a huge impact upon me: abstraction can play a role in the political process. The time is ripe for black abstract artist to take the lead.

It's time for me to stop thinking. Go on automatic pilot and allow presence to dominate. Relax the need to will. The key word is <u>aconceptual</u> . . . to go against the conceptual. I am bored with conceptual art! I want the original, primative instinct of art . . . . direct concrete—response to the world. I like the fact of every action in original art is devoted to survival. It was not about fashion!

<u>GONE FISHING</u>

—STUDIO LOG— '08

8 Sept. 08—Back to N.Y. The summer was quiet, very few tourist + no visitors except for Jurek wife + kids from Ireland. The garden was beautiful; Manolis's green house built to break the wind + sun worked. Did a neat wood carving "Socrates Tomb". Caught some octopi + small fish. O.K.

Now what? First, I must document all the early paintings for database. Second, Find art storage center. Third, back to work. I feel optimistic but not clear on next move. If I can say clearly . . . never know until I start but . . . . the painting 'Lateral Shift' completed last Fall is a positive statement about things in general but to be exact about painting: Everything has shifted in my behalf. I can feel this to be the case. Must act + take advantage. The last paintings completed before leaving for Greece, the bar code paintings are trying to tell me something. I've had time to think: The bar code paintings are the absolute end of 2$\underline{^{nd}}$ stage modernism. The 3$\underline{^{rd}}$ phase will be shaped by me! I plan to shift all of art history from my perspective. I wrote to Saul about my notion of 'dimensional light'. Dimensional light is a means of structuring the gap between painting and sculpture. The Multi-Dimensional worldview in which the <u>NOW</u> is located. I am proposing an organic 'as is' space defining spirit's allegiance to matter. The interaction of spirit and matter is the content. All I have to do is give a visual description of this interaction. It is not my job to explain. Dimensional light is my ticket to immortality!

—STUDIO LOG— '08

12 Oct: I've been thinking a lot about the word perceptual. All art is perceptual. Is it possible to isolate the perceptual from the other concerns and reduce i.e., compress all meaning into the perceptual? This would depend upon, ① reduction of all formal elements ② reduction of image ③ reduction of narrative ④ reduction of the conceptual Especially the conceptual. How does one bypass the conceptual? To seek the opposite of the conceptual. Which is? This is difficult and simulaneously not falling into the trap of automatism. Is there such a thing as <u>PERCEPTUAL ISM</u>? I feel like someone wanting everything and nothing at the same time! What would a purely perceptual painting look like? As a young artist, Bill Rubin told me "that there is no such thing as a perceptual painting" His point: The perceptual painting only exist in the mind. The Impressionists spoke of color that exist in the mind, and still managed to paint a picture. . .

FOR PERCEPTUALISM TO WORK IT CAN ONLY EXIST AS SPIRIT. SPIRIT EXIST ONLY THROUGH MATTER. MIND IS MATTER, THEREFORE, A PURE PERCEPTUAL PAINTING IS POSSIBLE THROUGH MATTER

THINGS TO CONSIDER →

① A PERCEPTUAL PAINTING IS MODE FOR CONTEMPLATION

② IT IS MADE TO SLOW THINGS DOWN:

③ NO CONCERN FOR SELF IDENTITY—NON AUTOBIOGRAPHICAL

④ NOT ABOUT MONEY

⑤ NOT ABOUT SEXUALITY

⑥ NOT ABOUT POLITICS

⑦ NOT ABOUT ILLUSTRATION (NON ILLUSTRATIONAL) the painting is not an illustration of an idea

⑧ NOT ABOUT DECORATION
⑨ MUST DENY THE HAND
⑩ THE STRUCTURE OF LIGHT IS MULTI DIMENSIONAL
⑪ COLOR IS NOT THE PRIME MOVER
⑫ SURFACE MUST BE TANGIBLE
⑬ THE SPACE IS MULTI-DIMENSIONAL
⑭ SCALE IS MOBILE + ADAPTABLE TO ANY ARCHITECTURAL SPACE
⑮ THE SUBJECT IS ONLY AN INSTIGATOR
⑯ TOTALLY DEPENDENT UPON FEELING
⑰ DEFYS ANY ATTEMPT AT DECODING
⑱ IS ANTI-CONCEPTUAL
⑲ MUST EXIST AS APRIOR STRUCTURE
⑳ PAINTING AS PRODUCT OF EVOLUTION
㉑ MUST BE NON-NARRATIVE—NO STORY—MUST HAVE ITS' OWN MEANING
㉒ NO ADHERENCE TO ANY PARTICULAR ART REFEFACE
㉓ CRAFT AS VEHICLE
㉔ THE FORMAL AS VEHICLE; THEREFORE, ANTI-FORMALISM
㉕ PAINTING AS OBJECT IS PARAMOUNT
㉖ NOT DEPENDENT UPON NATURE
㉗ COMPRESSION AS TOOL
㉘ NO EVIDENCE OF IDEA
㉙ NOT ABOUT RELIGION

14 NOV: "It's more than one way to Fuck a Duck" (Jeff Waite)
To <u>go against the conceptual</u> is another way to approach
perceptualism. Perhaps this method serves the most 'practical' +
therefore logical approach: TO CONSTRUCT SOMETHING +
THEN PROCEED TO DECONSTRUCT <u>IT</u>. THE Process of
CONSTRUCT + DECONSTRUCT IS <u>TRANSCENDED</u>
THROUGH RECONSTRUCTION i.e., <u>CONSTRUCT</u> +
<u>DECONSTRUCT</u> = <u>RECONSTRUCT.</u> TRANSCENDENCE IS
SUBLIME THOUGHT IN ACTION. SUBLIMITY IS AN ACTIVE
NOT PASSIVE ACTIVITY.
<u>OR</u> <u>MAYBE</u> <u>THE</u> <u>ACTIVE</u> <u>CANCELS</u> <u>OUT</u> <u>THE</u> <u>PASSIVE</u>.
Whatever, <u>it</u> is in the act of making. The more I make the more I
know . . . . so keep on making!

17 NOV: Leave for Chicago tomorow, Art Institute invited me to
talk. Hope to meet + connect with new people. Talk is on Wednesday.
Greg Bordowitz will be there.

<u>25 NOV</u>
Greg, Mary + I had dinner together at LULA'S CAFE IN HONOR
of OUR FORTY YEAR WEDDING ANNIVERSARY. VERY NICE
EVENING with two bottles of wine! [. . .] My talk went well, good
audience, large auditorium mostly filled. Very receptive. [. . .]
Chicago Art Institute is a neat place. After my talk a young man
introduced himself as Jeremy Whitten a student at CAI. He is
definately a cousin orginally from Mississippi. A beautiful surprise!
Good trip, Good experience but exhausting!

1 DEC: ART MUST GO BACK TO ITS' ORIGINAL SOURCE: IT
WAS A MYSTICAL EXPEIRENCE. THIS IS WHAT I WANT
FROM MY ART.

9 DEC: <u>IT'S</u> <u>WHAT</u> <u>I</u> <u>SEE</u> <u>+</u> <u>NOTHING</u> <u>ELSE</u>. <u>THAT'S</u> <u>FINAL!</u> <u>NO</u> <u>BULLSHIT!!</u>

10 DEC: IT'S THE NOT KNOWING THAT'S SO INTRIGUING.

17 DEC: Went to MoMA today. [. . .]
<u>GOOD TO SEE NORMAN LEWIS ON VIEW FACING
POLLOCK. RIGHT ON!!</u>

18 DEC: I am dealing with something that lies beyond me; therefore, my hand must not be visible. All shape, form, image, must occur without my hand . . . . the hand only directs the action. I am all constructed process. All actions including the space is compressed through matter. The perceptual happens as a result of vision i.e., it's only visible through mind. Mind is matter.

27 DEC: 1600 HRS. FINISHED E-STAMP #VI (42" X 42" VOURAY: FOR HARVEY QUAYTMAN)
It was a fun painting. Hope that Harvey is pleased. Rather touch + go toward the end . . . . aluminum, black, nickel yellow, wierd light emanates from aluminum when reacting to nickel. Harvey would understand this. Vouray was one of Harvey's favorite wines. He always served it for dinner. I miss Harvey. I sincerely miss speaking to him about painting. He was one of the few people who understood painting. He understood painters' obligation to history. We are indepted to history. . . It's our job to advance it.

Mary's birthday today. We are going out for dinner . . . maybe I'll order a bottle of Vouray! Next painting is for Mike Goldberg: <u>THREE SHAPES</u> *see 5 MARCH 09

Found myself on the floor today i.e., self portrait . . saves me some time . . . I don't have to make it. It's a 3" square, acrylic on canvas. Comes at a good time . . . . this is the essence of perceptualism: perceptualism exist beyond the notion of self; it is beyond the hand + only exist in the brain but can manifest itself through matter. Mind is matter. I am a perceptualist.

30 DEC: Art going back to its original source is also a formal issue. Yes it was mystical serving the need of survival; the formal was figure/ground. The figure was placed on support or cut into support. This was the beginning of <u>two dimensional</u> space.

30 DEC. '08 CONT'D: Today I am inlaying space. Mosaic is an inlaided space . . . . the space is built within i.e., constructed. Mike Goldberg's painting involves three shapes which I call spirits. They will be inlayed . . the space is compressed in the matter which is the paint. Mike's painting is specific figure/ground + I want it to be very clear + exacting . . . NO <u>FUZZY</u> <u>FOGGY</u> <u>BOTTOMS</u> . . . clear + specific. I am also exploring a new type of biomorphic form . . . an engineered bio-morphic form. . . . . a hybrid which is possible because of my presence in the modern technological society. My paintings are 100% contemporary. . . They engage the modern. Paintings of any significance must engage the present psychologically, spiritually, and plastically. Otherwise why bother!

31 DEC: Figure/ground is reversable. . . . It also operates as ground/figure. Either way is possible. It is not a chicken + egg syndrome; it's totally dependent upon the forces of nature in tune to space/time. I am very much excited by this discovery. I have expeirenced another extension of freedom. Freedom must continue to expand. As freedom expands, my consciouness expands. This is what I want. I absolutely refuse to accept any limitation upon my thinking. I will not allow race, sex, politics, religion or any known symbolic device to impose a limit. ART MUST BE FULL THROTTLE AHEAD. THERE IS NO SPEED LIMIT.

<u>3 JAN 09</u> Saw the Mary Heilmann show yesterday at the New Museum: bright—cheerful—most of the time good control of elements. I like them at their best. [. . .] Anyway its' good to see Mary getting her due. [. . .] Mary's insistence upon painting the sides of her canvases I do not agree with. Most of us experimented with that during the early seventies . . our emphasis was the object i.e., the painting as object. <u>THE OBJECT</u> <u>IS</u> <u>THE</u> <u>PHYSICAL</u>

PLACE OF THE PAINTING AND NOTHING ELSE! The plane
should be more than 3/16" of an inch. Everything is compressed
within the physical dimension of the plane. HAPPY NEW YEAR

STUDIO LOG FEB '09

5 FEB: the Africans, i.e., my ancestors, were very comfortable with their multiple realities. I must learn to become comfortable with the modern notion of multiple realities. I am acquainted with other realities because I have seen and experienced them. Originally I thought that the space was multi dimensional, which is correct but the next step was to see the reality. Saying that the space is multi-dimensional is only its' formal interpretion[s/p]. Through compression of the space other realities reveal themselves. Also, one must understand casualties can reverse themselves. They can unwind + go backwards. Reversable casualities are marvelous!

6 FEB: MOSAIC IS A COMPRESED SPACE: THIS IS WHY I AM ATTRACTED TO IT. AT FIRST I THOUGHT THE SPIRITUAL TO BE THE PRIMARY ATTRACTION, AS IN BYZANTINE ART. ALTHOUGH THE SPIRITUAL IS IMPORTANT, BUT ONLY IN TERMS OF ITS CONTEMPORARY APPLICATION. I OWE NOTHING TO BYZANTIUM!

13 FEB: WHAT INSPIRES ME THE MOST? THE GEOMETRY OF NATURE. I AM A PERCEPTUALIST + PERCEPTUALISM DEPENDS UPON STRUCTURALISM FOR ITS' PLASTIC INTERGITY. IT WAS NECESSARY TO APPROPRIATE NATURE'S GEOMETRY FOR MY USE. . . . THERE WAS NO OTHER WAY! I TOOK IT!

14 FEB: HAPPY VALENTINE DAY, MARY. . . I HAVE SUCCESSFULLY COMPRESSED THE TOTAL HISTORY OF ART! AMEN

18 FEB: I WANT A SHAPE/FORM THAT EXIST IN THE
WOBBLE i.e., THE GAP.

19 FEB: <u>EXTREME ABSTRACTION</u> IS ANOTHER NAME FOR
PERCEPTUALISM. IT GOES BEYOND ABSTRACTION AS WE
KNOW IT.

20 FEB: 1445 HRS. COMPLETED <u>THREE OPENINGS: FOR
MIKE GOLDBERG</u>
    SEE 5 MARCH * Hope you like it Mike. You were O.K. in
my book.
THE SPACE COMES OUT OF THE MATERIAL; THEREFORE,
IT IS NOT AN ILLUSIONISTIC SPACE IT IS REAL. . . . . . AS
REAL AS ANYTHING ELSE IN NATURE, IF NATURE
QUALIFIES AS REAL THEN MY SPACE IS REAL!

<u>NOTES FROM THE WOODSHED</u>

1 MARCH 2009: FROM THIS DATE FORWARD MY STUDIO LOG WILL BE KNOWN AS <u>NOTES</u> <u>FROM THE</u> <u>WOODSHED.</u>

I am a perceptualist. My movement is known as perceptualism. Perceptuaism as art runs parallel to life; indeed, it is analogous to life. In painting, which is my interest, the image maker, which is me, must be capable of compressing the total of the history of painting. It must be compressed into the flat skin of paint which makes a painting; therefore, it depends upon materiality i.e., paint as matter. Sense data which is confronted from the outside and forces the inside to act . . . . . action as emotion. Its' plasticity is tactile . . . classical in its' construction but possessing 100% autonomy of past plasticities. Perceptualism is recognizable in painting by its space: a multi-dimensional space which has been compressed into a skin of paint. My discovery of paint as collage in 1975 is the essence of this new space. This space has the 'appearnce' of photography but is not dependent upon photography The graphic content of the photograph is only an appearance of reality. Perceptual space is the reality. It is not the illustration of an idea. . . . It is the idea fused through action. <u>I ACT THEREFORE I AM.</u> The painting must embody the spirit. . . . Spirit is the life force. . . It's what make me human.

2 MARCH: HOW I PERCEIVE THE WORLD CONSTITUTE MY PERSONAL IDENTITY. MY PERSONAL IDENTITY IS THE TEMPLATE FOR WORLDVIEW. PERCEPTION . . . . PERCEPTION . . . . . PERCEPTION IS MY MANTRA.

NOTES FROM THE WOODSHED

TUES MAR 3: Perceptualism exist totally in the mind (Bill Rubin was right) I insist upon its manifesting itself through matter, which is paint and therefore existing as an object which is the painting. Perceptualism has the power to show the mind in all its' purity which exist in the brain. Mind is all . . . it is nature. Because of its' purity and absolute . . . . it must be left along . . . . <u>DO NOT INTERFERE WITH MIND</u>. Mind is an alternate reality therefore analogous with life . . . . not that they are separate . . . they run on parallel tracks. Art makes them touch . . . just enough to produce the painting. A better way to express this . . . . . through sensuality it 'allows' them to touch. ART IS A GIFT FROM NATURE. AMEN!

<u>PERCEPTUALISM IS A SYNTHESIS OF OPPOSITES:</u>
(1) FRACTAL GEOMETRY vs. EUCLID, i.e., PLANAR G.
(2) SPIRIT vs. MATTER
(3) EUDAEMONIA → EVIL vs. GOOD (PROPERTIES of SPIRIT)
(4) TRANSPARENCY vs. OPAQUE (PROPERTIES of LIGHT)
(5) GAS ↔ LIQUID ↔ SOLIDS (PROPERTIES of MATTER
(6) LOVE vs. HATE
(7) MALE vs. FEMALE
(8) PRIVATE vs. PUBLIC (POLITICAL)
(9) BULLSHIT NOTIONS of RACE: WHITE vs. BLACK (POLITICAL)
(10) INSIDE vs. OUTSIDE (PSYCHOLOGICAL)
(11) SOFT vs. HARD (PROPERTIES of MATTER)
(12) LIGHT vs. DARK (PROPERTIES of LIGHT) PSYCHOLOGICAL INCLUDING THE SPIRITUAL + THE PHYSICAL).

(13) SPECTRUM CHROMA vs. BLACK + WHITE
(DENSITIES of LIGHT INCLUDED PLUS WEIGHTS OF
COLOR → THE STRUCTURE OF LIGHT

"A NARRATIVE OF THE MOMENT TO FIT THE ZEITGEIST"

5 MARCH 09: MIKE GOLDBERG'S PAINTING <u>THREE
OPENINGS</u> CHANGED TO → <u>THE ZEITGEIST OF SHAPE:</u>
FOR MIKE GOLDBERG

NOTES FROM THE WOODSHED OR
<u>WOODSHED LOG</u>

10: MARCH 09

The important and primary definition of perceptualism is to receive information from the immediate world i.e., the world of the now, I must condition myself to be a recipient . . . . TO RECEIVE INFORMATION. I MUST LEARN TO <u>REACT</u> TO MY ENVIRONMENT. THIS IS THE ESSENCE OF PERCEPTUALISM.

<u>TODAY</u> I <u>SAW</u> THE 'BLACK' <u>SUBLIME</u>
AND I LOVED IT!

The perceptual operates in the brain:

In order to do what I am doing one must be capable of understanding what John Coltrane is doing. Not just listening to J.C. but understanding i.e., comprending. J.C. is operating on multiple layers of space/time. He is truly the 21ˢᵗ century man. I knew I this in the 1960's but its has taken me this long to compress what he is doing into a two dimensional plane of paint. Believe me. . . <u>This is not easy.</u> I am thankful for my health. . . . I need more time to continue my work. This I pray for.

17 MARCH: As you know, I have always been intrigued with the optical. The optical has been an element of my painting since the sixties. The optical is 'enclosed' within a matrix. . . . The matrix is planar. . . . . Next step . . . . can the matrix be optical? If so, the possibility exist for the planar optical i.e., the plane as optical. This is an extremely important breakthrough for me. <u>SHOW THE MATRIX!</u>

18 MARCH: <u>MEANING IS THE ENEMY OF ART</u>

NOTES FROM THE WOODSHED '09

26 MARCH: MOM'S BIRTHDAY IS TOMORROW, THE 27th MARCH,
BOY, DO I MISS MY MOM! I LOVE YOU MOM. I AM 69,
(WHAT A FUNNY NUMBER!) I'M GETTING CLOSER TO WHAT
I WANT BUT NOT CLOSE ENOUGH. THERE STILL REMAINS A
DISTACE BETWEEN & WHAT I WANT & IT'S NOT ABOUT MONEY.
I HATE MONEY. IF I EVER MEET THE MOTHERFUCKER WHO
INVENTED MONEY I WILL KICK THEIR ASS! I SAW SOMETHING
MY PAINTINGS HAVE FORCED ME TO BE HUMBLE. I SAW SOMETHING
IN THE EARLY 60'S AND I'VE BEEN CHASING IT FOR @ 50 YEARS.
IT IS SO LARGE, SO COMPLEX & DOWNRIGHT RUDE! IT HAS (WHATEVER
'IT' IS) WORKED THE HELL OUT OF ME, IT HAS REDUCED ME TO
MY KNEES. I AM NOT A BEGGER BUT AT TIMES I PRAY FOR
MY SANITY. MY HUMBLENESS IS TO EXCEPT WHATEVER AMOUNT
POSSIBLE. I CANNOT HAVE IT ALL; THEREFORE, I MUST ACCEPT
WHATEVER I AM CAPABLE OF. I'LL TAKE FROM 'IT' INCLUDING
THE CRUMBS LEFT SCATTERED ON THE WOODSHED FLOOR AND
MAKE DO: I WILL MAKE ANOTHER PAINTING, ANOTHER
PAINTING AND ANOTHER PAINTING. I DO NOT CARE
ANYMORE. I AM FREE OF HISTORY. FINALLY I HAVE
CONNECTED WITH THE PHILOSOPHICAL UNDERPINNING OF
JAZZ: THE EXPANSION OF FREEDOM. I CONTINUE TO
EXPAND; THEREFORE, MY PEOPLE CONTINUE TO EXPAND.
I AM DOING WHAT I WAS EDUCATED TO DO. MAY GOD
BLESS ALL THE PEOPLE WHO HAVE TAUGHT ME ALL OF MY
VARIOUS SKILLS. I LOVE ALL OF YOU.

1. MOM
2. DAD
3. MR. IVERSON DUDLEY
4. ALL OF MY GRADE SCHOOL
& HIGH SCHOOL TEACHERS
5. THE CHURCH OF GOD
6. COOPER UNION — TUSKEGEE - S.U.
7. JEFF WAITE
8. MARY & MIRSINI & KEITA & MY TWO GRANDSONS ELIAS & MALAKI
9. MY CLOSE FRIENDS
10. CAPTAIN YANNI &
THE CRETAN FISHERMEN
11. ART HISTORY
12. CARPENTERS STONE MASONS, TILE WORKERS, CEMENT
WORKERS, PLASTERERS, SHEETROCK WORKERS, ROOFERS, etc.

13. WOOD CARVING — *AFRICAN SCULPTURE
14. STRATI & THE GREEKS g CRETE
MRS. IRINI,
15. FARMERS (OL' MAN CARET)
16. JAZZ (J.C., BIRD, MONK, MILES, TRANE TRON
17. MR. WESLEY (HOW TO PICK COTTON,
CUT DOWN A TREE, HUNTING)

→ cont'd

<u>NOTES FROM THE WOODSHED</u> '09

26 MARCH: MOM'S BIRTHDAY IS TOMORROW, THE 27<u>th</u> MARCH, BOY, DO I MISS MY MOM! I LOVE YOU MOM. I AM 69 (WHAT A FUNNY NUMBER!) I'M GETTING CLOSER TO WHAT I WANT BUT NOT CLOSE ENOUGH. THERE STILL REMAINS A DISTANCE BETWEEN + WHAT I WANT + IT'S NOT ABOUT MONEY. I HATE MONEY. IF I EVER MEET THE MOTHERFUCKER WHO INVENTED MONEY I WILL KICK THEIR ASS!

MY PAINTINGS HAVE FORCED ME TO BE HUMBLE. I SAW SOMETHING IN THE EARLY 60'S AND I'VE BEEN CHASING IT FOR @ 50 YEARS. IT IS SO LARGE, SO COMPLEX + DOWNRIGHT RUDE! IT HAS (WHATEVER 'IT' IS) WORKED THE HELL OUT OF ME. IT HAS REDUCED ME TO MY KNEES; I AM NOT A BEGGER BUT AT TIMES I PRAY FOR MY SANITY. MY HUMBLENESS IS TO EXCEPT WHATEVER AMOUNT POSSIBLE. I CANNOT HAVE IT ALL; THEREFORE, I MUST ACCEPT WHATEVER I AM CAPABLE OF. I'LL TAKE FROM 'IT' INCLUDING THE CRUMBS LEFT SCATTERED ON THE WOODSHED FLOOR AND MAKE DO: <u>I WILL MAKE ANOTHER PAINTING, ANOTHER PAINTING AND ANOTHER PAINTING. I DO NOT CARE ANYMORE. I AM FREE OF HISTORY</u>. FINALLY I HAVE CONNECTED WITH THE PHILOSOPHICAL UNDERPINNING OF JAZZ: THE EXPANSION OF FREEDOM. I CONTINUE TO EXPAND; THEREFORE, MY PEOPLE CONTINUE TO EXPAND. I AM DOING WHAT I WAS EDUCATED TO DO. MAY GOD BLESS ALL THE PEOPLE WHO HAVE TAUGHT ME ALL OF MY VARIOUS SKILLS. I LOVE ALL OF YOU.

1. MOM
2. DAD

3. MR. IVERSON DUDLEY
4. ALL OF MY GRADE SCHOOL + HIGH SCHOOL
   TEACHERS
5. THE CHURCH OF GOD
6. COOPER UNION—TUSKEGEE—S.U.
7. JEFF WAITE
8. MARY + MIRSINI + KEITA + MY TWO GRANDSONS
   ELIAS + MALAKI
9. MY CLOSE FRIENDS
10. CAPTAIN YANNI + THE CRETAN FISHEREN
11. ART HISTORY
12. CARPENTERS, STONE MASONS, TILE WORKERS,
    CEMENT WORKERS, PLASTERERS, SHEET ROCK
    WORKERS, ROOFERS, ETC.
13. WOOD CARVING—*AFRICAN SCULPTURE
14. STRATI + THE GREEKS OF CRETE
    MRS. IRINI
15. FARMERS (OL' MAN CARET)
16. JAZZ (J.C., BIRD, MONK, MILES, KENNY, RON)
17. MR. WESLEY (HOW TO PICK COTTON, CUT DOWN A
    TREE, HUNTING)

CONT'D

28 MARCH: PERCEPTUALISM IS A NARRATIVE; IT TELLS THE STORY OF HOW I <u>REACT</u> TO THE WORLD. THE WORLD IS A MIND MADE OF MATTER. . I CONSTRUCT THAT WORLD WITH PAINT AS MATTER.

   * Mike, I must change the title of your painting for the second time, sorry about that but it's important. I'm sure you will understand. New title is:

   <u>ZEITGEIST TRAPS PSYCHEGRAPHS?</u> –PSYCHEGRAPHS—

31 MARCH:

   Did a set of 'PSYCHEGRAMS' today psychic grams are 2-D planar graphics that depend totally upon the manipulation of the material to produce an image. Their light source is perceptual, generated by the brain. It is an inner light. For the fax project at the Drawing Center, I have chosen Sunra as my subject. He was my homeboy. I always enjoyed talking with him. He had an oblique mind. . . Navigating with circular logic. He was unique.

   O.K. it must go beyond pattern. Only when pattern coalesce into form does perceptualism exist. Anyone who maintains an emphasis upon pattern will never be a perceptualist. Perceptualism is a brave new reality defined in painting through a specific quality of light i.e., the light is recognizable as such. And a specific quality of space that synchronize with the light. At this point, time becomes trapped. When time becomes trapped, . . . We experience the now. The now is all important. The now prevents a loss of energy. [. . .]

3 APRIL: I DON'T WANT MY PERCEPTUALISM TO BE ABOUT NOTHING IN PARTICULARLY BUT EVERYTHING IN GENERAL.

—NOTES FROM THE WOODSHED—

9 APRIL 09—The fractal is feminine and euclid is male. Mr. Euclid married Ms. Fractal and gave birth to 'TZAK'!* TZAK is black american with strong African blood. . he also has White, American Indian, + a host of other derivatives. It's all blood and it's all pure. Blood is pure. You see, it's good to know this; in my case . . . it keeps me sane and sane is good! Sane allows me to do my work. I am a maker of paintings. I like what I do. [. . .] I am a good wood carver, cabinet maker, spear fisherman, farmer. A lover of wine + good food. Sometimes I even like people. Most people bore me.

Perceptualism is not about how I see the world; it's about how I receive the world. I am a sponge. . . . . . . I soak in the world and sqeeze out what I don't want. What I keep is the raw material for my painting. I make paintings out of this 'stuff.'

Tzak (Whitten's nickname on Crete)

Parson's Branch in Bessemer, Alabama, did not have octopus, but I did learn to catch snapping turtles by hand. I grew up with a bamboo fishing pole in one hand and a .22 caliber rifle in the other. In 1969, while hanging out in Aghia Galini, Crete, I saw a young Englishman using a diver's mask and he invited me to try it. I had only seen a diving mask in movies. What I saw expanded my notion of nature as I knew it.

I am a certified scuba diver, but I can proudly say that I've never hunted a fish while wearing a tank. My passion is free-form diving using a mask, snorkel, weights and fins. Hunting octopus is my favorite sport. Millions of years ago the octopus had a shell, but slowly they lost it through the evolutionary process. Since then, the octopus is always looking for a home. They occupy the abandoned shells of other sea creatures, cans and car tires or make their own houses, which I call "octopus architecture." They are extremely smart animals with fast reflexes and are masters of camouflage. They are the Houdini of the sea; escape is their middle name. Being sly and elusive, they can open just about anything. Unfortunately, they are addicted to the color white like a bull is to red. They can't control themselves. Thus, I always keep a white handkerchief tucked into my wetsuit, which I use to seduce them from their lair.

When hunting for octopus, one must learn to recognize the morphology of the bottom of the sea. Octopus prefer a specific setting identifiable by a certain quality of stones, sand, and plant life. Octopus architecture is unique, constructed with stones, shells, wood, bits of sea glass, or anything available for building a nest. And of course, they prefer white stones. The nest is always semicircular and built at the base of a large rock, which serves as an anchor. They burrow a tunnel deep beneath the rock, usually with an exit for escape if attacked. The semicircular structure is built five, six or eight levels of rock high depending on the size of the octopus. It is masonry without mortar: closely fitted, tight, and fortified. Most of the time I only see the architecture. They feed

Originally published in *Art Lies* 61 (spring 2009): 30–33.

at night until early morning. During the day, they position themselves at the entrance of the nest, protecting their turf and soaking up the sun. When I locate an occupied octopus house, I can only see their eyes.

I hunt octopus with a *kamaki*, a simple tool made of seasoned wild olive wood cut during a waning moon and left to dry for several years. A strong metal trident measuring three inches across and six or seven inches long is secured to a customized wooden shaft carved from a single limb with decorative carvings. The trident can't be too small or too large. The correct size allows me to penetrate the front door. The critical phase of the hunt is thrusting the trident directly between the eyes of the octopus. I must stay cool and make sure that the trident is properly placed before attempting to pull the octopus from his house. Octopuses are strong; remember, they are all muscle with no bone structure. When hunting without a spear, I grab them by hand. I hold them tightly at the top of the head while being careful to prevent them from turning over. Directly beneath the head is a parrotlike beak capable of inflicting a vicious bite. I've been bitten more than once, and it's not fun!

A nerve runs directly between their eyes. When no spear or knife is available, I must bite them between the eyes to sever this nerve and kill them because they can otherwise be extremely difficult to control. I have had large octopuses wrap their tentacles up my arm and all the way to my neck. It's a weird feeling, and the welts from their suckers can last for weeks. After the nerve has been severed, I thrust my forefinger underneath the cap and invert the head. At the same time, I grab the larynx and pull from the head the liver, ink sac and other innards. A large octopus can discharge enough ink to render a diameter of two or three meters of water to invisibility. I am now surrounded by a cloud of black ink. I secure the octopus by threading a strong nylon string attached to a heavy wire through the head, like threading a needle. Only then can I relax: I have successfully caught an octopus.

Next step: the octopus must be tenderized by slamming it against a large rock at least a hundred times or more. When its natural color changes to white, I rinse it repeatedly in sea water and drag it back and forth over a rough rock surface with a rhythmic motion. A white foam is released, and this movement must continue until all the foam disappears. When the muscle has completely relaxed, the texture of the flesh changes and the color turns to a grayish white. I grab two tentacles and pull them apart gently. . . The flesh should tear. Then—and only then—is the octopus ready for cooking.

Octopus may be cooked by grilling over charcoal fire or a gas grill, boiled with herbs and served cold as a salad, in fresh tomato sauce with pasta or sun-dried as jerky, or *krasato*, with olive oil, bay leaf and red wine. For grilling, I hang the octopus outside in sunlight for a minimum of two days, which removes all the excess water. Octopus can be sun-dried for weeks, which concentrates the flavors and preserves the flesh for months.

Krasato is my favorite recipe: place the octopus in a covered pot with one cup olive oil, three fresh bay leaves and allow to simmer in its own juice for twenty minutes. Pour in one cup of red wine (I prefer a cheap, dry red wine with full robust flavor), leave the pot covered for another twenty minutes and test with a fork for tenderness. Remove the lid and reduce the sauce to a rich dark, red-velvet-cake color. The texture should have the sensual viscosity of cream. Krasato, when done right, should make your guests swoon!

I've caught octopus in one meter and as deep as 20 meters of water. At 68 years old, I can still hunt comfortably at 20 meters. I remember once finding two octopuses locked in mortal combat. They were literally eating each other. I caught and ate them both. Hunting octopus requires physical stamina, diving and breathing skills, tracking skills, and an unlimited passion for the hunt. Yes, at times I've felt a pang of guilt in killing such a smart animal, but after the first taste of krasato, any notion of guilt dissolves into the vastness of the Libyan Sea.

Notes from the Woodshed '09

15 Sept. 09—Space as object is extremely difficult to comprehend; It's a slippery notion. I don't know how to handle it <u>yet</u>. Hopefully through work I can grasp it, but maybe it's not 'graspable' I don't want the hassle of trying to catch a catfish with a gourd. My plan is to start working as soon as possible. I'll start with paper + see where it leads.

I've been thinking a lot about the Middle Passage. I am considering a large scale painting similar in scale to 9/11 but more rectangular @ 9' x 20'. It's a big investment in material + time designed to deal once and for all the caustic historical memory of displacement. There will be nothing cute about this painting: I want it to be <u>dark</u>, <u>loaded with pain</u>, <u>misery</u>, <u>fear</u>, <u>defeat</u>, <u>loss of family</u>, <u>community</u>, <u>language</u>, <u>religion</u>. . . <u>home</u>. Loss of love, Anger and the lust of revenge. I want it to be ME as universal man.

19 Sept: My show at Onyx Gallery in (1984?) dealt with conscioness conceptualized use of opposites → (out of psychological necessity) : hard edge geometry <u>v.s.</u> fluid organic geometry: the fractal vs. Euclid: the psychological + political implications of Black vs. White: Male vs. Female + etc. The notion of opposites is infinite, therefore, let's stop making an issue of them. The racial problem for example in America will never be resolved unless we stop this nonsense. My solution for dealing with opposites . . . . except them for what they are: they are a flaw in perception. We can not comprehend reality without their presence. This is a flaw in human consciouness. The transcendence of opposites is a myth, both spiritually and politically. Sexually it's a total myth! We are everything and then some! Let's start by accepting the world 'as is' . . . the world as given and proceed to correct what we don't like about it. I don't like suffering due to political concepts. I don't like hatred + descrimation. I don't like political dogma.

I don't like spiritual dogma. I don't like dogma of any kind. Religion has become political (it has always been politically) The acceptance of the world 'as is' is the only way out.

The Ribbons of Honor paintings, currently in the Alexander Gray Gallery, use hard edge forms and organic forms. They are different from the early 1980's paintings. The hard edge forms do not clash with the organic. Each form exist 'as is.' There is no psychological need to 'pronounce' their differences. Each form exist 'as is'.

I am hoping that this acceptance of opposites will help me in penetrating the notion of space as object. ALL of my energy must now be focused on space as object. This is the new frontier in painting.

—Could this new frontier be directed i.e., conceived of as the BLACK SUBLIME? No one has shown us what the BLACK SUBLIME Looks like. ALL of our Western notions of the sublime has been done by White artists. It's something to think about. Keep in mind that the sublime is a universal symbol. I think that Norman Lewis sensed this. it was not cognitive enough but he definitely sensed it. It's like owning GOD. The ultimate aesthetic from a Black point of view.

24 SEPT 09—

I have no choice but to accept the fact: art can be anything the artist wants it to be. I must clarify to the utmost of my ability: what is my art? First of all my approach to art is embedded within my southern sensibility. I am from Bessemer, Ala. This is very important. Not only am I from Bessemer I am black of African descent. Everything I do is informed by these simple facts. Therefore, my art is about identity. I want the world to know who I am. Unlike a lot of art by black artist, I am an abstractionist. I deal with the essence of life. I am not an illustrational-narrative painter. My identity is compressed into paint as matter. Paint as matter serves as a trap . . . . i.e., information is caught + coded in the material. For me, the painting is not an illustration of an idea. Idea is compressed (conceptuality + perceptuality) within action. e.g., action being the process of making which is plasticity. I make a painting I do not paint a painting.

Skin is the largest organ of the body. Skin is also the catalyst of race in America. My paint is my skin. Paint as skin is the foundation of my process. My 'processes' are all about skin. Paint as collage is the summation of modernist meaning in painting. This is why I speak of 3$^{\underline{rd}}$ phase moderism. I am an example of 3$^{\underline{rd}}$ phase until someone else surfaces, I am the only example of 3$^{\underline{rd}}$ phase moderism in painting.

TO <u>KILL</u> <u>TWO</u> <u>BIRDS</u> <u>WITH</u> <u>ONE</u> <u>STONE</u> is the psychological underpinning of my southern sensibility. Because of racial identities in the south and its resulting political structures . . . . . the black people's survival was + continues to be in informed by this fact of reality. We are a multi-dimensional people. We have always embraced reality within multiple meanings. Our ancient culture prepared us for this. The African belief system accomodated multiple notions of reality existing simultaneously. My psychic <u>is</u> and depend on complex interactions between fast + essence.

Recongnizing the complexity of my psychic, mosaic as structure, is a powerful tool in painting. It allows me 'gather' the pieces and build them into a whole. The beauty of this method allows me access to the <u>ancient</u> + the <u>contemporary</u> at the same time: I think that this is marvelous! Paint as collage extends the history of painting. At Tuskegee when I was an AFROTC cadet the mantra was 'we control the skies' whoever control the skies, control the battlefield. In painting, whoever controls space controls perception. <u>SPACE</u> <u>IS</u> <u>MY</u> <u>PRIMARY</u> <u>FORMAL</u> <u>ELEMENT</u> <u>IN</u> <u>PAINTING</u>. I SINCERELY DESIRE TO CONTROL THE SPACE.

25 SEPT: I visited 'Sam' today. He works outside. His wife has asthma + he can't work inside the house. I brought one painting . . . a dark cosmic backdrop with a rich purple . . . bluish . . . cosmic flower overlayed with galatical star-planet pattern. [. . .] Sam told me that he is 66 . . . fit . . . in good health . . . sane and accept this as proof of God's existence. I told him that I was 69. . . He said: 'there you go'! 'Proof that God exist + is watching over you' I enjoyed our meeting very much. I made my day.

—09—

10 DEC. A negation of the conceptual is extreme CONCRETEALITY (can I use this as a word?) I know that IT is concrete and I know that the concrete is physical i.e., physical as in matter which includes all aspects of matter. Earlier I wrote my interest in the gap that exist between FORM and MEANING; this is correct. Now, I have discovered gap between the CONCEPTUAL and the PERCEPTUAL. The conceptual must be negated. Through negation one discovers another space. Very strange thinking indeed . . . . . . but one of necessity. I am back to the beginning of time: to think but not to think. Somehow we humans eventually get it right!

12 DEC: TO REARRANGE NATURE IN MY IMAGE. . . . I LIKE THIS. . . IT'S LOTS OF FUN! MAN HAS FUCKED UP NATURE AND I WANT TO MAKE IT RIGHT!

19 DEC: [. . .] I FINALLY FIGURED OUT THE ANOLOGY TO THE PHOTOGRAPH: IT'S THE SPACE; THE COMPRESSED SPACE OF THE PHOTOGRAPH ATTRACTED ME! THE PAINTER'S SPACE MUST BE COMPRESSED. "AS IS"

28 DEC: Completed my 16' painting on saturday. . . what a relief! Almost two months of non-stop labor. It's strong. . even fierce. Must change the title from PIECES OF TIMES to THE MIDDLE PASSAGE. I knew from the beginning that the painting was about time, memory. . . pain + sorrow associated with grief of loss. . lost culture. . the experience of making this painting was one of excavation as in archeology. . to dig into the earth. . . into the sea + reveal the past. THE MIDDLE PASSAGE sums up what's the painting is about. Influences that informed the painting other than

basic concepts of culture are:
    ① George Kubler's book <u>THE SHAPE OF TIME</u>
    ② Trip to Berlin (a.) Ethnological Museum's African collection
    (b.) Ishtar Gate (c.) sidewalks + streets of Berlin
    ③ Zen rock gardens. . pebble, sand, etc.
(MADE OF GRAY GRANITE TESSERAE: TIME + MEMORY
IS INTERLOCKED. TIME HAS A SHAPE. IT'S THE THINGS
WE MAKE THAT GIVES TIME MEANING

    the notion of 'kinesis vs. 'stasis' influenced this painting. .
which lead me to a marvelous way of handling figure/ground.
Since the 1960's I have known the importace of figure/ground in
an all-over planar light structure. I have expeirmented with
different solutions but kinesis vs. stasis is a new way of dealing
with figure/ground. It is a 100% reciprocal space (an advancement
of strip painting) compressed within a skin of paint.

    The painting as object must exist <u>"AS IS"</u>. This qualifys the
<u>CONCRETENESS</u> of the object.

29 DEC: Here I go again. . . . . . . I do not like the title <u>THE
MIDDLE PASSAGE.</u> Therefore for the fifth . . . . maybe the sixth
time . . . it must be changed. Everything I have said previously is
correct: <u>TIME</u>, <u>MEMORY</u>, LOSS, PAIN, SORROW, LOST OF
CULTURE, RELIGION, LANGUAGE . . . all of this is correct but I
don't like the title! The painting for Mike Goldberg, <u>ZEITGEIST
TRAPS</u>, is a beautiful title . . . . . . to capture the spirit of time . . .
I like this. <u>ZEIGEIST TRAPS, II</u>, 2009 is an interesting thought;
this title encompasses everything I want. I'll think about it. . . There
is no rush!

30 DEC: In my sleep last night, the word <u>RECLAMATION</u> surfaced.
<u>RECLAMATION</u> is the whole narrative of this painting . . . . to
reclaim something that was lost . . . . to rescue or bring back . . . to

recover. My whole life is about this. My art is about this. . . I've been working all my life as an artist with one objective: TO RECOVERY WHAT WAS LOST DURING THE MIDDLE PASSAGE.

31 DEC: To recover what was lost is an interesting thought. To be more precise "what was lost"? Language? Custom? Religion? Political system? Fashion? Food? None of this suits my present need. I need something of value; something of practical use in shaping a modern worldview for the modern technological society. Perhaps worldview is the answer. AESTHETICS SHAPE WORLDVIEW; THEREFORE, FOR ME I WANT THE <u>ANCIENT</u> <u>AFRICAN</u> <u>AESTHETIC</u> . . . .TAKE THIS + USE IT TO CONSTRUCT A MODERN WORLDVIEW!

'10s

2010
NOTES FROM THE WOODSHED

2 JAN 010: TO RECLAIM THE SPIRIT THROUGH MATTER IS WHAT I WANT. THE SPIRIT OF THE MIDDLE PASSAGE IS TRAPPED WITHIN MATTER. ALL I HAVE TO DO IS RESCUE IT. ALLOW IT TO ESCAPE OUTWARD. YOU UNDERSTAND? THE SPIRIT IS PRESERVED IN MATTER. SET IT FREE! IT IS NOT ABOUT PICTORIAL ILLUSION OF ANY FORM … IT IS AS IS. THE ILLUSION IS A POSTERIOR BUT THE SPIRIT IS A PRIOR. AMEN! ALLOW THE MATTER TO SPEAK AND YOU ARE HOME FREE. IT'S A MATTER OF TRUST, — TRUST THE MATTER TO SPEAK FOR ITSELF. THE NARRATIVE IS COMPRESSED WITHIN THE MATTER. THE NARRATIVE IS WHATEVER YOU WANT IT TO BE. TRUST IT & PRAISE THE LORD!

~~20010~~

2010

<u>NOTES FROM THE WOODSHED</u>

2 JAN 010: TO RECLAIM THE SPIRIT THROUGH MATTER IS WHAT I WANT. THE SPIRIT OF THE MIDDLE PASSAGE IS TRAPPED WITHIN MATTER. ALL I HAVE TO DO IS RESCUE IT. ALLOW IT TO ESCAPE OUTWARD. YOU UNDERSTAND? THE SPIRIT IS PRESERVED IN MATTER. <u>SET IT FREE!</u> IT IS NOT ABOUT PICTORIAL ILLUSION OF ANY FORM <u>. . . IT IS AS IS</u>. THE ILLUSION IS A POSTERIOR BUT THE SPIRIT IS A PRIOR. <u>AMEN</u>! ALLOW THE MATTER TO SPEAK AND YOU ARE HOME FREE. IT'S A MATTER OF TRUST; TRUST THE MATTER TO SPEAK FOR ITSELF. THE NARRATIVE IS COMPRESSED WITHIN THE MATTER. THE NARRATIVE IS WHATEVER YOU WANT IT TO BE. TRUST IT + PRAISE THE LORD!

16 JAN: <u>PORT AU PRINCE</u> IS SUFFERING. . .

A human tragedy beyond comprehension. So many lives lost. These people are African descent—they are part of the diaspora. I have been struggling for a title for my 16' painting. Only after the fact of the earthquake can I read the symbols: ① black + white painting ② range of grays ③ 3-D African forms that read like masks or Ju-Ju bundles ④ Concentric rings around each 3-D form (as in earthquake sesmic readings. What am I to say "CONNECT THE DOTS"! The painting is ultimately about the Haitian earthquake. Roy de Carava's death as subject was the instigator. . . O.K. but the content is Haiti's suffering therefore I must be humble. . . The gods have spoken. . . Title is: <u>PORT AU PRINCE</u>, 2009

21 FEB: is it O.K. to change the title once more? Everything I've written is correct. . I am trying to be as truthful as possible . . . . but if Roy was the instigator . . . let's leave it at that: RECLAMATION: FOR ROY DE CARAVA. I received the news today that Carl Alexander (my high school buddy + college roomate at Tuskegee) passed. I have not seen Carl since leaving Tuskegee in 1959. It's been good to be in touch with him. We were close + I wish his 'spirit' a safe voyage home.

21 FEB. Alex has moved the gallery. [. . .] The opening last friday was very festive. People are talking. Things are happening + for once in my life I feel on top of things! [. . .] Things have changed + I <u>control</u> the space.

Working on a large 44" x 16', same size as <u>RECLAMATION: PORT AU PRINCE</u>: FOR THE HAITIAN PEOPLE. In spite of all the horror, this painting is for the maintenance of spirit + hope. All of humanity is praying for them. Hans Hofmann was correct: empathy is a very important ingredient in making art. (Necessary ingredient)

My mind is buzzing. So much is crystallizing now. Space is still defining itself with clarity. I am experiencing a <u>in+out</u> quality between 2-D + 3-D. As if one is affecting the other. The physical scientists speak of dark matter . . . . . one is dependent upon the other. There is something else out there that we do not know . . . . possible another kind of matter. Finally my insistence upon the photograph as analogy is starting to relax. . I don't need it as much. It has served me well for the past forty six years. Now <u>nature</u> as analogy makes more sense. Not that I should copy nature in any form but the processes of nature. It's not a 100% clear but I am on to something! Will keep you posted. Reality is mind.

25 FEB: THE CONSTRUCTION OF NATURE IN <u>MY IMAGE</u> THIS IS CLOSER TO THE POINT. THEREFORE I AM SUGGESTION A EXTREME NOTION OF THE AUTOBIOGRAPHICAL . . . . . <u>WORLDVIEW</u> AS <u>AUTOBIOGRAPHICAL</u>. THAT'S A NEAT IDEA!
I HAVE CONSOLIDATED THE <u>CONCEPTUAL</u> WITH THE <u>RANDOM</u>. THIS IS A NECESSARY STEP IN BECOMING A PERCEPTUALIST.

26 FEB: drawing + painting has become consolidated. Unfortunately, this eliminates the need to draw, except for fun!

—010—

2 MARCH: good news today: the Cleveland Museum bought RHO II. This sale will keep the wolf from the door . . . for a while!

12 MARCH: finished <u>PORT AU PRINCE: A PAINTING OF SPIRIT + HOPE FOR THE HAITIAN PEOPLE</u>. Yes, I gave a little money but what else can I do. Hans Hofmann said that empathy was a necessary ingredient in making art; I agree. Hope is important, spirit is important. . . . Without this plus financial aid . . . reconstruction is not possible. May their God be with them.

As usual, my paintings all have double meaning; I guess it's a Du Bois thing. . . Black folks are complicated! I read a declaration from Frank Stella that pissed me off. He said that "space in painting started with Caravaggio + ended with him." What bullshit! I've worked with space as primary formal element for fifty years . . . the nerve of him. Anyway . . . I shrunk i.e., to make smaller, as in a shrunken head . . . the essence of a Frank Stella painting . . . twisted it into knots. (By the way, I am the first painter to literally tie paint into knots) therefore reducing its' importance plastically + symbolically. The space in <u>third phase modernism</u> is mine + mine alone! If you own the space you own the battlefield: the battlefield is worldview.

I will start another painting immediately. Same conceptual approach to space. What's new is the reciprocal relationship of two dimensional plane + third dimensional object: there is a gap between 2-D + 3-D. The painting as object exist within this gap defined by a <u>particular</u> space. This is not a general art historical space. May the games begin!

—NOTES FROM THE WOODSHED <u>010</u>—

13 MARCH: I AM A PERCEPTUALIST. I RECEIVE PURE
SENSUAL INFORMATION FROM THE WORLD AT LARGE.
THIS PURE INFORMATION IS NOT FILTERED THROUGH
ANY SYMBOLIC DEVICE, I.E., IT IS NOT FILTERED
THROUGH THE ① AUTOBIOGRAPHICAL, ② SEXUAL
③ POLITICAL, NATURE ETC. IT IS PURE, IT FILTERS THE
WORLD AS IS. IT IS EVERYTHING + NOTHING!

15 MARCH: The painting as found object is what interest me:
<u>The painting is a found object</u>
Romare Bearden said "you are only as good as what you find"

19 MARCH: Perceptualism is governed by <u>ASYMMETRICAL
MIND</u>, i.e., it is the result of asymmetrical thinking; therefore, it is
non-linear. Do you understand? This is the historical difference of
the <u>now</u>. Time is non-linear.
<u>PRESENT = NON-BEING</u>
Non-being is the new worldview.
We must not be of this world; only in spirit am I here.
<u>ASYMPTOTOS</u>
We must learn to intersect the notion of self. Thelonious Monk had
an asymmetrical mind. . . That's why I like him. Charlie Parker—
John Coltrane—Bud Powell, all had asymmetrical mind—Ornette
Coleman has it! Miles Davis! Dizzy! <u>Mingus</u>
THE CIRCLE IS COMPLETE. <u>JAZZ IS THE EXPANSION OF
FREEDOM</u>. FREEDOM MUST EXPAND OR ELSE IT DIES.
"LET FREEDOM RING, LET FREEDOM RING" <u>MLK</u>

—010—

22 MARCH: Perceptualism is served by light, i.e., the painting as found object is built to receive light. In painting, all information is carried by light. Therefore, the painting is a <u>trap</u>. . . . It captures the light. Light is sequestered in the paint. . . Painters use paint to sequester the light.

27 MARCH: Saw the Whitney annual yesterday. It was so thin. . . Like walking through a MFA review. Becky* looked good. Pleased to see the good action she is getting. Harvey would be pleased. Also saw the Bob Ryman Show at Pace. Strick formalist structures . . . small scale fluctuations of light absorbing—light reflecting. Gallery was too dark. Not necessary. . The paintings themselves address the sublime content. Don't use lightning to make them appear holy. It was overkill. Otherwise O.K. I like Ryman. Milton Avery at Knoedler. . . Superb!! Obvious influence upon Guston + Rothko. Super dark red Rothko 5th fl of Whitney. A nice b+w Glenn Ligon + knockout earl Lee Bontecou.

Otherwise, the scene is thin.

—NOTES FROM THE WOODSHED 010—

8 MAY: saw the Monet show yesterday. I literally caught myself bowing before the paintings. . . . . I was practically on my knees! I share so much with him. His paintings are loaded with eidetic imagery . . . . the phenomological nature of being: our recognizing ourselves through nature. Nature is everything and everything is nature. Kant was right. Nature is extended through being . . . . thinking extends nature. I love Monet <u>but</u> I want it through a technological worldview i.e., technology as an extension of nature. Mind is nature. I see myself as a modern/contemporary equivalent of Monet. I am not an Impressionist, nature does not impress me! Nature inspires me but doesn't dictate. I receive my info through nature as mind. I am a perceptualist.

Saw Amy Sillman paintings at Sikkema. Interesteing. It's very encouraging to see younger painters beginning to think. Don't be afraid to think! She has good conrol of formalist issues + is developing a polemic on being. . . Very good sign. . . [. . .]

Joel Shapiro at Pace: very refreshing! Nothing we don't know . . . but refreshing. I loved his going back to his beginnings . . . . which had humor. At our age it's important to have fun!

9 MAY: went to William Pope.L's opening at Innes-Nash with Stuart H.* Pope is interesting + definitely <u>smart</u>, <u>intelligent</u>, <u>creative</u> but the 'negro' subject matter has become boring. [. . .]
WE MUST LEARN TO CANCEL OUT THE CONTRADICTIONS
LOCATE ALL CONTRADICTIONS + DESTROY . . . . SEARCH
+ DESTROY!

NOTES FROM THE WOODSHED

12 SEPT: back from fishing . . . not a good year for fishing. . . There are no fish worth hunting, only small fish few octopus. Plenty of germanie! Did a great sculpture of black mulberry + Gortina marble. I call it 'GRAY MATTER' a strange piece with extreme philosophical depth which I do not fully understand. Not understanding the full meaning of things could be a virtue. I refuse to speculate on meaning. I prefer to wait until meaning reveals itself on its own terms. I try to avoid imposing meaning. Meaning is something within its' self. Does a tree have meaning? A cloud? A man? The cat 'Meat Face' that came for food every day? Or 'Big Mouth Kitty'! These are serious questions + I don't know the answers.

First order of the day: clean studio + paint floor. This is my back to New York ritual. Every year I paint the studio floor.

Off to the Univ. Of Maryland, David Driskell Center to give a talk + present images of my work. Don't know what to expect. . . I go with an open mind with the primary objective of clarity. <u>I AM A TRANSPARENT MAN</u>.

Basel was a nice experience: the market place for art. I have trouble accepting art as market but what can I or any other artist do. We are part of the capitalist system. I don't like it but there is no alternative.

First painting of the season is for Louise Bourgeois. I sincerely admired her. A true champion of integrity. I want something of sly humor . . . brash + sincere . . . . bold + innovative . . . . sexy in a L.B. manner. Did anyone consider Louise to be sexy?

17 SEPT: Trip to D.D. Center was a success. . Lots of good down home folks. Black people. . .White people all giving good feedback. Thank you. . Thank you. My approach was correct—the source of abstraction—was a big hit. People need a 'hook' to help them to understand abstraction. They are afraid of it. Not knowing creates anxiety people need help. O.K. This was a grass root audience therefore I could approach it 'home grown' will it work at MoMA? I think so. People in genearl are not that different. Bill Hutson was there; it was good to see him. His eyes are better. So far so good. Spoke with David D. at length. [. . .]

Concrete abstraction as a category within perception. A thing— not necessarily an object . . but could operate as object. Concrete abstraction as event embodying time . . . therefore time as event . . not necessarily causal causality or better yet casuality as an entanglement of different systems i.e., symbols = symbol as factual matter simultaneously incorporating spirit. I want spirit as original pre- historical meaning as in life force. Must avoid transcendence + any attempt to transcend matter <u>must</u> <u>be</u> <u>as</u> <u>is</u>. How to avoid naturalistic interruptions? This continues to be a bitch! [. . .] Is it prudent to eliminate spirit? Do I need it? It's like asking do I need God.

Mel's show is terrific! Best installation ever! Small pieces are very compressed. I can imagined them more compressed + I highly reocmmend it. More compression will force them outside the Cubist mode. I would like to see more pre-Cubist content. David Smith + Gonzalez* were still present in the large piece but what a magnificent sculpture!

18 SEPT 10: [. . .] Note of interest: suspension is more than just paint method it's also philosophical + plastic as in formal element of space. Think about it: our planet is suspended. I must pay closer attention to this basic fact. It's concrete as in <u>concrete abstraction</u>.

19 SEPT: How does one approach concrete abstraction? Good question. First of all it is without design. Anti-design is the only way. There is no pre-conceived notion of shape—form—or function. That is all taken care of by detouring design. Concrete abstraction is a detour of history. One does not know where the detour will lead. It is truly a notion of journey. Design has become too burdened with cultural artifact. Bad art helps me to understand what I must do. Especially among black artist they carry too much baggage. We must get rid of the baggage. What must one do with memory? Should it be preserved? Is there a place for memory in concrete abstraction? I don't know, is there a place for God in concrete abstraction? Is God concrete abstraction? If so how do I recognize God? Is God a thing? Can concept be a thing? I am black and I am proud. Is blackness something that must be erased? Must my blackness be sacrificed in order to penetrate concrete abstraction? What about the self? That to must be sacrificed? There is so much I don't know. I am willing and ready to sacrifice anything.

24 SEPT: I must avoid the notion of transcendence at any cost. . .
Any notion of God must be avoided. Religion must be avoided. . .
Any notion of spirituality must be avoided. There is too much
baggage both historically + contemporary. I can live without this. . .
As long as I have empathy both for nature + people in general I can
survive. Transcendence can be replaced with translation i.e., what I
feel is correct, my worldview is correct for modern ethics + morality.
I simply have respect for my fellow beings as long as they are not out
to destroy me! The Republicans are evil racist people with no
empathy. I have no respect for them.

Art allows me to translate my feelings. My paintings are a
translation of my feelings. These feelings are concrete. . . they are
hard + durable like granite. I want my paintings to be concrete, hard
+ durable like granite. Compression makes things concrete.
Compress the space—compress the feelings—compress history—
compress the color structure—compress the surface—compress
everything into matter, and the spirit will exert itself. (Spirit is not
religious, spirit is free of all tangible notions, spirit is the energy that
drives the universe) <u>ALL IS SPIRIT</u>.

2 OCT: IT'S NOT THE PAINT, STUPID! LIGHT IS THE MEDIUM. I HAVE BEEN CONFUSING THIS FOR YEARS! THE PAINT IS ONLY A FORM OF MATTER THAT CARRY THE LIGHT I.E., + THEREFORE THE PAINT IS A METAPHOR FOR LIGHT.

CONT'D 2 OCT: In my case, since I believe in Vulcan philosophy: "INFINITE DIVERSITY IN INFINITE COMBINATIONS" I use light as a transporter of none specific feelings; I leave the specific to the illustrators. I have no interest in illustration. "ANYTHING TO ANYONE AND EVERYTHING TO EVERYONE" M. CASEY.* Sounds good to me. This is what I want. The ultimate expansion of freedom is found within this post-modern icon + it's not about religion it's about freedom.

3 OCT: COMPLETED <u>THE OTHER</u> 1900 HRS.
It's a troublesome painting. . . I always thought of the other as being outside of the self. . . My problem is: I have always spoke of ultimate freedom as the ability to nihilate the other to exhaust the need of the other. What have I done? This painting suggest the other as internal being; therefore, is the other the self? Have I nihilated the self?

4 OCT: This is confusing. I cannot afford the luxury of being confused. The artist likes confusion; it's romantic to be confused. Confusion means I have no responsibility: to no one, to anything, to society, to myself. . . . I am just a bubbly idiot floating in space! How marvelous!! Let's get real: I am a <u>structuralist</u> with lots of responsibility. Concrete abstraction is not about being confused.

5 OCT: The painting exist on the edge of comprehension; we can never know its' complete meaning. It's this not knowing that make the painting interesting. In concrete abstraction the paint as material

exist as physical fact. The material has its' own consciouness. We the viewer project our consciouness onto the material. Its' truly 'what you see is what you get' + then some! Bob was right "it's never enough"

11 OCT: POLLOCK HAD IT WRONG "I AM NATURE" THAT WAS A MISTAKE! WE ARE SIMPLY A PART OF NATURE. WE MUST REMOVE THE I.

10 DEC 10: My hand is hurting. . Difficult to write or work without pain but I must write + I must work. Good news. . . MoMA bought <u>SIBERIAN SALTGRINDER</u> Ms. Temkin* called yesterday. May the games begin!

11 DEC: A SHOT OF RAKI—A BURNING CANDLE—
AN INCENSE STICK LIGHTED. . . . RINGING BELLS,
    A SONG + A LITTLE DANCE
    IN THANKS TO JAMES MOODY
I AM ALWAYS IN THE MOOD FOR LOVE. . .
    LOVE YOU MR. MOODY!

16 DEC: Claire Gilman, curator from the Drawing Center just left [. . .] . . . especially interested in works from 1970's Xerox project. It's very difficult for me to explain this stuff. I know the process + I know the emotions that produced it . . . I don't know what it means. I know it's about matter. . . Matter is concrete + when paint is used as matter therefore the paint is concrete. I want to use paint as matter, which I am doing. . . This is a fact. . . But I also want to direct paint as matter to signifiy a specific subject. This is difficult. I hope this is not wishful thinking. Conceptual rigor is a necessity. Restraint is a necessity. Good health is a necessity. Economics is a necessity. At least I know my priorities. Meaning will have to get in line like all the other necessities! Another option: is meaning necessary? I don't know. Art is an abstraction of life. Is being also an abstraction of life? What is the role of time? Does time have a shape as sugested by Mr. Kubler? Maybe time has more than one shape? I am exploring this notion of time in my present painting. . . . Will keep you informed. [. . .]

30 DEC: My hand is hurting but I must write. When they ask what am I doing? <u>Tell them that I am directing matter</u>. I can direct matter toward any symbol of my choosing.

The most difficult thing for me is <u>restraint</u>. I know it's about <u>measure</u>. How much is enough? My southern sensibility is got me by the balls! Too much ham hocks, black eyed peas, collard greens, pig feet, ears, tails, gate lifters, maws, chittlings, corn bread . . . . . all heavy stuff! But I love it. . . What can I do? I want a worldview for the modern technological society + I am not going to get by taking Lipitor + Linospirol! I must learn to measure everything.

31 DEC: Improvisation i.e., the jazz language. How the jazz musicians use the word. After many hours of conceptual structuring + intense knowledge of plasticity . . both of theory + physicality of instrument + body . . the jazz musician let go into pure action. They are zen people! I want this in painting. . . I strive for this. I want pure action of the now. My materials are my instrument. Fifty years of knowledge go into what I do. It is all compressed into paint. Compression—compression—compression . . . . . . the $\frac{perceptual}{conceptual}$ is compressed in the paint . . . a synthesis of concreteness plus abstraction. I used to think that it was the gap between concreteness + abstraction but this gap has been transcended. <u>I AM ON MY OWN NOW</u>.

I speak of jazz as analogy which is correct. But also science as analogy is also correct, photograph as analogy is also correct. More than one arena defines what I am doing. Our present day culture consists of more than one arena (David Brooks in this mornings <u>Times</u>. Right on! I have chosen the right path.
HAPPY NEW YEAR! J.W.

11 JAN: Anti-design, i.e., to go against design. My thinking? Fractal patterns are not by design. They exist because of nature and nature is not by design. No one designed a tree or a frog or a people. We are here out of <u>pure process</u>. . . . There is no divine creation. We and we alone imposed the notion of the divine. I want my art to exist as an alternative to nature. Another thing that I must say: my art is a tool therefore it has use value. It instructs me on how I want to live. My art is a worldview. Hopefully, my worldview can help other people.

I've been working on rice paper soaked in Kremer's K-9 dispersion with graphite . . . very good results with unusual properties of light . . a photographic glow. I like the description of <u>PSYCHICGRAPHS</u>. Is this too corney?

16 JAN: PAINTERS USE PAINT . . . THAT'S WHAT MAKES US PAINTERS.

Paint is the medium + our notion of light comes from the paint. Light is what matters in painting. All the other shit is theterical props. A real painter do not need props. Subject matter is important but only important as a catalyst. My objective in painting is to reframe painting as we know it. i.e., I want to reframe the Western concept of painting. First I start by changing the verb . . . to paint . . . it must be changed to . I make . . this is the only way to bypass Western thought. Send it back to Africa where it came from! Especially abstraction must be sent back to Africa. I am very thankful to Picasso and all the other European Cubist + Expressionist painters. I am very thankful to Malevich he had the right idea. . . . Malevich's square is a unit. Western art history directed me to my roots, now I must repay it by showing the origin of the original unit. The original unit is a code embedded in African art. I have broken the code. All I have to do is <u>show</u> its' use value through painting. Theory is good but American Pragmatism demands functionality: it must have a use. My use is to construct a

useable worldview for now + the future. The past has served me a
bad hand. This is not the time to look back. <u>I WANT A BETTER
WORLD</u>.

3 FEB: ART IS AN AMAZING TOOL THAT CAN BE USED TO FIGHT OPPRESSION. THIS IS WHY IT FRIGHTENS FASCISTS—DICTATORS—FUNDAMENTALISTS OF ANY CAN. ART CAN BE USED TO RESTORE BALANCE BOTH IN SOCIETY + ONE'S PERSONAL LIFE.

3 MAY: A very nice evening with Jackie Winsor yesterday. I like her very much; she is a true artist. We finished our grading + I announced my retirement from teaching. Alice Ayock, John Newman, Tim Rollins, David Ross, J. Silverton, Suzanne Anker . . . all wished me well. The time has come to remove all the stops. I own the space; I have broken through casuality. Forty-two years of teaching is enough. I have given a lot. I've paid my dues. The rest of my life is mine + I plan to devote it entirely to my art.

What's new? The formal is a means to construct form + content; therefore, it instructs meaning. I've always known this but now it's much clearer. My subject is the world . . . . all of it! I can penetrate any aspect of it. I want it all! By the way . . . . Antwerp was a gas. Mary + I enjoyed every bit. What fun. Frank* + his crew were so nice to us. Alex + David* were fun to be with.

<u>I AM BLESSED</u>

11 MAY: Painting as an antidote to life: I like this. There is so much evil shit in life . . . you name it! Man's inhumanity to man . . . . . catastrophic natural disasters . . . probabily caused my man. Whether man made or not . . . it's all evil! I hate evil! I want a chance at living without life interrupting!

Pass the wine please.

Great art of significant form has no logic this is why it runs parallel to religion. Could art be used as a subsitute to religion? I am bored with the concept of religion as it exist in the modern world.

Religion has become political. Was it always political? Was Christ's death political?

Nice visit with Jackie at the studio; we have a lot in common.

11 MAY: COMPLETED <u>APPS FOR OBAMA</u> 1919 HRS.

22 MAY: COMPLETED <u>NEW YORK DELI FOR WAYNE THIEBAUD</u>. 1546 HRS

Wayne signed one of my reference papers for me when I applied for the John Jay Whitney Foundation grant in 1964. Romare Bearden signed one, Jacob Lawrence + Lawrence Calcagno. Just wanted to take my hat off to Wayne. For good counsel at that time + a great painter. Enjoy.

These are the last paintings for the season. I am going fishing!— these paintings broke with the last Greenbergian taboo . . . . . that of pictorial illusion. Pictorial illusionism is just another tool in the tool box!

I have retired from teaching; therefore, it's time to take out all the stops. Everything is free game. No subject matter is beyond my reach. I don't even rule out the figure . . . . . maybe I'll reinvent still life. Visual jazz: start with a known entity + transform it. Keep it abstract. Take abstraction back to its' original roots. Express yourself through the material. A funny thing has happened to identity: it's in the material.

Perception is my name and perceptionism is my game. Anyone who wants to play is welcome; it's a fun game!

<u>GONE FISHING!</u>

—NOTES FROM THE WOODSHED—
2011

13 SEPT: The summer was fantastic as usual . . . lots of raki, good eating . . . swimming everyday. My garden was beautiful this year: fresh arugula, bok choy, swiss chard, radishes, mustard + turnip, tatsoi . . . all of my favorites. The show with Nikos* was a big success. The villagers turned out including my fishing buddies. Capt. Yianni + Capt. Michael (a real treat!) Lots of young people saw the show. No fishing this year because of the show; that's O.K. Next year in Aghia Galini.

Back to the Big Apple. Go-go-go! None stop. A beautiful opening at Alex's . . gorgeous dinner party afterwards (I did not like the food, all veggie . . . but the vibes were good)

So, where do I start? I start by continuing i.e., it's not about starting + ending. It's always about continuing.

What's new? What if the patining is not an object? The object is secondary, just a piece of matter. The real painting is perceptual i.e., it exist in the brain. Did Jasper Johns led us wrong? Did Stella led us wrong? Somehow we must get back to the painting as a <u>VERB</u> not a <u>NOUN</u>. How do we do this? We do this by <u>bypassing</u> AB/EX's notion of action. Do not place an emphasis on action. It's about <u>STILLNESS</u>. All of us need time to stop + contemplate. <u>STOP</u>! You know the road sign? <u>STOP</u>. WE MUST LEARN TO <u>STOP</u>.

TO GO BEYOND ACTION INTO PURE MENTAL ACTIVITY. LEARN TO DECODE THE INFORMATION.

The information is coded. Every aspect of society carries coded information. The artist must be open and sensitive to vibrations emanating from signals generated by various energy sources. e.g. nature (both organic + inorganic), people . . . + things in general. These vibrations can only be accessed through the nervous system.

They are emotional. A stone generates signals. Water generates signals—people generate signals. Animals generate signals. We must learn to decipher the codes embedded in these signals.

I am rested and ready for actions. May the games begin!

—The French Impressionist said that their color was ceberal, i.e., the color one saw was in the brain. If this is true (which I think it is), consider a physical . . . . . . the painting as object exist in the brain . . . . the painting is an action not an object. <u>I MUST DEMATERIALIZE THE PAINTING</u>.

Remove the self. The notion of self is a sick Western notion. There is no such thing as the self! Identity has eluded me all of these years because of this sick Western notion! Genetics is a fact of science + I have a lot of faith in science. Genetics is also a fact of painting + I know a lot about the genetics of painting. Let science take care to explain the genetics of people + I will take care to explain the genetics of painting! Painting is organic + it continues to evolve. The codes that I speak of is a genetic code of painting. I must continue to decipher the genetic code of painting. That's my job. I am a painter.

23 SEPT: Yes, to dematerialize the painting. Therefore less dependence on the object . . . . I want its' perceptual qualities to exert itself on the viewer.

Everything is becoming clearer. I have always known painting to be organic. I believe that society is organic and I believe that history is organic. The end of history is a farce! Since history is organic, the history of painting is organic. I have been placing too much emphasis upon myself as organic (a literally truth) the emphasis must not be on me.

6 OCT: all of these years, I have been jealous of the photograph. Why am I so silly? There is no reason for anyone to be jealous of the photograph. The photograph converts three dimension into two dimension. This is so obvious I almost want to cry! <u>I am a painter</u>: I convert <u>an unseen</u> dimension into two dimension. I cannot see this dimension. I can only feel it. Remember the game 'Blind Man's Bluff'? It's very much like that. I can smell it; I can feel it but I cannot see it. Good meeting yesterday with Bennett Simpson. His show for L.A MOCA seems to be on track. He offered me the opportunity to write an essay for the catalogue. This is a great opportunity to get my ideas about jazz in print. I have a lot to say!

13 OCT: I had pig's feet for lunch today. They were fantastic! All chewy, fatty . . . lots of grizzle$_{s/p}$ gelantious. I made them Bessemer, Ala. style . . . . boiled whole until soft with garlic, onion, red + black pepper . . . . nothing fancy. My plan is to use the bones for a necklace. That's right . . . a pig's foot necklace!

<u>RIGHT ON</u>

14 OCT: COMPLETED <u>MS. FANCY PANTS</u> 2045 HRS.
For my summer kitty Ms. Fancy Pants. I hope that George's* mother is taking care of her. She is a spirit that came to me + pushed me to the next level. I love Ms. Fancy Pants!

19 OCT 1445 HRS. COMPLETED <u>SQUARE KNOT</u> (DOUBLE LOOP) 12" x 12"

27 OCT 1300 HRS. COMPLETED ~~TIME LOOPS~~ 12"X12"
SINGLE LOOP ~~OVERHAND LOOP~~ → ~~OVERHAND KNOT~~ ~~(that's what~~ it is!
> SIMULTANEITY: COMPETITION, RIVALRY, etc., TOGETHER OR AT THE SAME TIME
> CONTEMPORARY: LIVING OR HAPPENING IN THE SAME PERIOD OF TIME.
> MODERN: OF THE PRESENT OR RECENT TIMES
These three words all have time as a common denominator, therefore they are linked together, and they occur at the same time. Everything that I am feeling is about time. Since I believe that <u>art is structured feeling</u>; therefore my art is about structuring time. We know that time is connected to being (see Heiddeger); therefore my originally thinking is correct: if you can structure time you can structure space. Time and space is interconnected. These basic facts are cosmic. What was true a million years ago is true today. Time does not change . . . . we change!

7 NOV 2011—Completed <u>TRIPLE LOOP</u> 1230 hrs. 12" x 12"
Something has happened + I don't know what. Another level of
consciousness? I think but as usual I don't know what. I'm a little
shaky, as usual . . . . . . experiencing lots of anxiety. Very sensitive to
outside noise. Mary says 'no place is perfect' she is right . . . . but
noise bothers me.

<u>TRIPLE LOOP</u> is strange . . . a bit weird. . I don't know what to
think of it. Interesting color . . . interesting light . . . . interesting space
Hard to pin down i.e., hard to tie down!

<u>GO SLOW</u>

<u>SINGLE LOOP</u>, <u>DOUBLE LOOP</u>, <u>TRIPLE LOOP</u>
These three little paintings (12"x12") is about my attempt to
lasso time

<u>TIME IS A BUCKING WILD HORSE!</u>
+ I AM TRYING TO TAME IT.
IT'S A WILD WEST SHOW OUT THERE!

P.S. YOU MUST GO THROUGH TIME TO GET TO SPACE.

<u>UNDERSTAND?</u>

KEEP YOUR EYE ON THE PRIZE.

22 NOV: I received a frighten thought today + I don't know how to handle it: <u>GET RID OF THE SPIRITUAL</u>. I don't know what to do. I who have invested so much time into the spiritiual? To deny the presence of God? There is no one to advise me. If I get rid of the spiritual, what's left? I am stuck with a dumb piece of matter? Go back to the beginning of <u>time</u>: we the people gave meaning to the spiritual. We + only we said: <u>THERE</u> <u>IS</u> <u>A</u> <u>GOD</u>. It was our idea. Maybe it's time to re-establish the meaning of God without the baggage of history. What do I have to lose? It is not my history. <u>I PLEDGE</u> <u>NO</u> <u>ALLEGIANCE</u> <u>TO</u> <u>HISTORY</u> <u>AS</u> <u>IT</u> <u>IS WRITTEN</u>. Why should I? It has totally written me out of the discourse. I was never considered to be human. I was only chattel. <u>NOW IS THE TIME</u>!

We the people must take charge. Religion is totally disfunctional . . . . . it has become politcal; it is a means to power . . . . power over the weak . . . the dis-inheirited . . . . over people of color or anyone who do not agree with their agenda. The people must say, <u>I am the power</u>. The people must say <u>I</u> <u>AM</u> <u>THE</u> <u>POWER</u>. The people must take back <u>TIME</u>. <u>TIME</u> was stolen from us. Time belongs to the people. Time is a subtance of the soul. It has no color. It is transparent . . . . diaphanous . . . . translucent. Time is malleable. It can be hammered like water . . . . . . water is time. Time is congruent to water + likewise to matter in general. Our metaphor of time flows is correct. At present it has no perimeters therefore it is wasted. Someone must restore the parameters + maybe that someone is <u>ME</u>.

<u>P.S.</u> my knot paintings is a lasso . . . . a tool used to capture time. . . <u>TIE IT UP!</u> <u>HOG TIE IT!</u>

28 NOV 2011: COMPLETED THE <u>FOURTH LOOP</u> 1300 HRS.
And I think that there is a fifth loop . . . . .
. . . . . will start investigating immediately!
note: THE FOURTH LOOP is a circle with a circumference of @
30"; it turned four times to form this shape i.e., it's a circle that turns
in more than one dimension

2 DEC: completed the <u>FIFTH LOOP</u>. It is a circle also measuring
40" circumference. <u>PLEASE</u> <u>DO</u> <u>NOT</u> <u>ASK</u> <u>ME</u> <u>WHAT</u> <u>THIS</u>
<u>MEAN</u>! <u>I</u> <u>DON'T</u> <u>KNOW</u>!
I THINK THAT THERE ARE TWO MORE.
SOME ADVICE: <u>TAKE THE OTHER AND PACKAGE IT</u>.
<u>P.S.</u> THE OTHER IS A NEW FORM OF GEOMETRY.

5 DEC. COMPLETED THE SIXTH LOOP 1800 HRS. <u>HAPPY
BIRTHDAY</u>!
Omiros* called, Jesse called, brother called, Harriet Elam called →
for <u>Happy Birthday</u>!
<u>WHAT JOY!!</u>
→ 42" circumference circle <u>O.K. THE COMPASS OF FREEDOM
STARTING THE SEVENTH LOOP IMMEDIATELY</u>
The circumference must be 44" → this is my circle

8 DEC: COMPLETED THE SEVENTH LOOP 1500 HRS.
    There are probably more but I must stop; the others require
another level of consciouness. Elizabeth paid a visit just about three
quarters of completion; therefore, this set of seven little 12" square
paintings I give to her.
THE GIFT: (FOR ELIZABETH MURRAY) 2011
note: don't break this set . . . keep them together!
—THE FORMAL IS THE THING WITHIN THE THING. . . . I
WANT THE THING BEYOND THE THING.

10 DEC: I AM READY TO START THE BUD POWELL
PAINTING. A GOOD SOLID FOUNDATION HAS BEEN
LAID. THE TITLE IS FIVE LINES FOUR SPACES ; FOR BUD
POWELL. I HAD TO MAKE A SPECIAL TOOL, MADE OF
FIVE PENCILS SET INTO A SOLID PIECE OF PINE AT
3/4" INTERVALS   THIS ALLOWED ME TO DRAW
FIVE LINES   AT ONCE ... *THEY CURVE & LOOP (..changed
FROM ONE END   OF THE PLANE TO ANOTHER (..this
THE PLANE IS A GOLDEN MEANS THAT MEASURE 62¼" H X 46½" W
THE GROUND IS BUILT OF SPINEL BLACK. THE KEY TO SUCCESS WITH
THIS PAINTING IS SPONEITY /IMPROVISATION. THE TESSERA
          TAN
IS ALL PRE CUT. THE CONCEPTUAL IS COMPLETE ..... FROM NOW
ON IT'S PURE FAITH...... I WILL DUMP THE MIND AND
GO WITH THE PURITY OF SPIRIT. GOD BLESS.
11 DEC: I FORGOT TO TELL YOU HOW THIS PAINTING
GUTHRIE REMINDED ME & I WANTED TO DO
AN UPDATE OF BROADWAY BOOGIE WOOGIE BUT FROM
A BLACK PERSPECTIVE..... WARP THE GRID & MAKE
IT CURVE. ... I DON'T MIND IF A LITTLE
HIP-HOP GOT IN!

12 DEC ✳ IT'S NOTATION NOT IMAGE
          JAZZ MUSIC IS CODED. IT'S A LANGUAGE (PLASTICITY)
BEYOND THE NARRATIVE therefor VERY ABSTRACT. THE NARRATIVE
CANNOT BE ABSTRACT UNLESS IT'S AN ABSTRACT NARRATIVE... THERE IS A DIFFERENCE
· · · · · - - - - · · · · · / - - / · / - - - - / · · · · / - - / · - - / - - , etc.

          TIME IS WRAPED IN SPACE AS IF SPACE IS A BLANKET.
28 DEC. THE PAINTING IS A PERCEPTUAL OBJECT i.e, IT EXIST IN THE
BRAIN.... I CAN SEE IT BUT HOW MUST I PROCESS IT?
THIS IS THE HARD PART. SOMETIMES I WISH TO BE A CONCEPTUALIST
AND JUST LEAVE IT THERE... BUT I AM A PAINTER.... I NEED
THE OBJECT!
          TODAY I RECEIVED AN OLD FASHIONED ASS-WHIPING! THE PAINTING
WHIPPED MY ASS! YOU DON'T KNOW HOW HARD THIS SHIT IS.
WITH A WOOD CHISEL & MALLET I DESTROYED THE MOTHERFUCKER,
& GROUD IT OUT WITH MY GRINDER. THE PAINTING GOT TOO
CUTE, TOO CLEAVER, TOO SMART.... I WANT SOMETHING SIMPLE
NOT TOO COMPLEX & STRAIGHT FORWARD... DIRECT & BLUNT.
          I'LL RECACULATE & START OVER!
                    THAT'S THE NAME OF THE GAME!

—2011—

10 DEC: I AM READY TO START THE BUD POWELL
PAINTING, A GOOD SOLID FOUNDATION HAS BEEN LAID.
THE TITLE IS <u>FIVE</u> <u>LINES</u> <u>FOUR</u> <u>SPACES</u>: FOR BUD POWELL.
I HAD TO MAKE A SPECIAL TOOL, MADE OF FIVE PENCILS
SET INTO A SOLID PIECE OF PINE AT 3/4" INTERVALS
[drawing] THIS ALLOWED ME TO DRAW FIVE LINES AT
ONCE . . . .*THEY CURVE + LOOP FROM ONE END OF THE
PLANE TO ANOTHER (. . . changed this) THE PLANE IS A
GOLDEN MEANS THAT MEASURE $62\frac{1}{4}$" H X $46\frac{1}{2}$" W THE
GROUND IS BUILT OF SPINEL BLACK. THE KEY TO
SUCCESS WITH THIS PAINTING IS SPONTANEITY /
IMPROVISATION. THE TESSEERA IS ALL PRECUT. THE
CONCEPTUAL IS COMPLETE . . . . . . FROM NOW ON IT'S
PURE FAITH . . . . . . I WILL DUMP THE MIND AND GO WITH
THE PURITY OF SPIRIT. GOD BLESS.

11 DEC: I FORGOT TO TELL YOU KNOW THIS PAINTING
GOTHRIE REMINDED ME + I WANTED TO DO AN UPDATED
OF BROADWAY BOOGIE WOOGIE BUT FROM A BLACK
PERSPECTIVE . . . . . WARP THE GRID + MAKE IT
CURVE . . . . I DON'T MIND IF A LITTLE HIP-HOP GOT IT!

12 DEC * <u>IT'S</u> <u>NOTATION</u> <u>NOT</u> <u>IMAGE</u>
     JAZZ MUSIC IS CODED. IT'S A LANGUAGE (PLASTICITY)
BEYOND THE NARRATIVE therefore VERY ABSTRACT. THE
NARRATIVE CANNOT BE ABSTRACT UNLESS IT'S AN
ABSTRACT NARRATIVE . . . . THERE IS A DIFFERENCE
[drawing]
TIME IS WRAPPED IN SPACE AS IF SPACE IS A BLANKET!

28 DEC. THE PAINTING IS A PERCEPTUAL OBJECT i.e., IT EXIST IN THE BRAIN . . . . I CAN SEE IT BUT HOW MUST I PROCESS IT? THIS IS THE HARD PART. SOMETIMES I WISH TO BE A CONCEPTUALIST AND JUST LEAVE IT THERE . . . BUT I AM A PAINTER . . . . I NEED THE OBJECT!

TODAY I RECEIEVED AN OLD FASHIONED ASS-WHIPING! THE PAINTING WHIPPED MY ASS! YOU DON'T HOW HARD THIS SHIT IS. WITH A WOOD CHISEL + MALLET I DESTROYED THE MOTHERFUCKER, + GROUND IT OUT WITH MY GRINDER. THE PAINTING GOT TOO CUTE, TOO CLEAVER, TOO SMART . . . . I WANT SOMETHING SIMPLE NOT TOO COMPLEX + STRAIGHTFORWARD . . . DIRECT + BLUNT. I'LL RECALCULATE + START OVER. THAT'S THE NAME OF THE GAME!

29 DEC: Tell your particle physicists, your cosmologists, your astronomers + everybody else who is studying the universe that <u>dark matter</u> is the glue that holds the universe together. Without dark matter we will go back to the big bang! <u>I AM DARK MATTER.</u>

31 DEC: I am in a very bad mood. . . . I brunt my spare ribs! Fantastic Heritage Farms spare ribs + I brunt them! Mirsini + Mary will be upset. I ask forgiveness. New Years Eve . . . . what do I wish for? <u>Good health.</u>
Everything is possible with health.

A few painting problems to work on this year: (TEN POINTS)
1. I must continue to clarify my position.
2. Going back to the first gray paintings of the early sixties (photographic process paintings) "the image is photographic; therefore, I must photograph my thoughts" <u>SHOW THE END RESULTS OF THIS.</u> What does this mean today.
3. Explain i.e., show what I mean by the painting is a perceptual object.
    (a) I see the painting in my brain + must process it through matter. This is the meaning of the photograph as analogy.
4. Continue to clarify <u>PAINT AS COLLAGE.</u>
5. Remember my desire to do a non-relationship painting? I succeded in do this with my developer (the whole plane as one gesture) How do I continue to do non-relational concept without the aid of my developer? This is a tough problem. <u>THE ANSWER IS PURE MIND.</u>
6. Clarify my use of the word <u>SPIRIT.</u> What do I mean; <u>IT IS NOT DIVINE</u>. . . <u>IT IS HUMAN.</u> Being human is spirit. Spirit is not a hocus-pocus unknown. . . If I know myself . . . I know spirit.

7.   Perservence. Keep my eye on the prize.

8.   Avoid politics + religion at any cost!

9.   Support Alexander Gray

10. Make enough money to stay in the studio and to purchase any supplies necessary for work.

<u>HAPPY NEW YEAR</u>

2012 <u>NOTES FROM THE WOODSHED</u>

14 JAN: 1725 HRS. COMPLETED THE <u>EIGHTH LOOP</u>
That was tough! Nonstop . . . working in pain, but that's O.K. it takes pain to get what you want! My reward is a shot of raki. .
Plan to start the NINTH LOOP immediately.

15 JAN: Collage came out of Africa. Picasso saw it in African sculpture and took it. That's O.K. because his doing that gave me my freedom. It's a beautiful historical reference of one artist helping another artist. I needed that! Freedom has expanded through collage. It is good to know that freedom continues to expand. It gives me hope for the future + prevents me from becoming paranoid. <u>OPTIMISM IS MY BEST BET.</u> My accountant, Marty Melzer told me "whatever you are doing, keep doing it"

2012 <u>NOTES FROM THE WOODSHED</u>

OR: <u>WOODSHED LOG</u>

25 JAN: I saw the Buddha today; his image appeared on a piece of tessera. I was overwhelmed with joy! Now I definitely feel that I am connected to history . . . . just as Franz Kline said.
A messenger delivered two copies of February issue Artforum. Guess who is on the cover? A full reproduction of <u>PINK PSYCHE QUEEN,</u> 1973. [. . .]

GLORY TO ART!!!!! POWER TO ART !!!

31 JAN: 1620 HRS. COMPLETED THE <u>NINTH LOOP</u> 48" x 48"
151" circumference
Will start the <u>TENTH LOOP</u> immediately! → C=141" in ten loops it's a little tighter!

1 FEB: Absurd contradictions interest me. Is concrete realism absurd enough?

13 FEB: The painting has entered a phase whereas it paints itself. I think that this is what the Greeks means . . . Archeterios$_{s/p}$ . . . to paint without hands. Of course they are talking about the devine i.e., without human hands. A neat idea but I am not into that! For me, it's all human! Larry Miller certified me as human. . . Enough of the hocus-pocus; let get real!

I am working on the <u>TENTH LOOP</u> . . . long hours everyday, but this is what I do . . . it's my job. I am trying to avoid design, I want it to paint itself . . . I want it to design itself. The line, i.e., the strip of acrylic that is a linear surrogate dictates the curvature of space . . . even the light source is dictated by the curvature of space. Let's face it, it's all geometry!

14 FEB: HAPPY VALENTINE'S DAY!

Graham Greene, <u>Fabric of the Cosmos</u>, spoke of 'phase transition,' I like this. . . . Could the use of paint be thought of 'phase transition'? Think of it . . . . . we use this stuff as matter . . . . . we take it through different processes that transform its' character . . . thereby forcing it into a metaphysical realm. . . . Do you get my drift?

22 FEB: 1355 HRS. COMPLETED <u>THE TENTH LOOP</u>.

50" x 34¼" IT'S GORGEOUS!

I'LL HAVE A SHOT OF RAKI TO CELEBRATE!!

-2012-

21 MARCH:

I AM REARRANGING NATURE... BEING HUMAN ALLOWS ME TO DO THIS. WE HAVE INTERFERED WITH NATURE... IN ORDER TO RESTORE SYMETRY WE MUST TAKE RESPONSIBILITY. IT IS OUR DUTY TO RESTORE THIS PLANET!

P.S. IT OCCURED TO ME, FROM MY PERSPECTIVE BEING AFRICAN... IT IS, THE REVERSE OF PICKING COTTON & I WANT TO BE PAID FOR MY LABOR! GOD IS A CONCEPT CONCEIVED BY US WE & ONLY WE ARE RESPONSIBLE FOR THE MORAL & ETHIC BALANCE IN SOCIETY. WE MUST TAKE CHARGE!

24 MARCH: COMPLETED THE ELEVENTH LOOP 1900 HRS.

GOOD VISIT TODAY WITH HANS RUDOLF REUST. INTERESTING GUY... GOOD TALK.

25. I EXPLAINED TO HANS YESTERDAY THE SIGNIFIANCE OF THE 'LOOP'...... I GAVE HIM A DRAWING DONE ON A PIECE OF PLYWOOD... A SKETCH OF THE 'LOOP':

EUROPE
AMERICA
NOW
AFRICA

THIS IS THE LOOP.

I STARTED IN AFRICA, WAS BROUGHT TO THE AMERICAS... I HAD TO GO TO EUROPE.... BACK TO AMERICA & BACK TO AFRICA.. IN ORDER TO GET WHERE I AM TODAY, THEREFORE, THE 'LOOP' IS AUTOBIOGRAPHICAL. THIS EXPLAINS MY PRESENT IDENTITY..... I AM GLOBAL! THIS IS WHY I SPEAK OF THIRD STAGE MODERNISM. I AM THE THIRD STAGE. THE LOOP IS MY SYMBOL OF BEING.

—2012—

21 MARCH:

I AM REARRANGING NATURE . . . BEING HUMAN ALLOWS ME TO DO THIS. WE HAVE INTERFERED WITH NATURE . . . IN ORDER TO RESTORE SYMETRY WE MUST TAKE RESPONSIBILITY. IT IS OUR DUTY TO RESTORE THIS PLANET! P.S. IT OCCURRED TO ME, FROM MY PERSPECTIVE BEING AFRICAN . 'A'. IT IS THE REVERSE OF PICKING COTTON + I WANT TO BE PAID FOR MY LABOR! <u>GOD IS A CONCEPT CONCEIVED BY US</u>. WE + ONLY WE ARE RESPONSIBLE FOR THE MORAL + ETHIC BALANCE IN SOCIETY. WE MUST TAKE CHARGE!

24 MARCH: COMPLETED <u>THE ELEVENTH LOOP</u> 1900 HRS. GOOD VISIT TODAY WITH HANS RUDOLF REUST. INTERESTING GUY . . . GOOD TALK.

<u>25</u>. I EXPLAINED TO HANS YESTERDAY THE SIGNIFIANCE OF THE 'LOOP' . . . . . . I GAVE HIM A DRAWING DONE ON A PIECE OF PLYWOOD . . . A SKETCH OF THE 'LOOP':

[drawing; looping arrows proceeding through "AFRICA," "AMERICA," "EUROPE," and "NOW"]
THIS IS THE LOOP.

I STARTED IN IN AFRICA, WAS BROUGHT TO THE AMERICAS . . . I HAD TO GO TO EUROPE . . . . BACK TO AMERICA + BACK TO AFRICA . . IN ORDER TO GET WHERE I AM TODAY, THEREFORE, THE 'LOOP' IS AUTOBIOGRAPHICAL. THIS EXPLAINS MY PRESENT IDENTITY . . . . . <u>I AM GLOBAL!</u> THIS IS WHY I SPEAK OF THE THIRD STAGE MODERNISM. I AM THE THIRD STAGE, THE LOOP IS MY SYMBOL OF BEING.

26 MARCH: Bud is still whipping my ass! I had to go back into FIVE LINES FOUR SPACES: FOR BUD POWELL. It was not resolved. I discovered something that is very intriguing: THE ALL OVER HAS A GROUND. This is unbelievable! What would Clem say? Everybody, including myself, believed that the all-over was final i.e., no possible ground. That's why we thought of it as being sublime. Obviously Rothko suspected this . . . . that's why he put in a horizontal horizon divide. He was suspicious . . . beyond a doubt. And Pollock? He didn't have a clue! He simply thought it was more of himself. (A basic American mistake!) THIS SHIT IS NOT ABOUT US! It is beyond us. It's no wonder that particle physicists speak of other dimensions. They are correct.

27 MARCH: I AM A MÖBIUS STRIP.

I insist that soul + mind be the same thing. If all of us accept this proposition, it will cut through all the bullshit!

28 MARCH: I am a humanist first + second a möbius strip.

The most important is to be human. . . . Everything else takes second place. Being human: I love, I hate, I fuck, I eat, I fish, I make, I feel, I hear, I touch, I see, I shit, I fear, I plant, I plow, I water, I conserve, I protect, I fight, I laugh, I cry, I wonder, I inspect, I choose, I run, I walk, I stand, I smell, I drink, I pray, I think, I speak, I play, I hunt, I suck, I sleep. . . . . . . Have I forgotten anything?

If so, you understand my drift!

31 MARCH: 1752 HRS COMPLETED FIVE LINES FOUR SPACES (AN UPDATED VERSION OF BROADWAY BOOGIE WOOGIE): FOR BUD POWELL.

I am following the light. The light we now expeirence is from billions of years ago. . . . . It has just reached us!

The light I see now is from the time of the cave dwellers. I am going back in time. Humanity missed something and I want to know <u>what</u>!! Whatever was lost must be found. This is my worldview. . . to retrieve what was lost + make it useful for <u>now</u>.

Painting is showing me the way. Abstract painting is showing me the way. I have no need of illustation, rendering, design, smart-ass conceptual or other hyped-up bullshit masquerading as art. I want the real thing!

<u>THE DIVINE WAS A MISTAKE. CHRIST DIED FOR NOTHING: ONLY THE LIGHT CAN SET US FREE. FIND THE LIGHT AND YOU ARE FREE.</u>
<u>DON'T ATTEMPT TO ATTACH ANY MEANING TO THE LIGHT. IT IS WHAT IT IS. LEARN TO ACCEPT THIS. IT HAS NO NAME. IT IS NO DOGMA: IT IS IT.</u>

The conceptual is only a springboard for something much greater . . . it is a ramp . . . it is a launching pad . . . . . it is a diving board . . . . . it is a catalyst . . . . it is a detnator. What I am interested in lies 'beyond' the conceptual.

3 MAY: Art Frieze opens today. Mary + I are going to the VIP opening. Saw Richard Serra at the BOMB gala + asked him to see my paintings on view. He abruptly cut me off + said "I don't go to art fairs." I don't like going to art fairs either + I don't like the commerce of art. What is one to do? Every artist needs money to survive + do our thing. It takes money to make art. We have the same needs as everybody in society: a place to live + work, supplies, doctors, lawyers, accountants, food, clothing + all the necessities of life. Richard speaks from an extremely privileged position. . . one of money + power. He has always had support from commercial dealers, curators, major collectors, museum directors from all over the world, critics + historians. He is white + that means a lot in America. He is a good sculptor + I personally admire his work. <u>He is the one percent</u>. 'Don't be a hypocrite richard; you have always been a benefactor of art fairs!' White artists, especially white male artist overlook the importance of their whiteness . . . . they have an automatic entry into the art world. I am seventy two. I have maintained a studio in New York since 1960. . . Only now am I beginning to get some attention. I have survived with very little help from the 'art world' the white art world simply denies my existence. My adjenda_{s/p} is to paint; it is not political or commerce but all of this whether I like it or not becomes an issue. It's important that I am very clear of my objectives for being. What do I want from my art? I want a viable worldview.

4 MAY: THE PAINTING IS A TRAP DESIGNED + SET TO CAPTURE THE MOMENT. A LIGHT TRAP! <u>THE UNIT IS THE MOMENT</u>.

21 MAY: painting is about light. All information is carried by the light. The history of painting is the history of light. It's the artist choice to give light meaning. It can be anything the artist desires. It can be divine, i.e., sacred, addressing the sublime or it can be purely formal. Whtever you want; this is the ultimate freedom. I am interested in the sublime but I don't want anything to do with a particular religion. I am a humanist. The spirit is human.

My objectives in painting are somewhat clearer now. At seventy two my objective in painting is to use the light in order to go back in time. I am following the light to go back. . .before this history of art. Art history is tainted with the political and the cards are stacked against me. Destory the history of art! By destroying the history of art I have a better chance of directing the light in my favor.

The avant garde is a historical mistake! We must go back in time. . . Not forward!

I AM THE LIGHT.

30 MAY: I went to MoMA to see the Cindy Sherman show.

She is good. Lots of women viewers. . . both young + old: some of them actually looked like her photos. She in particular speaks to women. Her work is autobiographical identity photos. [. . .] Who is Cindy Sherman? The photos did nothing for me. They are extremely psychological; in painting we call this psychological space. Plastically they gave me something to work with: place more importance on the subject i.e., figure/ground . . . . more emphasis on the figure . . . . reduce the ground as being important. Any ground will do: as in photo backdrop paper. <u>REDUCE THE GROUND + INCREASE THE PRESENCE OF FIGURE</u>.

Figure could be presence as in African sculpture which is all presence. It's important to see everything! Even Satchmo said "you gotta listen to the Beatles!" Right on! Everything out there has something to offer. Everybody is important. Learn to recognize what people have to offer . . . this is part of the learning process and therefore a very important element of art.

We leave for Aghia Galini tomorrow. It's been a good year. I'm exhausted but feel good about my work. The show for Frank is ready to go. I can leave in peace. My body is aching to carve wood. The woodcarving means so much to me. My inspiration for painting comes from the wood. All of my ideas in painting come from the wood. My head is bursting!

Big problems in greece + we don't know what to expect. Stay close to home. . Support the locals as much as possible. Until next season. . . . .

<u>GONE FISHING!!</u>
TZAK

2 JUNE 2012

—Good news from Venice: my painting was well received. [. . .] What am I hoping for? M. Gioni's* concept for the show recognizes the desire for more substance in art . . . . more depth . . . . . more psychological presence. Today's art is lacking in all of this. The market driven aesthetic has wiped all the energy out of art. People are hungry for the real thing. <u>I AM THE REAL THING.</u>

<u>6 JUNE</u>: [. . .] —GONE FISHING!—

<u>NOTES FROM THE WOODSHED</u> 212

10 SEPT: Back to the big apple. My head is bursting with ideas. Good reading this summer: revisited Hegel's <u>Phenology of Spirit</u>, Husserl's phenomenological studies + commentaries, Gaston Bachelard's <u>The New Scientific Spirit</u>. More than ever I am convinced <u>THAT SPIRIT IS HUMAN; IT IS NOT DIVINE</u>. We invented the notion of God. Lost my sister Toots. . . . I am so sad but I am thankful that she did not linger. That was a blessing.

Lots to do: talk in Boston, talk in Amsterdam + show at Zeno X plus all the art fairs with Zeno X. For the first time I am not worried about money. . . .

Duchamp invented <u>readymades</u>. . . . I have invented <u>readynows</u>. Readynows are objects—shape—form built with acryic from many different sources. They allow me to work more rapidly + spontaneous without having to think. Making the painting is like making oriental cooking: everything including the support must be ready + available for instant construct. Barry White said "I don't like to think too hard!" I like this. . . . SET IT ALL UP CONCEPTUALLLY + ACT!

Abtract painting developed during first + second stage moderism plus the remants of post-moderism is over. I want an abstraction for third stage moderism. Abstraction has become generic. . . . The only way out is to go beyond abstraction. It's another mindset

13 SEPT: I have set a most difficult task for myself. My big mouth is getting me into trouble. For example: when I use the term molecular perception, how do I explain this without resorting to second haded scientific language? I am not a scientist at least not in the physical sense, but I know that what I am doing is parallel to science. What is my language? I can give a general description of what I am doing, but there comes a point when even description comes to a stop. What must I do? I feel like Ludwig Wittgenstein when he said "<u>I must show not say</u>. I have no problem with showing; I am a painter.

Materialization of matter is a difficult thing. How can I possibly explain this? I feel it but I can't say it i.e., explain in words. Mind is matter. How can I explain this? My next big problem in painting is the conversion of matter into energy. The scientist say that this is possible. How is it possible for painting? I have no problem with the idea as object. How can I remove the emphasis on physicality as matter (which is easy) and place the emphasis on the cerebral? I don't want the object as fact. . . . I want it as essence. Less matter more essence? Am I being dependent on paint as matter? I got involved with this line of thought through sensibility: <u>BLACK FOLKS ARE PHYSICAL</u>. Is my blackness starting to get in my way? Is painting asking me to give up something? If so, how much and what am I giving up?

Maybe <u>IT</u> is simple + I as usual am making <u>IT</u> more complex. I know this about myself. . . . . . I tend to make it difficult . . . . but difficult and complex is not the same thing. My problem is I tend not to trust anything if it is not hard. Never trust a limp dick! Ludwig said 'my ideas are like granite' I like this. If it's too soft + mushy, I don't like it!

There is no doubt in my mind that the loop paintings have thrust me into another orbit. I am out there now whether I like it or not!

14 SEPT:

I read an article in the <u>N.Y. Times</u> that was very interesting: it was an advertisement for a gadget that translates digital recording into analog recording. Sound travels in a wave. When we are listening to music it is the wave that strikes our ear. It made me think of John Coltrane when he said to me "it's like a wave" I remember his waving his arms in the air . . . . . "it's like a wave." Evidently the digital breaks this wave into bits and proceeds to connect the bits. Of course, something was lost with the digital. That's why the gadget was invented.

The best of Coltrane is the <u>thing within itself</u>. Later, someone dubbed this wave as a sheet of sound. Wave or sheet, is right on the money . . . . . . a continuous stream of sound. My early paintings were influenced by Coltrane's wave hence I called them 'LIGHT SHEETS'

I have learned a lot since 1968 but now I want to go back to my light sheets . . . . the concept of 'planar light.' Construct—deconstruct—reconstruct must be compressed into a sheet of light i.e., a plane of light.

15 SEPT: ANTI DESIGN—ANTI ILLUSTRATION—
ANTI IDEA—ANTI NATURALISM—ANTI CONSUMERISM—
ANTI WARHOL—ANTI KOONS—ANTI GAGOSIAN—
ANTI CONCEPTUAL—ANTI CLOSE—ANTI WASP—
ANTI RELIGION—ANTI RHETORIC—ANTI DOGMA—
ANTI FORMAL—ANTI NARRATIVE—ANTI PSYCHOLOGY—
ANTI AUTOBIOGRAPHICAL—ANTI DECORATIVE—
ANTI DEITCH—ANTI MEANING—ANTI RACE—
ANTI KNOWING—ANTI ART—ANTI ISMS —ANTI NOISE—
ANTI STRATEGY—ANTI-MONEY—ANTI MIND—
ANTI BODY—ANTI SOUL—ANTI SPIRIT—ANTI HUMAN—
ANTI SUBJECTIVE—ANTI OBJECTIVE, etc., etc., etc.

16 SEPT: I am not trying to be funny. Negation is an element of being. Through negation we discover other layers of consciouess. Negation is dangerous . . . . a risky undertaking. One must be careful not to negate being. I am therefore I am. There is nothing else to consider. What has happened to us? Are we still the people who were brought over in the hole of slave boats? Are my gods still with me? Who must I ask for guidance? There must be something left over . . . there must be something that we can salvage. Modern technology needs some competition. We have something to offer . . . . to bring to the table. We have something to say. What language must we use? Where are the words that have been missing from the dialogue of human rights? Where is the structure to say who we are? To whom must we speak?

Memory will not help us; we lost that a long time ago. Thinking could help: we must build a scaffold for thought. We must celebrate who we are. We must build an economic structure in order to implement our ideas. Sound ideas make sound people; sound people make a sound world.

18 SEPT: Meaning is the enemy of art. Artists must resist the temptation to give meaning to art. We are not politicians. Truth has no meaning nor can it be confined in tight spaces. In painting, the materials represent the truth; not the narrative. I trust red, yellow, ... all pigments embody truth. We must be careful and allow them to speak for themselves. Stop imposing meaning to colors. They don't need your help. You set-up the support i.e., the scaffolding and they will take care of the rest.

21 SEPT: I want an unpredictable color. This agrees with what I discovered in the sixties. . . . <u>FOUND COLOR</u>. This color does not come as a result of conceptual mixing. One must discover it during the act of making. It's fast to the eye therefore drawing as a means of

training the eye is the best exercise. Once we learn to recognize the light we can see the color. Molecular perception is located in the light.

CONT'D 21 SEPT:

SEE MOLECULAR PERCEPTION . . . . WE CAN ONLY FEEL IT. IT IS PURE PERCEPTION THAT EXIST IN THE BRAIN. PAINT AS MATTER IS THE ONLY MEANS OF STRUCTURING THE PAINTER'S LIGHT. OTHERWISE IT REMAINS PURE PERCEPTION e.g, ONLY IN THE BRAIN.

A FEW THOUGHTS ON THE CONCEPT of GOD:

1. NO ONE OWNS GOD.
2. CHRISTIANITY OWNS NO TRADEMARK ON GOD.
3. ISLAM OWNS NO TRADEMARK ON GOD.
4. BUDDAHISM OWNS NO TRADEMARK ON GOD.
5. HINDUISM OWNS NO TRADEMARK ON GOD.
6. <u>NO</u> <u>RELIGION</u> OWNS NO TRADEMARK ON GOD.
7. GOD IS THE ULTIMATE FREEDOM; THEREFORE, GOD IS ART.
8. I BELIEVE IN ART
9. I BELIEVE IN THE HUMAN SPIRIT
10. I BELIEVE THAT GOD IS A CONCEPT OF THE HUMAN SPIRIT.

28 SEPT 2012:

I have devoted all of my life to art. My retrospective in San Diego will be a celebration of my life. I want a big-fat book that covers my entire history. The documentation is what's important, of course I want the show to travel. [. . .]
This show is a great opportunity to set the record straight.

29: SEPT. I hate to admit it but to some degree I have underestimated the complexity of what I am doing. I have discovered a wall. The wall is built of an unknown sensibility. I have been to smug with the comfort of support known as black sensibility. The only way to penetrate this wall is to construct another. . . one of a can sensibility. It is not simply a matter of giving up what I have. . . . It is a matter of constructing on top of what I have i.e., what I have is a foundation. (This is hard to admit at 72!)

I've been rereading Meyer Shapiro's <u>Theory</u> + <u>Philosophy Of Art: Style Artist, And Society</u>. Meyer quotes the work of Alois Reigl (I have not read his works): <u>WILL, FEELING</u> + <u>THOUGHT</u> as the three constants used in the construct of worldview.

<u>SUBJECT + OBJECT</u>, <u>SPIRIT + MATTER</u>, <u>SOUL + BODY</u>, <u>MAN + NATURE or GOD</u>, <u>CONCEPTIONS</u> of <u>TIME + SPACE</u>, <u>SELF + COSMOS</u> as typical fields from which are derived the definitions of worldview. These are available themes which have been used by all artists throughout history. They are constants.

This ~~is~~ has been the basis of all my work up to this point. Now, what should I do? I have covered a tremendous amount of philosophical inquiries. I have asked many questions + I have answered many questions. Now, what should I do?

My use of acrylic tesserae is a unit. The tesserae provided me with a tool for structuring molecular perception. I am now investigating the <u>wave</u> structure of molecular perception. It is a more direct method without losing any of the <u>flow</u>: something was being lost in processing the tessera. I have learned a lot, but the wave is more complex and requires a much larger use of <u>risk</u>, both physically + mentally. I have an acquired taste for risk as long as it doesn't produce an abundance of anxiety that prevents me from working!

How is perceptual abstraction different from regular, generic 2nd stage moderist abstraction?

Good question. Tough question.

6 OCT CONTD:

I WILL TRY TO ANSWER YOUR QUESTION BY OFFERING A LIST OF SPECIFIC ELEMENTS THAT MAKE UP PERCEPTUAL ABSTRACTION.

1. THE FORMAL AS A MEANS RATHER THAN AN ENDS (WITHIN ITSELF)
2. SUBJECT AS PRENOMINATE ELEMENT
3. THE CONCEPTUAL AS CATAPULT
*4. COMPRESSION OF LIGHT AND SPACE
5. STRUCTURAL UNDERPINNINGS OF WILL, FEELING, THOUGHT
6. RECIPROCITY of FIGURE GROUND
7. MULTI-DIMENSIONAL SPACE
8. PLANAR LIGHT
9. MIND AS MATTER
10. THE PAINTING ~~OBJECT~~ AS TRUTH
11. SPIRIT AS ACTIVATOR
12. ABSENCE of SELF
13. THE PAINTING AS A PRIORI OBJECT ~~STRUCTURE~~
14. WORLDVIEW AS OBJECTIVE
15. MOLECULAR PERCEPTION AS UNIT
16. THE NOW (HERE!) AS BIBLE
17. REVERENCE FOR THE PAST
18. DISSOLUTION OF THE OTHER
19. GOD AS CONCEPT
20. INTEGRITY OF THE PICTURE PLANE
21. VOID OF NARRATION
22. NOT DEPENDENT ON RACE, GENDER, NATIONALITY
23. CHOREOGRAPHIC/SYNCHRONIZED SYMMETRY

*CONSIDER: The painting as apriori object and therefore a truth structure

how di ffrant? Does apriori object antecol locally trans/after its truth? Is a found object apriori? or occuring out the advent of experience?

OVER →

24. PICTORIAL ILLUSION AS SUCHNESS i.e., ACCEPTANCE OF EVENTS. w/o THE CAUSALITY

25. A SENSE OF MEASURE

26. EMPATHY AS NECESSARY INGREDIENT

27. CONSTRUCT, DECONSTRUCT, RECONSTRUCT AS PROCESS

28. PERSEVERANCE OF SPONTANEITY AND IMPROVISATION

29. FOUND COLOR STRUCTURE

30. SURFACE AS CONCRETE PLANE

31. LINE AND FORM AS RECIPROCAL ELEMENTS INCLUDING GESTURE

32. ANALOGY AS PARALLEL NOTION OF BEING

33. MODERN AND CONTEMPORARY AS ELEMENTS OF TIME
    (NOT THE SAME AS COSMIC TIME)

34. INTERRELATED FACT OF ALL GLOBAL SOCIAL STRUCTURES.
    (ECONOMIC BELIEF SYSTEMS, AESTHETICS, HEALTH, EDUCATION,
    HISTORY, POLITICS, WARFARE, FOOD, ENVIRONMENT, ENERGY,
    MEDIA, CULTURE IN GENERAL,)

35. PHILOSOPHICAL UNDERPINNINGS OF NEITHER/NOR.
    AS OPPOSED TO EITHER/OR

36. SENSUALITY AS PRIMARY CRITERIA FOR EXPEIRMENTATION

37. NO SECONDGUESSING : ESSENCE IS IN PRIMARY PROCESS

38. THE PAINTING MUST REPRESENT AN AFFIRMATION OF LIFE.

—2012—

6 OCT CONT'D:

    I WILL TRY TO ANSWER <u>YOUR</u> QUESTION BY OFFERING A LIST OF SPECIFIC ELEMENTS THAT MAKE US PERCEPTUAL ABSTRACTION.

1. THE FORMAL AS A <u>MEANS</u> RATHER THAN AN <u>ENDS</u> (WITHIN ITSELF.)
2. SUBJECT AS PRENOMINATE ELEMENT
3. THE CONCEPTUAL AS CATAPULT
*4. COMPRESSION OF LIGHT AND SPACE
5. STRUCTURAL UNDERPINNINGS OF <u>WILL</u>, <u>FEELING</u>, <u>THOUGHT</u>
6. RECIPROCITY OF FIGURE GROUND
7. MULTI-DIMENSIONAL SPACE
8. PLANAR LIGHT
9. MIND AS MATTER
10. THE ~~OBJECT~~ PAINTING AS TRUTH
11. SPIRIT AS ACTIVATOR
12. ABSENCE OF SELF
13. THE PAINTING AS <u>A PRIORI</u> ~~STRUCTURE~~ OBJECT

*Consider: The painting as aprior object and therefore of a truth structure →

How different? Does apriori object automatically translates as truth? Is a found object apriori? Occuring at the advent of experience?

14. WORLDVIEW AS OBJECTIVE
15. MOLECULAR PERCEPTION AS UNIT
16. THE <u>HERE</u> + <u>NOW</u> AS BIBLE
17. REVERENCE FOR THE PAST
18. DISSOLUTION OF THE OTHER
19. GOD AS CONCEPT
20. INTEGRITY OF THE PICTURE PLANE
21. VOID OF NARRATION

22. NOT DEPENDENT ON RACE, GENDER, NATIONALITY
23. CHOREOGRAPHIC / SYNCHRONIZED SYMMETRY
24. PICTORIAL ILLUSTION AS SUCHNESS I.E., ACCEPTANING THE CASUALITY OF EVENTS.
25. A SENSE OF MEASURE
26. EMPATHY AS NECESSARY INGREDIENT
27. CONSTRUCT, DECONSTRUCT, RECONSTRUCT AS PROCESS
28. ~~INSISTENCE~~ PERSEVERANCE OF SPONTANEITY AND IMPROVISATION
29. FOUND COLOR STRUCTURE
30. SURFACE AS ~~PHYSICAL~~ CONCRETE PLANE
31. LINE AND FORM AS RECIPROCAL ELEMENTS INCLUDING GESTURE
32. ANALOGY AS PARALLEL NOTION OF BEING
33. MODERN AND CONTEMPORARY AS ELEMENTS OF TIME (NOT THE SAME AS COSMIC TIME)
34. INTERRELATED FACT OF ALL GLOBAL SOCIAL STRUCTURES. (ECONOMIC, BELIEF SYSTEMS, AESHETICS, HEALTH, EDUCATION, HISTORY, POLITICS, WARFARE, FOOD, ENVIRONMENT, ENERGY, MEDIA, CULTURE IN GENERAL,)
35. PHILOSOPHICAL UNDERPINNINGS OF NEITHER/NOR. AS OPPOSED TO EITHER/OR
36. SENSUALITY AS PRIMARY CRITERIA FOR EXPEIRMENTATION
37. <u>NO SECONDGUESSING</u>: ESSENCE IS IN PRIMARY PROCESS
38. THE PAINTING MUST REPRESENT AN <u>AFFIRMATION</u> OF LIFE.

Five Lines Four Spaces

2012

Now is the time. When my white slave masters discovered that my drum was a subversive instrument they took it from me. My time was stolen. To steal a man's time is an attempt to steal his soul. The only instrument available was my body, so I used my skin: I clapped my hands, slapped my thighs, and stomped my feet in dynamic rhythms. I stretched my mouth wide open and allowed my vocal chords to strike a primal cry. I forced the world to listen. I discovered that my pain was a universal pain. Even those who could not understand my native language could understand my pain.

Born in the slave fields of the Deep South, call and refrain is the cornerstone of jazz and blues. Dialogue, however painful, starts between two or more people. . . . I call, you answer. How I feel is always about power: I, and only I, have control of my feelings. Empowerment serves identity and identity is an act of will. Beyond the political there is always the power of love. Whether in the guise of the divine or celebrated in the joy of sex, jazz and blues continue to inspire the power of love.

Time is a memory bank. The past, present, and future are encoded in time. Art can be used as a tool to decipher time. Break the code and consciousness will expand. When consciousness expands, freedom expands. The philosophical underpinning of jazz is the expansion of freedom. We have entered third-stage modernism, which is a global aesthetic based on otherness. Like jazz, thirdstage modernism insists on the expansion of freedom. Experimentation is the key. I believe that there are sounds we have not heard. I believe that there are colors we have not seen. And I believe that there are feelings yet to be felt.

Postmodernism was a welcome intermission. It allowed an opening for all the various multicultural, disinherited, and fragmented sensibilities to make their voices heard. First- and second-stage modernism did not acknowledge any artistic contribution by African Americans; such inclusion was simply not an issue worthy of consideration. Third-stage

Originally published in Bennett Simpson, ed., *Blues for Smoke* (Los Angeles: Museum of Contemporary Art, Los Angeles, and Prestel, 2012), 148–49.

modernism, with its emphasis on otherness and inclusion, offers the best scenario of hope for reconciliation. Without hope there is no reason for freedom. Anarchy is not a viable option, and romantic nihilism is only an immature, masturbatory response to the threat of total planetary chaos. We must learn to overcome our existentialist notion of being.

Abstract artists are attracted to jazz because of its expandable qualities. Jazz imposes no limit on feeling and its basic elements of spontaneity/improvisation preserve freshness of spirit. Spirit does not like stale air! Spontaneity/improvisation are necessary ingredients of art. The acceptance of spontaneity/improvisation does not reject the value of conceptual thought. Conceptualism is a tool in the service of spontaneity/improvisation. The multidimensional sheets of sound in John Coltrane's music could not reach cognition without the conceptual. As an abstract painter, I translate Coltrane's sheets of sound into sheets of light. Every emotion that ripples through my body is compressed into a plane of light.

My light is a physical fact: I freeze, boil, burn, hammer, sow, sand, grind, and glue sheets of acrylic paint with weights and clamps. The paint is the light. Being a physical fact, it is therefore concrete. The concrete must be transcended through sensibility in order to become abstract. For me, abstraction is a matter of choice, and transcendence is not attributed to any divine ordinance. I spoke of empowerment serving identity; likewise, transcendence empowers us to overcome. "We Shall Overcome" was not on arbitrary gesture of defiance. It was, and is, an act of identity.

Now is the time. Every day in the studio is an adventure. Formal materialism is only a means: it is not an end. Matter is dead meat without spirit. Spirit lives in sensibility. Sensibility, and only sensibility, makes art possible. Plasticity makes sensibility visual. My cosmic guides are: John Coltrane, Thelonious Monk, Charlie Parker, Miles Davis, Charles Mingus, Kenny Dorham, Bud Powell, Ron Carter, Fats Navarro, Dexter Gordon, Cecil Taylor, Ornette Coleman, Sonny Rollins, Coleman Hawkins, Eric Dolphy, Albert Ayler, Sun Ra, Clifford Brown. . . I am so blessed.

The historical continuity of jazz and blues is a valuable cultural asset. For the artist, especially the abstract artist, it is raw material, a resource of infinite possibilities available to anyone capable of deciphering its emotional codes. Good news, I found my stolen drum. I found it while experimenting with the formal element of space. Evidently, Rashied Ali, Alvin Jones, Philly Jo Jones, Art Blakey, Max Roach, Roy Haynes, Arthur Taylor, and others had retrieved it and stashed it in deep space.

[. . .]

26: I want that which goes against ① naturalism ② against fetish ③ against decoration ④ against narcissism. Am I asking too much?

Only through hard nose critical thinking can I overcome this. I have always known this. Have my brethen forgot how to think? Or maybe a warped notion of thought?

So many black people still think of themselves as Africans. Romantic primitivism is not going to get us any place. Yes, by all means I accept my African roots but I am a new people. We cannot not allow memory to imprison us!

An interesting thought on abstraction from late antiquity art: abstraction is that which goes against naturalism. I like this. I must concentrate more on dematerialization. Transparency is one beautiful means to dematerialize matter.

<u>MORE TRANSPARENCY + LESS OPAQUENESS.</u>
<u>EL NINO</u> is in Miami . . . . it's mostly transparent! I have a history of involvement with transparency. . . . . . <u>GO FOR IT</u>, <u>PUSH IT! I WANT TO SEE THROUGH LIFE.</u>

28 NOV: the difference between artists and people who write about art are: artists deal with a priori structures and art critics, art historians, art curators, decent folk by and large deal with a posterior structures. Philosophers are exempt from all other categories . . . . they along with poets are another breed.

I am beginning to disagree with James Dewey. Perhaps art is not expierence but an <u>erasure</u> of experience. True, nothing happens without expierence. Expeirence is a catalyst for thought or a better word . . . a detonator for thought. In order for expeirence to provide the raw material for action, . . . it must be erased! Erasure insures freshness of spirit. I have stated many times before 'spirit does not like stale air.' This is why sponeity is so important. Improvisation is a conceptual programing of the mind; information is stored (very much like a battery) at the proper time when needed, energy is released without the mind intervening. It's all in the act of making. I make therefore I am. Making is a personal manifestation of identity. Everything must be compressed into action. Everything includes: conceptual—perceptual—will—sensibility. All of my feelings must be compressed into action. I am a product of the other and third stage modernism provides the stage for me to act. My audience is the world.

I have reworked <u>FEEDBACK LOOPS</u>. Sandy threw me off balance. <u>FEEDBACK LOOPS</u> FOR THE BIG APPLE aka SANDY'S REVENGE, becomes <u>FEEDBACK LOOPS</u> <u>FOR CY TWOMBLY</u>. It took me this long to use the drawings for Cy. The expeirence had to be erased!

All of these years I have learned how to create matter. Now, I must learn how to dematerialize the matter which I have created. If I can do this, I will be able to see through life.

29: <u>BLUE SCRIPT, NOV.</u> 2012, 24" x 24" continues the expeirments of three dimensional gesture. This is new for painting: No one that

I know of has done this with paint. All of the loops are examples of three dimensional gesture. This includes line as gesture. David Smith's drawing in space is a good example of three dimensional gesture in sculpture which is already a three dimensional medium. This is a first for painting. I have been carving wood since 1962. My carveings have definitely influenced my paintings. . . The whole concept of making a painting as opposed to painting a painting came from my carving wood. African wood carvings dematerializes matter. Finally I understand my African heritage. <u>BLACK FOLKS EXCEED MATTER</u>! This is why we place so much emphasis on the notion of soul. Soul is dematerialized matter. Soul is all mind; it does not exist in duality. It is constantly in phase transition. This explains <u>my mind as matter theory</u>, but is no longer a theory: <u>IT IS</u>.

1 DEC: I am on a large sphere that's moving in celestial space at a very rapid speed. Gravity is the only thing that keeps me pinned to the planet . . . therefore I do not experience movement . . . only when I accelerate due to body movement or some sort of mechanical or animal energy do I experience movement . . . or speed, which I prefer! Therefore celestial space is a backdrop very much a photographers' backdrop. I want to incorporate this notion of space as backdrop in my paintings. I have been feeling this for a long time but now it is 100% cognitive.

It might interest you to know that a 13th century (<u>SIX PERSIMMONS</u>) Muqi was the detonator! [. . .]

2 DEC: Sunday and it's very quiet. I need quietness. . . It's a joy! To be quiet is a luxury. Alex sold <u>**BRIGHT MOMENTS**</u> in L.A. show and I am very sad. I never should have allowed it out of the studio. There are certain paintings that I need for my own use. I must learn to identify these paintings and remove them from the marketplace. My art is not about money. . . . Money is only a residue. It is the shit of aesthetics. <u>I hate money</u>.

I must learn to use money as a fertilizer . . . . use it to grow more shit! The world is full of shit!
I think that I have a painting for Toots . . . must wait until tomorrow . . . . . it looks good: YELLOW ORANGE LOOP FOR TOOTS.

SPACE IS TRANSPARENT.

3 DEC: <u>YELLOW ORANGE LOOP FOR TOOTS</u> 58" x 58"
I'll keep it. . A few minor adjustments to be made but its good; forgot to put the gorilla tape around the edge for release but managed to cut it from the perimeter.

Yes, space is transparent: I've expanded to another level of consciouness. I have more freedom of reaching my goal 'to see through life'.

I like the notion of abstraction being an antidote <u>to life</u>, <u>to politcs</u>, <u>to naturalism</u>, <u>to magical thinking</u>, <u>to evil in general</u> . . . . . all of this shit is poisonous!

I can't change anything, art cannot change anything. The best I can do is provide an antidote. Since I am an abstract paint~~ing~~er I want my paintings to serve as an antidote to evil.

13 DEC: Elaine* told me that Toots' favorite color was red. I have planned a loop for Toots but the original color was an orange yellow. . . This is why I couldn't get the painting to work. Toots' painting caused me a lot of grief . . . anxiety . . . lots of work. Back + forth it went until I reconstructed it by grinding out the entire picture plane. It was a nasty job. <u>RED LOOP FOR TOOTS</u> is successful. She fought me all the way but I hope she likes it.

I have discovered something quite startling with this painting: while removing the tape from the sides (I tape the edge in order to prevent any surface material from adhering, <u>IT'S ONLY ABOUT THE SURFACE PLANE</u>)

The tool I was using made a sound . . . . . intriguing. . . . I continued to tap the surface plane from the center to the outer edge. . . There is a scale . . . . the same as a stretched hide over a rim! <u>THE PAINTING IS A DRUM</u>!!
I was not kidding in my essay for Bennet Simpson:
<u>I FOUND MY DRUM</u>.

My consciouness has expanded to another level. I have worked so hard at painting since 1960 . . . including my student years at Cooper Union. It is starting too pay off now. The only thing I know for sure is work—work—work—work—work . . . . just like Mr. Mestrovic* told me. In my case, work did make me free. I am the freeist man on the planet!

BY THE WAY—ALL OF MY MEMORIAL PAINTINGS ARE GIFTS TO THE PEOPLE THAT INSPIRED THEM. . . THEY ARE NOT MERE DEDICATIONS. . . THEY ARE GIFTS.

15 DEC: Multi-dimensional space is identifiable by <u>COMPOUND PERSPECTIVE</u>. Compound perspective is a term for the quantum structure of multi dimensions. I use the word quantum because multi dimensional space is structured both as <u>point</u> and as <u>wave</u>. It operates simulantaneously, therefore it is not relative. (non-relational) In the early seventies when I spoke of non-relational space this is what I was feeling. I did my best with the tools available and I stand by those paintings. No one has even come close to this concept.

One point, two point, multiple point, both bird's eye and worm eye was used in the Italian Renaissance . . . . . but now because of quantum mechanics a compound perspective is needed to depict space in the modern technological society. All of my life I have insisted on a definition of world view for the modern technological society. I am now in reach of my goal: worldview.

Another way of describing compound perspective + perhaps a little clearer is: develop a mental picture of traditional-historical perspective from the ① Renaissance ② Oriental (position on the plane) ③ Cubism ④ AB/EX. . . . . Now compress this mentally and you would have a glimpse of compound perspective. Compoud perspective is pure perception. This is why I call myself a perceptionist and my movement is perceptionism. Very exciting stuff! I must continue to clarify.

18 DEC: The horizon is infinite in compound perspective + only depends on your position: space is a backdrop for object, therefore space is subject.

—NOTES FROM THE WOODSHED 2013—

1 JAN 2013: The last painting of 2012 is: <u>FORMAL IMPLANTS</u>

There is some confusion for implants vs. transplants. . . . I think that the correct word is implant but I am not sure. I am taking something from one source and transplating it into another source i.e., forms made through casting the bottom of plastic bottles, containers, etc. and implanting them into a formal structure. Both words apply but I am not sure. It's an interesting concept: to transplant something into the formal. One thing I am sure of: it's the reproduction of a concept not an illustration of a concept. The difference being something made without hands. I can't paint these structures I can only make them. Process becomes an extension of the hands. We are tool users and our tools are extensions of the hands and in the case of the computer, an extension of the brain. Painting evolves, the brain evolves. Therefore we evolve. It's a process of evolution.

I must use everything that I have discovered in the past fifty years of painting. I must continue to clarify my thinking. I am on the right track. I am a perceptualist and the name of my movement is perceptualism. Perceptualism is how I see the world. I feel that my time has come. Finding my drum made the difference. I've recaptured my time that was stolen from me. Pure abstraction is found in the perceptual. The perceptual is found in the brain. Abstraction has evolved. Space is the subject and the object can be anything I want it to be! <u>2013</u> <u>IS</u> <u>GOING</u> <u>TO</u> <u>BE</u> <u>AN</u> <u>INTERESTING</u> <u>YEAR</u>.

6 APRIL: [. . .]

Abstract painting that addresses subject is what I want. Before Western abstraction there was subject. I want something that goes beyond the notion of the 'formal' as subject. I want to use the formal as a means to arrive at subject. We live in a quantum world; everything is interealted. Nothing stands alone. There is no beginning + there is no end. Nothing is static . . . everything is fluid + mobile . . . . there is no center . . . the <u>icon</u> has shifted into multiple dimension which means that it can be centered if <u>one</u> desires it to be . . . but it can be centered + dispersed at the same time: <u>this is weird</u>!

If abstraction can be directed toward subject therefore, each painting can be totally different! I have always said that 'I am not a cookie-cutter painter'. Now I know why!

<u>SANDBOX; FOR THE CHILDREN OF SANDY HOOK ELEMENTARY SCHOOL</u>. is a good example. I wanted to do a painting for the living . . . not the dead, <u>INNOCENCE</u>, <u>PURITY</u>, <u>JOY</u>, <u>PLAYFUL</u>, <u>FUN</u> . . . . these are the signifiers!
<u>THE PAINTING WORKS</u>!

<u>NINE COSMIC CD'S</u>: <u>FOR JAYNE CORTEZ</u> . . . WORKS! + HOPEFULLY ALAN UGLOW'S PAINTING WILL WORK.
—KEEP YOU POSTED—

25 APRIL 13: Just returned from a visit to the Aldrich Mus. They are giving me a one-man show . . . new gallery space . . . no problem. Alex, Mary + I went . . . nice trip. . . [. . .]

—I AM A MAKER. I SHOULD REFRAIN FROM CALLING MYSELF A PAINTER. I CHANGED THE VERB TO PAINT → TO I MAKE. WHY NOT SIMPLY CALL MYSELF A MAKER?

26 APRIL: [. . .] The longing for fame, recognition, money is understandable <u>but</u> we must not succumb to the petty things of life. Art is not about fame. Art is not about fortune. Art is not about recognition. I is about developing a sustainable philosophy of life. Fame and fortune is a trap!

<u>STAY CLOSE TO GOD</u>.

28 APRIL 13: Jim* helped me to hang <u>REMOTE CONTROL</u>. <u>IT IS AMAZING</u>! It is so seductive but threating at the same time. . . . . Quantum emotions produces emotional geometry. Emotional geometry exist in the gap bewteen figure and ground. You cannot see it you can only feel it. This <u>is</u> and explains <u>why</u> it's taking me so long to clarify . . . . it is extremely elusive. It's a new specie of geometry. . It is not fractal + neither is it planar. It is some form of organic geometry like fractal but different. Anyway, I don't know what it is. . . I only know it's there . . . . sort of like dark matter . . maybe I am dark matter. That's why I'm so lovely!

— NOTES FROM THE WOODSHED —

13 SEPT 2013: GREAT SUMMER. NO FISHING ONLY WORK BUT GOOD WORK.. COMPLETED TWO SCULPTURES... CONTINUING THE THEME OF DIONYSIAN SWORD: WHITE MARBLE, CHARRED MULBERRY, LEAD.. METAL ROD.. STANDS TWO METERS... A TRULY POWERFUL PIECE. A SMALLER PIECE FOR MARY... SWEET.. FROM BLACK MULBERRY, SERBIAN OAK & IROKO WITH WHITE MARBLE & COPPER ROD TITLED 'ARRICHE' "THE CRETAN HAWK.

LEAVE FOR CALIF. ON MONDAY ... THIS IS GOING TO BE A FUN TRIP.. KATHERN IS EXICTED! FIRST RETRO SO IT BETTER BE FUN!

LOTS OF COMMITMENTS FOR 2013 & 2014: LARGE SCALE PIECE FOR MONS PLUS SHOW FOR FRANK IN MAY.... WORK — WORK — WORK — & MORE WORK!

I AM IN AN ANTI-CONCEPTUALIST MOOD.. SO MUCH 'IDEA' ART... EVERYTHING IS A CUTE ILLUSTRATED IDEA ... IT IS NOT PAINTING, IT IS ILLUSTRATION.

READ AN INTERESTING ARTICLE IN MY SCIENTIFIC AMERICAN ABOUT THE FOURTH DIMENSION... EXCITING STUFF! I FEEL SUCH A THING BUT HOW DOES ONE IMAGINE IT? ANOTHER DIMENSION COULD CHANGE THE HISTORY OF PAINTING. I'LL CONCENTRATE ON THIS THROUGH GEOMETRY..... .... SOME FORM OF GEOMETRY THAT GOES BEYOND FRACTALS.

HOW WOULD A FOURTH DIMENSION AFFECT PAINTING? IS MISSING MATTER PART OF THE EQUATION?

—NOTES FROM THE WOODSHED—

13 SEPT 2013: GREAT SUMMER. NO FISHING ONLY WORK BUT GOOD WORK . . COMPLETED TWO SCULPTURES . . . CONTINUING THE THEME OF DIONYSIAN SWORD: WHITE MARBLE, CHARRED MULBERRY, LEAD . . METAL ROD . . STANDS TWO METERS . . . A TRULY POWERFUL PIECE. A SMALLER PIECE FOR MARY . . . SWEET . . FROM BLACK MULBERRY, SERBIAN OAK + IROKO WITH WHITE MARBLE + COPPER ROD TITLED 'ARRICHE $_{s/p}$" THE CRETAN HAWK.

LEAVE FOR CALIF. ON MONDAY . . . THIS IS GOING TO BE A FUN TRIP . . KATHYRN* IS EXCITED! FIRST RETRO SO IT BETTER BE FUN!
LOTS OF COMMITMENTS FOR 2013 + 2014: LARGE SCALE PIECE FOR MONS PLUS SHOW FOR FRANK* IN MAY . . . . WORK—WORK—WORK— + MORE WORK!

I AM IN AN ANTI-CONCEPTUALIST MOOD . . SO MUCH 'IDEA' ART . . . EVERYTHING IS A CUTE ILLUSTRATED IDEA . . . <u>IT</u> <u>IS</u> <u>NOT</u> <u>PAINTING</u>. <u>IT</u> <u>IS</u> <u>ILLUSTRATION</u>. READ AN INTERESTING ARTICLE IN MY SCIENTIFIC AMERICAN ABOUT THE FOURTH DIMENSION . . . EXCITING STUFF! I FEEL SUCH A THING BUT HOW DOES ONE IMAGINE IT? ANOTHER DIMENSION COULD CHANGE THE HISTORY OF PAINTING. I'LL CONCEPTRATE ON THIS THROUGH GEOMETRY . . . . SOME FORM OF GEOMETRY THAT GOES BEYOND FRACTALS. HOW WOULD A FOURTH DIMENSION AFFECT PAINTING? IS MISSING MATTER PART OF THE EQUATION?

—WOODSHED LOG—

19 SEPT 2013: Returned from fishing 5 Sept + immediately non-stop activities. . My show opened at A.G. 11 Sept . . . very nice celebratory opening . . . lots of old friends came . . . it was fantastic! [. . .]

The Rose Museum opened on the 16 + 17 . . . another great opening! Lots of good cheer. Everybody loved the paintings including me! [. . .] For me to see paintings from 1971–73—<u>never stretched, never shown</u>. . . I was thrilled! [. . .]

Finally things are becoming clearer: I am dealing with something that cannot be painted. . . I can only establish a situation for something to happen. It lies beyond painting. To make as opposed to paint is correct. The only difference is: <u>DON'T EVEN TRY TO MAKE IT!</u> . . . <u>ALLOW IT TO BE!</u>
<u>IT IS THE PAINTING + THE PAINTING CAN BE ANYTHING I WANT IT TO BE.</u>

J.W.

24 SEPT. I am back to not knowing . . that is a very good thing. How could I possibly know? When Ron Gorchov spoke of doubt I was hard on him . . but maybe he is on to something. Doubt could be a good thing. Meaning is a bitch! What does meaning mean? I am too old for chasing riddles. My ass is still floating but that's O.K. I am a good swimmer!

25 SEPT: OMPHALOS: a central point. A rounded stone in Apollo's temple at Delphi, regarded as the center of the world by ancients.
—I AM THE CENTER OF THE UNIVERSE—
* I AM TRYING TO LOCATE THE CENTER OF THE UNIVERSE. I FOUND IT IN MYSELF.

2013
<u>1970</u>
43

Forty three years have passed since I made the slab paintings of the early seventies. The slab paintings are the foundation of what I am doing today. The Developer with its analogy to photography is still in use. Recognizing the fact of photography's dynamic influence on painting since its invention I continue to struggle with a parallel plasticity in paint without resorting to photographic illustrational reproductions. I want the paint to speak for itself.

I accept Technology as an additional symbol in painting. Our modern sensibility is rapidly evolving as a direct result of technology's intrusion into every aspect of our daily lives. I have devoted my entire life to the preservation of a viable vital anthropological philosophy. A Scientific philosophy based on the ~~absolute premise of sciences~~ absolute omnipotent universal law of science is unacceptable. Science is only a part of being human.

3 OCT: If mind is matter then matter must be some sort of phase transition. What was matter's previous state? It's an interesting question and I don't know the answer but it is worth pursuing.

[. . .] IS IT POSSIBLE THAT ENERGY IS ANOTHER SORT OF MATTER? I WILL KEEP YOU POSTED.

7 OCT: The symposium at the Rose Museum was very good. [. . .] It's interesting how people from different disciplines reframe the paintings. Each speaker was helpful. [. . .] Arthur,* the photographer from Taiwan spoke of "accumulation" of light. . . . I like this. It imples light as fetish which is something I never thought of. (Or could be used as fetish) Technological fetish? Based on photon + not societal debris?

—DISTORTION FIELD—a psychological reordering of reality . . . . . . to reframe the whole notion of reality . . . . through use of multiple spatial dimensions . . . . light aquifers as retainers of memory . . . . . again I say . . . some kind of weird phase transition is at play.

* Correction: phase transition is not weird in its' physical state i.e., as its' concreteness . . . . it becomes weird when it applies to its' metaphysical state. In its' concreteness . . . . it is the paint + what happens to paint as skin. . . . . . . It is the process of drying that alters its concreteness.

Metaphysically, it is like hammering water. The metaphysical is a phase transition when applied to matter. All <u>meta</u> devices run into metaphysics.

Being is a thing within itself. If being becomes a necessity of survival (as it should be) then we must construct our notion of reality. The construction of being is a reframing of reality; therefore, it is a <u>structural reality</u>. Structural reality is a very good sound foundation for worldview.

→ * being is a notion + therefore can act as object.

Now, I have something to say: I have a language. Glissant* claims
that poetry is a language that exist inside of language. My space is a
symbolic space. Symbolic space is the ~~plastic~~ formal foundation for
abstraction as symbol. Space in third stage moderism is a symbolic
space and I can direct it toward any subject I desire. If you control
the space . . . all is possible. Abstraction as symbol is a higher form of
abstraction . . . it exist 'beyond' the generic abstraction of first +
second stage moderism. <u>I</u> <u>AM</u> <u>THE</u> <u>NEW</u> <u>SENSIBILITY</u>.

All matter functions in the metaphysical realm when confronted
with human consciouness: consciouness and only consciouness
<u>allows</u> matter to function metaphysically. Without the intervention of
human consciouness matter will remain in an <u>inert</u> state. No manner
how many trees are in the forest + how many trees will fall in the
forest . . . . . a tree will never hear the sound of a falling tree!

The concept of flatness in painting is not only a formal concept;
it is one of compression i.e., the totality of ~~life~~ history must be
compressed into a sheet of light. Compression could be another type
of formality. . . . . I must think about this . . . . possibly a new
type of 'formal' for third stage modernism? I don't know.

29 Dec 2013

Asymmetrical structures are formed out of fractal geometry. In painting asymmetrical structures coincide with asymmetrical color structures, which are ~~formed out of~~ made from found color i.e., a color structure that is dependent on process. Asymmetrical structures and asymmetrical color structures cannot be painted. They are not illustrated through conceptual 2-D pictorial illusions. → They must be made i.e., to make a painting the verb must be changed to <u>make</u> not <u>paint.</u> Both asymmetrical structures and asymmetrical color structures are a prior in the most classical Kantian sense: they exist outside of expeirence. Even though they are constructed out of fractal geometry they do not exclude other means of geometry such as the Euclidian model or other types of geometry. Asymmetrical structures have the universal ability of all inclusive geometrical dimensions, therefore they are truly multi-dimensional.

All states of matter ~~are~~ can be compressed into asymmetrical structures and can modify their behavior through phase transitions. Phase transitions are also present in the metaphysical realm of matter. Through the use of symbol, the artist can direct matter toward any degree of subject. The ancient notion of substance must be substained out of necessity to avoid the oversimplification of content + meaning. If the artist is not capable of giving substance to a work of art, surface tactility is reduced to fashion. Fashion's epherimal appeal is seductive and serves the purpose of instant gratification. In our Capitalist Christian materialist culture, Fashion ~~is in the services~~ provides ~~the contemporary society's~~ our lust for instant gratification and supports the success of Extreme Capitalism. We need fashion and when it remains in its' proper place it balances out the dreadness of contemporary life. However, it is not to our collective ~~interest~~ well being to confuse it with art.

Art is a sanctuary. It provides refurge for all of us in need of R+R from the absurdities of modern life. Only in art can we place

trust in the substainablitiy of the human spirit. We and only we
are responsible for the health of planet earth. We and only we are
responsible for the health of our moral and ethical values. The
dysfunctional state of affairs in politics and our various religious
belief systems has eroded the public's trust in institutional governance.
As Adrienne Rich so eloquently stated "Art means nothing if it
simply decorates the dinner table of power which holds it hostage"

The artist survival is always on the edge. We are truly the canary
in the coal mine. We must remain forever diligent in sensing the
slightest shift in perception. Perception is a double edged sword ~~that
can be use for defense and offense~~ and our survival depends on its
proper use. It is important to know that perception can be
structured, it is mallable. It can be stretched like a rubber band.
Perception is an energy field with vast resources. Learn how to
structure perception and the discovery of art will be your reward.

Long live painting!

31 DEC 13

THE light is coming from two different locations:

① An Outer light i.e., it's coming from the outside and has been
traveling since the birth of the cosmos

② An Inner light that has been traveling since the birth of man.
I don't know positively if the birth of man coincided with the
birth of the universe. . . . . . . I think not.

Man, I think is a by-product of the big-bang. I accept
Science's notion of the big bang, but to say why, what, when,
where, how?. . That remains a mystery. I don't know.

At times I speak metaphorically of being on a
threadmill. . . . That threadmill is <u>light</u>. I am just trying to keep
up! If I could only let go, stop trying to keep up and let the light
carry me. I must work on this. Giving up and let the light carry
me is my New Year's resolution!

1 JAN 14: <u>I FEEL GOOD.</u>

POARCH COLLONDADE —
A COVER SUPPORTED BY
COLUMNS + WALL

STOA — ZENO —

STOIC — ZENO A FOUNDER OF A
GREEK SCHOOL OF PHILOSOPHY (@ 308 B.C.,
HOLDING THAT ALL THINGS, PROPERTIES,
RELATIONS, etc. ARE GOVERNED BY
UNVARYING NATURAL LAWS, AND THAT THE
WISE MAN SHOULD FOLLOW VIRTUE ALONE,
OBTAINED THROUGH REASON, REMAINING
INDIFFRENT TO THE EXTERNAL WORLD
AND TO PASSION OR EMOTION.

ENARTHROSIS — JOINTED, A JOINT
    ARTHRO — JOINT
ART — HUMAN ABILITY TO MAKE THINGS;
CREATIVITY OF MAN AS DISTINGUISHED FROM THE
WORLD OF NATURE.

— ART'S CIRCLE — (THREE JOINTED SEGMENTS)

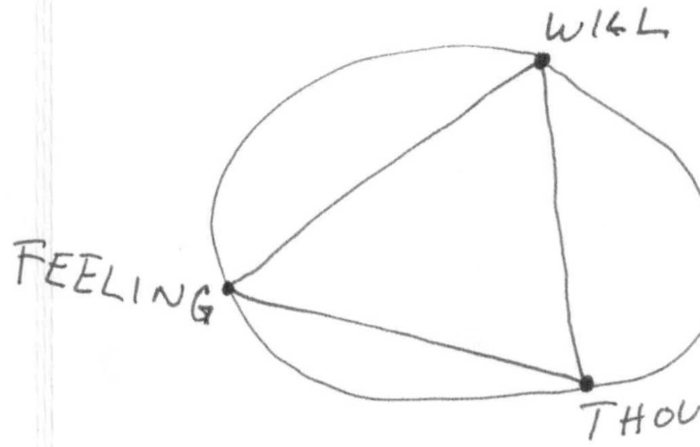

PORCH COLLONDADE—
A COVER SUPPORTED BY COLUMNS + WALL
STOA— ZENO—

STOIC—ZENO A FOUNDER OF A GREEK SCHOOL OF
PHILOSOPHY @ 308 B.C., HOLDING THAT ALL THINGS,
PROPERTIES, RELATIONS, etc., ARE GOVERNED BY
UNVARYING NATURAL LAWS, AND THAT THE WISE MAN
SHOULD FOLLOW VIRTURE ALONE, OBTAINED THROUGH
REASON, REMAINING INDIFFERENT TO THE EXTERNAL
WORLD AND TO PASSION OR EMOTION.

ENARTHOSIS—JOINTED, A JOINT ARTHRO-JOINT
ART—HUMAN ABILITY TO MAKE THINGS; CREATIVITY OF
MAN AS DISTINGUISHED FROM THE WORLD OF NATURE

—ART'S CIRCLE— (THREE JOINTED SEGMENTS)

[drawing; triangle inscribed in a circle with points labeled, "WILL,"
"FEELING," and "THOUGHT"]

5 JAN 14: I have rendered the term 'abstraction' to be meaningless. It is no longer a significant form. It has run its course in Western society . . . . . no longer revelant. The light weight formalists both black and white are left over scraps of Greenbergian formalism. There is a new order in painting and it's called <u>painting</u>. Artists have forgotten how to paint or mostly likely they never knew! The art schools are churning out smart-ass conceptualists who know how to package 'idea' as illustrational design motifs. <u>It is not painting</u>. A painting can not be painted it must be made. Art is simply the human ability to make things. To make is not to illustrate. To make is an event that takes place in spacetime. It has nothing to do with how smart you are! We are all suspended in the cosmos and the only umbilical cord available is our soul. Black people were correct in emphasizing and relieng on soul . . . it is our salvation. <u>THERE</u> <u>IS</u> <u>NO</u> <u>GOD</u> <u>THERE</u> <u>IS</u> <u>ONLY</u> <u>SURVIVAL</u>.

—NOTES FROM THE WOODSHED 2014—

30 JAN 14: Good trip to Houston. [. . .] The Rothko Chapel + the Cy Twombly Museum affected me very much. They are both great for different reasons. If I had my ultimate pick . . . it would be Rothko. I am at a critical position in time about my work. It occured to me that no black artist has penetrated the sublime. Tanner* came close but I cannot accept his dependence on Christianty and Duncanson* + Bannister* was close (however somewhat academic) with his nature as symbol. Nature served him well but I have no interest in nature as a means to the sublime; too many artists have already exploited that! And besides, nature is a beast!

I do have an interest in the sublime from a blackman's perspective. A worldview based on the sublime is a good thing and I am capable of sturcturing this. I don't see anyone else whose capable. <u>I MUST ACT ALONE.</u>

12 FEB 14: CONCEPTS:

1. FOUND COLOR—found color cannot be painted . . . it comes as a result of process and is a pure a prior color structure. It exist the same as found object i.e., the artist must be able to recognize its presence. . . . <u>IT IS</u>.

2. PLANAR LIGHT—when I spoke with John Coltrane he told me "it's like a wave" The first gray paintings which were made by trapping black + white acrylic paint between a layer of stretched cotton duck and a fine netting of silk, rayon + other fine mesh fabric. The excess paint was removed with a metal scraper. This was my first encounter with photographic imagery. I say photographic imagery because they looked like blurred photographs.

3. ENERGY FIELD—my discovery of planar light (the entire picture plane as a sheet of light) in reference to John Coltranes 'sheet of sound', is constructed of energy. Energy as spirit can be conceptualized. Therefore it can be used to structure any symbol.

4. MULTI-DIMENSIONAL SPACE—an extension of the everyday use of practical <u>one</u>, <u>two</u> <u>+ three</u> dimensions to include time as <u>fourth</u> dimension which opens the door to <u>non casual</u> multiple dimensions. Multi-dimensional space is constructed by <u>compressing</u> multiple dimensions into a place of light.

5. CONCRETE LIGHT—light as matter on par with all physical matter. Concrete light is constructed through process . . . . it cannot be 'painted' . . . . it must me 'made.'

⋆ planar light is concrete light used as a plane. (see my paper that list the various qualities of light.)

6. MOLECULAR PERCEPTION—recognizing the fact that all art of any medium depends on human perception: perception is the holy grail of art. Perception, like consciouness, exist in layers. Through the process of evolution these layers expand. Expansion produces deeper layers of consciouness which in term pruduces

deeper layers of perception. Primarily, due to the influence of modern technology (which has altered our sense of perception) we are capable of receiving more visual data than ever before in the history of humanity. We have become 'data gatherers' as opposed to 'hunter gatherers'. We see more and we feel more.

7. ~~THREE DIMENSIONAL GESTURE—~~

7. PAINT AS COLLAGE—the removal of paint from the surface of the canvas. By changing the verb to 'paint' to the verb to 'make', paint becomes a physical three dimensional skin . . . . . . with this skin I make the painting.

8. CONSTRUCT, DECONSTRUCT, RECONSTRUCT— parallel thinking as process used in the making of a painting.

9. THREE DIMENSIONAL GESTURE—same as three dimensional line i.e., gesture constructed of paint collage.

10. SPECIFIC GROUND—a 'slab' of paint built specifically as foundation support for specific symbol.

28 FEB 14: [. . .]
 —I am rushing but I must write this:
 <u>THE</u> <u>PAINTING</u> <u>EXIST</u> <u>OUTSIDE</u> <u>OF</u> <u>SPACE/TIME.</u>

1 MARCH 14: the trinity has become one: compression has occured. The meaning of this is . . . I no longer have to worry about everyday phenonom. I exist beyond space/time. It is not the painting as object that has been my obsession all of these years . . . . . it is I, therefore the 'I' is no longer revelant. My mother would say that I am a child of God . . . perhaps, but whatever, <u>it</u> <u>is</u> <u>a</u> <u>good</u> <u>feeling</u>! I have achieved what I've always wanted:

To take art back to its original place in society. The painting is only a sounding board for dialogue with the self. What's more important? I don't know being a dialogue with communication for the self . . . . . . if the dialogue offers useful information in the form of constructive data . . . . it could be used to benefit society. I understand the political nature of this. This is a lot to think about . . . truthfully it is frightening!
Do I want to give up my autonomy for the sake of society? I don't know . . . yet.

4 MARCH 2014: Photonics is the best physical example of what I am doing (that is other than the painting as object i.e., physical object). The photograph has always been the physical example, but now that my perception has become molecular the photograph has become to literal. Photonics which explains the interaction of light with matter is a much better analogy.

Yun Gee and his 'diamondism' and the color stnchronicity of Macdonald-Wright* + Delaunay* felt this but had no language for it (other than the formal). Science has given me the language and I am capable of structuring it through painting. Yes, the paint is the light, now precede to structure light that has been filtered through perception. At the molecular level lights' interaction with matter is a crystal . . . . . the crystal is a lense and the lense is used to project symbol. The symbol can be anything I want. Abstraction is a manner of choice but I can, if I want to, project the figure as symbol, the landscape as symbol . . . . nature in general as symbol . . . . but thought i.e., mind as $\frac{symbol}{matter}$ . . interest me much more! I am attracted to mind as symbol because of its promise of 'expansion of freedom.'

<u>FREEDOM MUST EXPAND.</u>

<u>JAZZ IS MY HOLY GRAIL</u>

[. . .] Big time revelation: the choir came down to greet the family . . . those faces I have seen all my life! Their faces are what touched me . . . as I looked around the church . . . . . the faces is what I saw in the 1960's paintings . . . . the faces in the paintings are not spirits of the dead . . . . they are the faces of my people!

It is nothing weird, nothing esoteric, nothing bazaar. . . they are simply my people and they are trying to tell me that they are with me! I don't have to be afraid of anything or anybody because God is with me!

Met Jesse Jackson today at the airport in Chicago. I went to him + introduced myself . . . told him about the Brooklyn Museum show . . . . . . told him about Baton Rouge in 1960 + told him about meeting King in Montgomery in 1957. I am blessed!

17 MARCH 2014 1348 HRS.:
COMPLETED: <u>BLACK MONOLITH#</u>
<u>FULL CIRCLE</u>: <u>FOR LEROI JONES A.K.A. AMIRI BARAKA</u>
2" x 84" x 63"

ROI WORKED THE SHIT OUT OF ME! I FEEL HIM
LAUGHING. . . <u>WORK NIGGER,!</u> <u>WORK!</u> O.K. I HOPE HE
LIKES IT.

LOTS OF WORK BUT IT WAS FUN . . . A BIT HAIRY
TOWARD THE MIDDLE BUT I GOT A HANDLE ON IT BY
REDUCING IT TO THE CIRCLE. THE CIRCLE IS COMPLETE
NOW. . . IT TOOK @ 500 YEARS.

25 MARCH: Without passion art is reduced to illustration and
design. I am bored with seeing so much smart conceptual art. . . . . .
Everything I see is smart-ass MFA art!
I want the primitive. . . . that which is not tainted by the smart brain.
I want passion in it's rawest state. Locate the subject and let the
mind do its job . . . . do not interfere with mind . . . . . only the mind
knows. The painting is a thing within its' self . . . . interelated with
the world but ultimately has its own look . . . do not impose i.e., the
artist must learn not to impose other <u>logics</u> derived from other
disciplines to painting.
THE PAINTING MUST EXIST <u>AS IS.</u>
*COMPLETED: <u>THE QUEEN BEE</u> <u>FOR JEANNE SIEGEL.</u>
IT WAS A HELLUVA RIDE!

↔ 26 MARCH: ARRIVED IN THE STUDIO EARLY. . . IT WAS A
PIECE of SHIT!
HAD TO REWORK IT. . . . . WILL KEEP YOU POSTED
I AM STILL RIDING THE <u>B</u>ITCH! (PUT ON HOLD)

FRIDAY 4 APRIL 1530 HRS
     COMPLETED BLACK MONOLITH #
     MASK (UPDATED VERSION) FOR TERRY ADKINS
—OFF TO THE JEANNE SIEGEL MEMORIAL—

—NOTES FROM THE WOODSHED—

1757 HRS SAT 9 APRIL: I finally completed Jeanne Siegel's painting.

This painting exhausted me . . . but at least I finished it in time for Easter. The leg of lamb is marinating. . . . Mary did the eggs (red)(blood of Christ) that's O.K. I don't fight religion but in due respect I don't want it fightning me! I am in the world an I do what the romans do.

THE RITE OF SPRING: FOR JEANNE SIEGEL

*not sure of this title original title was CRYSTAL PALACE

[. . .]

1 MAY 2014: MAYDAY. . . . . . THIS IS NOT A S.O.S.! AT LEAST I DON'T THINK SO. I'm tired . . . exhausted an irritable$_{s/p}$ The paintings have pushed me into another realm of thought. I don't understand what's happening but it is something very positive . . . . my consciouness has expanded . . . . it appears to be another dimension of mind . . I think that my investigation of photonics open another door. One thing that I know for sure is: the symbol is the sublime i.e. it's rooted in transendence but this time around transcendence is not about the holy. Traditionally transcendence referenced the spiritual triggered by nature but the transcendence I speak of is of the mind. IS MIND SPIRIT? I DON'T KNOW BUT IF MIND IS SPIRIT I AM O.K. WITH THAT.

There is so much I don't understand but I feel it to be correct. My gut is right and my gut agrees with my mind. I am comfortable with this.

Received an e-mail from MoMA. SIBERIAN SALT GRINDER is hanging on the fourth floor [. . .]

FULL CIRCLE. . . . . . a lot is coming together.

2 MAY 2014: Completed <u>DU BOIS'S LEGACY</u> BLACK MONOLITH #?

1824 HRS. FOR W.E.B DU BOIS. This is truly a fantastic painting!!!!

Everything that I want is in this painting. It is sublime. It is worldview. It is space. It is light. It is new + it's African American. . . . . I have arrived at the station. . . . I don't need the train anymore. . . The universe will take me wherever I want to go. . . . There is no more desire. I want for nothing. . Art is my guide. . . <u>LONG LIVE PAINTING</u>. I fear nothing. . W.E.B. Du Bois would be pleased this is what he wanted for black people. <u>I THANK GOD FOR W.E.B. DU BOIS.</u> His words were my inspiration.

30 MAY 2014: THE DIFFICULTY IS: I AM DEALING WITH SOMETHING SO COMPLEX AND SO ELUSIVE. I HAVE KNOWN THIS FOR YEARS BUT IT HAS BECOME MORE EVIDENT THAN EVER. STRUCTURALLY IT IS THE SAME AS QUANTUM MECHANICS.... IT CAN BY ANYTHING .... AT ANY TIME ..... AT ANY PLACE. IT IS DEFINITE NOT EITHER·OR! IT IS NEITHER·NOR AND AS HENRY WOULD SAY "AND THEN SOME". IT CAN BE ANYTHING TO ANY ONE. IT IS NOT DEPENDENT ON RACE.... OR SEX .... OR NATIONALITY. IT IS BEYOND ALL KNOWN ART HISTORICAL REFERENCES BUT IT IS NOT DIVINE! IT IS A MAN MADE PHENOMENON. THIS IS WHAT BOTHERS ME.... CAN I PLACE THAT MUCH TRUST IN BEING HUMAN? THERE ARE TOO MANY FLAWS IN BEING HUMAN...HOW CAN ANYONE TRUST BEING HUMAN? I AM NOT A CREATIONIST... I DON'T BELIEVE IN THAT SHIT! BUT YET I HAVE A BELIEF IN GOD.... IS THIS A CONTRADICTION? CAN ONE HONESTLY SAY THAT THEY BELIEVE IN GOD AND AT THE SAME TIME SAY THEY WERE NOT CREATED BY GOD? I AM NOT A HYPOCRITE! GOD IS A CONCEPT INVENTED BY US. I DO NOT BELIEVE IN THE VIRGIN BIRTH of CHRIST & I DO NOT BELIEVE IN THE RESURRECTION..... CAN I STILL CALL MYSELF A CHRISTIAN? I DO NOT ACCEPT ZIZEK'S NOTION OF A CHRISTIAN MATERALIST & YET I AM NOT SIMPLY A MATERIALIST. WOULD HUMAN MATERALIST SUFFICE? I ACCEPT THE TITLE HUMANIST BUT AM I PREPARED TO ACCEPT THE POLITICAL FALLOUT OF THIS ACCEPTANCE? I PROMISE YOU: THERE WILL BE FALLOUT.
ALLAN STONE WOULD SAY "JACK YOU ARE THINKING TOO MUCH" O.K, BUT THINKING IS NECESSARY... ALL PHILOSOPHICAL INQUIRY STARTS WITH A QUESTION. WHO AM I DOES NOT BOTHER ME MUCH...THIS IS NOT THE

30 MAY 2014: THE DIFFICULTY IS: I AM DEALING WITH SOMETHING SO COMPLEX AND SO ELUSIVE. I HAVE KNOWN THIS FOR YEARS BUT IT HAS BECOME MORE EVIDENT THAN EVER. STRUCTURALLY IT IS THE SAME AS QUANTUM MECHANICS . . . . IT CAN BY ANYTHING . . . . AT ANY TIME . . . . . AT ANY PLACE. IT IS DEFINITE NOT EITHER – OR! IT IS NEITHER – NOR AND AS HENRY WOULD SAY "AND THEN SOME". IT CAN BE ANYTHING TO ANY ONE. IT IS NOT DEPENDENT ON RACE . . . . OR SEX . . . . OR NATIONALITY. IT IS BEYOND ALL KNOWN ART HISTORICAL REFERENCES BUT IT IS NOT DIVINE! IT IS A MAN MADE PHENOMENON. THIS IS WHAT BOTHERS ME . . . . CAN I PLACE THAT MUCH TRUST IN BEING HUMAN? THERE ARE TOO MANY FLAWS IN BEING HUMAN . . . HOW CAN ANYONE TRUST BEING HUMAN? I AM NOT A CREATIONIST . . . I DON'T BELIEVE IN THAT SHIT! BUT YET I HAVE A BELIEF IN GOD . . . . IS THIS A CONTRADICTION? CAN ONE HONESTLY SAY THAT THEY BELIEVE IN GOD AND AT THE SAME TIME SAY THAT THEY WERE NOT CREATED BY GOD? I AM NOT A HYPRICRITE! s/p GOD IS A CONCEPT INVENTED BY US. I DO NOT BELIEVE IN THE VIRGIN BIRTH of CHRIST + I DO NOT BELIEVE IN THE RESURRECTION . . . . . CAN I STILL CALL MYSELF A CHRISTIAN? I DO NOT ACCEPT ZIZEK'S NOTION OF A CHRISTIAN MATERIALIST + YET I AM NOT SIMPLY A MATERIALIST. WOULD HUMAN MATERIALIST SUFFICE? I ACCEPT THE TITLE HUMANIST BUT AM I PREPARED TO ACCEPT THE POLITICAL FALLOUT OF THIS ACCEPTANCE? I PROMISE YOU: THERE WILL BE FALLOUT.

ALLAN STONE WOULD SAY "JACK YOU ARE THINKING TOO MUCH" O.K., BUT THINKING IS NECESSARY . . . ALL PHILOSOPHICAL INQUIRY STARTS WITH A QUESTION.

WHO I AM DOES NOT BOTHER ME MUCH . . . THIS IS NOT THE

CONT'D

6 JUNE 14: GONE FISHING!

It's been a great year . . . lots of work . . . lots of success but I, as usual this time of the year am tired . . . need a rest. Everyone must learn to listen to their bodies. . . When the body tells you to stop . . . . . . pay attention.

Back in N.Y. + out to San Diego. for the opening of my first retrospective . . . very exciting! [. . .]

See you in September.

22 SEPT 2014: Back in the Big Apple: I am very pleased with the show. [. . .] . . . . beautiful installation. The small gray paintings (framed to perfection) are the big surprise. [. . .] Great feedback from everyone. [. . .]

50 years is a long fucking time! It sends a message: I've always been in it for duration and there is more to come. The paintings show a remarkable consistency. . My ideas are intact through every stage of development

What now? Stay on track. Do no deviate. The public is slowly beginning to understand what these paintings are about. Hold steady + keep doing what you are doing.

6 OCT: <u>ARTOPOLIS</u> IS UP ON THE WALL: 10'4" x 20'8"

It's big! Slightly larger than 9•11. I've started with a drawing made by rolling lead buckshot over stretched black primed canvas . . . this is my substructore. The lines will guide me + keep the subject on track. The buckshot was submerged in golden white gesso + simply rolled across the surface. In the early 1970s, I was inspired by hydrogen bubble chambers which showed the tracks left behind by subatomic particles . . . . it's quite beautiful + I've already done a series of drawings using this technique on rice paper with great success. These drawings are for <u>ARTOPOLIS</u> it is now 1428 hrs . . . . the first tesserae will be applied in half hour from now.

11 OCT: It's becoming clearer: the lead buckshot taught me another quality of line . . . . a drawing that reproduces an 'organic grid' . . . . yes, that's right! . . . an organic grid. The organic grid is equivalent to the euclidean grid which is the basis i.e., foundation of first + second stage modernism. The organic grid is the foundation of third stage modernism. From now on this grid will serve as the plastic under-rinning of everything I do. This organic grid is the underlining structure of African sculpture. <u>I HAVE RETURNED HOME.</u> [. . .]

14 OCT: There must be some reason for doing this shit. Every day
is voluteered slavery . . . . thanks to Roland Kirk! Mestrovic put
a curse on me: WORK—WORK—WORK + MORE WORK! MY
ART IS AN ANTIDOTE TO MADNESS + EVERYTHING THAT
IS WRONG WITH WORLD SUCH AS RACISM—EVIL—
POLLUTION OF ALL KINDS—HATE—REPUBLICANS—
TALIBAN—ISIS—DISTORTED BELIEF SYSTEMS—DISEASE
OF ALL KINDS INCLUDING EBOLA

I am tired of the bullshit of being human. How about something
that transcends human? How about becoming a spirit? A non-being
human? I like the notion of art as antidote, perhaps this concept will
inspire people to change their ways. Can republicans learn to like
Obama? I am no simple minded fool . . . there is evil in this world . . .
there is racism . . . there is hate . . . . people suffer from everything
imaginable . . . . but art survives and art is the only tool I have to
transcend the bullshit!

POWER TO ART

[. . .]

17 OCT: A horrorable day in the studio . . . spilled a fine particle
aluminum . . . . disgusting + dangerous! Bad spill difficult to clean
up . . . painting took a drastic turn . . . I don't know what it wants +
I cannot see it. I was close but for now 'IT WHIPPED MY ASS'!
BIG TIME!

21 OCT 14:

Took time off today to read Richard Shiff's <u>Doubt</u> It's interesting. . . He is a smart, intelligent writer/thinker well versed in the history of art. . . I enjoyed it. Ron Gorchov mentioned doubt as something to consider and I did not acknowledge its importance. For me doubt is a luxury I can not afford. . . . Everything is always so pressing that I have no time to doubt anything I do in painting. . . . Time is precious and I have no time to doubt. The painting <u>FAST FORWARD</u> instructed me: FULL STEAM AHEAD! DO NOT LOOK BACK AND DON'T QUESTION. . . . . MINE IS NOT TO REASON WHY. [. . .]

R.S. mentions physicality, concrete, the making of Art vs. Theory, materiality . . . . all the things I work with. How is my thinking different from other artists whom I admire like Irwin—Judd? They all depend on empirical data so do I. The history of painting is at a crossroad and its time to shit or get off the pot!

31 OCT 2014 1630 HRS. COMPLETED ATOPOLIS:
    FOR EDUARD GLISSANT 10'4"X20'8"
"A CONTRACTION OF ATOPOS AND POLIS" REVERBERATES WITH THE IDEAS OF
EDUARD GLISSANT AND HIS LONGTIME COMMITMENT TO TRY TO ARTICULATE
A THOROUGHLY INTERCONNECTED AND EGALITARIAN RELATIONSHIP BETWEEN
HUMANS, COMMUNITY AND NATURE, BETWEEN ANIMATE AND INANIMATE THINGS,
BETWEEN IMAGINARY, THE SYMBOLICAL AND THE REAL"
    DIRK SNAUWAERT
        IS IT POSSIBLE TO NAME SOMETHING ABSTRACT REALISM?
THIS IS WHAT I AM DOING .... IT IS ABSTRACT BUT IT'S REAL ....
REAL AS IN CONCRETE. HOW CAN SOMETHING (INCLUDING A
CONCEPT) BE REAL AND ABSTRACT SIMULTANEOUSLY??
THIS CONCRETENESS EXIST AS MATTER ... MATTER BEING THE
MATERIAL WHICH IS THE PAINT: PAINT AS MATTER. I INSIST
ON THE MATERIAL TO BE INFUSED WITH THE SPIRIT ... HENCE
SPIRIT AND MATTER. IS IT POSSIBLE TO SEPERATE SPIRIT FROM
MATTER OR IS IT SIMPLY A 'MATTER' OF CHOICE? I DON'T
KNOW AND I DON'T WANT TO PRETEND THAT I KNOW ...
WHICH I AM CAPABLE OF. IS SPIRIT A 'MATTER' OF
WILL? DO ALL HUMANS HAVE SPIRIT?
        THE PLASTIC UNDERPINNING OF PAINTING, I CALL THE UNIT.
THE UNIT IS ANALOGOUS TO THE STRUCTURES OF PARTICLE PHYSICS AND
REPRESENT THE HOLY GRAIL OF PAINTING. IT IS ORGANIC AND HAS ITS'
OWN UNIQUE GEOMETRY. THE CLOSEST GEOMETRY THAT I CAN
IMAGINE IS FRACTAL GEOMETRY BUT I SINCERELY THINK THAT
THERE IS ANOTHER FORM OF GEOMETRY SOMETHING THAT I DO NOT
HAVE A NAME FOR. I CAN FEEL IT AND I CAN SEE IT IN
MY BRAIN. MY JOB AS A PAINTER IS TO STRUCTURE THE
PICTURE PLANE USING THIS FORM OF GEOMETRY. I KNOW
THAT THIS GEOMETRY COMPOSED OF LIGHT. IT DEPENDS ON
LIGHT TO MANIFEST ITS' SELF. IF I CAN SEE THE LIGHT

31 OCT 2014 1630 HRS. COMPLETED <u>ATOPOLIS</u>:
FOR EDOUARD GLISSANT 10' 4" X 20' 8"
"A CONTRACTION OF ATOPOS AND POLIS"
"REVERBERATES WITH THE IDEAS OF EDUARD GLISSANT
AND HIS LONGTIME COMMITMENT TO TRY TO
ARTICULATE A THOROUGHLY INTERCONNECTED AND
EGALITARIAN RELATIONSHIP BETWEEN HUMANS,
COMMUNITY AND NATURE, BETWEEN ANIMATE AND
INANIMATE THINGS, BETWEEN IMAGINARY, THE
SYMBOLICAL AND THE REAL"
DIRK SNAUWAERT
IS IT POSSIBLE TO NAME SOMETHING <u>ABSTRACT
REALISM</u>? THIS IS WHAT I AM DOING . . . . IT IS ABSTRACT
BUT IT'S REAL . . . REAL AS IN CONCRETE. HOW CAN
SOMETHING (INCLUDING A CONCEPT) BE REAL AND
ABSTRACT SIMULTANEOUSLY?? THIS CONCRETENESS
EXIST AS MATTER . . . MATTER BEING THE MATERIAL
WHICH IS THE PAINT: PAINT AS MATTER. I INSIST ON THE
MATERIAL TO BE INFUSED WITH THE SPIRIT . . . . HENCE
SPIRIT AND MATTER. IS IT SIMPLY A 'MATTER' OF
CHOICE? <u>I</u> <u>DON'T</u> <u>KNOW</u> AND I DON'T WANT TO PRETEND
THAT I KNOW . . . . WHICH I AM CAPABLE OF. IS SPIRIT A
'MATTER' OF WILL? DO ALL HUMANS HAVE SPIRIT?
THE PLASTIC UNDERPINNING OF PAINTING, I CALL
THE UNIT. THE UNIT IS ANALOGOUS TO THE
STRUCTURES OF PARTICLE PHYSICS AND REPRESENT
THE HOLY GRAIL OF PAINTING. IT IS ORGANIC AND HAS
ITS' OWN UNIQUE GEOMETRY. THE CLOSEST GEOMETRY
THAT I CAN IMAGINE IS FRACTAL GEOMETRY BUT I
SINCERELY THINK THAT THERE IS ANOTHER FORM OF
GEOMETRY SOMETHING THAT I DO NOT HAVE A NAME
FOR. I CAN FEEL IT AND I CAN SEE IT IN MY BRAIN. MY

JOB AS A PAINTER IS TO STRUCTURE THE PICTURE PLANE USING THIS FORM OF GEOMETRY. I KNOW THAT THIS GEOMETRY COMPOSED OF LIGHT. IT DEPENDS ON LIGHT TO MANIFEST ITS' SELF. IF I CAN SEE THE LIGHT

CONT'D FROM 31 OCT 14:

then I am able to construct the picture plane. The narrative/ subject/object/symbol . . . . . all is carried by light and Hans Hofmann was correct: "the only light you have as a painter is the paint" Hofmann was also correct about emmpathy. . . "It's a necessary ingredient of making art"

By all means necessary I must be consistent with my thinking . . . . stay focus and stay in the studio! <u>THE SHIT IS ABOUT TO HIT THE FAN</u>.

3 NOV: It was not tight enough . . . . had to go back into it . . . I think it's O.K. now. [. . .]

24 NOV 14: MARY & I WENT TO THE JEWISH MUSEUM TODAY TO SEE LEWIS/KRASNER SHOW. WHAT A TREAT! A HISTORICAL SCHOLARY EXHIBITION. I AM THANKFUL THAT THE JEWISH MUSEUM DID THIS SHOW. IT IS GOOD FOR NORMAN... GOOD FOR LEE & GOOD FOR THE PUBLIC.

I MISS NORMAN. I WILL ALWAYS BE THANKFUL TO ROMY FOR INTRODUCING ME TO NORMAN. ABSTRACTION IS THE KEY TO THE UNIVERSE, UNLOCK THE UNIVERSE AND ANYTHING IS POSSIBLE. FOR ME, THERE IS A PERSONAL NORMAN LEWIS'S LEGACY THAT I AND ONLY I MUST FULFILL. THERE IS NO ONE ELSE. I MUST OVERCOME MY EXISTENTIAL DREAD AND BT BRAVE ENOUGH TO TACKLE THE UNIT. I AM ALONE AND NO SENTIMENTAL 'DESIRE' WILL HELP THIS. I AM ALONE. NORMAN FELT THE IMPORTANCE OF SCIENCE AND TECHNOLOGICAL... NOW I MUST DEFINE SCIENCE AS THE DETERMINATE PHILOSOPHY FOR A MODERN WORLDVIEW. RACISM, BLACK IDENTITY, RELIGION ARE SYMBOLS TO OVERCOME. THERE IS A BRAVE NEW WORLD OUT THERE AND I WANT TO BE THE ONE WHO PAINTS IT! "CUT THROUGH THE BULLSHIT AND BE HONEST WITH YOURSELF.... YOU ARE THE ULTIMATE TRUTH."

(AN UNKNOWN VOICE FROM THE UNIVERSE. I HEARD IT IN THE MUSIC OF JAZZ... IT WAS CODED BUT I'VE MANAGED TO DECIPHER IT) "STAY ON TRACK... BE CONSISTENT... CONCENTRATE AND COMPRESS ALL OF YOUR ENERGY INTO PAINT." ART WILL TAKE CARE OF ITS' SELF. ALL ART ASK OF ME. IS TO MAKE IT SO!

THANKS TO RICHARD STAFF FOR EXPLAINING THE DIFFERENCE BETWEEN MAKING & FINDING.....IT'S JUST ANOTHER BINARY OPPOSITE ...... COMPRESS IT INTO ACTION!

24 NOV 14: MARY + I WENT TO THE JEWISH MUSEUM TO SEE LEWIS/KRASNER SHOW. WHAT A TREAT! A HISTORICAL SCHOLARY EXHIBITION. I AM THANKFUL THAT THE JEWISH MUSEUM DID THIS SHOW. IT IS GOOD FOR NORMAN . . . GOOD FOR LEE + GOOD FOR THE PUBLIC.

I MISS NORMAN. I WILL ALWAYS BE THANKFUL TO ROMY FOR INTRODUCING ME TO NORMAN. ABSTRACTION IS THE KEY TO THE UNIVERSE, UNLOCK THE UNIVERSE AND ANYTHING IS POSSIBLE. FOR ME, THERE IS A PERSONAL NORMAN LEWIS'S LEGACY THAT I AND ONLY I MUST FUFILL. THERE IS NO ONE ELSE. I MUST OVERCOME MY EXISTENTIAL DREAD AND BY BRAVE ENOUGH TO TACKLE THE <u>UNIT</u>. I AM ALONE AND NO SENTIMENTAL 'DESIRE' WILL HELP THIS. I AM ALONE. NORMAN FELT THE IMPORTANCE OF SCIENCE AND TECHNOLOGICAL . . . NOW I MUST DEFINE SCIENCE AS THE DETERMINATE PHILOSOPHY FOR A MODERN WORLDVIEW. RACISM, BLACK IDENTITY, RELIGION ARE SYMBOLS TO OVERCOME. THERE IS A BRAVE NEW WORLD OUT THERE AND I WANT TO BE THE ONE WHO PAINTS IT! "<u>CUT THROUGH THE BULLSHIT AND BE HONEST WITH YOURSELF</u> . . . . <u>YOU ARE</u> THE <u>ULTIMATE TRUTH</u>."

(AN UNKNOWN VOICE FROM THE UNIVERSE. I HEARD IT IN THE MUSIC OF JAZZ . . IT WAS CODED BUT I'VE MANAGED TO DECIPHER IT) "STAY ON TRACK . . . BE CONSISTENT . . . . CONCENTRATE AND COMPRESS ALL OF YOUR ENERGY INTO PAINT." ART WILL TAKE CARE OF ITS' SELF. ALL ART ASK OF ME: <u>IS TO MAKE IT SO</u>!

THANKS TO RICHARD SHIFF FOR EXPLAINING THE DIFFERENCE BETWEEN MAKING + FINDING . . . . IT'S JUST ANOTHER BINARY OPPOSITE . . . . . <u>COMPRESS IT INTO ACTION.</u>

1606   26 NOV 14: COMPLETED <u>ESCALATION</u> 48" x 48"

It's a message to any painter who attemps to follow my lead . . . . be prepared for a difficult confortation: . . . you must do your homework you must know a lot about the history of painting . . . you must know how to paint . . . . understand paint as matter . . . . able to read the density of light . . . . . know all of the basic formal elements . . . . . cut through the hype of money + fashion . . . . . know the meaning of substance . . . . . . be prepared for the long haul . . . . have lots of guts . . . . . must have the spirit on your side . . . . . be comfortabe with lonliness and accept the fact that you are alone . . . . . work—work—work + more work! You can't be lazy + do this . . . . . overcome race—religion—gender—politics—identity on any level—family . . . . . . be true to yourself + remember: <u>THIS SHIT IS BEYOND LIFE.</u>

P.S. <u>ESCALATION</u> is a 100% multi-dimensional painting. . . There is no top or bottom it may be hung in any direction including on the diagonal. I suggest that you change its' direction periodically. Have fun with it!

27 NOV.—HAPPY THANKSGIVING – I have a 16 LB. Free range turkey in the oven. The fucking thing cost $65! . . . It better be worth it. Got to run Mary will be angry if I am late.

30 NOV: <u>IT WAS WORTH IT</u>
<u>VERY GOOD!!!</u>

1843 HRS. 30 NOV 2014: I HAVE JUST EXPERIENCED A MAJOR BREAKTHROUGH IT WAS BREATH TAKING: GEOMETRY AS SPACE. I AM PRESENTLY DOING A PAINTING FOR ALEXANDER GROTHEN-DIECK.... SOMEONE I SINCERELY ADMIRE. AFTER READING HIS OBITUARY IN THE N.Y. TIMES FOR THE FOURTH OR FIFTH TIME, EDWARD FRENKEL, A PROFESSOR OF MATHEMATICS AT UNIVERSITY OF CALIFORNIA, BERKELEY SAID "THAT ALGEBRAIC EQUATIONS CAN PRODUCE ALGEBRIC GEOMETRY TO DESCRIBE GEOMETRIC SHAPES, OR SPACES" THIS IS WHAT I HAVE BEEN LOOKING FOR... A GEOMETRY THAT CAN DESCRIBE A SPACE. I KNOW A LOT ABOUT NATURAL SPACE. I KNOW A LOT ABOUT POETIC SPACE BUT GEOMETRICAL SPACE? THIS IS AMAZING. THANK YOU MR. FRENKEL AND OF COURSE THANK YOU MR. GROTHENDIECK. I PROMISE YOU THAT YOUR PAINTING WILL BE AS GREAT AS YOU ARE. MY WORLDVIEW HAS ADVANCED TO ANOTHER LEVEL OF CONSCIOUNESS,

1 DEC: PERHAPS THIS GEOMETRICAL SPACE IS A PHILOSOPHICAL SPACE?

2 DEC.: YASMIL RAYMOND JUST LEFT... MY FIRST TIME MEET-ING HER... ENERGETIC.. A TRUE SPIRIT... ENGAGED IN THE POSSIBILITES THAT ART HAS TO OFFER..., I LIKED HER. AESTHETICS IS THE LAST FRONTIER

4 DEC: IT'S CONSCIOUNESS THAT IS EXPANDING..., THIS IS THE DIFFICULTY FOR ALL OF US: HOW DO WE KEEP UP WITH THIS EXPANSION? THAT IS THE QUESTION. EVOLUTION IS FEEDING THE EXPANSION. HOW DOES THIS EFFECT PAINTING? IF I CAN MANAGE TO SHOW THIS... THEN I HAVE EXPANDED THE HISTORY OF PAINTING. 1900 HRS MY PAINTINGS ARE TRAPS BUILT TO CATCH THE LIGHT.... LIGHT TRAPS

1843 HRS. 30 NOV 2014: I HAVE JUST EXPEIRENCED A
MAJOR BREAKTHROUGH. IT WAS BREATH TAKING:
GEOMETRY AS SPACE. I AM PRESENLY DOING A PAINTING
FOR ALEXANDER GROTHENDIECK . . . . SOMEONE I
SINCERELY ADMIRE. AFTER READING HIS OBITUARY
IN THE <u>N.Y. TIMES</u> FOR THE FOURTH OR FIFTH TIME,
EDWARD FRENKEL, A PROFESSOR OF MATHEMATICS
AT UNIVERSITY OF CALIFORNIA, BERKELEY SAID "THAT
ALGEBRAIC EQUATIONS CAN PRODUCE ALGEBRIC
GEOMETRY TO DESCRIBE GEOMETRIC SHAPES, OR
SPACES" THIS IS WHAT I HAVE BEEN LOOKING FOR . . . A
GEOMETRY THAT CAN DESCRIBE A SPACE. I KNOW A LOT
ABOUTT NATURAL SPACE. I KNOW A LOT ABOUT POETIC
SPACE BUT GEOMETRICAL SPACE? THIS IS AMAZING.
THANK YOU MR. FRENKEL AND OF COURSE THANK YOU
MR. GROTHENDIECK. I PROMISE YOU THAT YOUR
PAINTING WILL BE AS GREAT AS YOU ARE. MY WORLDVIEW
HAS ADVANCED TO ANOTHER LEVEL OF CONSCIOUNESS.

10 DEC: PERHAPS THIS GEOMETRICAL SPACE IS A
PHILOSOPHICAL SPACE?

2 DEC.: YASMIL RAYMOND JUST LEFT . . . MY FIRST TIME
MEETING HER . . . ENERGETIC . . A TRUE SPIRIT . . .
ENGAGED IN THE POSSIBILITIES THAT ART HAS TO
OFFER . . . I LIKED HER. <u>AESTHETICS</u> <u>IS</u> <u>THE</u> <u>LAST</u>
<u>FRONTIER</u>

4 DEC: IT'S CONSCIOUNESS THAT IS EXPANDING . . . THIS
IS THE DIFFICULTY FOR ALL of US: HOW DO WE KEEP UP
WITH THIS EXPANSION? THAT IS THE QUESTION.
EVOLUTION IS FEEDING THE EXPANSION. HOW DOES THIS

EFFECT PAINTING? IF I CAN MANAGE TO SHOW
THIS . . . . . . I HAVE EXPANDED THE HISTORY OF
PAINTING
<u>1900 HRS</u> MY PAINTIGNS ARE TRAPS BUILT TO CATCH THE
LIGHT . . . . <u>LIGHT TRAPS</u>

8 DEC 2014 1616 HRS. COMPLETED <u>ESCALATION II</u> $(x^2 + y^2 = 1)$:
FOR ALEXANDER GROTHENDIECK   O.K.!

~~20 DEC 2014 1600 HRS. COMPLETED ESCALATION III (THE CIRCLE OF DESIRE) AKA THE GREEN SQUARE~~ (I DON'T KNOW)
20 DEC.   SOME THOUGHTS: THE COLOR STRUCTURE IS
DIMENSIONAL.... SPACE IS DEPENDENT ON COLOR AND
COLOR IS DEPENDENT ON LIGHT...LIGHT IS CONSCIOUSNESS.
    ALL of THIS SUPPORT MY NOTION OF A MULTI-DIMENSIONAL
SPACE. I FEEL O.K. ABOUT THIS.
21 DEC. I THINK ITS' O.K...... NEEDED SOME ADJUSTMENTS
OR AS THE OLD TIMERS WOULD SAY "PUT IT BACK IN THE OVEN"
THIS SHIT IS HARD! THAT'S THE REAL MEANING OF 'HIGH TIMES-
HARD TIMES' IT'S LIKE TRYING TO BREAK IN A WILD HORSE!
OR BETTER YET A CONEY ISLAND ROLLER COASTER..... 'UP &
DOWN SHE GOES WHERE SHE STOPS NOBODY KNOWS'. SPEAKING OF
TRUTH... THIS IS THE TRUTH. THERE IS NO SUCH THING AS
ABSOLUTE TRUTH OR ABSOLUTE PURITY... IT'S ALL A
BUNCH OF MULE SHIT! I CAN'T WASTE MY TIME ON
ABSOLUTES. I AM ABSOLUTE & THAT'S THE DAMN TRUTH!

     THERE ARE <u>TWO BASIC CENTERS</u>: ONE IS MANMADE
AND THE OTHER IS COSMIC. ULTIMATELY, THERE ARE MANY
CENTERS i.e., WHEN THE NOTION OF SELF INTERVENES.
I DEAL WITH ALL OF THEM BECAUSE I LIKE IT
  LIKE THAT. MULTIPLE CENTERS ARE MORE ENJOYABLE.
THAT'S WHY I LIKE NEITHER-NOR PHILOSOPHICALLY...
  IT'S MORE ENJOYABLE. THIS IS THE CRUX OF MY
IDENTITY..... I LIKE IT LIKE THAT!

8 DEC 2014 1616 HRS. COMPLETED <u>ESCALATION II</u> ($x^2+y^2=1$):
FOR <u>ALEXANDER GROTHENDIECK</u>   O.K.!

~~20 DEC 2014 1600 HRS. COMPLETED ESCALATION III,~~
~~(THE CIRCLE OF DESIRE) AKA THE GREEN SQUARE~~.
(I DON'T KNOW)
20 DEC. SOME THOUGHTS: THE COLOR STRUCTURE IS
DIMENSIONAL . . . . SPACE IS DEPENDENT ON COLOR AND
COLOR IS DEPENDENT ON LIGHT . . . LIGHT IS
CONSCIOUNESS.
ALL OF THIS SUPPORT MY NOTION OF A MULTI-
DIMENSIONAL SPACE. I FEEL O.K. ABOUT THIS.
21 DEC: I THINK ITS' O.K. . . . . . . NEEDED SOME
ADJUSTMENTS OR AS THE OLD TIMERS WOULD SAY "PUT
IT BACK IN THE OVEN" THIS SHIT IS HARD! THAT'S THE
REAL MEANING OF 'HIGH TIMES-HARD TIME' IT'S LIKE
TRYING TO BREAK IN A WILD HORSE! OR BETTER YET A
CONEY ISLAND ROLLER COASTER . . . . 'UP + DOWN SHE
GOES WHERE SHE STOPS NOBODY KNOWS.' SPEAKING OF
TRUTH . . THIS IS THE TRUTH. THERE IS NO SUCH THING
AS ABSOLUTE TRUTH OR ABSOLUTE PURITY . . . IT'S ALL A
BUNCH OF MULE SHIT! I CAN'T WASTE MY TIME ON
ABSOLUTES. I AM ABSOLUTE + THAT'S THE DAMN TRUTH!
THERE ARE <u>TWO</u> BASIC CENTERS: ONE IS MANMADE
AND THE OTHER IS COSMIC. ULTIMATELY, THERE ARE
MANY CENTERS i.e., WHEN THE NOTION OF SELF
INTERVENES. I DEAL WITH ALL OF THEM BECAUSE I LIKE
IT LIKE THAT. MULTIPLE CENTERS ARE MORE ENJOYABLE.
THAT'S WHY I LIKE NEITHER-NOR
PHILOSOPHICALLY . . . . IT'S MORE ENJOYABLE. THIS IS
THE CRUX OF MY IDENTITY . . . . I LIKE IT LIKE THAT!

30 DEC 14: Ms. Lynne Cooke visited me yesterday. [. . .] She is interested in the connection of outsider art (she wants to get rid of the label) to fine art. . . . I think that she means painting. There is some connection. My understanding is: the only difference between outsiders and painters is "the outsider does not develop dialogue with the history of painting" I think that this is correct. As far as the label . . . . . . call all of us artists + the hell with it! (Is this what Bill Williams meant when he said to me "I do not to be part of the dialogue" Does he see himself as an outsider?

2 JAN 2015: Stuart H. called with bad news: Jake Berthot died. I was expecting it . . but its always very painful. Jake was the real deal. His brutal honesty about painting . . . . the absence of hype is what I admired about him. My little painting, <u>ODE TO JAKE</u> was done last year. We have lost a great painter . . . but we learned a lot from him.

22 JAN 2015: Completed <u>APOLLONIAN HAYRIDE</u> (FOR ALEXIS TSIPRAS) GOOD LUCK!

62" x 62" ∴ I have five paintings for Zeno-X show which opens 25 April. <u>DON'T GET COMFORTABLE!</u> IT'S NOT OVER YET. KEEP PUSHING. THESE PAINTINGS REQUIRE LOTS OF REST . . . . A FULL EIGHT TO TEN HOURS SLEEP. THEIR COMPLEXITY IS OVERWHELMING . . . . AT TIMES I HAVE TO TAKE A WALK. IT'S THE ONLY WAY FOR NOW . . . I SEE NO OTHER WAY OF DOING THIS . . . . THE PAINTING DEMANDS COMPLEXITY. I GUESS IT'S THE NATURE OF OUR TIMES.

Good news: the Whitney Museum brought <u>SORCERER'S! APPRENTICE!</u> It was one of the paintings in my Whitney show. It took forty years! Not bad . . eh? For me . . . . it's been a long-slow-hard-treacherous climb. Mine is an epic adventure. I have never been bored! [. . .]

—NOTES FROM THE WOODSHED—

20 FEB 15: [. . .]

I've completed four small <u>COMPRESSED SPACE</u> paintings + two other small paintings <u>QUEEN BEE</u> + the <u>PROTANGIST</u>. I am very pleased with all of them. . . . <u>NO DOUBTS</u>! But what these paintings have taught me is I have been making a mistake for several years: it is not a topographical space it is a topological space. . . big difference! I must correct this. How? By converting the energy from a naturalistic source to a mathematical source or to be precise energy quanth. I have no knowledge of mathematics but I have something more valuable: I can sense its presence intuitively <u>GO WITH THE INTUITION</u>. Grothendieck's* research into algebraic geometry is the signifier. I think that this is the type of geometry that I've been looking for. One thing for sure: we live in a quantum universe and I want a worldview that reflects this universe. "Objects now follow different rules depending on their size, and we can never be sure where they are or what they are doing." Dr. Robert P. Crease + Dr. Alfred Scharff Goldhaber.

I am energized. My only problem is my health. . . . . . I hope for the best.

On Willem de Kooning's *Door to the River*
May 28, 2015

I met Langston Hughes when I was a student at Tuskegee Institute during my sophomore year of 1958. He was artist-in-residence for more than a week, and gave informal readings of his poetry followed by questions from the students and faculty. He was very engaging, and it was my first time meeting a "certifiable poet." Meeting him was a rare treat. My greatest memory of him occurred when I bravely gave him some of my poems to read. He was nice, patted me on my head and said, "Son, you have to just keep trying!"

His poem, "The Negro Speaks of Rivers," inspired me tremendously. The river is a powerful metaphor. I grew up in Alabama, fishing and swimming in the Alabama River, The Black Warrior River, and The Cahaba River. Some of my best memories growing up in the South are about rivers. Metaphor is a Greek word, and it means "to carry something." Bill de Kooning is a painter whose historical roots are located in the history of materiality. Painters of this aesthetic persuasion must learn to carry their meaning in the paint. All means of narration, if any, must be compressed into the paint.

I knew Bill de Kooning when I was an art student at The Cooper Union. I first met him in 1961. For me, it was enough to hear him say, "Hi kid, how are you doing? Are you learning anything at that school?"

I came to New York to study at Cooper Union in 1960. It was the first time I sat in a classroom next to a White person, or had a White teacher. At first, being with White people in a public setting was very difficult for me. My experiences growing up in the Deep South were ones of hate, violence, and total subservience to Whites . . . real American Apartheid. Fortunately, my instructors at Cooper Union were all a bunch of humanists, and I did not sense racism in any of them. Robert Gwathmey, my first year drawing instructor, was particularly helpful. A Southerner, with a heavy Southern drawl, he went out of his way to make me feel at ease.

Originally given as a talk at the Whitney Museum of American Art, New York, NY, May 28, 2015.

I was attracted to Bill de Kooning: the way he talked, his gestures, the way he dressed, his down-to-earth composure. . . Because of my experience in Alabama with people drinking moonshine whiskey, I did not approve of his heavy drinking. As I learned more about painting, his signature gesture in painting not only attracted me but I became obsessively entwined in his method. I struggled to wean myself from hero worship. It took me 10 years to bypass his influence.

The color structure in *Door to the River* (1960) is a master's use of high-density color. Density is the painters' method of measuring light. Yes, light in painting can be measured. Unlike the physical science of physics or mathematics, painters do not have access to any physical tool for measuring light. We only have our feelings. The measure of light is not an intellectual exercise. There are no conceptual formulas. *Door to the River* is not a fluke. Paintings such as *Rosy-Fingered Dawn At Louse Point* (1963), some of the *Clam Diggers*, and some of the late 1980s *White* paintings are other examples of high-density color structures. We usually feel de Kooning's color in our gut. . .therefore we use the word *visceral*. A good example of the visceral would be another painting in the Whitney's collection, from the *Woman* series, *Woman And Bicycle* (1952–53). We feel *Door To The River* in our head . . . . to be exact . . . . we feel it at the base of our skull.

Sexuality and sensuality is not the same thing. Bill de Kooning was no saint, and I have no memory of his expressing any notion of God, spiritual leanings, or feelings of sublimity. I do know that his paintings are not one-liners, i.e., they invite multiple meanings and *Door to the River* is no exception. His use of high-density color is symbolic of sensuality. This is why we feel it in our head as opposed to our body.

No one can speak of Bill de Kooning's paintings without acknowledging the role of speed. Speed of gesture was the only way possible for him to capture the intensity of emotion. As a young painter interested in photography's influence on painting, I equated speed to the split second timing of the camera's shutter. Light was not only carried by paint but also trapped in a split second.

A couple of weeks ago, I was delivering a lecture at the Art Institute of Chicago. Whenever I am in Chicago, I always spend time with Bill de Kooning's *Excavation* (1950). It's so different from *Door to the River*. Here we see Bill's mythic struggle with Picasso coming to a close. Bill is desperately trying to free himself from Cubism. *Excavation* is a wrestling match, a heavyweight-boxing match. It is Jacob wrestling with the Devil! The canvas has become an archaeological dig site, and he knows if he's not careful . . . it will become his burial ground. Here Bill is fighting for his life . . . clawing himself out of the stratified weight of Art History. *Door to the River* has air. It has light . . . . atmosphere . . . it is a diaphanous, sensual veil of cosmic reverie. And finally, it has the awe of discovery that offers us the gift of the sublime.

At this point, I would like to go back to Bill de Kooning's influence on me. Norman Lewis spoke of the single brushstroke as "unit": Meyer Schapiro wrote of the single brushstroke as "unit" and I remember Haywood "Bill" Rivers using the word "point." I think that they were all speaking of the same thing. The brushstroke as unit in Bill de Kooning's painting was a radical departure from the history of painting. I understood this in the mid-sixties but I could not do anything about it until 1970. However radical Bill de Kooning's paintings were, I realized that they were still using a residue of Cubism, i.e., relational mark making. If I could destroy the relational, then I would be home free! It was Ad Reinhardt who gave me the clue.

I grew up with guns . . . hunting and fishing was my thing. I am a spear fisherman. I go underwater with powerful spear guns and lights hunting for cave-dwelling fish. My target is always the eye. Large fish can only be controlled by placing the spear in their skull. In 1970, my target in painting became the concept of non-relational painting. Bill's brushstroke was fast, but I had to go faster! After a devastating critique by an older painter who said, "You have some very nice de Kooning's here." I got rid of my brushes and built a large drawing board on the studio floor. It measured 12' x 20', made of 2' x 4's placed at 16" center honeycomb grid, covered with ¾" construction grade plywood, and topped off with a layer of industrial linoleum for easy cleaning. The drawing board was built absolutely flat, level, and square to prevent any arbitrary flow of paint. In answer to Bill de Kooning's house painting brush, I built a large "T", 12' wide of 2' x 4's which I called the *Developer.* My studio became a laboratory for experimentation into the nature of paint as matter. My first objective was to rake a continuous slab of acrylic paint that measured ¼" thick. These paintings are known as the *Slab* series. The whole picture plane had become a single gesture, i.e., a line. This was a radical departure from relational painting, with no notion of "touch." I had destroyed my target.

Young painters who are hungry, ambitious, and eager to make a name for themselves need someone to push against. For Bill de Kooning, it was Picasso. For me, it was Bill de Kooning. Deep within one of Bill de Kooning's brushstroke is the door that leads to the river, and deep in the river is another door that leads to molecular perception. But one must dive deep, deep, deep, and *still deeper* until you cannot see with the naked eye. Only mind can lead the way. One must learn the concept of mind as matter.

I am thankful to Bill de Kooning for being there when I needed him. I am thankful that he took the time to say, "Hi kid, how are you doing?"

Jack Whitten
New York City
May 2015

<u>1960'S!</u> TO BE CONTINUED. . . I am meeting Mel and William T.* for lunch. . . <u>NOHO STAR 1:30</u> I'll take the 'R' to Bleecker St.

1630 HRS.: Very nice lunch: Mel had mussels in tomato sauce with pasta (spaggetina), Williams had a hamburger + a glass of lemonade (no wine) Mel + I had a Riesling and I, a poached arctic char . . . . perfectly cooked. I am so glad we were to meet for lunch . . . lots of fun. [. . .]

This conversation is excerpted from two interviews conducted between Whitten and Campbell on September 6, 2015, and November 9, 2015.

CAMPBELL   I am filling out what some of these interactions between artists were like because there's little to no history recorded.

WHITTEN   No history?

CAMPBELL   A scant amount. What I really want to do is to build a rich history that elucidates Norman Lewis' connections to artists. Now it's difficult because those early histories that should have included him, they did not.

WHITTEN   I used to ask Norman about why Black artists were not included in the history books. And his answer—always, in all clarity—his answer was, "Jack, if they had to include our achievements"—particularly about him; he was talking about abstract painting now—"they would have to rewrite their history books, and they ain't gonna do that."

CAMPBELL   Yes, but that was then and this is now. We are now correcting the oversights and that which was available for study in plain sight like Lewis's praxis.

WHITTEN   In all clarity, that's something I remember and it made a big impact on me.

CAMPBELL   So, in what year did you meet Lewis?

WHITTEN   We have to go back to the beginning. As a student at Cooper Union I was the only Black kid there. Robert Blackburn, have you heard the name?

CAMPBELL   Of course, the artist and printmaker.

WHITTEN   Robert Blackburn, seeing that I was the only Black student there, reached out and took me to Romare Bearden. But, it was Romy afterwards who extended himself to introduce me to other artists—you know, "you've gotta meet Jacob Lawrence." Now we're going to Brooklyn to see Lawrence because of Bearden. "We got to go uptown to meet Norman Lewis." So I met Norman coming as result of what Bearden said—"You've gotta see these people." So it was Bearden who started giving me this broader introduction to the Black community in 1962, '63.

CAMPBELL   And at that point Lewis was still showing with Willard?

WHITTEN   No. He didn't have commercial representation when I met him. Norman got most of his attention in the '50's. I didn't go up to the studio until '65, '66.

CAMPBELL   He was still represented but not getting exhibitions until around 1964. So what was he working on in the studio?

WHITTEN   Well, first of all, his studio was on 125th street. I don't even know if it was legal for living. It was not a tenement, though.

CAMPBELL   No, it wasn't a tenement.

WHITTEN   Like an office block building. He lived and worked in the same spot. Even the bathroom was out in the hallway.

CAMPBELL   Yes he rented a studio at 136 W. 125th Street. It was near the former Koch & Co. department store. There's a Walker Evans photograph in the Lewis Pennsylvania Academy of the Fine Arts catalogue. And then, when you walked into his studio, were there paintings on racks?

WHITTEN   He had painting racks built. It wasn't that large a space. And, of course, the size of the studio has a lot to do with the size of the paintings—he was very much aware. "Hey, man, that's the size of my studio."

CAMPBELL   What did he say about scale? What about scale inside the picture?

WHITTEN   What we were talking about are paintings that might be
             24 inches, 18 inches, 12 inches. But mentally, it has a way
             of thrusting your mind outward, where it expands. This is a
             little big painting. Very few artists can do that, but Norman
             could do it.

CAMPBELL   Would you describe the conversations you had in the studio?
             Would you talk about his artistic influences and interests? He
             kept an extensive library of these. Did he mention any of that
             to you specifically?

WHITTEN   A lot of it was social stuff. The difficult thing was, "How does
             one survive? How do you make money?" That was one of the
             first things I wanted to know from Norman beyond the
             painting. How do you make a living out of it? Norman wasn't
             making any money when I met him.

CAMPBELL   True.

WHITTEN   I remember once he told me something very funny. He says, "I
             go to the track a lot." [laughs]

CAMPBELL   It's true; he was a gambler. He bought the loft at 64 Grand
             Street in SoHo with his winnings. One of the biggest
             difficulties for Lewis was that he and Lawrence knew each
             other quite early on in Harlem, and there were newspaper
             articles that would discuss both of them as being the future of
             the art world. I think when Lawrence gets the solo show at
             MoMA, Lewis thought he had a shot. Eventually he realized
             that it was about the abstraction. A Black artist could not
             make abstract work in the 1950s and be recognized.

WHITTEN   My attraction originally to Norman was the fact that he was an
             abstract painter. Except for peers of mine, the only other Black
             painter I knew that was doing abstraction from the older
             generation was Haywood "Bill" Rivers.

CAMPBELL   I love those.

WHITTEN   Bill was the only other one. But Norman was the *only* one that
              had a substantial presence in the community as a black
              abstract painter. That was my attraction, and that's why I
              wanted to speak with him. There's something from a formal
              point of view that should be explained a little bit more. It was
              the first time I'd heard someone use the word "unit." I didn't
              know what that meant.

CAMPBELL   And what did it mean when he used it?

WHITTEN   The stroke is the unit that goes together to build form. Norman
              knew about this and he understood it in relation to his own
              work. In painting it refers to artists who depend upon the small
              flecks of pigment that coalesces to make something
              superlative. In art history, the best example would be
              somebody like Seurat or Cézanne or even Van Gogh with in
              his brushstroke.

CAMPBELL   Yes, the broken brushstroke we see in Impressionism,
              Divisionism, and even the little daubs of the Fauvists. And
              what was Lewis's understanding of the unit in terms of its
              relationship to his own work?

WHITTEN   Well it was his calligraphic brushstroke. All brushwork is
              relational thinking. Meaning that the artist puts down a point
              and it goes to another. For me it was Bill Rivers who helped
              to clarify this; Bill who understood this; Bill, who pointed out
              the terms of the brush stroke as a unit. There's a history to
              that in painting. So that was very helpful. That was probably
              the main formal point of view in talking with Norman that was
              a big help for me.

CAMPBELL   That reminds me so much of his interest in movement, the way
              that a line can move on the canvas. Did you ever talk about that?

WHITTEN   Not really. I mean, some things that are obvious, painters don't
             talk about. A lot of talk between painters—and this is beyond
             Black and White—painters period. If you get two or three
             painters together, our conversations are along the lines of
             grunts and groans and "yeah" and "no." It's not as spoken and
             laid out as an academic person would lay it out. We get our
             vibes from the act. . . "You know what I mean by that," or, "You
             know, the kind of a thing?"

CAMPBELL   But you're an intellectual, and to paraphrase Norman speaking
             about Spiral and this divide in the 1960s, "When Black artists
             get together, we talk about money. And when I hang out with
             White artists, they're talking, they're talking about theories
             of painting."

WHITTEN   This is true.

CAMPBELL   I thought if anyone actually talked about painting with him, it
             would be you.

WHITTEN   We did, and that's why I want to emphasize the use of the
             word "unit." But Norman is right. That's been one of the
             downfalls in the Black community, because the social issue
             and the politics have been so pressing then discussions of
             ideas and of concepts just come up with less urgency.

CAMPBELL   And therefore, when people write about the work, they fall into
             the same trap. I think that it doesn't allow for the richness of
             possibility within the work itself.

WHITTEN   There are reasons for that, though. Because, again, the
           political pressures, the pressures of survival of a whole history
           as a people here in America. That's the pressing issue. And
           still, today, in the Black community, the pressure is economics.
           I remember listening to Mark Bradford give a talk once. He
           was so straightforward. Mark said, "You know, I grew up with
           a lot of love. My family, my mother," right? "A lot of support and
           love, but we didn't have no money." [laughs] I remember
           clapping my hands and say, "Yeah, I hear you, man."

CAMPBELL   That is certainly true.

WHITTEN   This is the first time in the history of artists with
           representation—because of what the younger Black artists are
           doing, and the successes they are having on the commercial
           gallery scene—that there is a little bit of money's coming in.
           Now, what I'm hoping for is that will bring us to a discussion
           where it's not so much about the politics of race and survival.
           We can talk about concepts and ideas.

CAMPBELL   This is something that I want to inject (as Ann Gibson, Kobena
           Mercer, and Katy Siegel have done already begun to do) into
           the scholarship around Lewis as well.

WHITTEN   When I talked to Norman, we could talk about painting. Not
           that "the problem," as we call it, didn't come up. The problem
           was always there. Always there. He understood. Here is a
           man who is clarifying through abstraction, the notion of Black
           sensibility. Now, when I talk, I can say definitively to any-
           fuckin'-body who's willing to listen: there's such a thing as
           Black sensibility and I have a history to prove it, and if I have
           to, I can back into the history and point it out A, B, C, D,
           where it comes from. I can do that. Everybody should be able
           to do that by now. The minute you clarify the Black sensibility,
           it allows you to link it to the notion of form, the plasticity, and
           then you're in the position to do something fantastic.

CAMPBELL   I think Black sensibility could even be about something
            structural rather than being just social. Painters and especially
            ones that are friends and of a generation tend to share
            coincident sensibilities. You were attracted to Lewis's work
            just as he mingled with the other Abstract Expressionists.
            Structures can be fluid and do overlap.
WHITTEN   Well, you could make Black sensibility into a structure.
            Abstract painters like Norman Lewis (and I have to include
            myself) will have shown that it may be structural.
CAMPBELL   That's what I'm talking about.
WHITTEN   We have learned that we can structure this. We know that
            now. We know that. The thing that gives me great pleasure is
            to say there's a historical source for what I do within the Black
            community. I can say that in all pleasure. That's fantastic.
CAMPBELL   Do you remember anything else that sticks with you for those
            early years?
WHITTEN   Well, I'll go back a little bit, just go back a little bit in time. The
            Americans, when abstract expressionism hit and after, they
            extended gesture, historically. We were the people that
            extended gesture and Norman was a part of that. I also
            became attached to Bill de Kooning for example because of
            the radicalness that he had exercised in gesture. I'm still a
            student.
CAMPBELL   No, I don't think so.
WHITTEN   And like being a very ambitious student and following de
            Kooning, following Norman, I just had to make this statement.

— NOTES FROM THE WOODSHED → 2015

3 OCT: THE PAINTING MUST BE ALLOWED TO MAKE ITSELF i.e., <u>IT = SELF</u> AS OPPOSED TO <u>MY = SELF</u>

IT = SELF ⟩ MY = SELF   <u>THE SOUL MAP IS:</u>

∥

WORLDVIEW

BODY = MIND = SOUL = SPIRIT
THESE ELEMENTS ARE INTERCONNECTED AND AT <u>NO</u> TIME SHOULD WE ATTEMPT TO SEPARATE THEM.

I DON'T HAVE MUCH TIME LEFT THEREFORE I MUST NOT WASTE TIME.... ALL ELEMENTS ARE SUSPENDED IN TIME. IT IS O.K. TO THINK OF TIME AS THE FOURTH DIMENSION i.e., CLASSICAL HISTORICAL NOTION OF TIME, BUT I HAVE LEARNED THAT TIME IS ONLY A DOORWAY INTO MULTIPLE DIMENSIONS. BODY = MIND = SOUL = SPIRIT ARE THE COORDINATES THAT ALLOWS US TO VISUALIZE MULTIPLE DIMENSIONS. SPACE IS WHAT GLUES TIME TOGETHER, WITHOUT SPACE THERE WOULD BE NO TIME + WITHOUT TIME OR SPACE THERE WOULD BE NO SOUND NOR WOULD THERE BE LIGHT. THESE ELEMENTS EXIST ONLY BECAUSE <u>WE SAY THEY EXIST.</u>

I HAVE STARTED ORNETTE'S PAINTING. THERE WILL BE <u>NO</u> PRELIMINARY DRAWINGS. THE CONCEPTUAL HAS ALREADY BEEN TAKEN CARE OF. REMEMBER WHEN I FINISHED THE <u>COSMIC BOPPER</u> FOR DIZ? I WAS LOOKING OUT OF MY STUDIO WINDOW ON LISPENARD ST AND SAW ORNETTE... I RUSHED DOWNSTAIRS AND TOLD ORNETTE ABOUT THE PAINTING... "ORNETTE YOU MUST SEE THIS"/ ORNETTE CAME UPSTAIRS, HE STOOD IN MY DOORWAY AND SAID "I CAN HEAR IT, JACK.. I CAN HEAR IT"

→

3 OCT CONT'D. 2015 I WANT ORNETTE TO HEAR HIS PAINTING.....KNOWING ORNETTE, HE DOESN'T HAVE TO SEE IT. MY BROTHER WORKS WITH SOUND!

PHOTONIC LIGHT PRODUCES A SOUND. IT'S A VIBRATION THAT HAPPENS WITHOUT TWO THINGS STRIKING... OF COURSE, IT'S A BUDDHIST CONCEPT THAT I DISCOVERED THROUGH JAZZ. I WILL REMOVE MYSELF & ALLOW THE PAINTING TO MAKE ITSELF. MIND IS THE MEDIUM & PAINT IS THE MATTER BY EXTENSION; THEREFORE, MIND IS MATTER.

THIS IS MY SECOND ATTEMPT IN MAPPING THE SOUL & I HAVE A LONG WAY TO GO! (I SHOULD SAY THE THIRD TIME BECAUSE THE BIRTH OF JAZZ WAS REALLY THE FIRST BUT I DID NOT KNOW IT, ONLY NOW I REALIZE THIS TO BE TRUE.)

COGNITION IS MOST DIFFICULT, IT HAS ITS OWN AGENDA! LUCKILY, I CAN RECOGNIZE IT WHEN IT HAPPENS. A LOT OF CANNOT RECOGNIZE NOR ARE THEY AWARE OF ITS PRESENCE, COGNITION OCCURS OUTSIDE OF THE SELF THEREFORE IT'S OBJECTIVE. IF WE DO NOT LEARN TO CULTIVATE OBJECTIVITY, WE ARE FOREVER TRAPPED IN THE NOTION OF SELF. WITHOUT OBJECTIVITY, IT IS NOT POSSIBLE TO STRUCTURE WORLDVIEW.

—NOTES FROM THE WOODSHED— 2015

3 OCT: THE PAINTING MUST BE ALLOWED TO MAKE ITSELF i.e., <u>IT = SELF</u> AS OPPOSED TO <u>MY = SELF</u> [drawing; labeled "IT=SELF," "MY=SELF," and "WORLDVIEW] <u>THE SOUL MAP</u> IS: BODY = MIND = SOUL = SPIRIT THESE ELEMENTS ARE INTERCONNECTED AND AT <u>NO</u> TIME SOULD WE ATTEMPT TO SEPARATE THEM. I DON'T HAVE MICH TIME LEFT THEREFORE I MUST NOT WASTE TIME . . . . ALL ELEMENTS ARE SUSPENDED IN TIME. IT IS O.K. TO THINK OF TIME AS THE FOURTH DIMENSION i.e., CLASSICAL HISTORICAL NOTION OF TIME, BUT I HAVE LEARNED THAT TIME IS ONLY A DOORWAY INTO MULTIPLE DIMENSIONS. BODY = MIND = SOUL = SPIRIT ARE THE COORDINATES THAT ALLOWS US TO VISUALIZE MULTIPLE DIMENSIONS. SPACE IS WHAT GLUES TIME TOGETHER. WITHOUT SPACE THERE WOULD BE NO TIME + WITHOUT TIME OR SPACE THERE WOULD BE NO SOUND NOR WOULD THERE BE LIGHT. THESE ELEMENTS EXIST ONLY BECAUSE <u>WE</u> SAY THEY EXIST.

I HAVE STARTED ORNETTE'S PAINTING. THERE WILL BE <u>NO</u> PRELIMINARY DRAWINGS. THE CONCEPTUAL HAS ALREADY BEEN TAKEN CARE OF. REMEMBER WHEN I FINISHED THE <u>COSMIC BOPPER</u> FOR DIZ? I WAS LOOKING OUT OF MY STUDIO WINDOW ON LISPENARD ST. AND SAW ORNETTE . . . I RUSHED DOWNSTAIRS AND TOLD ORNETTE ABOUT THE PAINTING . . . "ORNETTE YOU MUST SEE THIS"! ORNETTE CAME UPSTAIRS, HE STOOD IN MY DOORWAY AND SAID "I CAN HEAR IT, JACK . . I CAN HEAR IT"
3 OCT CONT'D: I WANT ORNETTE TO HEAR HIS PAINTING . . . . KNOWING ORNETTE, HE DOESN'T HAVE TO

SEE IT. MY BROTHER WORKS WITH SOUND!

PHOTONIC LIGHT PRODUCES A SOUND. IT'S A VIBRATION THAT HAPPENS WITHOUT TWO THINGS STRIKING . . . OF COURSE, IT'S A BUDDHIST CONCEPT THAT I DISCOVERED THROUGH JAZZ. I WILL REMOVE MYSELF + ALLOW THE PAINTING TO MAKE ITSELF. MIND IS THE MEDIUM + PAINT IS THE MATTER BY EXTENSION; THEREFORE, MIND IS MATTER.

THIS IS MY SECOND ATTEMPT IN MAPPING THE SOUL + I HAVE A LONG WAY TO GO! (I SHOULD SAY THE THIRD TIME BECAUSE <u>THE BIRTH of JAZZ</u> WAS REALLY THE FIRST BUT I DID NOT KNOW IT, ONLY NOW I REALIZE THIS HAS TO BE TRUE.)

COGNITION IS MOST DIFFICULT, IT HAS ITS' OWN AGENDA! LUCKILY, I CAN RECOGNIZE IT WHEN IT HAPPENS. A LOT OF CANNOT RECONGIZE NOR ARE THEY ARE OF ITS PRESENCE, COGNITION OCCURS OUTSIDE OF THE SELF THEREFORE IT'S OBJECTIVE. IF WE DO NOT LEARN TO CULTIVATE OBJECTIVITY, WE ARE FOREVER TRAPPED IN THE NOTION of SELF.

WITHOUT OBJECTIVITY, IT IS NOT POSSIBLE TO STRUCTURE WORLDVIEW.

7 OCT: Idenity is like neutrinos i.e., it is plural (not like <u>pluralism</u>) There are many catgorigies of identity and they all have mass which make them concrete. They are transparent + have the ability to pass through anything. Like photons which are particles of light, they have color. Identity is fluid, mallable → this is my idea of a see through space in painting, like hammering water which is another form of mallability, it is elusive, slippery and operate like a cloaking device i.e., it can change + adopt to a particular environment or different form of matter. Randomness is name of the game but does <u>not exclude</u> exact conceptualize patterns. They can switch back + forth like wave to particle. There are many types of pattern (patterns are infinite) *Pattern painters of the 1970's missread the vibrations, the decrotive is only one form of pattern and they manifest themselves through chaos or controlled delibrate positiong. . . . . They all operate at the molecular level and the macro-cosmic level. (ALL OVER THE PLACE!)

Sensibility is encoded through pattern i.e., patten gives us a structural basis to structure feelings; therefore, ~~is the~~ pattern serves as the "tabla rasa" of art making. Without recognition of pattern (which is a template of feeling) artists could not make art.

Is there a need for identity? It depends . . . . if one is not comfortable with themselves in the cosmos then it's best to have an identity. Depending on the political situation . . . . identity can be a necessity. The political can undermine identity and prevent its' rise to maturity. Identity is like an American Express card. . . . 'Don't leave home without it'. Considering the fact that evil is woven throughout our society identity is a good insurance policy!

I know that I will be attacked on my theory of quantum geometry because no one has defined its' meaning . . . . yet. I will defend my position based on the fact of: every historical significant cosmic shift in perception has been accompanient by a definitive geometry. Contemporary perception is shaped by quantum theory;

therefore. There has to be a geometry. Quantum geometry is structured out of all the known classical geometries but through 'mathematical transdence' transforms itself into another entity: it is a new kind of geometry.

18 OCT 15: The geometry that I work with, I call it quantum geometry because its' the geometry of multiple dimension. Every major shift in perception i.e., historical shift has an accompaning geometry. For the early Greeks it was Pythogrian i.e., planar + therefore Euclidean after Euclid. Planar geometry was the norm throughout the renaissance for art, architecture, music, mathematics + science. Cubism introduced us to another form of planar geometry which was influenced by African sculpture + textile. Even though this geometry was planar it included another dimension of time which was not evident in Euclidean thought. The Africans were aware of other dimensions of time. Picasso + others were attracted to this + acted accordingly. It was not a manner of stealing it was simply influence. Influence is a powerful human element + it propels consciouness i.e., it is the vehicle that expands consciouness.

Painting has always reacted to these major shifts in perspective and through 'form' give a structural visuality . . . . . . this is what painting does. I was attracted + therefore influenced by Jackson Pollock because he showed me another geometry . . . which is the fractal. There are many forms of geometry + I like it because no one owns geometry! It is a thing within itself. This is also why I like the cosmic. . . . No one owns the cosmos!

My plan or stragety (if you want to call it that) is to structure my paintings with quantum geometry.

Saw the Richard Serra show at Gagosian last Friday. The guy is doing my early drawings! Maybe this is a good thing. . . I did it 40 yers ago + finally someone is catching up with me. This could help develop the current dialogue around abstract painting. Its' good that someone is starting to feel what I have been feeling for fifty years. RIGHT ON!

23 OCT 15: 1654 HRS.

When the spirit enters the painting: I stop working on it. The painting is a resting place for the spirit. The spirit is distinct from science + technology. It has always been here therefore the spirit is ancienct The spirit has been present in all phases of human development. Spirit is attracted by matter, in truth, matter is a magnet for spirit. This attraction can be man made, i.e., an object made by man purposefully to attract spirit as in art i.e., art as matter or it can be attracted by nature, in truth, nature was the first attraction before the advent of man. . Due to consciouness man was able to attract spirit. Therefore since man is matter man is also a magnet. Evil matter cannot attract spirit (this is my ultimate optimism!) I am not evil. Saying that the painting is a resting place for spirit does not negate the painting as reproduction of a concept . . . . . the spirit is a concept . . . . . . this concept is not of man but of the cosmos . . . . the cosmos is spirit.

    The spirit does not have an image. . . one can only feel its presence. It is absent of color, absent of sound + absent of movement . . . . it has no smell NO ONE CAN SEE SPIRIT. Again, we can only feel its' presence. COLOR—SOUND—MOVEMENT—SMELL—TASTE—SIGHT—TOUCH ARE ELEMENTS OF MATTER THAT CAN BE USED TO SEDUCE THE SPIRIT. I LIKE THE NOTION OF PAINTING AS OBJECT USED TO SEDUCE SPIRIT!

1 NOV 15: [. . .] I was sent here to make a difference + I am succeeding. TRULY WHAT I AM DOING IS <u>FULFILLING A HISTORICAL DESTINY</u>. . . <u>MY PEOPLE WILL OVERCOME</u>!

4 NOV: For the sake of clarity . . . . let me make myself clear . . . . I must repeat myself: the revolutionary change in my thinking is the correction of my original concept of light as planar (the light is multi-dimensional) I will continue my concept of space as multi-dimensional . . . . which is correct and exist as an absolute.

Obviously speed and time is a factor . . . . speed I have no problem with (I must be careful here, I've just purchased a new car, the 2015 Subaru Outback . . . it likes to go fast!) New York State only allows me 65 MPH but my soul likes 100 MPH! Time remains problematic . . . . . . I am not sure of its' purpose. . . . Can time be an unnecessary thought projection? Maybe it simply takes care of itself like all cosmic events. Sound is another element, but I have no problem with sound. . . It is a vibration made without two things striking. In painting sound is produced through the optical + the optical exist as the result of color densities. . . This is my connection to jazz. . . . Jazz is a vbration that epands consciouness. Wen consciouness expands freedom expands . . . . we all want the expansion of freedom. Completed Ornette's painting: can you hear it Ornette?

POSSIBLE TITLES FOR ORNETTE'S PAINTING

OPEN CIRCLE

SIGHT LINES

OPEN ENDED

THE SOUND of ORNETTE

ORNETTE'S CIRCLE

POLYRHYTHMIC CIRCLE

ORNETTE'S HIDEAWAY

SOUND of the CENTURY

HARD DRIVE
PROXIMITY

<u>POSSIBLE TITLES FOR ORNETTE'S PAINTING</u>
OPEN CIRCLE
SIGHT LINES
OPEN ENDED
THE SOUND of ORNETTE
ORNETTE'S CIRCLE
POLYRHYTHMIC CIRCLE
ORNETTE'S HIDEAWAY
SOUND of the CENTURY
HARD DRIVE
PROXIMITY

19 NOV 15

O.K. ..... WE NEED MORE CLARITY FROM YOU WHITTEN ..... WHAT ARE YOU DOING? O.K. I UNDERSTAND THE NEED FOR MORE CLARITY... BUT GIVE ME A BREAK! THE SHIT IS COMPLICATED! I HAVE MANAGED TO AT LEAST CLARIFY THE AESTHER: IT IS A JAZZ AESTHETIC. I KNOW THE PHILOSOPHICAL UNDER-PINNING OF JAZZ.... IT IS THE EXPANSION OF CONSCIOUNESS WHICH IN TERM PROVIDES FOR THE EXPANSION OF FREEDOM. WHEN CONSCIOUNESS EXPANDS FREEDOM EXPANDS. EVERYBODY DESIRE THE EXPANSION OF FREEDOM. IN PARTICULAR FOR ME CONSIDERING THE FACT THAT I WAS SOLD INTO SLAVERY THE EXPANSION OF FREEDOM GAVE ME THE TOOLS NEEDED IN THE CONSTRUCTION OF A NEW IDENTITY. THE IRONY IN THIS IS THE NEW IDENTITY HAS BECOME GLOBAL i.e., EVERYBODY WANTS THE SAME THING. HOW IS IT POSSIBLE FOR A SLAVE TO CONNECT THE DOTS FOR A GLOBAL INTERGALATICAL IDENTITY WHICH IS THE AESTHETIC FOR A MODERN WORLDVIEW? WORLDVIEW IS THE PRIZE. IF I CAN MAKE A LITTLE MONEY IN THE PROCESS; GREAT! BUT IT'S NOT MY PRIME OBJECTIVE. MONEY IS ONLY A BY-PRODUCT OF WHAT I DO.

NOW THAT I HAVE CLARIFIED THE AESTHETIC, CAN I GET BACK TO WORK?

✳ SAW THE BARNES COLLECTION LAST FRIDAY... FANTASTIC! THE CEZANNES WERE MARVELOUS + MATISSE..... WHAT A MASTER! I HAD A BEAUTIFUL REVELATION WITH THE MATISSES: I CAN USE FIGURATION BY REDUCING MATISSE TO A SINGLE THREE-DIMENSIONAL LINE

✳ SEE A SWEET LITTLE ANGEL, FOR B.B. KING

'NOTES FROM THE WOODSHED'

19 NOV 15

O.K. . . . . . WE NEED MORE CLARITY FROM YOU WHITTEN . . . . . WHAT ARE YOU DOING? O.K. I UNDERSTAND THE NEED FOR MORE CLARITY . . . BUT GIVE ME A BREAK! THIS SHIT IS COMPLICATED! I HAVE MANAGED TO AT LEAST CLARIFY THE AESTHEIC: <u>IT</u> <u>IS</u> <u>A</u> <u>JAZZ</u> <u>AESTHETIC</u>. I KNOW THE PHILOSOPHICAL UNDERPINNING OF JAZZ . . . . IT IS THE EXPANSION OF CONSCIOUNESS WHICH IN TERM PROVIDES FOR THE EXPANSION OF FREEDOM. WHEN CONSCIOUNESS EXPANDS FREEDOM EXPANDS. EVERYBODY DESIRE THE EXPANSION OF FREEDOM. IN PARTICULAR FOR ME CONSIDERING THE FACT THAT I WAS SOLD INTO SLAVERY THE EXPANSION OF FREEDOM GAVE ME THE TOOLS NEEDED IN THE CONSTRUCTION OF A NEW IDENTITY. THE IRONY IN THIS IS THE NEW IDENTITY HAS BECOME GLOBAL i.e., EVERYBODY WANTS THE SAME THING. HOW IS IT POSSIBLE FOR A SLAVE TO CONNECT THE DOTS FOR A GLOBAL INTERGALACTICAL IDENTITY WHICH IS THE AESTHETIC FOR A MODERN WORLDVIEW? <u>WORLDVIEW</u> <u>IS</u> <u>THE</u> <u>PRIZE</u>. IF I CAN MAKE A LITTLE MONEY IN THE PROCESS, GREAT! BUT IT'S NOT MY PRIME OBJECTIVE. MONEY IS ONLY A BY-PRODUCT OF WHAT I DO.

NOW THAT I HAVE CLARIFIED THE AESTHTETIC, CAN I GET BACK TO WORK?

* SAW THE BARNES COLLECTION LAST FRIDAY . . . <u>FANTASTIC</u>! THE CEZANNES WERE MARVELOUS + MATISSE . . . . . WHAT A MASTER! I HAD A BEAUTIFUL

REVELATION WITH THE MATISSES: <u>I</u> <u>CAN</u> <u>USE</u> <u>FIGURATION</u> <u>BY</u> <u>REDUCING</u> <u>MATISSE</u> <u>TO</u> <u>A</u> <u>SINGLE</u> <u>THREE-DIMENSIONAL</u> <u>LINE</u>.
*SEE <u>A SWEET LITTLE ANGEL,</u> <u>FOR</u> B.B. KING

6:00→1800 HRS. 9 DEC 15:

Went to see the Frank Stella retrospective today. They looked good in the new Whitney . . . better here than at MoMA. It's unfortunate timing that the Picasso sculpture is up at MoMA. One cannot help but make a comparison. Picasso knew instinctily about three dimensional concepts in painting + sculpture. Stella <u>tries</u> to push it into multiple dimensions which is a good thing because we live in a multiple-dimension world. For me, personally, the early Black Paintings remain the best. These paintings were helpful . . . . . a beautiful introduction into something other than AB/EX. I was also invited to the Dia Foundation to see Robert Ryman's show. The opening + dinner was a classic New York evening. Both Ryman + Stella has helped me but I owe neither of them. They are good painters who have contributed a lot to the history of painting but they are not God's gift to painting. [. . .]

I have always clearly understood F.S.'s paintings. We share some of the same attributes: ① systemic thinking when needed, ② we are both structuralist i.e., we understand how something is built + have the mentally capacity to make it so ③ love for the history of painting. ④ a good balance between conceptual/perceptual ⑤ interest in multi-dimensional space ⑥ workaholics!

The guy is good but his is <u>not</u> the last word in painting. My painting do what his sculptural forms are trying to do . . . . . but they are only illustrations of a multi-dimensional. The paint must be dimensional not its' support! Beyond the materiality of paint, it is the light that is multi-dimensional. There is so much that F.S. do not know about abstract painting: he might arrogantly think that the history of space ends in F.S. . . . . . he is making a big mistake.

It seems like that I am the only who understanding what way the wind is blowing . . . . . to participate in the <u>new</u> abstract painting one must be able to visualize multi-dimensional space, light and

molecular perception . . . otherwise you are only an illustrator
of ideas!

There are a lot of smart ass conceptual thinkers producing a
lower form of art. I do not like design + illustration poseing as
painting. Painting is not about design + illustration. . . . . Painting
is pure vision, conceptual thinking is only a diving board that
leads to the magic of painting. If you can't use a diving board stick
to walking!

14 DEC 15: Synapse: the point of contact between adjacent neurons, where nerve impulses are transmitted from one to the other. In a multi-dimensional space there is an equivalent to this biological function. . . . . When different dimensions clash at the quantum level . . . . . they jump from one dimension to another . . . of course light plays a role in this since light is an adjunct to matter. Clem insistence on the flattening of the picture plane just took on another meaning i.e., several dimensions can be flatten by light . . . ironically due to the topology of a given object/mass . . . particularities take over and produce a topographical appearance of space . . . . this explains why my paintings have always had a topographical "look". Of course I had no way of understanding in the nineteen seventies, 80's, 90's 2,000. I only dealt with it as frontal vs. topographical as explained by the history of pictorial illusion. Kant's concept of autonomy has finally manifest its' self in painting. Notions of concretness were just notions, never arriving at the true meaning of notion: <u>THE IDEA AS OBJECT</u>.

    <u>I MUST EXPLOIT THIS TO THE FULLEST EXTENT.</u>
THERE IS NO ONE STANDING NEXT TO ME.
I MUST LEARN TO FIND COMFORT IN LONELINESS.

15 DEC: I have been mistaken (indeed all of recent art history including Hans Hofmann, Bill de Kooning and other expressionist painters who insist on spontaneity. . . . . . Spontaneity helps but is not the issue . . . . the issue is <u>IMMEDIACY</u>. Early Clyfford Still was closer to the point. . . . . Immediacy was achieved by freezing the light . . . . but later . . . he lost it. He allowed the light to thaw out + it melted! The light must remain frozen or go through a complete phase transistion i.e. light as steam
→ or light as water or light as absolute energy as in nuclear fusion or its' conversion into mass (Einstein explained this)

Now, all of this shit is interealted . . . . right down to the cells of our bodies and of course our genes: <u>WE</u> <u>ARE</u> <u>ALL</u> <u>ONE</u>. IT'S POLITICS AND RELIGION THAT HAVE FUCKED THINGS UP! <u>GET</u> <u>RID</u> <u>OF</u> <u>POLITICS</u> / <u>GET</u> <u>RID</u> <u>OF</u> <u>RELIGION</u> / <u>GET</u> <u>RID</u> <u>OF</u> <u>RACE.</u> ALL WE NEED IS OUR ORIGINAL IDENTITY AND THE PRESENT WILL TAKE CARE OF ITSELF.

Immediacy explains my attraction to the photograph. What started in 1964 has become full circle. In 1964 it was pure vision. . . . I still have the vision but now I am in a position to employ the conceptual.

19 DEC 1900 HRS: Just completed eight works on paper made with spinel, black and Renaissance Wax. I'll have to wait a few to see if this shit is stabile. It appears to be stabile. I should know within a week. I have named them <u>PSYCHICGRAMS</u> this is the most apporiate term. They are part of a series called <u>PORTALS</u> i.e., the portal series . . . . . openings into another dimension . . . . other dimensions because portals as in dimension are plural

22 DEC: 1900 hrs. ① <u>IT</u> <u>LIES</u> <u>BEYOND</u> <u>THE</u> <u>CONCEPTUAL</u> ② <u>IT</u> <u>IS</u> <u>PURE</u> <u>SPIRIT</u> ③ <u>IT</u> <u>IS</u> <u>THE</u> <u>TRUTH</u> ④ <u>IT</u> <u>IS</u> <u>UNIVERSAL</u> ⑤ <u>NO</u> <u>ONE</u> <u>KNOWS</u> <u>WHAT</u> <u>IT</u> <u>IS</u> ⑥ <u>IT</u> <u>IS</u> <u>DIVINE</u> <u>THEREFORE</u> <u>IT</u> <u>IS</u> <u>SPIRITUAL</u> ⑦ <u>STOP</u> <u>TRYING</u> <u>TO</u> <u>AVOID</u> <u>IT</u> ⑧ <u>IT</u> <u>BELONGS</u> <u>TO</u> <u>NO</u> <u>ONE</u> ⑨ <u>THE</u> <u>INDIVIDUAL</u> <u>CAN</u> <u>ONLY</u> <u>DISCOVER</u> <u>IT</u> ⑩ <u>IT</u> <u>IS</u> <u>BEYOND</u> <u>SELF</u> ⑪ <u>IT</u> <u>IS</u> <u>NOT</u> <u>RACIAL</u> ⑫ <u>IT</u> <u>HAS</u> <u>NO</u> <u>NATIONALITY</u> ⑬ <u>IT</u> <u>IS</u> <u>LOVE</u> ⑭ <u>IT</u> <u>DOES</u> <u>NOT</u> <u>EXIST</u> <u>IN</u> <u>TIME</u> ⑮ <u>IT</u> <u>IS</u> <u>ETERNAL</u> ⑯ <u>IT</u> <u>BELONGS</u> <u>TO</u> <u>NO</u> <u>RELIGION</u> ⑰ <u>IT</u> <u>IS</u> <u>NOT</u> <u>POLITICAL</u> ⑱ <u>IT</u> <u>HAS</u> <u>NO</u> <u>GENDER</u> ⑲ <u>IT</u> <u>HAS</u> <u>NO</u> <u>COLOR</u> ⑳ <u>IT</u> <u>IS</u> <u>MULTI-DIMENSIONAL</u>

NOTES FROM THE WOODSHED—2016

17 JAN 1632 HRS.

[. . .] I need a larger presence in Europe. All of us must remember that modernism started in Europe. My third stage modernism is an evoluntary fact: abstract painting being a product of the human mind evolves like all other organic structures . . . its' all about mind. The evolution of Western abstract painting is what I do an am betting on this to construct a truly modern worldview. Power be to painting!

I have something to say considering pictorial illusion in painting: historically pictorial illusion was a pre-conceived condition of painting i.e., painters constructed an illusion of what they saw in nature. As painting evolved, pictorial illusion was no longer a priority. . . . The painting as object was the dominant issue in modernism (both first stage + second stage). In third stage modernism there is no necissity as the painting as object. We accept it as a given. The photograph was the main influence on painting and this influence was a gift of freedom! The painting is a concrete object (at least abstract painting is a concrete object) therefore something quite marvelous has happen: the painting as concrete object is obviously an a-priori object. Being a-priori, any pictorial illusion becomes aposteriori. [. . .]

Once the painting establishes itself as concrete it gains one hundred percent autonomy. I AM AN AUTONOMIST AND AUTONOMISTS DO NOT START OUT CREATING PICTORIAL ILLUSIONIST PAINTINGS! [. . .]

NOTE FROM THE WOODSHED

5 JUNE 2016:

[. . .] It's been a long time since I've written anything. . . . .
Painting everyday has exhausted me . . . . no time to write. Anyway
what's happening? [. . .]

Mentally I am in a good spot. . . . . All the pieces are falling
together. . . . I must maintain the momentum. THE NINETEEN
SEVENTIES BELONG TO ME: I am the only one who clearly
understand what the seventies were. It is important that I continue to
clearify the meaning of the 'SLAB' paintings. The 'SLAB' is the raw
material. The notion of perception is trapped within the slab. This
allows me to do anything that I want: it is the third entity that I want.
It is a structure that is not dependent on abstraction or realism. The
third entity lie beyond abstraction and representation. I like Hilary
Putnam's 'internal realism' or 'pragmatic realism' it reminds me of
Jung's 'psychic realism' whatever, these are old fashion notions. The
quantum world has changed all of that. My molecular perception is
the traditional art historical UNIT in painting that is visible at the
quantum realm: light changes hand with matter. . . . It is the
nanosphere. Only those people who have the ability to reach another
level of consciouness can 'see' with molecular perception. In third
stage modernism, very few people are at this level of consciouness.
In painting, I do not know of anyone other than I.
MY WITTGENSTEINIAN MOMENT HAS COME: I MUST
SHOW

GONE FISHING!

<u>NOTES from THE WOODSHED</u>

23 Sept. 2016: I received the medal of honor from Obama yesterday at the White House. They call it the Medal of Honor for the Arts but in my case: THE MEDAL of HONOR. I have been on the battlefield all of my life and I continue to fight: I AM A WARRIOR. Obama is truly a special person. Shaking his hand I knew that he was a soul Brother! The man is sincere; I wish we had him for another four years.

The sculptures are arriving in New York on Monday. Everything tells me I made the right decision to bring them home. Tate is excited. Chris B. is excited. Kathy is excited. A lot of people are going to support this. Hauser & Wirth are ready to rumble and I want to give them a lot of rope! My time has come & there is no reason to slow down. The painting and the sculpture have come together... there is no longer a gap between painting & sculpture are drawing for that matter ... my thinking has consolidated into one mass of energy. I have the money and support that I've always waited ... the main issue now is health... I want to stay healthy in order to complete what I've started.

2 OCT   Reconstructed process is an advanced notion of process. With reconstructed process I am not hindered by scale. This is the best method of tackleing the complexities of multipe dimensions of both space & time.

8 OCT 16   COMPLETED THE BIRTH of MOHAMMED ALI
           BLACK MONOLITH #___. IT WAS A
           THRILLER IN WOODSIDE THAT DID IT...
           BRUTAL TO THE END... TOTAL EXHAUSTION
           IT'S A TOUGH PAINTING.. ALI WOULD BE
           PLEASED, 1900 HRS. → GOING HOME

18 OCT   Nice trip to Boston over the weekend...
           gave a lecture at the grad center of Boston
         Univ... great bunch of students — professors of art
         very appreciative audience. My lecture: Closing
           the Gap Between Painting + Sculpture.
         A big surprise: John Walker was present
         it was such a treat to see him! Came with
         his wife... very nice lady... half Irish +
         Iranian. What a mixture. Stuart Diamond
         was also there. It was like a SOHO
         reunion!
             Something that I must write down:
         You know the Periodic Table of elements?
         These are elemental units of matter and we
         add them to the chart as they are discovered.
         Scientists are still discovering elemential matter.
         The 'painting' as elemential matter is an
         intriguing theory. All of my fifty years of
         research into 'paint as matter' could this
         possibly be what I've been looking for?   .

18 art cont'd: The painting existing in the world as other forms of 'elements.' I like this. It solves a lot of problems and at the same thing extends the meaning of a thing within itself without the historical baggage of Greenbergian formalism or any other kind of social construct including race, gender all psychological content. An element is indivisable ... it is what it is. Like gold, Like lead, like carbon, Oxygen Hydrogen, Helium, etc.

⟨18⟩

If This is correct its just a matter of finding out what yo can do with this element. What is it good for? I know what lead is good for. I know what gold is good for. I know what iron is good for. What is a painting good for? I said in my lecture that art is perception. Could my paintings be good for changing the perception of racism in America? In the world?

I speak of symbols that have existed throughout the history of art such as: Nature – Sexuality – Politics – Autobiographical, etc. What if Perception is a symbol? Therefore 'beyond' any thing it is perception that sparks my imagination. TO BELL RUBIN FIFTY YEARS LATER: THERE IS SUCH A THING AS A PERCEPTUAL PAINTING!

21 Oct: I don't like how Mr. Hegel treated me in his ~~Phenomenology~~ Philosophy of Mind but he is correct about the spirit. He forgot to mention that Black Folks or as he calls us NEGROES also has spirit. Considering the fact that we all came out of Africa We possess the original spirit. The spirit is universal no one can argue that. Again with all clarity ... BLACK FOLKS ARE THE FIRST CONCEPT of SPIRIT..., WE ARE SPIRIT.

I don't illustrate ideas I reproduce ideas. CONCEPT = IDEA = SPIRIT = MIND = MATTER

7 Nov The only way to penetrate multiple dimensions of space time is through the mind.....it cannot be penetrated through illustration. Illustration is for illustrators and designers & I am neither. I am a Painter! I am correct in saying that my paintings are the reproduction of a concept and reproduction is not the same as illustration. The meaning is in the paint as matter. Mind is matter and mind is elemental. There are different categories of matter all available to the artist for experimentation. I can signify anything I want through matter.....The subject is in the paint and not vice versa.

<u>NOTES from THE WOODSHED</u>

23 Sept. 2016: I received the medal of honor from Obama yesterday at the White House. They call it the Medal of Honor For the Arts but is in my case: THE MEDAL of HONOR. I have been on the battlefield all my life and I continue to fight: I AM A WARRIOR. Obama is truly a special person. Shaking his hand I knew that he was a soul Brother! The man is sincere; I wish we had him for another four years.

The sculptures are arriving in New York on Monday. Everything tells me I made the right decision to bring them home. Tate* is excited. Chris B. is excited. Kathy is excited. A lot of people are going to support this. Hauser + With are ready to rumble and I want to give them a lot of rope! My time has come + there is no reason to slow down. The painting and the sculpture have come together . . . there is no longer a gap between painting + sculpture are drawing for that matter . . . my thinking has consolidated into one mass of energy. I have the money and support that I've always wanted . . . the main issue now is health . . . I want to stay healthy in order to complete what I've started.

2 OCT Reconstructed process is an advanced notion of process. With reconstructed process I am not hindered by scale. This is the best method of tackleing the complexities of multipe dimensions of both space + time.

8 OCT 16 COMPLETED THE BIRTH OF MOHAMMED ALI BLACK MONOLITH #__ IT WAS A THRILLER IN WOODSIDE THAT DID IT . . . BRUTAL TO THE END . . . . TOTAL EXHAUSTION IT'S A TOUGH PAINTING . . ALI WOULD BE PLEASED, 1900 HRS. → GOING HOME

18 OCT Nice trip to Boston over the weekend . . . gave a lecture at the grad center of Boston Univ. . . great bunch of students—professors of art very appreciative audience. My lecture: Closing the Gap Between Painting + Sculpture. A big surprise: John Walker was present it was such a treat to see him! Came with his wife . . . very nice lady . . . half Irish + Iranian. What a mixture. Stuart Diamond was also there. It was like a SOHO reunion!

Something that I must write down: You know the Periodic Table of elements? These are elemental units of matter and we add them to the chart as they are discovered. Scientists are still discovering elemental matter. The 'painting' as elemental matter is an intriguing theory. All of my fifty years of research into 'paint as matter' could this possibly be what I've been looking for?

18 oct cont'd: The painting existing in the world as other forms of 'elements' I like this. It solves a lot of problems and at the same thing extends the meaning of a thing within itself' without the historical baggage of a Greenbergian Formalism or any other kind of social construct including race, gender all psychological content. An element is indivisable . . . . it is what it is. Like gold, Like lead, like carbon, oxygen, Hydrogen, Helium, etc.

If This is correct its' just a matter of finding out what yo can do with this element. What is it good for? I know what lead is good for. I know what gold is good for. I know what iron is good for. What is a painting good for? I said in my lecture that art is perception. Could my paintings be good for changing the perception of racism in America? In the world?

I speak of symbols that have existed throughout the history of art such as: Nature—Sexuality—Politics—Autobiographical, etc. What if perception is a symbol? Therefore 'beyond' any thing it is perception that sparks my imagination. TO BELL RUBIN FIFTY YEARS LATER: THERE IS SUCH A THING AS PERCEPTUAL PAINTING!

21 OCT: I don't like how Mr. Hegel treated me in his <u>Philosophy of Mind</u> but he is correct about the spirit. He forgot to mention that Black Folks or as he calls us NEGROES also has spirit. Considering the fact that we all came out of Africa we possess the original spirit. The spirit is universal no one can argue that. Again with all clarity . . . BLACK FOLKS ARE THE FIRST CONCEPT OF SPIRIT . . . WE ARE SPIRIT.

I don't illustrate ideas I reproduce ideas. CONCEPT = IDEA = SPIRIT = MIND = MATTER

7 NOV The only way to permeate multiple dimensions of space time is through the mind . . . . . it cannot be penetrated through illustration. Illustration is for illustrators and designers + I am neither . . I am a painter! I am correct in saying that my paintings are the reproduction of a concept and reproduction is not the same as illustration. The meaning is in the paint as matter. Mind is matter and mind is elemental. There are different categories of matter all available to the artist for experimentation. I can signify anything I want through matter . . . . . The subject is in the paint and not vice versa.

2016

8 NOV: Now is the time...... My SASA
           has arrived on time
       I am in the orbit of my ancestors
       We dance together
         We eat & drink together
          we rejoice together
              & sing together ~~ ZEKIEL
       The wheel of ~~EZEKIEL~~/sp. is no
           longer Christian
           it is African ....
              it is the beginning ~~& it is~~
                      of time
             & it IS MINE!
       "ZEKIEL SAW DE WHEEL, WAY UP IN THE
          MIDDLE of THE AIR"

12 NOV:

       QUANTUM EXPRESSIONISM.... QUANTUMISM
          > The contemporary existence of being modern <
       I Am A Quantum Expressionist. I work at the
       molecular level i.e, I play with atoms and photons
       I collaborate with Nature. i.e., Nature as it
       exist at the MICRO < — > MACRO: I AM
       IN THE MIDDLE HOLDING BOTH EXTREMES
       IN MY HANDS. I HAVE LEARNED TO DANCE
       WITH THE UNIVERSE, I HAVE ARRIVED AT
       ANOTHER LEVEL OF CONSCIOUSNESS AND THERE IS NO
       END IN SIGHT. I SEE ONLY LIGHT AND

AND IT'S A BEAUTIFUL LIGHT! I MUST LEARN TO USE THIS LIGHT FOR THE BENEFIT OF MANKIND. THE LIGHT IS MY SOURCE OF ENERGY AND I MUST LEARN TO USE IT WISELY.... IT IS NOT TO BE WASTED ON NONSENSE & FOOLISH ENDEAVORS. MY FIRST THOUGHT IS TO USE IT AS AN ANDTDOTE TO ALL THE EVIL THAT SURROUNDS ME. WHETHER I LIKE IT OR NOT WHAT I DO IS POLITICAL : UNCERTAINTY - AMBUIGITY - RANDOMNESS CHAOS THEORY - QUANTUM MECHANICS DEALS WITH ALL OF THIS & MORE ... IT IS NOT STATIC BUT FOREVER IN MOTION WITHOUT A FIXED STATIONERY CENTER. IT DEPENDS ON INTERACTION IN ORDER TO BE 'ACTIVE' THEREFORE IT IS POLITICAL. WE DID NOT INVENT THE POLITICAL... IT HAS ALWAYS BEEN THERE!

2016

8 NOV: Now is the time . . . . . My SASA
         has arrived on time
        I am in the orbit of my ancestors
        We dance together
            We eat + Drink together- - ZEKIEL
        We rejoice together
            + sing together
        The wheel of Ezekiel $_{s/p}$ is no
            longer Christian
              it is African . . . .
                  it is the beginning + ~~it is~~ of time
                  + it is MINE!
        "ZEKIEL SAW DE WHEEL, WAY UP IN THE MIDDLE
        of THE AIR"

12 NOV:

Quantum EXPRESSIONISM . . . . QUANTUMISM
  > The contemporary existence of being modern <
I AM A Quantum Expressionist. I work at the molecular level i.e., I
play with atoms and photons I collobrate with Nature i.e., Nature as
it exist as the MICRO ↔ MACRO: I AM IN THE MIDDLE
HOLDING BOTH EXTREMES IN MY HANDS. I HAVE
LEARNED TO DANCE WITH THE UNIVERSE. I HAVE
ARRIVED AT ANOTHER LEVEL OF CONSCIOUNESS AND
THERE IS NO END IN SIGHT. I SEE ONLY LIGHT AND

12 NOV

AND IT'S A BEAUTIFUL LIGHT! I MUST LEARN TO USE
THIS LIGHT FOR THE BENEFIT OF MANKIND. THE LIGHT
IS MY SOURCE OF ENERGY AND I MUST LEARN TO USE IT

WISELY . . . . IT IS NOT TO BE WASTED ON NONSENSE +
FOOLISH ENDEAVORS. MY FIRST THOUGHT IS TO USE IT
AS AN ANDTIDOTE TO ALL THE EVIL THAT SURROUNDS
ME. WHETHER I LIKE IT OR NOT WHAT I DO IS POLITICAL:
UNCERTAINTY-AMBIGUITY-RANDOMNESS.

CHAOS THEORY—QUANTUM MECHANICS DEALS WITH
ALL OF THIS + MORE . . . IT IS NOT STATIC BUT FOREVER
IN MOTION WITHOUT A FIXED STATIONERY CENTER . IT
DEPENDS ON INTERACTION IN ORDER TO BE 'ACTIVE'
THEREFORE IT IS POLITICAL. WE DID NOT INVENT THE
POLITICAL . . . IT HAS ALWAYS BEEN THERE!

— NOTES FROM THE WOODSHED —

26 MARCH 2017: TO REPEAT MYSELF: I AM A THIRD PHASE MODERNIST. I UNDERSTAND THE DIFFICULTY IN ANYONE TRYING TO PIN ME DOWN i.e., TO LABEL WHAT I AM DOING. NOT BEING PINNED DOWN IS A GOOD POSITION... IT KEEPS THEM GUESSING AND GIVES ME TIME TO CULTIVATE MY OWN SPACE. THERE IS NO ONE STANDING NEXT TO ME. I AM ON MY OWN.... THAT'S THE WAY IT SHOULD BE.... THE BEST POSITION IS THE TO BE ALONE.... THERE AND ONLY THERE DO I FIND SILENCE... SILENCE IS A GOOD THING; ONLY IN SILENCE CAN ONE CONTEMPLATE.
        I AM PLEASED WITH MY FIRST SHOW AT HAUSER & WIRTH. FOR THE FIRST TIME IN MY LIFE... EVERYTHING WAS SOLD WITHIN TEN DAYS OF THE OPENING! THAT IS UNBELIEVABLE. I WILL USE THE MONEY WISELY: INVEST IN WHAT I AM DOING. THE REVIEWS HAVE BEEN EXTREMELY POSITIVE. THANKS TO PHONG BUI of THE BKLYN. RAIL — VILLAGE VOICE — PARIS REVIEW & THE CULTURE magazine THANKS TO JOHN YAU. LOTS OF FANTASTIC FEEDBACK FROM OTHER ARTISTS... PAINTERS WHOM J RESPECT.
        WHAT.S NEXT.??

CONTINUITY — CONSISTENCY — COMMITMENT — CLARITY STAYING TRUE TO THE CAUSE: IT IS IMPORTANT THAT THE WORLD KNOW THAT THERE ARE BLACK PEOPLE COMMITTED TO THE CAUSE OF RESTORING THEIR COSMIC SENSE OF BEING. THIS IS WHAT KEEPS ME IN THE STUDIO.
    MY PAINTINGS ARE PHENOMENOLOGICAL OBJECTS. THEY EXIST WITHIN THEMSELVES. WHAT'S HARD FOR ME TO UNDERSTAND IS CONTRADICTION... MEANING THEY ARE A COLLECTION OF SENSE DATA... BUT HOW CAN THEY BE SIMULTANEOUSLY BE BOTH.... AT THE SAME TIME? IS THIS SOME SORT OF QUANTUM PUZZLE? OR IS IT SIMPLY: THAT'S THE WAY IT IS.

—NOTES FROM THE WOODSHED—

26 MARCH 2017: TO REPEAT MYSELF: I AM A THIRD PHASE MODERNIST. I UNDERSTAND THE DIFFICULTY IN ANYONE TRYING TO PIN ME DOWN i.e., TO LABEL WHAT I AM DOING. NOT BEING PINNED DOWN IS A GOOD POSITION . . . IT KEEPS THEM GUESSING AND GIVES ME TIME TO CULTIVATE MY OWN SPACE. THERE IS <u>NO</u> ONE STANDING NEXT TO ME. I AM ON MY OWN . . . THAT'S THE WAY IT SHOULD BE . . . . THE BEST POSITION is TO BE ALONE . . . . THERE AND ONLY THERE DO I FIND SILENCE . . . . SILENCE IS A GOOD THING; ONLY IN SILENCE CAN ONE CONTEMPLATE.

I AM PLEASED WITH MY FIRST SHOW AT HAUSER + WIRTH. FOR THE FIRST TIME IN MY LIFE . . . EVERYTHING WAS SOLD WITHIN TEN DAYS OF THE OPENING! THAT IS UNBELIVEABLE! I WILL USE THE MONEY WISELY. <u>INVEST IN WHAT I AM DOING</u>. THE REVIEWS HAVE BEEN EXTREMELY POSITIVE. THANKS TO PHONG BUI of THE BKLYN. RAIL—VILLAGE VOICE—PARIS REVIEW + THE CULTURE MAGAZINE. THANKS TO JOHN YAU. LOTS OF FANTASTIC FEEDBACK FROM OTHER ARTISTS . . . PAINTERS WHOM I RESPECT.

<u>WHAT'S NEXT</u>??

CONTINUITY—CONSISTENCY—COMMITMENT—CLARITY

STAYING TRUE TO THE CAUSE: IT IS IMPORTANT THAT THE WORLD KNOW THAT THERE ARE BLACK PEOPLE COMMITTED TO THE CAUSE OF RESTORING THEIR <u>COSMIC SENSE OF BEING</u>. THIS IS WHAT KEEPS ME IN THE STUDIO.

—MY PAINTINGS ARE PHENOMENLOGICAL OBJECTS.

THEY EXIST WITHIN THEMSELVES. WHAT'S HARD FOR ME TO UNDERSTAND IS CONTRADICTION . . . . MEANING THEY ARE A COLLECTION OF SENSE DATA . . . BUT HOW CAN THEY BE SIMULTANEOUSLY BE BOTH . . . . AT THE SAME TIME? IS THIS SOME SORT OF QUANTUM PUZZLE? OR IS IT SIMPLE: <u>THAT'S THE WAY IT IS</u>.

— NOTES FROM THE WOODSHED —
2017

3/MARCH: MET WITH RICHARD S. YESTERDAY..... AS USUAL GREAT TALK. HE IS QUICK TO UNDERSTAND. I DO MY BEST TO SPEAK CLEARLY, TO WRITE CLEARLY WITHOUT "GOOBEELY GOOK" PHILOSOPHICALLY, I THINK THAT WE ARE CUT FROM THE SAME 'SLAB.' HE LIKES CASSERIER, HUSSERL, DEWEY, BACHELARD, KANT. HE ALSO UNDERSTAND 'l/p' CEZANNE'S BRUSHSTROKES AS 'UNIT' AND THE ARCHITECTRONICS i.e., their MEANS OF STRUCTURING. WE ARE ON THE SAME PAGE HISTORICALLY. HE DID NOT BLINK AN EYE AT MY SUGGESTION OF MALEVICH'S BLACK SQUARE AS 'UNIT.' TO REPEAT MYSELF, THE UNIT IN PAINTING IS THE DIRECT EQUIVALENT OF PARTICLE PHYSICS & THE MOLECULAR. I AM VERY CLOSE. WHY HAS IT TAKEN SO LONG? RICHARD S. RESPONDED TO MY SAYING "I WANT THE PAINTING TO PAINT ITSELF" BUT, AS USUAL, HE PUT IT IN PERSPECTIVE: MY SAYING THAT IS WHAT PRODUCES THE PHOTOGRAPH. THE PHOTOGRAPHER ACTS AS A CATALST WITH HIS CAMERA, LIGHT + ABSENCE OF LIGHT, CHEMICALS, PAPER AS SUPPORT THE IMAGE MANIFESTS ITSELF THROUGH PROCESS. I MORE THAN ANYONE HAVE THE REAL GOODS! THE 'GHOST PAINTINGS' ARE WHAT STARTED IT..... THEY WERE THE BEGINNING, THE GENESIS of THIRD PHASE MODERNISM. I HAVE DONE ALL THE NECESSARY REBEARCH.... NOW I MUST USE WHAT I HAVE DISCOVERED. MOLECULAR PERCEPTION IS THE KEY. WITH THIS KEY I CAN OPEN ALL DOORS (PORTALS) INTO ANOTHER UNIVERSE. THE OTHER UNIVERSE IS MY WAY OF EXPANDING CONSCIOUSNESS....... WHEN CONSCIANESS EXPANDS FREEDOM EXPANDS. REMEMBER, JAZZ IS THE EXPANSION OF FREEDOM AND I AM THE SON of JAZZ.
— LET THE PAINTING PAINT ITSELF —

1 APRIL: REAL ART IS GOT NOTHING TO DO WITH LOGIC; THE REAL ARTIST ONLY PRETENDS THE NOTION OF LOGIC BECAUSE IT OFFERS A PRATICAL WAY TO GET STARTED.... IT'S LIKE A CATALTST.. IT CAN SPEED UP OR SLOW DOWN THE PROCESS OF MAKING. BILL GATES NEEDS LOGIC MORE THAN I BECAUSE HIS SYSTEM IS BINARY.

—NOTES FROM THE WOODSHED—
2017

31 MARCH: MET WITH RICHARD S. YESTERDAY . . . . .
AS USUAL GREAT TALK. HE IS QUICK TO UNDERSTAND.
I DO MY BEST TO SPEAK CLEARLY, TO WRITE CLEARLY
WITHOUT "GOOBEELY s/p GOOK." PHILOSOPHICALLY,
I THINK THAT WE ARE CUT FROM THE SAME 'SLAB.' HE
LIKES CASSIRER, HUSSERL, DEWEY, BACHELARD, KANT.
HE ALSO UNDERSTAND CEZANNE'S BRUSHSTROKES AS
'UNIT' AND THE ARCHITECTRONICS, i.e., their MEANS OF
STRUCTURING. WE ARE ON THE SAME PAGE HISTORICALLY.
HE DID NOT BLINK AN EYE AT MY SUGGESTION OF
MALEVICH'S BLACK SQUARE AS 'UNIT.' TO REPEAT MYSELF,
THE UNIT IN PAINTING IS THE DIRECT EQUIVALENT OF
PARTICLE PHYSICS + THE MOLECULAR. I AM VERY CLOSE.
WHY HAS IT TAKEN SO LONG?
    RICHARD S. RESPONDED TO MY SAYING "I WANT THE
PAINTING TO PAINT ITSELF" BUT, AS USUAL, HE PUT IT IN
PERSPECTIVE: MY SAYING THAT IS WHAT PRODUCES THE
PHOTOGRAPH. THE PHOTOGRAPHER ACTS AS A CATALST
WITH HIS <u>CAMERA</u>, <u>LIGHT</u> <u>+ABSENCE OF LIGHT</u>,
<u>CHEMICALS</u>, <u>PAPER AS SUPPORT</u> THE IMAGE MANIFESTS
ITSELF THROUGH PROCESS. I MORE THAN ANYONE HAVE
THE REAL GOODS! THE 'GHOST PAINTINGS' ARE WHAT
STARTED IT . . . . . THEY WERE THE BEGINNING, THE
GENESIS OF THIRD PHASE MODERNISM. I HAVE DONE ALL
THE NECESSARY RESEARCH . . . . NOW I MUST USE WHAT I
HAVE DISCOVERED. MOLECULAR PERCEPTION IS THE KEY.
WITH THIS KEY, I CAN OPEN ALL DOORS (PORTALS) INTO
ANOTHER UNIVERSE. THE OTHER UNIVERSE IS MY WAY
OF EXPANDING CONSCIOUNESS . . . . . . WHEN

CONSCIOUNESS EXPANDS FREEDOM EXPANDS.
REMEMBER, JAZZ IS THE EXPANSION OF FREEDOM AND
I AM THE <u>SON of JAZZ.</u>
    —LET THE PAINTING PAINT ITSELF—

1 APRIL: REAL ART IS GOT NOTHING TO DO WITH LOGIC;
THE REAL ARTIST ONLY PRETENDS THE NOTION OF
LOGIC BECAUSE IT OFERS A PRACTICAL WAY TO GET
STARTED . . . . IT'S LIKE A CATALYST . . IT CAN SPEED UP
OR SLOW DOWN THE PROCESS OF MAKING. BILL GATES
NEEDS LOGIC MORE THAN I BECAUSE HIS SYSTEM
IS BINARY.

—NOTES FROM THE WOODSHED—

9 APRIL 2017. Yesterday we had a chmpagne toast with mezes to celebrate the closing of my show. Sara's* record show that 15,000 people saw the show. <u>This is incredible!</u> Katy* was there, Tom* + Jess,* Winnie* + Paul,* Suzanne Randolph, Thelma* + her husband* (nice + smart fellow), Susan Stedman + Alfred, Tarin* + her husband The campagne was Perrier Jouet with plenty go around. H+W are very generous. I have done my job. The paintings go into the world where they will complete the circle.

William T. had a very nice opening everybody was there. [. . .] I congratulated him + wished him luck. Thankfully he has taken good care of his work. They looked fresh.

—NOTES FROM THE WOODSHED—

WED. DEC 27 2017: Finally I have something to say that is significance enough to enter the log-book.
It has been a really tough year . . . . couldn't go to Greece. [. . .]

Richard* got a selection of works together from the 1980's which I agreed to for the London show. My doctors did not give an O.K. to travel until last chance for London. The show was beautiful the book was on time + looks terrific! I am very pleased. A much needed vacation from New York and doctors! They also allowed me to travel to Aghia Galini for two weeks. Mary and I went to Kriti opened up the house and spent two glorious weeks of good weather—good food + good wine. We set on our newly finished porch had our coffee and basked in the sun. [. . .]

Finally Euclidean geometry loosens its grip. We knew in in the early 1900s but no one would speak about its' implications to Western civilision. But we knew . . . . . it was no longer a dualistic system, no one wanted to accept it including Einstein.

The pythagorean system has collapsed. Euclidean geometry system is not relevant to the new worldview. Quantum mechanics + particlele physics has replaced it. Multiple dimensions which we cannot see is where the action is. The new geometry is embedded deep within quantum mechanics. It is not a binary system. Dualism has been dissolved in time. Christanity is no longer revelant. All organized state approved religions have been reduced to the politics of power, therefore no longer spiritual. Must be reconstructed or otherwise they will die out. At the quantum level there is no dualism. There is no substance . . . it is only a cosmic soup with our minds serving as a container.

Philosphically, we have entered a new age of development: I call it <u>third phase modernism</u>. Aesthcally for the arts it has huge implications . . . . especially in geometry: any artists today who continue to rely on Euclidean based geometry are not prepared for this level of consciouness. <u>TPM</u> is none dualistic—it has no sex, no race—no color. It's spiritual footings are deep—it's all based on perception $\rightarrow$ therefore metaphysical therefore, as Kant explained . . . nature is the brain + if we can comprehed it . . . it can qualify as nature. There is no best of all. <u>NO ONE OWNS IT!</u> IT'S FREE FOR THE TAKING!

We still do not know its geometric pattern. . . . . I think it's something so close . . . . . like hiding in your back pocket. . . Something so natural + so close we cannot see it. The pop artists are still trying to tell us something. We must learn to listen to Andy . . . especially <u>me.</u>

<u>I ask the Lord for ten more years</u>. . . I NEED TEN MORE YEARS.

I am close . . . . but not close enough and I will not pull the trigger until I can see the eye. My first mistake was to misunderstand how many years it took the light that I am working with, @ one millon years to reach plant Earth. I am working with that goes back in time. Before the Greeks, before the Egyptans, before the Africans (both North + Subsaharan Africans) (I could still be off another 500 light years).

I use this time period because there was no binary system in place. M. Heidegger did a blistering critique of the early Greeks. M.H. said the Greeks made a cosmic mistake when they separated the idea from the actions. Husserl also knew this. Nietzsche loved this because it opened to capitalism, a new form of power where the will could enforce its self. So much for history. But we are still stuck with capitalism.

Art is the only spiritual form that we can depend on. When politics goes amok, when organized religions become political . . . we can always depend on art to pull us through. We must make sure the arts will survive for the benefit of all. Support the arts without any forms of restrictions. Art is what artist do. And we are the canaries in the coal mines. So all of the artists out there, keep sniffing the air for warning signs of any polluntants. [. . .] ART IS OUR COMPASS TO THE COSMOS.

Afterword

A Conversation on Jack Whitten's Writings with
Matilde Guidelli-Guidi, Glenn Ligon, and Zoé Whitley

PUBLISHER'S NOTE In October 2024, on the occasion of an exhibition of Whitten's paintings, works on paper, and sculptures from the 1970s, curators Matilde Guidelli-Guidi and Zoé Whitley and artist Glenn Ligon gathered for a public conversation about Whitten's life and work.* Though wide-ranging in its themes, their discussion returned repeatedly to Whitten's notes and their richness both as an art historical resource and as guidance for other artists. An excerpt of the conversation appears here, edited for clarity and length, offering readers of this second edition of Whitten's studio logs some additional points of departure for thinking about the artist's writing and work.

WHITLEY I first had the privilege of meeting Jack Whitten in 2015 in the lead up to *Soul of a Nation: Art in the Age of Black Power*. We are sitting among what was an incredibly transformative period in the artist's way of thinking about making, and we can't take for granted the fact that these works are here—at the time that I first met Jack, many of the works were still in the studio. Some had never been shown in public. We may think that these works have always been like this, but that isn't the case. It was incredibly hard-won.

Whitten was born in Bessemer, Alabama, and even as a young man, he'd always thought of himself as an artist. But that didn't necessarily seem like a viable career path, so he was going to be a doctor and pilot, studying at Tuskegee. Then he transferred to Southern University, so that he could actually study art. At that time, he became very active in the civil rights movement organizing marches, but because of his incredible eye and facility with graphic design, he was also in charge of the many protest posters and the visual identity of this movement. As a profoundly spiritual person, he was really tested in a way that I don't know most of us

Jack Whitten: Speedchaser was on view at Hauser & Wirth London from October 7–December 21, 2024. The conversation between Guidelli-Guidi, Whitley, and Ligon occurred on October 10, 2024, in the gallery space.

will ever be tested, and that has to do with what it means to be part of nonviolent action.

Then he moved to New York, where he was able to study at Cooper Union. One of the beautiful things about Cooper Union in the arc of so many artists' careers is the fact that the tuition was free, and they were able to be part of this wider community of artists and thinkers and even those who were established by that point, Willem de Kooning among them—it wasn't such a closed world. You could be a young artist and be in dialogue with these other artists, and at the same time, absorbing all these different kinds of readings, too—for example, Gaston Bachelard had only recently published *The Poetics of Space*. There's this way of thinking about these theoretical things and how an artist puts them into practice.

It was really toward the end of the '60s that a number of things happened. Jack completely transformed his studio, and he met his wife Mary and started traveling to Greece. All of a sudden, he's making this instrument called the developer, thinking, "How can I make the line, the gesture, the composition?" Jack turned the whole studio into a completely different practice, also through his peerless skill in carpentry. And in 1969, Whitten had a dream about a tree: he was commanded to go find this tree and carve it. Then he and Mary went to Crete, they got off this bus that had arrived in a village, and he saw exactly the tree he had dreamed of. They would go on to spend almost every summer going to Greece, where he started to develop a sculptural practice alongside the painting practice. And something awesome happened there: he starts to paint like a sculptor and sculpt like a painter—the way he's thinking about light and density and all of these things. He is also really thinking about things that would otherwise be impositions: we may think of yellow as happy or blue as sad or red as angry, and he really wanted to strip away all of these connotations or thinking that there had to be a narrative that carried the work.

And even though some of these works wouldn't come into a kind of public awareness for many, many decades—through the important work of curators like Katy Siegel—there were also moments where individuals did recognize what Jack was doing. In 1975, Henry Geldzahler acquired one of the works for the Metropolitan Museum of Art, and at the end of the '70s Kynaston McShine acquired another work for the Museum of Modern Art.

LIGON I recently reread *Notes from the Woodshed*, the part from the '70s. It's fascinating because he talks about what it means to be an artist in New York at that moment—the difficulty of getting people to look at and buy work. He went for years selling very few works. There's another amazing part in the diary where he talks about Barnett Newman's wife, Annalee, giving him a carpentry job—that just blew my mind. But that's what he had to do to survive, because the work wasn't selling in a way that could support the studio practice and his family.

The other thing that is really interesting about his diaries is that he talks about how he makes the paintings. Everyone wants to know how these things are made—it's still quite mysterious to me as an artist how they were actually constructed. And he's very explicit—about what paints he's using, what gel medium, what the developer is as a tool to make the lines on the paintings. And I was wondering, who is he writing for? In some ways, he's writing for the future. He's writing for someone like me—you know, Jack Whitten was not taught in my art history class. He's someone I had to find later. And we overlapped a little—I knew him a little bit when he was alive, but it's

almost like the diaries are providing me a mentor that
I didn't have and didn't know that I needed.

I'm particularly interested in his series of paintings
called the *Black Monoliths*. The first one is dedicated to
James Baldwin, who has been a touchstone of my practice.
And Whitten says, "Baldwin is in the painting"—but this
painting is quite abstract. It's not figurative in any sort of
conventional way. What does that mean to say a person,
an essence, is in the painting? It's been really instructive to
look at the diaries and tease out what he means by that.

GUIDELLI-GUIDI The diaries are quite extraordinary, also, because, as you
said, there's this clear intention to be his own first art
historian. There's this kind of great awareness that he had,
that what he was doing was really important. There's this
ambition. He was looking around at what he was seeing
in New York and was extremely aware of what was
happening, extremely well read in terms of new theories
within and outside of art and art history, such an avid
reader of philosophy as well as technology.

And at the same time, many of these studio notes were
written when he was extremely down—yet again, he's being
included in a segregated show, or yet again, his work is not
being understood. Or he keeps on talking about the specter
of landscape, something that he is really trying to get away
from, to this new space in painting that he finds in the '70s.
Then you get to this dialectical moment in each of his
studio notes that is like, "And yet, I am doing this." And then
sometimes, "I'm packing in a month, and I'm going to Greece."

And there are these beautiful metaphors he uses
with his tools, like what we've been talking about with his
developer. Early in the '70s, he starts thinking about how to
make paintings without a brush, and "What is the relationship
of the hand to the canvas?" And he also shifts to using acrylic

rather than oil paint. There are huge changes in the studio
that make it both a chemistry lab and a carpentry shop.
He's there to make a painting rather than paint the painting.

In 1975, he starts the suite that he called the *Greek
Alphabet* paintings, which we had the pleasure to exhibit at
Dia Beacon. We didn't even know how many paintings there
were when we started. Now we know that there are perhaps
about sixty—ten are untraceable, but fifty, we know where
they are. It was very much detective work, with the help of
Mirsini Amidon and Ruby Lawrence from the Estate, who
shared with us all of Jack's incredibly meticulous studio notes,
both on how he would move from one letter in the series to
another as well as the idea of where the paintings were going.
Lucky for us, he kept these notes for the future, almost like
a time capsule. He knew that this moment would be coming.

LIGON   I want to think about making your own discourse—not waiting
for art historians who are not looking at the work to write
about the work, to validate it. So he writes about it himself,
and he, through those diaries, makes his own discourse. Also,
he knows when he's had a breakthrough—several times in the
diaries, it's like, "This was a breakthrough. I figured something
out about my work." And he's very clear about those moments,
which is really interesting. He knows his work well enough
to know when he's leapt somewhere in the practice.

WHITLEY   To think about that: the additional labor that had to go into
being his own archivist—to keep those things, knowing
that at some point, this will be something that we need
to have. In *Notes from the Woodshed*, because there had
been a fire in his studio and what was going to be his
family's home, he talks about these three years of "sweat
equity" he had to put into fixing the building. I think Jack's
whole life was this sweat equity.

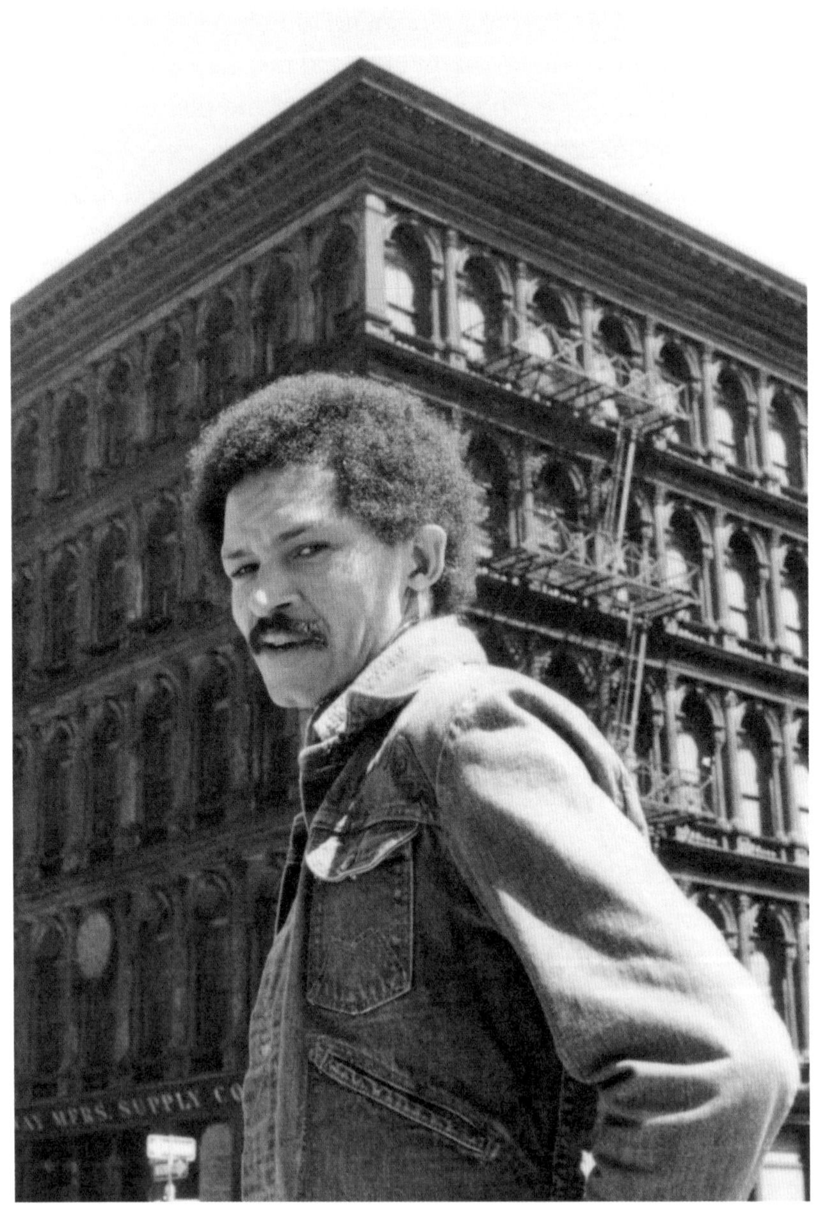

Jack Whitten

1939–2018

Editor's Acknowledgments

The most obvious and heartfelt thanks are for
Jack Whitten, who first trusted me to read his
studio logs, and later to publish them. Close
behind Jack is his daughter and studio manager,
Mirsini Amidon, who organized, scanned, and
reviewed the logs with meticulous care and
generosity. Mary Whitten, Jack's wife, answered
many questions, and in the wake of Jack's death
in January 2018, continued to support the project
during a difficult time. At Hauser & Wirth, Iwan
and Manuela Wirth, together with Marc Payot,
were unstinting in their advocacy of this project
from the outset, immediately understanding
its historic importance after Tate Dougherty,
Diana Murphy, and Michaela Unterdörfer initially
welcomed the proposal. Most concretely, Jake
Brodsky oversaw the publication, and worked
extremely hard on every detail; he was an ideal
partner. I thank Rita Jules and Miko McGinty for
their deep feeling for the form and content of
the logs, and for translating that feeling into this
beautiful book.

I always pictured *Notes From the Woodshed*
as a gift from Jack Whitten to other artists; I hope
it finds you, wherever you are.

—K.S., 2018

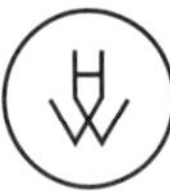

Jack Whitten: Notes from the Woodshed © 2018, 2025 Hauser & Wirth Publishers
First edition 2018. Second edition, fully transcribed with a new afterword, 2025.
hauserwirth.com

Editor: Katy Siegel
Publisher: Michaela Unterdörfer
Managing editor: Jake Brodsky
Assistant editor: Susannah Faber

Book design: Rita Jules and Miko McGinty, Miko McGinty Inc.
Typesetting: Tina Henderson, Miko McGinty Inc.
Production coordination: Poppy David; first edition, Christine Stäcker
Prepress: prints professional, Berlin
Printing and binding: Printer Trento s.r.l., Italy

Cover Paper: Fedrigoni Acqua Materica 250 g/m^2
Paper: Munken Print White 100 g/m^2
Typefaces: Akzidenz Grotesk and Plantin

Jack Whitten's writings and archival material © The Estate of Jack Whitten
Introduction © 2018 Katy Siegel
Afterword © 2025 Matilde Guidelli-Guidi, Glenn Ligon, and Zoé Whitley

Page 518: Jack Whitten in the early 1970s on the corner of Broadway and
Broome Street, New York. Courtesy The Estate of Jack Whitten

Distribution:

North & South America
ARTBOOK | D.A.P.
75 Broad Street, Suite 630
New York, NY 10004
artbook.com

All other territories
Thames & Hudson Ltd.
181a High Holborn
London WC1V 7QX
thamesandhudson.com

ISBN: 978-3-907493-11-3
Library of Congress Control Number: 2024949326

This edition of *Notes from the Woodshed* is produced using FSC-certified materials.

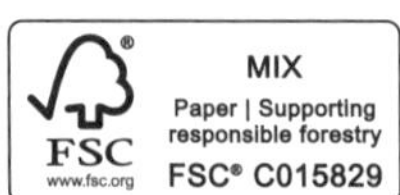

Printed and bound in Italy